GOVERNANCE, GROWTH AND GLOBAL LEADERSHIP

Modern Economic and Social History Series

General Editor: Derek H. Aldcroft

Titles in this series include:

Governance, Growth and Global Leadership

The Role of the State in Technological Progress, 1750–2000

ESPEN MOE
Norwegian University of Science and Technology, Norway

ASHGATE

Published by
Ashgate Publishing Limited
Gower House
Croft Road
Aldershot
Hampshire GU11 3HR
England

Ashgate Publishing Company
Suite 420
101 Cherry Street
Burlington, VT 05401-4405
USA

Ashgate website: http://www.ashgate.com

British Library Cataloguing in Publication Data
Moe, Espen
    Governance, growth and global leadership : the role of the state in technological
    progress, 1750-2000. – (Modern economic and social history) 1.Industrial policy –
    History 2.Industries – History 3.International economic relations – History
    I.Title
    338.9

Library of Congress Cataloging-in-Publication Data
Moe, Espen.
    Governance, growth and global leadership : the rise of the state in technological
progress, 1750-2000 / Espen Moe.
        p. cm. – (Modern economic and social history)
    Includes bibliographical references and index.
    ISBN–13: 978–0–7546–5743–9 (alk. paper)
    ISBN–10: 0–7546–5743–4 (alk. paper)
  1. Industrial policy–History. 2. Technology and state–History. I. Title.

    HD3611.M555 2007
    338'.064–dc22

                                                                                2006018531
ISBN–13: 978–07546–5743–9

Printed and bound in Great Britain by MPG Books Ltd. Bodmin, Cornwall.

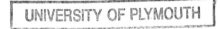

Contents

List of Tables

Modern Economic and Social History Series
General Editor's Preface

Economic and social history has been a flourishing subject of scholarly study during recent decades. Not only has the volume of literature increased enormously but the range of interest in time, space and subject matter has broadened considerably so that today there are many sub-branches of the subject which have developed considerable status in their own right.

One of the aims of this series is to encourage the publication of scholarly monographs on any aspect of modern economic and social history. The geographical coverage is world-wide and contributions on the non-British themes will be especially welcome. While emphasis will be placed on works embodying original research, it is also intended that the series should provide the opportunity to publish studies of a more general thematic nature which offer a reappraisal or critical analysis of major issues of debate.

Derek H. Aldcroft
University of Leicester

Acknowledgements

This book has already led a long and convoluted life. My interest in long-term growth and development was sparked as a graduate student at the Department of Sociology and Political Science at the Norwegian University of Science and Technology in Trondheim, and so my first attempt at writing what would eventually become this book started almost ten years ago. However, it was not until I arrived at the Department of Political Science at UCLA in 1999 that things started picking up speed. Hence, this book is a focused, shortened and revised version of what essentially started out as a dissertation project at UCLA.

This project would never have turned out the way it did if not for the competence, support and inspiration from a number of people—faculty, fellow students and staff— at UCLA, who all deserve special mention. Ron Rogowski has been my mentor and Chair of my dissertation committee, and a man whose range of knowledge is truly breathtaking. His advice and suggestions have all been helpful and of the highest quality, and while being bombarded with what at times must have seemed like an endless stream of (almost always exceedingly lengthy) drafts and emails, he always remained positive and optimistic. I have been truly grateful for his guidance and friendship as well as for his trust in me and his willingness to let me run with my own ideas.

Also, on my committee, a heartfelt thanks to Jean-Laurent Rosenthal for picking a number of fairly serious holes in my original project and for forcing me into an extensive theoretical and methodological re-think. At a time when I thought that the format was essentially there, he forced me back to the drawing board. For a while, it left me theoretically stranded. Needless to say, he was right on all accounts, and by the time the re-think was over, conceptually, theoretically and methodologically, the project had become far sounder and more promising. The book that has eventually emerged out of this is no doubt far better than it would have been without his input.

Art Stein's input has been valuable throughout my years at UCLA. Art is one of the UCLA faculty that I have gotten the most from. I have enjoyed his courses, I have worked for him, and he has provided guidance to me on papers, one of which has partially found its way into the last of the empirical chapters in the book. He is someone that I have tremendous respect for and feel honored to have worked with. This leaves me with the final member of my committee, Marc Trachtenberg. As the resident historian of the UCLA political science department, his course on historical methods proved extremely useful. It was a great comfort to have him on the committee. And not to be forgotten, he was the one who suggested Governance and Growth as the title of the dissertation (Ashgate later suggested adding Global Leadership). Thanks!

At UCLA, I would also like to thank Deborah Larson, Robert Brenner and Perry Anderson. Deborah has been a huge influence on me during my years at UCLA. I worked for her for two full years, and in the US there are few people that I have sought out for advice on papers, committees, oral exams and so on more often. I have drawn on what I have learnt in her classes on countless occasions both in teaching and in my own writings. Robert Brenner and Perry Anderson, both with the History Department also deserve credit. Perry Anderson's inputs can be seen primarily in the final empirical chapter, Robert Brenner's in the first two. Furthermore, a thank you to Robert Brenner for having me as Visiting Fellow at his Center for Social Theory and Comparative History.

There are also a number of people in Norway that deserve their fair share of credit for this book. At the Department of Sociology and Political Science at the Norwegian University of Science and Technology in Trondheim, no one has had a greater influence on me than my long-time adviser, mentor and friend, Torbjørn L. Knutsen. During the above-mentioned theoretical and methodological re-think, he was extremely conveniently located in the US on sabbatical, more specifically in Washington DC. Spending a few days with him and his family in May 2003 helped me get back on theoretical track at a time when I was at my most wayward. Back in Norway a year or so later, co-teaching a methods course with him and Jennifer Bailey, I picked up new methodological impulses at a stage where I had mistakenly assumed the rest of the dissertation merely to be a wrap-up. Methodologically, I have also received valuable input from Gunnar Fermann. Equally important is the emotional and moral support that I have steadily received and drawn upon from the above-mentioned people, whether it be through regular conversations, dinners, projects or even mountain climbs. At the same university, a final thanks to Edgar Hertwich for making me feel welcome at my new employer, the Industrial Ecology Programme.

Erik Reinert also deserves special mention. While I have not been regularly in touch with Erik over the past few years, it was he who originally pointed me in the direction of evolutionary reasoning. Through his writings, he was the one who got me started. He was the one pointing me in the direction of a literature that is sometimes a little obscure, but almost always fascinating, and encouragingly rapidly growing, as it is being discovered by ever more scholars.

While it is easy to acknowledge that there are a number of people to be thanked for their substantive inputs, it is easy to forget that without funding, this project would never have gotten off the ground. My five years at UCLA, and hence this book, would never have materialized if not for the funding of the Fulbright Foundation, the Norwegian Research Council, and UCLA. Without the Fulbright grant I would never have been able to go in the first place. Without the three-year Research Council Grant, which fortuitously arrived as the Fulbright money was running out, I would not have been able to stay. Equally important, scholarships and tuition waivers at UCLA managed to keep me afloat. They were all willing to take a chance on me and I am most thankful for the trust that they have shown me. Hopefully, this book means that I have now been able to repay at least some of their faith in me. And hopefully, there is still more to come.

Writing a dissertation is one thing, publishing a book a wholly different matter. My main problem in this respect was that my manuscript was horribly long—two to three times longer than what would make it publishable. This meant that most publishers would not even want to entertain the idea of looking at it, unless I got back to them with a version about a third of the original length. Hence, a special thank you to Rasmus Gjedssø Bertelsen, who I met for the first time at a conference in the US. A few conferences and a number of emails later we decided to submit papers for a common panel at the BISA conference in Warwick, UK, December 2004. In between submitting and writing papers and actually going to the conference, I managed to finish my dissertation, and I arrived bringing with me some very recently printed copies in the distant hope that anyone would be remotely interested. In the meantime, Rasmus had gone from panelist to Chair of the panel, and as he informed me, one of the other members of the panel happened to know someone at Ashgate, and so if I passed on a copy to him, maybe he could pass it on to his friend at Ashgate. Hence, a heartfelt thanks to Steven Morewood, for bringing my manuscript to the attention of Ashgate. A couple of months later Derek Aldcroft informed me that he wanted to publish it in the *Modern Economic and Social History* Series, for which he is the series editor (granted that it could be considerably shortened and somewhat sharpened). Thus a special thanks to him for seeing the potential of the manuscript and being willing to work with me.

Having a book published is a drawn-out process involving a number of steps. Ashgate has made this process easy for me, and in addition to Derek Aldcroft, this has been due to the help and guidance of Commissioning Editor Tom Gray and Desk Editor Emily Ebdon. Finally, proofreader Anthea Lockley has made sure that the book is more readable and less embarrassingly riddled with typos, grammatical errors and other interesting linguistic constructions that belie my origins as a Norwegian speaker. Thank you to all of you.

Also, thank you to David Johnson, Lars Morten Rimol and Stefanie Yow for reading parts of the manuscript and for making suggestions, both with respect to substance, cuts and language. Also, thank you to Mary Prestløkken and Glenda Jones. Academics are supposed to be forgetful and absentminded, at least in practical matters. I easily fulfill this requirement. I am afraid Mary and Glenda have had to endure the same stupid questions from me over and over again whenever I have been grappling with some kind of practical issue. And then having to repeat their answers the following day as I have predictably failed to comprehend what they were actually telling me the day before (probably already then repeating what they had told me on an earlier occasion). Hopefully I was not too much of a burden.

A lot of people deserve mentioning. I have received inputs from so many, and I have probably left out several. Hopefully not too many. And obviously, despite an abundance of excellent advice, I am still solely responsible for whatever flaws and errors have crept into the book. Almost last but definitely not least, I have to thank my family, for encouragement, trust and support and all that they have meant to me throughout the years. A final generic thanks goes out to all the people that were there for emotional support and that helped me remain (remotely) sane, both in the US and in Norway. There are a lot of you. Hopefully, you know who you are.

Espen Moe
Trondheim, 2006

Chapter 1

Introduction

Economic Growth, Technological Change, and Industrial Leadership

The story of long-term economic growth and development is an alluring one. The might of great powers has waxed and waned. Periods of peace and stability have been followed by turmoil and large-scale warfare. New dominant powers have risen from military victory, or peacefully, from economic prosperity. The most obvious observation that can be made about the international system is that for centuries, it has been in a state of flux. International leadership comes and goes. Today's dominant powers are not the ones that controlled world politics 250 years ago.

Leadership is in many ways what this book is all about. How can leadership be preserved and maintained over larger periods of time? Why is it that some countries have been able to rise to a position of international leadership? And why is it that some countries have been able to maintain this position for so much longer than others? Is it inevitable that a country's rise will ultimately lead to its demise, or can this cyclical waxing and waning of power somehow be stopped, so that the inevitability of the fall may be prevented?

The type of leadership that is the focus of this book is *economic* leadership. Obviously, economic and political leadership is intrinsically intertwined. Hence, economic leadership undoubtedly serves as one of the best predictors of political leadership. One of the reasons why we should be interested in economic leadership in the first place, is because of the consequences of economic growth and development for power relationships in the international system. Few things are more destabilizing to the international system than different powers growing at different rates. This is what makes weaker powers catch up and what ultimately dethrones the stronger power. It has happened on numerous occasions in the past, and it has happened to the countries whose stories I will tell over the next few chapters.

To explain economic leadership is to explain long-term economic growth and development. Economic growth is one of those apparently straightforward notions that nevertheless seem to elude us whenever we seek to investigate it more thoroughly. Countless books have been written, numerous theories advanced, and tons of empirical material produced. Economic growth has been a concern for historians, economic historians, economists, sociologists, political scientists, etc. It is the goal of any worldly ruler with the least bit of concern for his subjects, but it still seems so hard to achieve and so easy to miss.

However, economic leadership can mean a lot of things. Hence, instead of using for instance GDP, GDP per capita or GDP per capita growth as the yardstick for economic leadership, this book disaggregates the economies into singular industries. This means that the focus really is on *industrial* leadership. However, this is inextricably connected with overall economic growth and development. To a plethora of scholars, different growth industries have put their distinctive stamps on different time periods. In one sense the point is trivial. The growth industries of yesteryear are not the same as the growth industries of today. In a day and age where computer technology has revolutionized the way we do business, communicate, search for information, etc., it would have been very odd if the cotton textile industry of the early Industrial Revolution was still the world economy's main engine of growth. New technologies give rise to new industries, to growth and prosperity. But eventually, they grow old and obsolete, and are replaced by newer industries that draw on more recent technologies.

In a different sense, the point is not equally trivial. This is a perspective that privileges certain industries over others, singling these out for particular analysis for the reason that they are deemed more important for overall growth and development than other industries. They are the industries that have been engines of the world economy. They have been important first, because in general they have been generic industries, drawing on generic technologies. In other words, they have been industries with multiplier effects on the overall economy through their contribution to other sectors. The real reason for the importance of for instance early to mid-nineteenth-century iron industry was not that iron smelting in itself was such a huge industry, but because iron was utilized by so many other industries and for so many purposes. Second, because they are industries that as a rule have drawn upon revolutionary technological breakthroughs. Technological breakthroughs have allowed major productivity improvements. But also, stemming from such breakthroughs, entire new industries have risen. Some of these new technologies have been so groundbreaking that they have transformed entire economies.

Why cannot just every country start employing new technology right away? This is the perspective taken by a host of textbook economic theory. Technology is a public good. Once a new technology has been invented, it is there for everyone to use (e.g. Fagerberg 1994:1149). However, diffusion of new technology is never immediate. It is usually a drawn-out process, since among other things, firms will try to protect the advantage provided by new technology to as great an extent as possible. Also, the necessary knowledge base for adopting new technology may not always be available yet to other firms. Moreover, diffusion across national borders is normally far slower than diffusion within a country. Hence, new and revolutionary technologies may give rise to growth industries, but not necessarily anywhere. Different economic growth rates in different countries lead some countries to forge ahead or catch up, and others to fall behind or be caught up with. Technological breakthroughs give rise to new and prosperous industries that can grow and develop relatively unhindered within a country. By innovating and staying technologically ahead a country can in certain industries, for all practical purposes, carve out for itself a monopolistic position, by steadily raising the bar for competitors. In such a way, new technology effectively serves as an entry-barrier against other actors. Hence, industrial leadership is inextricably linked to *technological* leadership. Consequently, this book is not only about industrial leadership, but about *technological and industrial* leadership.

This means that despite only focusing on specific industries, this book is about growth and development on a more overarching level. The industries singled out for analysis are industries that have been of particular importance. They are the industries that have been instrumental in the rise of some countries, and the demise of others. From this perspective, a country's economic growth and development hinges on performing well in certain crucial industries, in particular industries drawing upon new technology. And from this perspective, this book is really about the technological and industrial rise and fall of the great powers.

The Role of the State: Governance and Growth

But the book is not just about technological and industrial leadership. It is about *the state*, or rather, the *role of* the state in promoting technological and industrial leadership. The state has for centuries been the dominant actor in international relations. It has also been the most important political actor in general, and while its importance has waxed and waned, it has always been among the main actors. Since the Industrial Revolution, technological change has become the most important source of economic growth, and thus of power and leadership in the international system. Different rates of technological change lead to unequal rates of growth in different countries. This destabilizes the international system. It is hugely beneficial for the countries that take advantage of it, but leads to stagnation, backwardness and ultimately obscurity for those countries less skilled at it. Drawing on the obvious observation of the rise and fall of the great powers in the international system; is there something that the state can do in order to prevent the fall? Is there something that it can do in order to encourage and promote technological change and industrial leadership? And is there something that the state might conceivably do in order to prevent technological and industrial dominance from being only a one-shot success? Is there a role for the state in achieving long-term economic dominance, beyond singular technologies and industries, and beyond specific time periods?

There are valid theoretical reasons why this should be the case. While the role of the state in technological progress and industrial leadership is by no means an angle ignored by any majority of scholars, consensus on how the state relates to issues of technological progress and industrial leadership keeps eluding us. The approach chosen here is a *combined focus* on the state *and* on technological progress and industrial leadership. The role of the state is one of creating conditions that are conducive to unlocking the creative potential of the population, to stimulating and diffusing knowledge and innovation, and promoting the growth of new and promising industries.

Which are the technologies and industries that will be analyzed over the following chapters, over what time interval and for which countries? The book covers a time-span of 250 years, starting with the Industrial Revolution and ending with the present.

Going back to the start of the Industrial Revolution, there is no doubt that the first major growth industry was cotton textiles. Obviously, by picking the Industrial Revolution as the starting point, one suggests that this event represents something special, a take-off-point of some kind. Contemporary economic research has de-emphasized the role of the Industrial Revolution in that respect, stressing gradual rather than revolutionary change. No mechanical revolution happened overnight, and the Industrial Revolution may be a less obvious starting point for a study of industrial leadership than the name suggests. Still, while less than a revolution, it counts as a milestone in human history, and for that reason alone is a worthy and obvious point of departure. The British cotton textile industry is routinely considered the world's first *real* industry, inherently intertwined with the Industrial Revolution.

When growth in cotton textiles could no longer spur on the British economy in particular, the iron industry took over. Hence, the choice of cotton textiles for the early Industrial Revolution, starting around 1760–1780 and running out of steam some time after the end of the Napoleonic Wars, followed by iron for the early to mid-nineteenth century, were obvious. For the third growth industry, stretching from the late nineteenth century on toward World War I, the task was trickier. Toward the mid- to late nineteenth century, three new major industries emerged, growing to become as important as iron had once been—steel, electric industry and chemical industry. Steel and electrification would have been worthy choices. However, while not the only possible choice, the chemical industry was as natural a choice as steel or electricity. First, chemicals is a generic industry, and thus has major multiplier effects on the economy as a whole, although this is also the case with steel and electricity. Second, the chemical industry is often referred to as the first science-based industry, representing a shift in the sense that for the first time, a university education was now essential in order to achieve industrial success. Then again, electric industry can also be said to have been science-based. Third, in the chemical industry, it is possible to discern quite different approaches to economics and to industry in different countries. This makes it easier to tease out potential causal variables. For the interwar years, the main new development was mass-production. However, since this is a mode of production, and not an industry, an industry still has to be selected, and the automobile industry is an easy choice. Finally, the present-day period sets the stage for a chapter on industries derived from information and communication technologies (ICTs).

Through five time periods, the book covers the growth experiences of Great Britain, France, Germany, the US, and Japan. They have not been included for each and every time period and industry—for that there would have had to be both a volume II and III ... However, they are all countries that have possessed or aspired to industrial leadership. They are, or have all been, great powers, at some stage either dominating or aspiring to global leadership. Britain was the first industrial superpower, and is an obvious inclusion, but is also interesting because its powers ultimately waned. First, how was it that a small, and for long inconspicuous and peripheral, island nation grew to become the world's economic and industrial powerhouse? And how was it that this power, which at its peak produced more than

50 per cent of the world's iron, two thirds of the coal, 50 per cent of world cloth production and generating roughly a quarter of world trade, half a century later was surpassed not just by the US, but by Germany as well? France was the perennial challenger, with aspirations of both economic and political domination. It was more populous than Britain, had a larger territory, an abundance of good soil, and a huge army. Still, it found itself losing out to Britain on most accounts and then gradually also to other countries. Germany very rapidly became the industrially and militarily dominant European power toward the end of the nineteenth century, rising from the utter political fragmentation of the Holy Roman Empire in record time.

Still, German efforts were in many respects overshadowed by those of the US, which after the Civil War industrialized extremely rapidly. And this growth only continued, persisting until the present day, making the US the prime example of a power that has forged ahead, but not yet started its possibly inevitable decline. Finally, there is Japan, which rose from the ashes after World War II, challenging the US for leadership in mass manufacturing, but ultimately failed to translate its manufacturing prowess into leadership in ICTs.

From a historian's point of view, these are all interesting countries, industries and time periods in and of themselves. However, there is a more overarching purpose. Each country and industry provide us with pieces to a larger puzzle: Why is it that some countries have been able to ride the waves of technological change, in the process fostering new and prosperous growth industries, whereas others have not? Why is it that some countries have been able to preserve their power, whereas other countries rose *and fell*?

Technological Progress and Long-Term Economic Growth

Theories of Economic Growth

Despite the enormous literature in the field, holes still remain to be filled. With respect to the state and technological change, there is a solid strand of literature organizing its subject matter in terms of case studies of particular periods of technological change and/or industrial growth. For instance, there exists a massive amount of *case studies* on the Industrial Revolution. And there are studies comparing industrialization in for instance Britain with similar processes elsewhere. There are also numerous studies on other periods of technological change. The story of Germany and the late nineteenth-century chemical industry is a familiar one, as is that of the rise of Japan to an industrial superpower. In other words, there is a wealth of literature on specific processes of structural change. What is lacking is knowledge about the causes of technological change in general, on an overarching level. In other words, a number of studies have provided causal arguments about specific countries and time periods, but there is a relative scarcity of attempts at causal inference about the *general phenomenon of technological change* (and industrial growth).

On the other hand, there is also a literature on general technological change. Historians and social scientists have identified *epochs of technological change*, and sought to come up with general characteristics of these epochs. Often, these studies are organized according to historical periods, seeking to outline the contribution of technological change to long-term growth and to international economic hegemony. However, while these accounts make inferences about technological change and industrial leadership, they rarely seek to explain what it is that causes change and leadership *per se*. In other words, in one sense, what is supposed to be explained—long-term growth and development—is essentially left unexplained by using a proxy for growth, namely technological change and industrial leadership, as the independent variable. Further, these accounts rarely have an institutional side, and they seldom make any conjectures about the role of the state beyond vague references to the importance of education, openness, cohesion etc. What is also often lacking is a comparative perspective. They do not compare processes of change between countries in order to explicate why change happened in one country and not somewhere else. They explain the role of technological change for economic growth, but do not go further.

Hence, one strand treats technological change as what is to be explained, but chooses its cases so that conclusions can only be drawn about technological change and industrial leadership within one particular time period. And a second strand tries to make inferences about technological change and industrial leadership in general, but treats technology as the *cause*, and is thus better able to make inferences about the *effects* of technological change, rarely touching upon any role of the state. Both strands cover interesting ground, but leave plenty of room for a different project: Is it possible to say something about the role of the state in promoting technological progress and industrial leadership in general, across time and space? What are the conditions that are conducive to technological change and industrial prowess, and how does the state go about promoting this? This is the project that unravels over the next few chapters.

Regarding technology and growth, this book draws particular inspiration from a few scholars that deserve special attention: Works by Nelson (1995; 2002), Nelson and Winter (1982), Freeman and Perez (1988); Freeman and Soete (1999); Freeman and Louçã (2001) and Perez (2002), are invaluable with respect to evolutionary economics, technological change and important sectors. Works by Modelski (1996; 2001) and Thompson (1996; 2000) are extremely important for their international relations perspective on leading sectors and technological change. North (1990) deserves special mention, not so much for his focus on institutions, as for his explicitly linking institutions to long-term growth, suggesting that institutional differences between countries can explain difference in long-term growth performance. Doing this, he is one of comparatively few people to link evolutionary economics and institutions. Mokyr (1990; 2002a) is significant for similar reasons. His treatment of knowledge and his emphasis on its use and diffusion is placed in an evolutionary setting. Also, his exposition of evolutionary economics—its biological roots, main assumptions and relevance—is exemplary. Finally Landes (1969; 1998) is less explicitly evolutionary, but important for his clear emphasis on innovation and creativity, on the unlocking of the human potential as the key to long-term growth and development.

Numerous approaches and scholars could (and should) be mentioned. Just a few will have to suffice. For 50 years, neoclassical economics has been the dominant economic framework. But for most of this period, economic growth has been poorly understood. Moses Abramovitz (1956) and Robert Solow (1956) provided early attempts at growth theories,[1] but these seemed more than anything else to show the inability of neoclassical indicators to provide a satisfactory explanation of growth. When Abramovitz set forth to investigate how much of American economic growth could be accounted for by traditional neo-classic economic indicators, he found that capital *per se* could only explain a measly 10–20 per cent. The rest, a residual of 80–90 per cent, he discontentedly called 'a measure of our ignorance' about the causes of economic growth. Robert Solow came up with approximately the same result—88 per cent of the variance was left unexplained by the model. Back in 1992, *The Economist* (1992:17) wrote: "True enough: economists are interested in growth. The trouble is that, even by their standards, they have been terribly ignorant about it. The depth of that ignorance has long been their best-kept secret." True, a wealth of research and economic theorizing over the past decade has moved the understanding of growth far beyond what used to be the case. Mankiw, Romer and Weil (1992) serve as just one example that this approach still has many proponents. However, there are areas that are still not well understood.

Neoclassical economics has been challenged by the *endogenous growth* school, which emphasizes technological change and knowledge, criticizing the neoclassical lack of a long-term perspective, while otherwise drawing on the same theoretical foundations.[2] *Endogenous* refers to core concepts like technological progress, learning by doing and knowledge spillovers. Unlike traditional neoclassical models, knowledge and technology are endogenous, not exogenous, innovations driven by conscious investment decisions and knowledge treated as a factor of production alongside capital and labor (Gilpin 2001:112p; Hodgson 1996:392; Romer 1994:3). Because of this, the theory does not predict diminishing returns. Instead, knowledge and new technology may lead to increasing returns—historically the case on several occasions.

One school focuses on learning by doing (Romer 1986; Lucas 1988; Rebelo 1991), yielding an aggregate production function exhibiting constant or increasing returns to scale, with spillovers from learning by doing leading to a social rate of return on such activities more than twice that of the private rate of return, weakening the convergence assumption of neoclassical economics.[3] A second school focuses

---

1   The basic model: $Y = AK^{\alpha}L^{1-\alpha}$.

2   Verspagen (2001:3) identifies four prototypes of endogenous models: Romer (1990), Lucas (1988), Aghion and Howitt (1992), Rebelo (1991).

3   Neoclassical models predict economic convergence among all economies. If output per capita differences are caused by differences in capital–labor ratios, capital flows from capital-rich to capital-poor countries will close the gap. If they are the result of differences

on technological change, and on returns from R & D (e.g. Aghion and Howitt 1992; Howitt 2000). The costs of inventing decline as society accumulates ideas. Breakthrough technologies and products, or *macroinventions*, are very often produced by newcomers rather than by existing industry leaders. This goes with assumptions that industrial leaders often have a stake in existing best technology, arising from large investments made for instance in machinery. This allows for a model of leapfrogging: Follower firms and nations may overtake previous lead firms and nations (Barro and Sala-i-Martin 1995; Brezis, Krugman and Tsiddon 1993).[4] The rejection of numerous constraining assumptions of neoclassical models makes the endogenous growth school better able to deal with issues of long-term economic growth. The rate of economic growth in advanced economies will not by necessity decline, and the gap between rich and poor countries will not by necessity converge, as rich countries invest in human capital to preserve their initial advantage (Gilpin 2001:115p).

A third strand concerns the question of growth as a result of destiny or policy, "nature or nurture". Acemoglu, Johnson and Robinson (2001) focus on developments since 1492, and side with institutions rather than geography.[5] But various authors have tried to explain growth by pointing to demography, geography, climatic conditions, natural resources, etc.: Great Britain probably benefited from its peripheral geographic position, sheltered by the seas, unlike France, which seemed to fight in every war in Europe. Climatic conditions may be important. Harsh winters teach people to build solid houses; it gives them incentives to innovate, to conquer nature. On the other hand; too harsh conditions makes growth impossible altogether. Extremely warm weather affects one's ability to work hard. It also stimulates numerous sorts of dangerous bacteria and larvae, which may damage health, reduce physical well-being, strength, stamina and life expectancies. The European diet as well as a lack of microparasites made Europeans healthier (thus, more energetic and creative) (Crosby 1986; Landes 1998; McNeill 1977). Europe's geography made it conducive to trade (Crouzet 2000), and at the same time hard to conquer,

---

in technology, technological know-how will flow from the technologically advanced countries. All nations should eventually grow equally fast in the most simplified version of the neoclassical world. Empirical evidence suggests that the absolute convergence hypothesis does not hold, but that data are compatible with conditional convergence and club convergence (that is, convergence among groups of countries developing in the same direction) (Galor 1996:1056).

4   The model promises no advantages from backwardness *per se*. The model needs to be combined with assumptions of diminishing returns to experience in order to accommodate leapfrogging: That is, the leader has a stake in the current best technology, and sticks to it instead of innovating. Thus, it is being leapfrogged once the follower nation develops a decisive advantage in a new technology (Barro and Sala-i-Martin 1995).

5   Although part of the story has to do with how mortality rates determined which colonies were good for settling, and which colonies could only be used for resource extraction. Good institutions (protection of private property) typically occurred in areas that attracted white settlers, hence geography still plays a part.

ensuring a European interstate system inherently competitive, eventually giving rise to a technological lead over other continents (Landes 1998; Taylor 1996). A lack of natural resources may be crucial. Pomeranz (2000) is one of several Sinologists blaming China's eventual backwardness primarily on an absence of coal. And for an extreme long-term view, see Diamond (1997), who suggests that geography—for instance the physical shape of the continents—is important. The east–west shape of Eurasia was much more conducive to the spread of agriculture than the north–south shape of the Americas.

In this book, I draw on several of the above categories, but without quite fitting any of them. Neither of the three include a specific role for the state. The latter—"nature vs. nurture"—does at least implicitly include institutions as opposed to geography. While geography is obviously interesting, it is less relevant here. My purpose is to say something about human interactions, and about the role of the state. Geography is a constant as much as a variable. There is not much one can do about it! Instead, the story of long-term growth and development is probably one of circumventing such (and other) obstacles through human creativity, invention and organization.

On the other hand, my concern is not with the state *per se*, but rather with the role of the state in *fostering long-term growth and development* through technological change. The focus on technology fits endogenous theories, as they are better at dealing with technological change than neoclassical theories are. Part of the reason for this is their rejection of diminishing returns, and the focus of neoclassical theories on economic convergence. This book focuses on periods of technological change and the rise of new growth industries, in other words on exactly those periods in history where we would not see diminishing returns. And the focus is, for more or less the same reason, on economic divergence rather than convergence: Countries that are successful in implementing technology and making good use of it will forge ahead. Eventually, the technology will grow mature and commonplace, with convergence setting in, but until this occurs, the name of the game is divergence, with one or a few countries forging ahead of the others because of their successful application of the new technology. This favors endogenous theories.

However, these theories do not really deal with the state. They have also been criticized for their treatment of technological change, knowledge and human capital for being mechanical and unrealistic. They routinely consider technology a public good, and hence easily transferable, both within and between countries. The same goes for knowledge. Endogenous theories have a tendency to treat technology and knowledge as tangible, easily quantifiable and accessible. However; technology is not a public good, but embedded in organizational structures. It is not necessarily easily transferable. Firms often do what they can to keep other firms from acquiring technology in order to stay competitive. Moreover, transfers between countries are more difficult than within a country (Hodgson 1996:393; Metcalfe 2001:7).

Hence, while drawing on established theories, these are not sufficient. Mokyr (1990; 2002b) refers to the kind of growth based on technology and knowledge as "Schumpeterian". Schumpeterian hints at a different set of theories, namely evolutionary theories. Despite outward similarities with endogenous theories, and despite convergence between endogenous and evolutionary theories, evolutionary theories are organic and biological where endogenous theories are mechanical. Evolutionary theories have a more realistic take on the accumulation of technology and knowledge, as well as the diffusion of these. Also, the growth process in evolutionary theories is more uncertain. Radical innovations are hard to predict, and institutional and historical contexts affect the way and the extent to which they successfully filter down into the economy. Thus, path-dependencies and historical accidents often play as significant a role in long-term technological trajectories as does the standard neoclassical assumption of rational actors with perfect foresight.

Another advantage of evolutionary theories is that from the outset these were conceived as *disequilibrium* theories. That is, unlike neoclassical theories, they do not see the economy as first and foremost characterized by a steady march toward economic equilibrium. Instead, they focus on periods of transition, on processes of structural change, on path-dependencies, and on the extreme long run. Endogenous theories, despite relaxing numerous neoclassical assumptions, are still equilibrium theories.[6] Thus, they have major difficulties explaining long-term economic transformation and technological change. As equilibrium theories, they can cope with microinventions. However, evolutionary theories take greater interest in those breaks and discontinuities that arise from radical inventions (or macroinventions). Technological discontinuities and economic transformations are macro phenomena that require a richer framework than the neoclassical (including endogenous) (Fagerberg 1994:1147; Gilpin 1996:411pp; 2001:106; Nelson 1995:68pp; Verspagen 2002:1). Hence, it is important to be true to the historical narrative provided by each and every case. Each case goes through a historical evolution involving complex interactions and evolutionary relationships between different actors, the state often (but not always) being the most important one.

Schumpeterian Growth and Evolutionary Theory

Technological progress is crucial for its effects on long-term economic growth. However, there are several kinds, and they are not all equally interesting. *Ceteris paribus*, a nation's GNP will rise when its population grows. More subjects means higher overall production, more people to tax, a potentially larger army, etc. But it does not imply increased productivity. Clearly, the growth induced solely by population increase is not what is interesting. Instead, what we regularly look for is average real income per capita increasing together with demographic growth, in other words some form of increase in per capita GNP. Yet, per capita GNP growth figures tell a very imperfect story. In particular, they do not tell us much about what goes on behind the figures. Economic statistics are like sports scores. They tell us the result, maybe even who scored the goals, but absolutely nothing about the game

---

6   However, very much in line with evolutionary theories, endogenous theories reject constraining neoclassical assumptions like asymmetric information, economies of scale and entry-barriers.

itself! The kind of growth that is interesting usually entails some form of *structural change*, not normally captured by aggregate statistics. To better understand the focus of this book, it is necessary to present a short typology of different types of growth.

First, there is investment-led, or Solovian growth (after Robert Solow). Economic growth takes place when capital accumulates more rapidly than the growth of the labor force, thus leading to higher output per capita through increased productivity (although only temporarily). The second is Smithian growth, based on commercial expansion, also known as gains from trade—a more specialized division of labor leads to productivity growth. Third is growth based on scale or size effects. Without downgrading the importance of these types of growth (and while recognizing that in most cases growth consists of several components at the same time), this book deals with so-called *Schumpeterian* growth, based on increases in the stock of human knowledge and technological innovation (Mokyr 1990:4pp; 2002b:3pp).

There are several reasons to focus on Schumpeterian growth: The first is obvious. Traditional neoclassical theories cannot account for more than modest amounts of long-term growth. The rest is a residual, routinely associated with technological progress. Most analyses attribute such significant portions of overall growth to technological progress that while acknowledging the importance of non-Schumpeterian growth, technological change is in itself important enough to justify a focus on this aspect of growth exclusively.[7]

The second reason is less obvious, but equally important. Without technological change, the three other forms of growth will sooner or later (granted that no exogenous shocks take place) run into diminishing returns. Only Schumpeterian growth may escape this. Theoretically, one might conceive of processes where markets could grow ever bigger, and where specialization grows ever more extreme. But for all practical purposes there are limits as to how far such processes can run. Contrary to this, technological change is more rapid and more important than ever, showing no signs of slowing down. One could of course conceive of a world in which technological progress came to a halt because there was essentially nothing left to invent. In that case, technological progress would run into diminishing returns as well. However, there is no indication that this is happening. As long as technological progress occurs, no diminishing returns set in.

A third reason is intricately intertwined with international relations. Technological progress has, at least since the Industrial Revolution, been linked with leadership in the international system. While there are examples of countries with impressive growth spurts not based on technological change, and while there are examples of militarily powerful and influential countries that have *not* been at the technological frontier, political dominance has been associated not only with international leadership, but with economic prowess stemming from technological sophistication (Modelski and Thompson 1996).

---

7   For the G–5 countries (US, Japan, Germany, France, Great Britain) 50–75 per cent of post-war growth was due to "technical progress" (Kim and Lau 1994).

Historically, evolutionary thinking can be traced back to people as diverse as Alexander Hamilton, Friedrich List and Karl Marx, although the one that has done the most to promote this tradition is probably the Austrian economist Joseph Schumpeter. There is a host of different evolutionary theories. Biological models and metaphors have been the main starting-point. The theory of evolutionary *economics* finds its modern roots in Nelson and Winter (1982:6), who distinguish between *evolutionary economic* theory on the one hand, and *orthodox* theories[8] on the other. *Orthodox* theories are rejected for being blind to phenomena associated with historical change. Verspagen (2001:6) identifies four main characteristics fairly generic to evolutionary economics. One of these is about structural change. Radical innovations create new industries, but incremental innovations are the driving force behind the growth of these. Incremental innovations tied in with the radical innovation, make it possible for the radical innovation to have an impact on the overall economy.

There are numerous strands of evolutionary theorizing. In this book, I draw extensively on Schumpeter. The neo-Schumpeterian school refers to a set of theories that pay particular attention to the role of, and relationship between, technology and institutions in the process of economic growth, with Schumpeter's disequilibrium dynamics a main contribution (Verspagen 2001:5). At the core of most explanations is the intertwining of the techno-economic and the socioinstitutional (e.g. Dosi (1982), Freeman and Perez (1988), Freeman and Soete (1999), Gilpin (1996)). The world economy is in a constant state of flux. Technologies and institutions change over time. What drives growth in one era is most likely not equally important in the next.

The neo-Schumpeterian tradition has a somewhat heavy technological bias. Hence, while a useful starting point, it is not in itself enough. Schumpeter (1939) adopted the Russian economist Kondratieff's view of the world economy as having gone through successive waves of industrial revolutions of empirically 50–60 years each. While this is far too deterministic to be credible,[9] most historians will admit that cotton textiles, water power and steam power were important with respect to explaining the late eighteenth- and early nineteenth-century British economy. Evolutionary economists (e.g. Freeman and Perez 1988; Freeman and Louçã 2001; Mokyr 1990; 2002a) argue that different historical epochs have been characterized by different types of technology, giving rise to new, important growth industries; iron and railroads; steel, chemicals and electrification; Fordism and the production of consumer durables (cars in particular); and industries based on ICTs. The same sectors are also routinely identified by historians and social scientists—Bairoch

8   See the following list of theorists representing the broader tradition of Western economic thought: Smith, Ricardo, Mill, Marshall, Walras (Nelson and Winter 1982:6pp).

9   A significant amount of early evolutionary theorizing arose from a fairly deterministic, more or less strictly cyclical, interpretation of long waves. However, the overwhelming amount of authors adhere to a weaker, non-deterministic version of the theory, in which they adopt Schumpeter's clustering of innovations and periods of creative destruction, but reject the position that waves have a predetermined duration (Freeman and Soete 1999; Freeman and Perez 1988; Reinert 1994b; Verspagen 2001).

(1982), Cameron and Neal (2003), Hobsbawm (1969), Landes (1969; 1998), Gilpin (1981; 1987), Modelski and Thompson (1996) and Rostow (1978). While not altogether uncontroversial, there is solid support and justification in the literature for choosing a focus on periods of technological change and economic transition.

Radical innovations create new and prosperous industries, while incremental innovations tie in with the radical innovations and add economic weight to them. When the new industries become saturated, running out of further opportunities for investment and growth, the world economy drifts into a structural depression that can ultimately only be resolved when (or if) new growth industries, based on new breakthrough technologies, occur to provide the world economy with a new industrial engine. As this happens, industrial and overall economic leadership of one country may falter, and another country rises to industrial and overall economic prominence. To use Schumpeter's (1942:81pp; 1983 [1934]) own terminology: The world economy goes through "waves of creative destruction". Depression leads to the destruction of a multitude of old firms and industries, but also to the creation of new ones. For a country to be economically successful in the extreme long term, both the creation phase and the destruction phase must be allowed to play themselves out. Seeking to prevent the phase of destruction only leads to economic rigidities and to long-term failure.

Technological progress is not a neutral process of gradual accumulation of incrementally more efficient technologies. We do not just add one extra unit of "technology" to achieve so and so amounts of economic growth. To neoclassical theories all technologies are essentially the same. Technological progress is good because it enables us to produce what we previously did at a lower cost—productivity has improved. But to evolutionary economists, technological progress also has qualitative effects. In addition to improving productivity, evolutionists argue that some innovations are particularly important as they have the potential to transform the economy. Radical innovations disrupt existing economic structures and force new institutional setups and routines on the economy. They give rise to new growth industries and destroy old ones (Freeman and Soete 1999:329pp; Nelson 1995:76pp; Verspagen 2001:5p).

This implies an understanding of economics, technology and institutions as part of the same framework. In order to achieve long-term growth a country requires a set of institutions compatible with and supportive of the new technologies in order to be able to make good use of them. Institutions well suited for an earlier paradigm may be completely inappropriate for the new one (Freeman and Perez 1988:50pp; Gilpin 1996; Nelson 1995:80).[10]

In other words; some economic activities are more important than others. Countries that have mastered the core technology of a particular historical era, and have been successful in setting up industries employing this technology, are the ones

---

10 Different scholars have framed this in different ways. Nelson (1995:79) speaks of *technological regimes*, Dosi (1982) of *technological paradigms*, Freeman and Perez (1988) of *techno-economic paradigms*.

that have forged ahead, grown in power, stature and economic strength. Hence, it is crucial for a country to perform well within those technologies and industries that are linked with the core technologies of a techno-economic paradigm.[11] This among other things has to do with the rejection of evolutionists of two important assumptions of orthodox neoclassical models—the absence of economies of scale and entry-barriers—and also ties in with Schumpeter's ideas about imperfect competition and temporary monopolistic conditions.

Schumpeter reasoned that a monopoly position might be more conducive to technological progress than perfect market competition.[12] It is the dynamic, imperfect competition in markets controlled by a limited amount of suppliers that fuels growth. Monopolistic conditions are necessary in order to promote the rapid adoption and innovation of new technologies. Large firms introduce new methods of production beyond the reach of smaller firms, and are thus able to produce cheaper goods in larger quantities than under conditions of free competition. Industrial activity within old, established businesses and methods of production rarely yields great returns. The greatest profits are made in new industries or in industries that adopt new methods or technologies (Scherer 1984:vii; Schumpeter 1997a:200 [1946]; 1997b:258pp [1949]).[13]

Hence, unlike neoclassicists, evolutionary theories recommend that an economy specialize within sectors that are particularly growth-inducive. These are typically sectors that require advanced technologies and/or specialized human skills and knowledge. Being the first firm to enter a new sector or employ a new technology, makes it easier to expand freely, in the process making it harder for competing firms to gain a foothold. Also, if a sector requires advanced technologies and skills, any new firm that wants to establish itself must also have these. Thus, an established firm can effectively raise the entry-cost of any new firm by consistently being at the technological frontier, for all practical purposes creating entry-barriers and temporary monopolies by innovating.

On a nation-wide scale: A country's prospects for long-term growth and development depends on its ability to perform well within new technologies, new

---

11 This is also indicative of an inherent relationship between International Relations theory and economics. Evolutionary economic theories are theories, not of economy, but of *political* economy. In evolutionary theories the link between economics and the international system is widely recognized. Economic power translates into overall power. For an attempt at combining these two aspects, see Modelski and Thompson (1996).

12 With perfect competition, there will be no investments, no R & D expenses and no profits—a consequence of the fact that a price-taker in a perfect market will set its price equal to the unit cost (Nelson and Winter 1982:284pp).

13 This weakens Ricardo's theory of comparative advantage. One may still have a comparative advantage within certain sectors, but these sectors may not be very profitable. A comparative advantage in potato chips is not as favorable as a comparative advantage in micro chips. As anyone can produce potato chips cheaply, prices remain low, and no one grows rich, while monopolistic market conditions imply numerous gains to be had from a prospering micro chip industry.

industries and particularly growth-inducive sectors. And it depends on its ability to find sectors from which it can reap monopoly gains. A country can forge ahead and stay there by being at the technological frontier, continuously creating new entry-barriers and benefiting from economies of scale by being first (Reinert 1994b:12p).[14] This suggests a role for the state. A country, in order to be successful, needs a state that is willing to ride the waves of technological change, of causing them, catching them, or at least creating conditions conducive to catching them. The question becomes one of tracing these conditions.

The State: Mancur Olson and Preventing Sclerosis

There is a virtually complete consensus that secure and effective property rights and well-functioning markets are among the most important conditions for long-term growth (e.g. Bethell 1998; Epstein 2000; North and Weingast 1989; Pipes 1999; Roll and Talbott 2001). Thus, a number of scholars have focused on how the state can be instrumental in securing such rights.

Among the most-cited accounts on the role of the state and the rise of the west, is North and Weingast (1989), and their treatment of the 1688 English Glorious Revolution. The role of the state should be limited, so as to prevent the arbitrary abuse of power by the sovereign, thus improving stability, predictability and reducing transaction costs. This happened with the Glorious Revolution. Property rights and the expansion of markets laid the necessary foundations for the Industrial Revolution, which followed under a century later. Epstein (2000) presents a very different argument. The main political-regime barriers usually arose from a state's inability to enforce a unified, non-discriminatory fiscal and legal regime. Jurisdictional fragmentation and monopolies inherited from medieval days increased negotiation, enforcement and exaction costs. *Limitations to state sovereignty* constrained property rights and the rise of competitive markets. Fierce competition in the European state system ensured that empirically, the arbitrary abuse of power was less of a problem. Hence, what was needed was a strong state, with full sovereignty.

However, these very different arguments both belong in a pre-industrial context. Pre-industrial growth has been primarily Smithian. But this logic does not necessarily apply to industrialization, which implies technological growth, which is Schumpeterian. Granted, property rights and well-functioning markets are crucial. It is hard to imagine a country where property rights were systematically abused and

---

14 This is *not* synonymous with the strategic trading schools of among others Robert Reich and Lester Thurow (Krugman 1994). Paul Krugman's criticism is valid: If everyone identifies the same strategic businesses, these will attract so much investment that capacity moves ahead of the market and profits plummet. It may also lead to firms entering into sectors in which they have no core competency (ibid.:253). Although a version of this argument plays some part in evolutionary thinking, for success it is far more important to exploit new (and often generic) technologies to improve one's productivity in those areas where one already has an advantage, in other words use the new technologies to increase one's potential for economies of scale.

long-term growth still the outcome. However, if we were to analyze the causes of present-day long-term growth and development in industrialized countries, property rights would give us little leverage for the obvious reason that most countries are doing fairly well in this respect already. In other words, as long as the countries analyzed are fairly developed, for success or failure we need to look beyond background variables. While preconditions like well-functioning markets, property rights, infrastructure are necessary parts of a framework for industrial growth, this is not where the extra intellectual effort should be put in.

Instead, for the industrialized era and for Schumpeterian growth, the role of the state is about the promotion of new technology and industries. Hence, the first component that needs to be in place in a theoretical framework for Schumpeterian growth is human capital. Surely, if well-endowed in human capital, a country is more likely to enjoy a technological advantage. There is an obvious role for the state in promoting such skills through primary and higher education and by setting up technical institutes, cross-disciplinary research facilities, sponsoring technology support, marketing and internationalization efforts, etc.

However, without the *diffusion* of knowledge, a country will not gain much from its human capital, and no large-scale technological change will occur. The role of the state thus also becomes one of promoting diffusion, that is, of seeking to put knowledge to good use. Diffusion has often been the domain of actors not normally associated with the state. Still, we cannot focus exclusively on the production of knowledge, not caring about how or if it is being utilized. Producing the best experts in the world counts for precious little if one is unable to make good use of them. Technology often diffuses distinctly slowly, especially across borders. There are numerous examples that countries with excellent knowledge-bases have been unable to benefit (Freeman 1995, Lundvall 1998; 2002, OECD 1997).

Human capital can only be a start and a foundation. Success is never permanent. Technological progress allows for new industries to grow, and for old ones to fade into oblivion. And consequently, it allows for the rise of some nations and the fall of others. One might think that the lead country within one set of technologies and industries would naturally be the one with the greatest chance of succeeding within the next breakthrough technology (and subsequent industries) as well. However, it has often been the case that a country that has done well within one set of technologies and industries, has not been equally successful when the next industrial revolution has come along. With Gilpin:

> ... a society can become locked into economic practices and institutions that in the past were congruent with successful innovation but which are no longer congruent in the changed circumstances. Powerful vested interests resist change, and it is very difficult to convince a society that what has worked so well in the past may not work in an unknown future. Thus, a national system of political economy that was most "fit" and efficient in one era of technology and market demand is very likely to be "unfit" in a succeeding age of new technologies and new demands. (1996:413)

There will always be opposition against inventions and new technology. New knowledge displaces existing skills and reduces rents. Technological change leads to losses for those that have specific assets tied in with the old technology—formal skills, tacit knowledge, reputation, specialized equipment, ownership of natural resources, barriers to entry that ensured monopoly positions, etc. Through history, sclerosis has materialized in different ways, as opposition to the implementation of new technology has taken different forms (Mokyr 1990): Outright physical resistance against new technology, as in riots, strikes, and the destruction of new machinery. Opposition has also taken the form of laws and regulations restricting the implementation of new technologies, as well as barriers of entry—guild systems, trade unions, labor unions, lobby groups, state monopolies etc. Finally, once powerful interests have formed, they have managed to shield themselves against competition and change by pushing through protection and favorable treatment—tariffs and subsidies.

In addition to providing the proper knowledge base for innovation, there are thus numerous tasks that the state needs to perform in order to prevent vested interests from blocking new technology. The argument is one that blends Schumpeter and Mancur Olson, and should for practical purposes be considered like something of a balancing act. Unlike Schumpeter, Olson's view of the economy was not cyclical. Also, Olson did not focus on technology in particular. Olson's (1982) by now famous argument has to do with interest groups and vested interests. Too much institutional stability leads to institutional rigidity. Societies that have had to start over again, reforming their institutions and breaking up old monopolies of power and economic vested interests, are the ones that have been economically prosperous. Stability on the other hand, has led to a silting up of vested interests, to stasis, sclerosis and to an inability to alter the status quo. Economic policy becomes trivial as it is controlled by vested interest, unwilling and uninterested in change. As a result, the country gradually drifts into economic obscurity.

However, the argument can easily be applied to technological change, as a dynamic argument rather than a static one. This happens when we mix in Schumpeter, and the dynamic, or cyclical, Schumpeterian world economy. Technologies come and go, and industries and interest groups come and go with them. Unlike the Olsonian world, the Schumpeterian world is in a constant state of flux. Hence, the first mover in Schumpeter's world is not institutional stability or rigidity (causing stagnation), but technological change (or its absence). When technological change, or for that matter, creative destruction, is allowed to occur, sclerosis from institutional rigidities will not happen. When the process of creative destruction is blocked, it will.

As with Olson, rigidities silt up in the Schumpeterian world too, but here because of vested interests springing from new technologies. New technologies sooner or later mature, becoming commonplace and obsolete, and thus give way to newer technologies and newer industries. This is the Schumpeterian dynamic, which gives the original Olsonian argument a different twist. It now allows for the state to actively promote and protect new technologies and new industries while they are still young and vulnerable, both against foreign competition and against blocking efforts by vested interests attached to old technologies and traditional industries. But if this promotion and protection is allowed to go on for too long, we are stuck in an Olsonian trap, where vested interests have once again been allowed to rise and grow economically and politically influential.

Hence, the role of the state entails at least two tasks, seemingly at odds: The state needs to promote new and potentially promising industries—that is promote structural economic change, away from old and stagnant industries and into new and promising ones (or at least preventing old and stagnant industries from blocking the growth of new and promising ones). However, the state must also prevent these new industries from becoming so powerful that a few decades down the line, they themselves have a vested interest—as well as the political and economic influence— in blocking further structural economic change, and new and promising industries from arising. In other words, stagnant and obsolete industries should not be unduly overprotected. Tariffs and subsidies to such industries would harm the economy and reduce the chances of a successful shift toward production in new and promising industries. To frame this in terms of product cycle theories, in an early stage of a technology or an industry's product cycle, it is important to promote that industry, or the diffusion of that technology. Toward the end of the product cycle, it is important *not* to support that very same industry, as it will impede upon structural change, and harm the chances of future success in new industries. To frame it in terms of Schumpeter, the state must see to it that both the "creative" and the "destructive" part of the process of *creative destruction* are allowed to happen. The state needs to prevent technological progress from creating the forces that will eventually destroy it. It must recognize that technological progress, and economic growth, is not a situation of stasis, and that what works today probably does not work equally well in 50 years. In many ways, the role of the state becomes one of avoiding institutional rigidities, or to use the language of Mancur Olson (1982; 2000), of avoiding *sclerosis*.

What Kind of State has the Ability to Prevent Sclerosis?

Outlining what the state needs to do in order to prevent sclerosis is one thing. The more pressing question is; how does the state do this? What kind of state is better able to counter sclerosis?[15]

---

15 Definitions of the state have tended to focus on two separate issues. First, to what extent does the state have the necessary political autonomy to implement policy? The question has normally been raised within a temporally static framework, with the state considered an exogenous variable. Second, congruity: How do institutional structures change in response to changes domestically or abroad? This is a question that has normally been answered within a temporally dynamic framework, with the state as an intervening variable (Krasner 1984:224). Here, I end up somewhere in-between. First, I draw on static approaches. I suggest a role for the state that has to do exactly with the implementation of government policies. The extent to which the state has the necessary autonomy to carry out policy is crucial. The state *is* an independent actor as in the statist model. This corresponds to the Olsonian part of the framework. But second, there is a dynamic focus, corresponding to the mix of Schumpeter and Olson. Unlike statists, I am concerned with processes of change. To what extent is the

North and Weingast (1989) argue that a weak state is more conducive to growth, Epstein (2000) pleads the case for centralization and "full" sovereignty. However, these arguments run into problems when extended to the industrial era: Although probably underestimating the amount of change in the pre-industrial (Smithian) world, there is little doubt that the pace of change began to accelerate fairly dramatically with industrialization and Schumpeterian growth—not so much during the first years, but gradually ever more. Centralized states may be better at promoting technological change, but can also more easily adopt anti-technology regulations and more effectively protect or cater to vested interests than a state that is endowed with less than "full" sovereignty. For the pre-industrial era this was less of a problem, as the pace of change was slower. Political instability arising from structural change was less likely to occur. But technological change and structural economic change at a greater pace, implies a much greater degree of overall change to a society and a much greater challenge to a government than does the extension of markets or the establishment of secure property rights. That centralization is good for markets does not by extension mean that it is good for technological change, which depends on creativity as much as regulation. Hence, Mokyr (1990) makes the observation that the weaker the state, the less its ability to block innovation. Some centralized and autocratic regimes like Germany and Japan accepted the challenge in a very deliberate attempt to modernize. But without the incentive, authoritarian governments are too concerned with political instability to risk large-scale structural change. While strong states may be better able to implement change once they have decided on it, it may be easier to find the willingness to do so in weaker states. Similarly, political fragmentation is no guarantee that creativity will persist. In countless cases, fragmentation has led to stagnation rather than the advance of technology.[16] But where Mokyr is right, is that centralized states, as in authoritarian

---

state able to affect these processes, and to what extent is it able to adapt to them? In this context, the state becomes an intervening variable, in a framework that is temporally dynamic. This is a framework in which institutional change is abrupt, and where stasis is the norm for long periods of time, but where crisis gives rise to sudden change and to efforts to meet challenges (ibid.:234) presented by new breakthrough technologies.

Krasner (1984:224) suggests four different conceptualizations of the state. 1) The state as government: "the collective set of personnel who occupy positions of decisional authority in the polity". 2) The state as "public bureaucracy or administrative apparatus as a coherent totality and as an institutionalized order". 3) The state as a ruling class. 4) The state as normative order. While I do refer to the state as ruling elites, the ruling class, and as political elites, there is nothing Marxist to this, as opposed to 3) above. Rather, the definition of the state employed here falls closer to 2). The state is an administrative apparatus and a legal order. Also drawing on 1), the most important actor within this apparatus is the government. However, the state is more than just the government, and while being the most important actor, by no means the only actor. A country's political elites encompass more than just the government, hence terms like "political elites" rather than just government.

16 However, Mokyr's (1990) weak state is not the conceptual opposite of Epstein's (2000) centralized state. Likewise, centralized does not have to imply any degree of authoritarianism.

states, are better at decisively screwing up. Thus, what is needed is more than just acquiring a capacity for regulating the economy, striking down on resistance against the implementation of new technology, etc. The regime must also harbor some form of willingness or tolerance toward change, something found less often with authoritarian rulers.

If for instance centralization were the sole redeeming variable, we would soon run into diminishing returns. The secular trend over the past 250 years has been one of most states having ever more control and sovereignty. Thus, if for the sake of argument we assume that Britain's industrial head start can be explained by centralization and sovereignty, how do we explain Britain's eventual and gradual industrial waning? Did Britain become less centralized? On the one hand, this makes intuitive sense, as other countries were more centralized than Britain at the time. On the other hand, by the late nineteenth century, Britain was in absolute terms stronger than it had ever been before, more centralized than during the early Industrial Revolution. Thus, it is hard to use for instance centralization as an explanatory variable when the secular trend is one of continuous centralization.

It is also the case that very different regimes have been able to achieve technological progress, industrial leadership and long-term growth. States as dissimilar as laissez-faire Britain and laissez-faire (although highly protectionist) US, authoritarian Germany and Japan have been among the most successful states ever, and a common denominator is hard to find if the measure applied is too rough. Measures like centralized vs. decentralized, authoritarian vs. democratic etc. do not make sense.

An insight derived from De Long (2000) provides a better clue: Contrary to popular belief, long-term growth is not a high priority of the state. Rather, politics consists of millions of seemingly trivial decisions. Before any decision can be made on abstract and overarching issues, countless minor concerns have to be addressed and satisfied. True, technological change and long-term growth are concerns, but mainly of high-flying rhetoric, and with a focus often decidedly short-term (as in reelection). This is true of present-day democratic policy-making where politics often comes down to administration, bureaucracy and negotiations, but equally true in regimes of yesteryear, where assorted different interests took priority over growth and development, and where very concrete military issues usually took precedence over more abstract and long-term issues like technological change and economic growth.

Maybe it is possible to frame the strong vs. weak states argument in a light that makes it more useful? Knutsen (1999:168) argues that there is a distinct difference between being a strong *state* and being a strong *power*. Being strong as a power

---

The main point: Centralized states and authoritarian states both have the ability to implement change once they have decided on it, but they also have the ability to block such change to a far greater extent than a fragmented state. Then again, the politically fragmented state may not have the necessary autonomy to implement change at all. Conclusion: These are in all likelihood all the wrong kinds of variables.

hinges on economic and military might, but does not preclude weakness as a state. Of the two Cold War superpowers, only one, the United States, was a strong state, even if both were undisputedly supremely strong powers. The Soviet Union was fraught with corruption, internal instabilities, a stalling economy and a population less than utterly convinced as to the benevolence of the regime. A state is strong because of *social cohesion*—because of what holds it together. This implies a state where rulers have authority whether they are being authoritarian or not, a state which is permanent, and does not change radically; it also implies a state which is perceived as one community, with an implicit social contract, instead of harboring several competing communities (Holsti 1996:104pp).

One of the ideas of this book is that the more cohesive the state, the greater the chance of preventing sclerosis, and the greater the chance of preventing vested interests from gaining control over the state and from creating institutional rigidities favoring the status quo. As mentioned above, with concepts like centralization, secular trends present problems of interpretation. Another weakness of theories of long-term growth and of the state is that, at a time where most scholars have rejected Rostow's (1960) notion of a take-off into sustained growth as simplistic (or downright wrong), what a number of theories seem to be looking for is exactly that, namely take-off conditions! With social cohesion, we avoid these kinds of problems. Countries have gone through both cohesive and less cohesive periods, with no discernible secular trend. Cohesion is something that seemingly very different regimes may conceivably have in common.

If we accept De Long's (2000:139p) point, that ultimately, technological change and long-term growth is not very high on the list of the state's priorities, the likelihood that the state will successfully pursue policies that seriously go against the interests of powerful vested interests (that is, policies of structural economic change), is small indeed, unless there is a fairly strong *consensus* about what policies to pursue. A truism of political science is that the most immediate concern of a regime is its own survival.[17] The likelihood of survival diminishes greatly if controversial decisions, with potentially grave effects—concrete and obvious losers vs. less than concrete winners—have to be made (e.g. Pierson 1996). Hence, decisions with potentially grave redistributive effects are politically risky, and will with a much greater likelihood be made if there is a solid political consensus surrounding these policies. Consensus means less room for vested interests to exploit fragmentation within the political apparatus.

Since there are different kinds of regimes, we should allow for different forms of cohesion, and at different levels. In a democracy, or at least a fairly representative regime (after all, how many democracies do we find in eighteenth- and nineteenth-century Europe?!), strong and permanent political alliances and a comparative lack of

---

17 For two classical, but very different expressions of this view, see Downs (1957) and Waltz (1979).

political fragmentation would be one situation in which sclerosis could be avoided.[18] In authoritarian regimes, political alliances would have to take different forms. Here, one would instead have to focus on the kind of power alliances the ruler would have to keep satisfied in order to stay in power.

Does cohesion apply to the population? In democracies it is fairly obvious that it does. In order to stay in power, political parties need at least to some extent to cater to the voters. And it is easier for the populace to accept political decisions with potentially large redistributive effects if there is already a healthy amount of cohesion, and a general perception that the government is legitimate, the rules of the game acceptable, and there is a healthy amount of trust in the government and in central political institutions. Under such conditions, it is less risky for politicians to undertake controversial policies with potentially large redistributive effects. The importance of the populace was probably less before the franchise extensions of the nineteenth century. At the same time, popular dissent was often voiced through non-institutional channels, as riots and strikes. Thus, even without institutional channels, lack of cohesiveness has made it harder for regimes to survive.

Does cohesion apply only to democracies? One might imagine that authoritarian states are better able to prevent sclerosis, since their decision-making structure is simpler, and since a dictator can more easily make decisions without adhering to the whims of vested interests. However, dictators like other rulers are supported by power alliances that need to be persistently satisfied. Whereas governments in democratic countries merely go out of power, dictators routinely get killed if and when deposed. Hence, authoritarian regimes may actually be less happy about structural economic change than democracies, as their legitimacy is derived in a more tenuous manner, and therefore more cautious about upsetting the status quo. Thus, for an authoritarian state, avoiding sclerosis probably requires a more obvious commitment. This also goes for cohesion in the people. Because of the tenuous basis for legitimacy,[19] dictatorships are skeptical about upsetting the status quo, and potentially even more so than democracies.

For practical purposes, I have divided the notion of social cohesion into two. First, there is *political consensus*, which applies to the political elites. Second, there is *social cohesion*, which applies to the people. To spell the implications out: 1) A

---

18 Although a cautionary note from Olson (1982) should be added. The countries that are the most stable are also the ones where institutional rigidities are more likely to build up. Thus, the lack of political fragmentation cannot be understood as the permanent rule by one party, as this might very possibly lead to the dominance of one or a few strong vested interests, and the permanent build-up of rigidities. Instead, what is important is that during periods of structural economic change, political decisions are made in a way that does not conform to the pressures of old and powerful vested interests. For this, cohesion is useful.

19 Although again: Is a dictator more susceptible to requirements of cohesion than a democratically elected leader? A dictator could probably live with serious amounts of discontent in the people as long as no open revolt took place, as long as he felt secure, and as long as the economy kept running fairly smoothly. In contrast, he might be more dependent on the support of core power alliances than a democratically elected leader.

lack of political consensus and/or a lack of social cohesion in the people, make it easier for vested interests to pursue their own interests. A lack of political consensus makes it easier to exploit differences of opinion between different parties or decision-makers. A lack of cohesion in the people makes it more risky for political parties or other decision-makers to pursue policies with potentially large redistributive effects (with concrete losers and not so concrete winners). 2) Political consensus and/or social cohesion in the people make it easier to promote structural economic change, that is, making decisions that are in the interest of society at large, going against those of vested interests. For practical purposes, this means an end to favoring old and stagnant industries on behalf of new promising ones. Political consensus makes it more difficult for vested interests to pursue continued protection and it makes it less risky for political parties or other decision-makers to pursue policies with potentially large redistributive effects. Social cohesion in the people makes it less risky for political parties or other decision-makers to pursue policies with potentially large redistributive effects.

Two qualifications need to be made. Nothing has been said about *how* social cohesion arises. While in itself an interesting problem, it is not my focus. The concern is with whether or not social cohesion is strong, not on how it happened. The second qualification has to do with political consensus and decision-making. Consensus does *not* by necessity lead to technological change, industrial growth and economic development. A consensus might easily center from around distinctly dumb choices! Even if we assume strictly rational actors, situations where individual rationality does not yield results, socially optimal results are easy to find. It is not hard to envisage situations where it was economically irrational for businessmen to invest in new technology, even if in the long run this effectively doomed their domestic industries. However, this is not the problem focused on in this book. Consensus and cohesion does not by necessity lead to technological change and industrial growth. Rather, consensus and cohesion greatly increase the chances of such transitions being successfully overcome. Without consensus and cohesion, the chances of missing out are much greater, as politically daring and controversial decisions have much graver consequences for the government, and will not be made for fear of being overthrown or losing the next election.

The Argument and the Structure of the Book

Summarizing the argument, the remaining chapters seek to show the following: First, that human capital has been crucial for technological progress and industrial leadership. An emphasis on new industries and on breakthrough technologies, naturally invite a focus on human capital. The different industries are not all equally research-intensive, but having the appropriate skill base has still been of vital importance.[20]

Second, that the countries that have successfully risen to industrial leadership are countries where the state has been able to resist the pressures of vested interests against structural change. Unlike Schumpeter, Mancur Olson has no cyclical understanding of the economy, and his focus is on the overall economy, not on specific technologies or industries. However, Olson and Schumpeter fit neatly together. Schumpeter provides an understanding of long-term cyclical macrotrends in the economy and the rise and fall of industries from shocks to the economy. Olson provides a mechanism by which these shocks occur. Structural change in an economy is always a thorny and tenuous process, and routinely meets with resistance from vested interest groups that perceive of their group as threatened by change. Olson (1982) warns us that long-term stagnation in an economy is the result of a process of vested interests over time accumulating political influence, eventually becoming so powerful that they can use the influence to block structural economic change in order to preserve the existing status quo, but in the process dooming the economy to long-term decline.

Hence, there is a role for the state in preventing vested interests from growing so powerful that they can effectively block structural economic change, thus seeing to it that the destruction of inefficient industries is allowed to unfold. But the state also needs to encourage the creation part. Thus, there is a role for the state in promoting new and potentially promising industries, in other words channeling resources away from old and stagnant industries and into the growth industries of the future. And finally, this means that there is a role for the state in preventing these new industries that the state has encouraged and promoted from eventually becoming so powerful that a few decades down the line, they have now become the new vested interest and the new powerful force working to block structural change. In short, the state needs

---

20 What is more important; primary or higher education? 1) The industries included here are not equally knowledge-intensive, despite the fact that they all rest on technological breakthroughs. This in particular applies to the car industry. While the US possessed a clear human capital advantage in car manufacturing, higher education was of less importance. 2) There is an obvious secular trend in the direction of greater state involvement in knowledge production. This means that for the later time periods, differences in primary education is of little importance, since all the countries already score well in this respect. For the more recent time periods, the sciences have become so advanced that the more relevant differences between countries must be attributed to higher education. 3) While industries like cotton textiles and iron required considerable human capital, they did not rely very explicitly on human skills acquired through the formal education system. Education systems were not yet well developed and the sciences sufficiently primitive for adequate and relevant human capital to be accumulated outside of the formal system. Hence, I need to focus less on the formal education system as opposed to trying to make an overall assessment of the country's general level of human capital.

to prevent technological change from creating the forces that will ultimately stifle future change.[21]

Thus, the role of the state can be rephrased along Schumpeterian and Olsonian lines: It is to ensure that no vested interests become so powerful and influential that they can effectively block processes of creative destruction. What the following chapters will show is that this is what happened in those countries that rose to industrial leadership, and it is what failed in the countries that did not.

Either human capital *or* a lack of vested interests is not sufficient. They must appear in conjunction. The absence of vested interests will be of little benefit if the country does not have a human capital base sufficiently developed to take advantage of opportunities arising from new technologies. Likewise, a strong human capital base is not enough. If vested interests can block change, the country will still be unable to provide conditions conducive to industrial growth.

Third and finally, the book seeks an answer to the question of what kind of state this really is. Why is it that some states have been able and willing to control its vested interests, whereas others have patently not? The answer provided in this book takes into account the political difficulties associated with political decisions that go against the interests of powerful societal actors. Often, those losing out from structural change are more visible than the ones benefiting. The number one priority of most regimes is survival. In order to maximize its chances of survival, the regime will seek to avoid controversial political decisions with potentially large redistributive effects. De Long's (2000:139p) point that policies of technological change and long-term growth are not very high on the average regime's priorities, means that there will always be political concerns that are more concrete and pressing. Politics consists of a multitude of small and fairly trivial decisions and a number of interests that have to be satisfied before more overarching goals can be pursued.[22]

---

21 I do not identify particular vested interests *a priori*, although certain vested interests are by default more crucial than others, hence economic interests have been privileged. In particular; have political elites been receptive to the needs of new and vulnerable industries, or have these industries been at the mercy of policies designed to protect the interests of older and more established industries against a change to the status quo? For each time period, I identify the major economically and industrially related political issues, relevant vested interest groups, and to what extent they were successful in influencing government policies. Hence, industrial lobby groups figure prominently, whether lobbying for or against protection, for change in the education curriculum, etc. The variable contains both a deductive and an inductive component. It is deductively derived from theory, but there are a multitude of vested interests, and we cannot a priori derive which interest is the most important for each period. This must be accomplished inductively, through a thorough examination of the historical record.

22 I have divided the variable into two components, consensus and cohesion. A state characterized by both consensus *and* cohesion is better off than a state that is low on consensus and high on cohesion, or the other way around. Whether "low on consensus and high on cohesion" is better or worse than "high on consensus and low on cohesion", strikes me as an empirical question. Because the variable is hard to operationalize, I have tried to shy away

If this is true, most regimes will shy away from policies of structural economic change, unless they have a clear mandate for such policies. Hence, there are only under certain comparably rare conditions that a regime will be strong enough to pursue such policies. What this book seeks to demonstrate is that only regimes characterized by a high degree of *political consensus and social cohesion* have had the ability to undertake potentially controversial and politically risky projects like policies of structural change. They have not always done so, even when they have had this ability, but it is certainly the case that a high degree of consensus and cohesion have been necessary in order for the state to pursue structural policies independently of vested interests.

For an exhaustive treatment of the methodology, I refer the reader to Moe (2004). A few comments are still in order. The following chapters employ a mixture of historic and comparative methods. The one more or less presupposes the other. Without the comparative method, we would be left with only descriptive inference. Without the historical method, the comparative method for all practical purposes leaves us with a set of correlations, but without a large enough sample to make valid inferences. The descriptive inferences drawn out of the historical method provide a foundation for causal inferences when employing the comparative method—historically tracing the micro mechanisms specified by the macro variables in the theoretical framework, and thus creating a foundation for causal inferences about the invariances discovered

---

from controversy, and instead treat the subject matter in such a manner that there should be a great deal of overall consensus as to the variable values. Nevertheless, ultimately the assessments as to whether a country exhibits a high or a low degree of consensus and/or cohesion are mine.

Political consensus: I am looking at broad consensus among the ruling elites as to the major economically and industrially relevant political issues. For practical purposes, this means the government and parliament. However, it is not always this simple, especially when looking at less representative regimes. Bismarckian Germany was less than democratic, but there were still very obvious alliances supporting the regime, for instance involving the Junkers. The Kaiser was closer to omnipotence than most Western monarchs, but considerable wheeling and dealing went on behind his back. When the ruler relies on implicit political alliances in order to remain in power and to implement policies, "ruling elites" becomes a very fluid notion.

Social cohesion: It can be thought of as the bonds that tie a country together (Knutsen, 1999:168). Societies founded on networks of trust and cooperation help realize human potential (OECD, 2001b:39p). Putnam (1995a; 1995b) laments what he sees as a decrease in *social capital* in the US, and Fukuyama (1995) focuses on how successful economies are economies with a high degree of *trust*. Dayton-Johnson (2001:8, 35, 59) defines it as the degree of interconnectedness and trust among a group of people. He refers to "a community of shared values, shared challenges and equal opportunity," and suggests indicators like democratic institutions, an effective judiciary, and a bureaucracy free of corruption. I have sought to make overall assessments as to the general level of social cohesion in the people, based on the historical literature, and the evidence of trust, the record of unrest and turbulence in the population. However, as reliable and valid data on social cohesion are harder to get hold of than for political consensus, privilege has been given to consensus.

through the comparative method. Each and every chapter (with the exception of the automobile chapter) focuses on two countries, comparing one case of success with a one case of (at least relative) failure. While each chapter can be taken as a completed narrative, the full story can only be understood reading the chapters as a whole. For each time period and industry, the juxtaposition of two by two cases yields a design with negative degrees of freedom. Hence, strong inferences should not be made based on each and every chapter, but drawn from all the five time periods put together, where a total of nine cases rule out problems regarding degrees of freedom.

Chapters 2 through 6 comprise the bulk of the book. Chapter 2 analyzes the rise of the cotton textile industry during the early Industrial Revolution and contrasts the overwhelming success of Britain with the far more moderate achievements of France. In chapter 3, the focus is on iron during the early to mid-nineteenth century, where again the overwhelming success of Britain is contrasted with the very partial success of France. The focus of the third time period and chapter 4, late nineteenth century on toward World War I, is on the chemical industry. The number one success case in this chapter is Germany. In addition to the success of Germany, the chapter also contains the failure of Britain, whose industrial power was now waning.

Chapter 5 differs in the sense that it only includes one case—the US. The automobile industry is an easy choice. Choosing the right time period of analysis is harder. For the reason that the chapter seeks to explain the rise of the US car industry instead of European catch-up, the focus has been primarily on the interwar years. Other scholars have chosen to concentrate on the postwar era.[23] There are good reasons for this. 1950–1973 was a period of unprecedented growth, not just in one or two lead countries, but for the entire Western world. However, since my purpose is to explain industrial leadership, it makes less sense to focus on a historical period where US leadership is waning (postwar era) rather than the period when it actually arose, that is the interwar years. The automobile industry of the US reigned so supreme during the interwar years that it is really hard to find any cases with which the US can credibly be contrasted. With respect to automobiles, Europe and Japan emulated the US, but not until quite some time after World War II. Instead of there being a major contrast between the US and its competitors, it is probably more correct to say that European and Japanese manufacturers went through some of the same stages as the US, but with a time delay. Europe and Japan were tremendous successes—but not until after the war. More on this later.

Chapter 6 focuses on industries stemming from breakthroughs in ICTs, and deals with problems of a different nature. First, there is the problem of analyzing a time period that has not yet come to an end. We are very much still in the beginning of the ICT era, and the future is obviously uncertain. It is too early to make any final judgments, and we cannot with certainty predict the outcome of policy decisions made just a few years ago. Second, ICT industries are different in the sense that they

---

23 See Thompson (2000:11p): Motor vehicles, aviation, electronics; 1945–1973. Growth peak: The 1950s.

represent a transition away from mass production manufacturing toward the service industries. Hence, what becomes obvious in the ICT chapter is that the impact of ICTs on the overall economy has had less to do with the manufacturing of ICT equipment, and far more to do with the utilization of such equipment. Thus, I have had to trace ICTs along a dual path. The two countries analyzed in this chapter is the US and Japan. A striking contrast here is how Japan, despite being supremely adept at ICT manufacturing industry, has been a laggard in utilizing its ICTs, very much unlike the US.

Finally, since the book spans a time period of a quarter of a millennium, there is no such thing as a perfect match between theory and empirical findings. However, the final chapter shows that there has been a very distinct pattern to how states have risen and fallen. This is the pattern outlined by the above theory.

Chapter 2

The Cotton Textile Industry

Introduction: Cotton Textiles and the First Industrial Revolution

In many ways the cotton textile industry needs no introduction. It is intrinsically intertwined with the notion of the Industrial Revolution, an event often thought of as a genuine watershed in human history, symbolizing the transition to inanimate power sources. Economically, the period saw British industrial dominance, with dynamic industries like cotton textiles and iron, organized in factories and driven by water and later steam power. Politically, it was a period that spanned both the French Revolution and the Napoleonic Wars—developments that stifled French growth, making Britain's ascendancy to industrial hegemony even more obvious. The British industrial breakthrough combined with French political turmoil, signaled an end to France's challenge for leadership in Europe, thereby cementing the already perceptible British lead.

A number of scholars have warned against the tendency to assume that Britain was by necessity headed for prosperity and France with equal necessity for stagnation, and present-day economic historians tend toward downplaying notions of British peculiarity, instead stressing the continuities in British economic and social history. However, many scholars consider the edge that Britain had on France rather minute. There were clear signs of a proto-industry evolving in France at the time when British industrial growth began to accelerate, and as a whole, there were many progressive tendencies in the French economy of the late eighteenth century. Britain was not even the richest nation in Europe.[1] As late as 1780, the Dutch were probably still ahead in terms of per capita GDP (Kindleberger 1996:126p). Some sources claim that this lasted as long as 1848 (Maddison 2003:59).There is disagreement as to how fast and widespread structural transformation was. To Crouzet (1990:46p), France and Britain advanced at the same pace during the eighteenth century, with annual growth at slightly above one per cent. David Landes (1969:13) thinks it is reasonable to suppose that income in France was moderately lower, but that it kept pace fairly well. Britain was more developed at the beginning of the eighteenth century, and the gap never closed. Impressive French eighteenth-century growth (1715–1789) may really only have been a recovery from abnormally low levels during Louis XIV (Landes 1969:53; Rostow 1975:171). Then again, we may well have underestimated the level of British industrial development prior to the Industrial Revolution. Hence,

---

1   In 1688 Gregory King estimated income per capita to £8 1s 4d in Holland, £7 18s in England and £6 3s in France (Kindleberger 1996:109).

the industrial sector of 1770 may have been twice as large as previously estimated (Jones 1988:22), with the period 1770–1815 therefore exhibiting growth rates quite a bit lower than what has been popular belief.

In any case, most contemporary scholars agree that change was limited primarily to cotton textiles and iron. Structural change was slow, bar within a few sectors, where it was revolutionary. Overall growth rates were very modest by modern standards, although still representing a marked increase over pre-industrial times. Hardly a metamorphosis, the Industrial Revolution was really a slow evolution of preexisting features present in most European economies, although particularly so in Britain. Overall growth rates were low, and the rate of technological progress unimpressive (as measured by *total factor productivity* (TFP) growth). If TFP growth rates are to be taken literally, technological progress made no impact on growth until 1780, and was hardly noticeable between 1780 and 1801 (representing 8–10 per cent of total GDP growth[2]), only gradually picking up from the nineteenth century onwards.[3]

Does this mean that "the Industrial Revolution" is a flawed starting point for this analysis? After all, the focus of this book is on periods of technological change and structural transformation, and the Industrial Revolution does not seem to have been much of a revolution. However, this is actually exactly the pattern one should expect. The rate of technological change in Britain was uneven, concentrated in a few sectors, only negligibly impacting services. Typically, even the greatest of inventions have only a very slight *initial* impact. Also, at such an early stage of mechanization, scale effects were relatively unimportant. Cotton mills may have had a minimum efficient size as low as one hundred and fifty workers. Britain, being the pioneer could not catch up by emulating others (Crafts 1998:196p). Mokyr (1999:12pp) admits that overall growth and productivity rates were not impressive, but reminds us that the traditional economy was still very large (average of 79 per cent, 1780–1860). Revolutionary changes in the modern economy (21 per cent) thus should not be expected to have large effects on overall growth rates.[4] Finally, industrial production trend-growth figures indicate that actual change *did* take place. The best guess series

---

2   Annual GDP growth: 1760–1780 0.6 per cent, 1780–1801 1.3 per cent, 1760–1801 1.0 per cent (Crafts and Harley 1992:718; Crafts 1996:198).

3   There are multiple TFP estimates for Britain. Most estimates support the overall story, namely that technical change was modest, and limited to a few sectors only. Early estimates by for instance Deane and Cole (1962) are commonly considered too optimistic. TFP growth for the era stretching from the 1760s to 1800, ranges from 0.0 per cent to 0.27 per cent, and accounts for somewhere between 0 and 23 per cent of overall growth for the period. (Antràs and Voth 2003; Crafts and Harley 1992; Crafts 1995b; 1996; 1998; Harley 1999; Hoppen 1998). Widely cited figures can be found with Crafts and Harley (1992:718): TFP growth for 1760–1780 was 0.0 per cent, 1780–1801 0.1 per cent, 1760–1801 0.1 per cent.

4   Estimates are from McCloskey (Mokyr 1999:13). Productivity growth in the traditional sectors: 0.6 per cent annually; non-traditional sectors: 1.8 per cent. If we add weights of 79 per cent to the traditional and 21 per cent to the modern economy, this yields 0.79*0.6%+0.21*1.8 %=0.852%. In other words, despite rapid change in the modern economy, overall productivity growth was bound to be modest as long as the traditional economy remained large.

industrial output data of Crafts and Mills (1994:770) and Crafts (1995b:758), reveal three structural breaks: 1776, 1834 and 1874. Industrial production accelerated sharply upward from 1776 onwards, reaching a peak in 1834, with a continuous but more moderate slowdown setting in after 1874.[5] Also, industrialization figures from Bairoch (1982), suggest that already by 1800, Britain was ahead of the rest, even if not by enormous amounts.

Table 2.1 Per Capita Levels of Industrialization (Great Britain in 1900=100)[6]

	1750	1800	1830	1860	1880	1900	1913
Great Britain	10	16	25	64	87	100	115
France	9	9	12	20	28	39	59
Germany	8	8	9	15	25	52	85
US	4	9	14	21	38	69	126
Japan	7	7	7	7	9	12	20

Source: Bairoch (1982:294, 330).

There are those that speak of sweeping overall changes to the economy. Peter Temin (1997) argues that Britain for a protracted time period managed to compete internationally not only within a few sectors, but over a broad range of manufacturing goods, indicating that change was widespread. David Landes (1999:132pp) considers the Industrial Revolution a "rupture". The fact that growth figures do not reveal major change does not counter an understanding of the Industrial Revolution as machines substituting for human skills and strength, the invention of new materials, and a new mode of production. It is true that growth per capita was only around 0.3 per cent. However, Britain simultaneously underwent a population explosion, and being able to do this without any Malthusian checks coming into play is itself evidence of the power of new technology.[7] Bairoch (1982:289) uses the somewhat vague concept of "new technology" industries to make the point that Britain by 1830 had a marked lead over any other country. New technology industries accounted for roughly one-

---

5   Greasly and Oxley (2000:105) suggest that an upward acceleration started around 1795 and peaked around 1825.

6   Bairoch's (1982:321p) indicator of industrialization is manufacturing industry, which covers all forms of industry except mining, construction, and electricity, gas, water and sanitary services. Bairoch (1982:327p) estimates the margin of error to 25–30 per cent for Western countries at the eve of the Industrial Revolution. From 1830 onwards the average margin of error for Europe is 20–30 per cent, and around 20 per cent by 1913.

7   Hudson (1992:42) argues that giving the government sector a more realistic weight (12 per cent instead of eight), doubles Crafts' estimates of 1760–1800 GDP per capita growth rates.

third of British manufacturing output by 1830, as opposed to 6–10 per cent for other western countries.

Despite less than impressive growth and TFP growth figures, the Industrial Revolution is a fruitful starting point. If nothing else, cotton textiles experienced dramatic growth; as did the second main branch of early industrialization, iron. Greasley and Oxley (2000:111pp) find that no industry had more causal links with other industries than cotton textiles. Cotton played a leading role in stimulating coal, cotton yarn, iron and steel goods, pig iron, paper, shipbuilding and sugar; and iron became increasingly important after 1815. However, cotton was the unrivaled number one industry of the early Industrial Revolution, probably accounting for half of all productivity change in manufacturing (Hudson 1992:38).

Table 2.2 Annual Growth, Cotton vs. Iron, Great Britain[8]

Percentage Annual Growth	Cotton	Iron
1700–1760	1.37	0.60
1770–1780	6.20	4.47
1780–1790	12.76	3.79
1790–1801	6.73	6.48
1801–1811	4.49	7.45
1811–1821	5.59	-0.28

Source: Freeman and Louçã (2001:154).

British cotton textiles were far more successful than French cotton textiles. This does not mean that late eighteenth-century France was stagnant. Between 1716 and 1788, French overseas trade accelerated more rapidly than British overseas trade. French industrial output growth (1700–1790) largely matched that of Britain. France produced more linen, silk, woolens, maintaining a total industrial production considerably higher than that of Britain (even if Britain had been ahead in per capita terms ever since the seventeenth century) (Crouzet 1990:21p; Greenfeld 2001:143; Modelski and Thompson 1996:99; Schama 1989:190; Trebilcock 1981:112). Still, it is hard to find reliable data measuring productivity growth and the overall growth of the French economy. This was a period of extreme political turmoil, with revolution followed by the war. Tentative estimates suggest that 1789–1815 was "a lost generation for economic growth" (Le Goff and Sutherland quoted in Hoffman 1996:194). If growth occurred at all, it was just a continuation of that of

---

8   Crafts and Harley (1992:713) compare cotton textiles with a few other sectors (annual growth rates 1770–1815): Cotton textiles 7.0 per cent, other textiles 1.1 per cent, iron 3.2 per cent, coal 2.5 per cent, others 0.8–1.2 per cent.

previous centuries. Hoffman (1996:195) suggests that agricultural TFP may have actually declined and that it is unlikely that the Revolution boosted productivity. Most scholars do not want to speak of any French industrial revolution until the 1830s–1850s. To quote Landes (1994:654): Some of the most used French data exhibit "exemplary fragility … On a scale of 1 …, estimates of French output might be indexed at 0.2 or 0.3." At best, this is a story of slow growth, more realistically one of stasis. Structural transformation was very limited. Still, if unimpressive by British standards, cotton and woolen textiles saw developments of a scale that was unprecedented on the Continent (Trebilcock 1981:115, 140).[9]

Despite the British state being less than eager to invest in education, Britain had a considerable human capital advantage. The pool of mechanically skilled craftsmen and tinkerers was far greater than in France, despite the fact that these did not normally stem from any formalized education system. France was behind in terms of people skilled in machine construction, repair and maintenance. Britain's advantage was in the application of technology and science to industry, and in the close links that existed between entrepreneurs and mechanically skilled experimenters and tinkerers. The major innovations in the cotton textile industry were made in Britain, and then slowly diffusing across the Channel. The French Revolution and the Napoleonic Wars put an end to diffusion. Prior to the Revolution, France had been only moderately behind. By 1815, the gap was huge, with France still using equipment that had been obsolete in Britain since the 1790s. Human capital, combined with revolution and war, thus played an important part in Britain's industrial rise.

Vested interests played a major role. Toward the end of the eighteenth century, French kings faced great difficulties in pursuing policies of structural change. Louis XV and Louis XVI were aware of the necessity of large-scale reform in order to avoid financial collapse. However, they found themselves blocked by nobility that wanted political influence in return for concessions. British ruling elites did not have these problems. Moreover, British ruling elites, unlike French elites, were nearly unanimously pro-industry, and so physical resistance against industrialization was decisively and persistently struck down by the authorities. In France, resistance was no less fierce, but where the attitude of the British government was decisive, that of the French was vacillating. In France no political consensus existed on the importance of industry and technological progress. Also, social cohesion in the populace was low—evident by the simple fact that the late 1780s crisis found no solution short of revolution. While social cohesion was low in Britain too, the political consensus of the ruling elites was great. In the years prior to the Industrial Revolution, the interests

---

9   Of the regions analyzed, only Paris shows any increase in late eighteenth-century TFP rates compared to TFP rates going back to the early sixteenth century. A tentative estimate for all of France for the whole of the eighteenth century gives a range of 0.04–0.19 per cent annually, with several regions exhibiting negative rates (Hoffman 1996:130p). Hoffman (1996:197) suggests annual TFP growth of 0.12–0.17 per cent for 1810–1815 (agricultural TFP), whereas British figures for the same period hovered around 0.4–0.5. However, Hoffman suggests that if the assumptions behind the French figure are replaced with more realistic ones, TFP rates might actually have been negative.

of the ruling elites more or less merged. Also, social cohesion rose as Britain came under military threat. Popular resistance against new machinery subsided when the war was at its most intense, not flaring up again until the last few years of the war.

Cotton Textiles

Cotton had started from modest beginnings, wool being the dominant industry,[10] and the first mechanical innovations in the textile industry were originally developed for wool. However, cotton was stronger and more resistant to the abuse of machines, and most inventions were more successful when applied to cotton. As a result, cotton textiles became the fastest growing and most rapidly modernizing of the early industries in Britain and in France. Developments were more rapid in Britain, and the story of early industrialization and of cotton textiles is one of France losing out to Britain, despite the considerable success that France could show compared to the European Continent. Compared to Britain, French technological progress was slow, and heavily reliant on applying British breakthroughs to the French industry (Brose 1998:34pp, 43; Landes 1969:82).

The technological breakthroughs were almost without exception British. John Kay's flying shuttle (1733) enabled one weaver to do what had previously been the job of two.[11] However, as the spinning wheel (spinning) was a much less efficient device than the hand loom (weaving), the main problem was that the spinning wheel could not supply weavers fast enough. Three to four spinners were required to keep one weaver occupied, with bottlenecks often occurring. The solution came in 1764, when James Hargreaves designed the spinning jenny.[12] It enabled one spinner to operate eight spindles simultaneously, spinning several threads at once, through a hand-based machine with several spindles rotating yarn. Richard Arkwright's water frame (1769) enhanced the jenny by allowing water power to work several spindles at once.

The real breakthrough arrived in 1779, when Samuel Crompton managed to fuse the jenny and the water frame, combining the quality product of the spinning jenny with the strength of the thread from the water frame. His hybrid—hence the name; the spinning *mule*—though continuously refined, remained the backbone of the British cotton textile industry for more than a century to come. Steam power was soon applied to the mule. Hence, cotton yarn now cost a fraction of what it

---

10 As late as 1783, wool accounted for 77.2 per cent of the overall value of the textile industry, and cotton only 4.4 per cent. In 1741, the value of imported raw cotton was somewhere around £55,000. The value of the materials consumed by the wool industry was somewhere around £1,500,000 (Landes 1969:82).

11 Most accounts of the Industrial Revolution begin somewhat later, as in somewhere around 1760, with Hargreaves' spinning jenny and Arkwright's water frame the two first main inventions. Still, Kay and the 1712 Newcomen steam engines were contributions leading up to Hargreaves and Arkwright. Hence, the periodization 1733–1825.

12 Patented in 1770 (Landes 1969:85).

did before, and was of far higher quality. Further improvement came in 1825, with Richard Roberts's self-acting mule (Beaudoin 2003:xviii; Griffiths, Hunt and O'Brien 1998:124pp; Hobsbawm 1969:58p; Mokyr 1999:21p; Morgan 1999:41p; Pugh 1999:29).

The spinning jenny and the water frame increased productivity enormously. The spinning jenny could produce 6–24 times as much as a normal spinning wheel (increasing to around 80 in later years), the water frame several hundred times. The mule produced 200–300 times more than a spinning wheel, which meant that by the end of the century the once revolutionary spinning jenny had already become obsolete (Brose 1998:36; Landes 1969:85). Arkwright's cotton mill in Derbyshire had been the first important British factory, opened in 1769 with around 300 workers. By 1788, more than 300 Arkwright-type mills existed, driven by 10 hp water wheels, and with roughly 1,000 spindles. By the turn of the century, there existed around 900 British cotton-spinning factories (Freeman and Louçã 2001:158; Mokyr 2002a:124; Morgan 1999:39p).[13] Costs and prices fell dramatically, from 38s in 1786 to 6s 9d in 1807, and almost down to 3s by 1837—5 per cent of what it had been in 1760.[14] Between 1780 and 1850 the price of cotton cloth fell by 85 per cent (Cuenca 1994:101p; Freeman and Louçã 2001:155; Landes 1999:151; Mokyr 1990:111).

Fewer strides were made in weaving. A multiplication of hand looms and manual weavers saw to it that weaving kept pace with spinning. Edmund Cartwright patented a power loom in 1785, but no significant mechanization took place until after the Napoleonic Wars. Power looms did not become commonplace until the 1820s (Crouzet 2001:104; Griffiths, Hunt and O'Brien 1998:130; Hobsbawm 1969:59pp; Magraw 1999:339).[15]

A parallel series of inventions also took place in Britain: The first working steam engine was built by Thomas Savery in 1698. The design was perfected by Thomas Newcomen in 1712, who used it for pumping water out of mines. The next major improvement was James Watt's 1769 steam engine, and 1802 saw Richard Trevithick's high-pressure engine. By 1800, water power was still dominant, but by 1835 steam power fueled 75 per cent of the British cotton industry. This can be compared to France, which as of 1850 only had 24 per cent of the steam power of Britain. Watt's engine had been introduced in France in the late 1780s, but had

---

13 Most of these in Lancashire, with the subsequent result that by 1800, money wages in Lancashire typically exceeded those of London (in itself astonishing, considering London was the capital, the financial center, business center etc.), sometimes by more than 50 per cent (James 1996:3pp; Perkin 1969:135).

14 Lancashire cotton yarn No. 100 (Landes 1999:151).

15 As late as 1813, there were only 2,400 power looms in Britain. From thereon the amount increased rapidly: 55,000 in 1829, 85,000 in 1833 and 224,000 in 1850. The amount of hand loom weavers continued to rise until the 1820s (reaching 250,000), then fell rapidly as the power loom rapidly diffused (Hobsbawm 1969:64).

negligible impact on manufacturing (Freeman and Louçã 2001:200; Jacob 1998:73; Magraw 1999:338; Mokyr 1990:90).[16]

Table 2.3 Spinning Costs per 100 Pounds of Cotton, 1780–1830[17]

	£	Index
1780	2.10	100
1790	1.07	49
1795	0.57	23
1810	0.21	5
1830	0.13	4

Source: Freeman and Louçã (2001:156).

Table 2.4 Cost and Selling Price of 1 Pound of Spun Cotton

Year	Raw materials	Selling cost	Margin for other costs and profits
1784	2s	10s 11d	8s 1d
1812	1s 6d	2s 6d	1s
1832	7½d	11¼d	3¾d

Source: Hobsbawm (1969:76).

While less influential, French dynamism could also be found in cotton textiles. Decretot's 1789 textile mill at Louviers was the world's finest. The Overkampfs of France employed 1,200 at their factory at Rouen, making finer colors than could be dyed in Britain (but showed no interest in steam power or in further mechanization). The cotton giant Richard–Lenoir was a spectacular success, with 39 establishments and 15,000 employees (Jacob 1998:70; Trebilcock 1981:140).[18] The one invention emerging from France was the technologically revolutionary Jacquard

---

16 Jacob (1998:73) makes the comparison between Troyes and Manchester, and is struck by the greater reluctance of the French in using mechanical power, primarily stemming from a lack of understanding, and not from higher fuel cost. Despite high fuel prices, for two decades, few if any modifications were made on Watt's engine, in a country where the incentives should tend highly toward making it more efficient.

17 English Cotton number 80.

18 In 1833, a medium sized combined British mill employed 319 workers (Boot 1995:288).

loom, introduced in 1804. It used instructions embedded in chains of cards, with holes prodded by special rods, to weave complicated patterns into fabric. Despite essentially inventing the binary system for coding of information, the invention had marginal economic influence, and was relevant largely with respect to high-quality, expensive products, mostly in silk. It diffused into Britain in the 1820s (Beaudoin 2003:xviii; Magraw 1999:346; Mokyr 1990:100pp; 1999:22). Unlike Britain, which manufactured for the mass market, the French industry was consistently more successful as a skill-intensive, small-scale and high-quality trade (Sewell, Jr. 1980:154).

The French cotton sector grew by five per cent annually (1780–1850), becoming twice as large as any continental rival. The first water-powered cotton mills arrived in 1802. The number of cotton enterprises in Mulhouse, which became France's industrial center, tripled between 1786 and 1810. The cotton spun by France increased fivefold between 1806 and 1812 (Lyons 1994:270pp; Magraw 1999:352; Trebilcock 1981:140). Textiles employed 40 per cent of the total labor force in manufacturing (Magnac and Postel-Vinay 1997:20). Still, as can be seen from Table 2.5, French cotton textiles did not experience growth on the scale of Britain. Some (Marczewski 1960:176) see cotton as the most dynamic element in early French industrial development. Others (Crouzet 1970:273) surmise that French industrial weakness stemmed primarily from the slow growth of sectors like cotton and textiles. It was the textile industry (textiles overall, not just cottons) that was the primary laggard, averaging a growth of only 1.5 per cent a year (although there may be a downward bias to this figure) (ibid.:269pp). This was in any case no match for Britain, whose industrial growth was far greater during this first phase of industrialization. From being roughly on a par with France in 1780, by 1810 Britain represented more than 75 per cent of the world's raw cotton consumption. From 1760 to 1820, the British cotton textile industry grew by seven per cent a year. While the industry never accounted for more than 7–8 per cent of national income, it was technologically progressive, larger than all other industries, and expanded much faster. Starting from scratch, with wool the dominant industry, British cotton textiles grew to comprise more than 50 per cent of British exports by 1831. When cotton ceased to expand, so did the rest of the British economy (Crouzet 2001:105; Hobsbawm 1969:69; Modelski and Thompson 1996:99; Sullivan 1989:441).

Napoleon brought a temporary upswing to French industry, as his Continental System removed rival manufacturers and kept British goods out of Europe. This led to a spectacular artificial boom contingent on the exclusion of British goods in the east. However, in terms of modernization, there was little progress. The wars also almost completely halted the process of technology diffusion across the Channel, which France had been dependent on for technological progress. By the war's end, the French cotton textile industry lagged even further behind (Lyons 1994:268pp; Price 1993:143; Wright 1995:148).[19] The modern sector of French

---

19 Structural transformation was restricted to a few cities. Half of France's power looms could be found in Mulhouse, as well as one-third of all steam-driven spindles. Even in

textiles employed equipment that Britain had abandoned in the 1780s–1790s. Steam power was virtually unknown. Textile mills were consistently two or more decades behind Britain, and the power loom, commonplace in Britain in the 1820s, was not introduced until the 1860s (Freeman and Soete 1999:51; Landes 1998:280; Magraw 1999:346; Trebilcock 1981:132, 145).[20]

Table 2.5 Shares of Raw Cotton Consumption (metric tons)

	Great Britain	France
1760	*1,100*	
1780	3,000	4,000
1790	14,000	4,000
1800	24,000	7,000
1810	56,000	8,000
1820	54,000	19,000
1830	112,000	34,000
1840	208,000	53,000
1860	492,000	115,000
1880	617,000	89,000

Source: Landes (1969:41 [italics]); Modelski and Thompson (1996:99).

Table 2.6 Shares of major exports, Great Britain (%)

	Cotton	Wool	Iron/steel
1700	0.5	68.7	
1750	1.0	46.7	
1801	39.6	16.5	9.3

industrial cities hand looms outnumbered power looms by two and three to one (Trebilcock 1981:145).

20 Power looms were hard to adapt to the production of fine cloths—France's specialization. Hence, among the reasons why France was slow to adapt to the power loom was an industrial structure that was different than Britain's (Sewell, Jr. 1980:156). There were exceptions: In Alsace, water frames and hand mules were exchanged for power-driven mules and power looms as early as 1815–1830 (Amsden 2001:32).

	Cotton	Wool	Iron/steel
1831	50.8	12.7	10.2
1851	39.6	14.1	12.3
1870	35.8		16.8

Source: Hobsbawm (1969:110); Hudson (1992:183).

The Role of the State

Human Capital

Knowledge and education have not always had much of an effect on technological change. In the seventeenth and eighteenth centuries—periods that saw dramatic advances in both scientific knowledge and industrial techniques—there was no great exchange of ideas between scientists and industrialists. Before 1750, education and science probably had larger effects on social and political theory than on industry: Attitudes and behavior were transformed, people were developing an interest in the outside world, positive values were put on education and technical skills, etc. But not until the nineteenth century did education become genuinely important for *industrial development*. The first truly science-based industry was the chemical industry in the late nineteenth century. In contrast, the early Industrial Revolution is routinely thought of as the product of tinkering and experimenting by practically minded men without much formal education. Science and technology had not yet advanced to a stage where it required scientific understanding of physical processes to an extent that would render it incomprehensible to people without formal training. Significant technological breakthroughs were not yet beyond individual geniuses strong on practical skills and mechanical intuition (Freeman and Louçã 2001:156p; Hobsbawm 1969:59p; Mathias 1969:3; Mokyr 1990:113).

There is disagreement as to how advanced the inventions of the cotton textile revolution were. However, what is true is that early industrial growth was to a significantly lesser degree Schumpeterian than was later to be the case. The Industrial Revolution marks a transition to an era where Schumpeterian growth was gradually *becoming* the dominant mode of economic growth. Human knowledge was undoubtedly an important part of the Industrial Revolution, but less so in the late eighteenth century than later. At this early stage, Smithian processes were relatively more important than later.

Education Systems   Neither primary nor higher education can explain why Britain, rather than France, took the lead in cotton textiles. What marked the English education system (omitting Scotland),[21] was the genuine lack of state interest and the amateurism of English education institutions. In contrast, French institutions were consciously designed to educate engineers with the aim of producing scientific and technological progress. Yet, in terms of literacy and school enrollment, Britain was no laggard. Ever since the sixteenth century, England had astonishingly high levels of literacy. London was one of the most literate cities in the world (Graff 1987:97).[22] Data on British and French grooms writing their signatures on the marriage register support this:

Table 2.7 Percentage of British and French Grooms Writing their Signatures on the Marriage Register[23]

	Ca. 1750	1786–90	1816–20	1841	1854	1865	1876
Great Britain	(60)	(60)	(63)	67	70	77	84
France	(40)	47	54	–	69	73	81

Sources: Cipolla (1969:121pp); Graff (1987:195, 232, 313).

Table 2.8 Adult Male Literacy (1760–1830)

	1760	1780	1788	1800	1830
Great Britain[*]	62	62	60	65	70
France[**]	–	–	47	48	53

Sources: Crafts (1995b:754, 766); Vincent (2000:9).

[*]   Figures for England and Wales. Estimates from Crafts (1995b:754). Crafts uses 20 and 30 year intervals. For comparison purposes I use the start date of each interval. This might give British figures an upward bias. However, the bias is only slight, as for all practical purposes the literacy rates did not change much in any case! The choice of the starting year for each interval was made for comparison purposes.

[**]   Estimates from Vincent (2000:9)

---

21 Scottish and English education policies were highly different, and while this chapter focuses on Britain, when it comes to human capital, I generally refer to *England* only. Scotland institutionalized compulsory education as early as the seventeenth century. This did not happen in England until the late nineteenth century (Evans 1983:324).

22 Obviously, reliable data are hard to come by, but Graff (1987:95) states that literacy was on a par with the most developed areas of Europe. Crouzet (1990:72) claims that England and Scotland acquired a lead in literacy as early as the seventeenth century, and although France later advanced at roughly the same pace, it could never close the gap.

23 Figures in parenthesis are from Graff (1987:232). A parenthesis signifies a somewhat larger margin of error, although no margins of error have been explicitly stated.

While there is more to literacy than being able to write one's name, male literacy figures tell the same story as marriage register signatures, though general literacy rates fall below the figures in Table 2.7.[24] France was behind, and did not catch up until the mid-nineteenth century (Vincent 2000:9). This does not mean that the English school system was particularly good. English elites did not push for literacy. British primary school enrollment rates may have been ahead of those of France (although not by much), but not by virtue of any effort on the part of the state. In both countries, education was overwhelmingly provided by the Church. Compared to the US and Germany, Britain was far behind as early as 1830 (Easterlin 1981:18p; Lindert 2001). By the late eighteenth century, numerous countries were outperforming the English education system, as for instance the Nordic countries, Scotland and Geneva. Vincent (2000:8) puts England behind these countries, in the same category as among others France, suggesting that the difference between Britain and France was fairly marginal.

Table 2.9 Estimated Primary School Enrollment Rate, 1818–1882 (per 10,000)[25]

	1818	1830	1850
Great Britain*	600	900	1,045
France	–	700	930
USA	–	1,500	1,800
Germany	–	1,700	1,600

Source: Easterlin (1965:426; 1981:18p).
* Figures for Great Britain comprise figures from 1818 and 1850: England and Wales. 1830 and 1882: England and Wales, Scotland and Ireland.

France had made considerable strides. In the 1680s only five out of 83 French departments had literacy rates above 40 per cent. A century later, most departments in the north and east were above 50, with two of the Norman departments exhibiting male literacy above 80 per cent. In Normandy, nearly 70 per cent could sign their names, as opposed to Vannetais, where the corresponding figure was less than 10. The French Revolution led to some change. However, high ideals as to human

---

24 Going back in time, male literacy figures are generally more reliable than overall figures. Also, the working population, including potential inventors and investors would for practical purposes be male. The impact of women on technological progress, industrial and economic growth was probably only slight. In any case, female literacy figures suggest that the gender gap was smaller in Britain than in France, with British female illiteracy dropping off sharply after 1845 (Vincent 2000:9pp).

25 Easterlin (1998:59) considers rates above 1,200 synonymous with complete enrollment. Different kinds of distortions make figures above 1,200 less than comparable.

progress and cultivation through education were notably difficult to realistically implement. Most evidence suggests that the impact of the Revolution on elementary education was minor. Lower-class children were still effectively excluded from post-elementary schooling (Crouzet 1990:xvii; Graff 1987:266; Lindert 2001). Reforms during Napoleon had more impact on higher education (Collins 1995:193p; Lyons 1994:103pp; Roche 1998:428pp; Trebilcock 1981:127). Until the 1830s, the state was highly indifferent toward elementary schooling. Conditions were deplorable, with schools lacking proper books (Furet 1995:335; Wright 1995:148).

Regarding universities, England was the laggard. England only had two universities[26]—Oxford and Cambridge (commonly referred to as "Oxbridge")—and even these were in decline. By the mid-eighteenth century, enrollments were lower than at any time between 1650 and 1850. There was a very clear distinction between "pure" sciences and their practical counterparts (Elbaum and Lazonick 1984:572; Kindleberger 1996:146). The Industrial Revolution had been a revolution for those who were *not* gentlemen, for the practically minded with no more than a decent basic education. Out of 498 applied scientists and engineers born between 1700 and 1850, only 50 were educated at "Oxbridge". Three hundred and twenty-nine had no university education at all, whereas 91 were educated in Scotland, which had a much better education system. Of Cambridge students between 1752 and 1849, 61 per cent joined the Church, *none* into banking or business. Only 0.8 per cent of those educated at Winchester (born 1820–1839) went into engineering, 6.2 per cent into business and almost 67 per cent joined the Church, the law or the military (Crafts 1995b:764; Mokyr 1999:37).

France, before the French Revolution, already had more than 20 universities (McCloy 1977:410 [1946]).[27] The late eighteenth century was the heyday of French scientific accomplishment. Until the 1830s, France possessed global scientific leadership, and was the world's center of science (Cameron and Neal 2003:232; Chesnais 1993:194). France pioneered the system of higher technical education in Europe, with the explicit purpose of creating growth by improving the national industry (Ahlström 1982:30p; Keck 1993:117). Obviously, military and naval goals were also prominent. Despite rather unremarkable performance with regard to elementary education, there was a clear activist aspect to higher education policies, in stark contrast to England. Hence, France led Britain in formal technical education, in engineering textbooks, encyclopedias and in other developments (Mokyr 2002a:74).

---

26 This lasted until 1826, when the University College of London was built. Fourth was Durham University in 1833. In contrast, the far less densely populated Scotland had four universities: St. Andrews, Glasgow, Aberdeen and Edinburgh (Evans 1983:317). These universities took a far more practical approach than Oxford and Cambridge and had a more distinguished faculty.

27 The figures listed by McCloy are 21, 22 and 29 (1977:410 [1946]). Whichever is correct, it is vastly superior to England.

The state actively promoted expert level science, producing a type of senior technician little known elsewhere: The technical expert elite of engineers, were meant to function in a multitude of top-level positions—as industrial managers, high level political and administrative personnel. The French system of *Grande Ecoles* produced the best engineers in the world. The *Ecole Polytechnique* was established in 1794 as the finest science school in Europe, and was meant to train scientists and engineers. However, technical schools had been in existence ever since the 1720s, when artillery schools had been founded, followed by schools for military officers in the 1740s (*Ecole des Ponts et Chaussées*, *Ecole du Génie*). Another technical school of the revolutionary years was the *Ecole des Mines*, while the purpose of the *Ecole centrale des arts et manufacture* (est. 1829) was to increase the supply and quality of engineers available for business. The curriculum emphasized mathematics and science, differing greatly from the humanities offered in England. However, while French governments had taken an interest in science ever since the 1660s, French colleges had been slow in shifting their curricula to the new Newtonian worldview. By 1790, only 31 of 105 new French central schools (students aged 15 and upwards) had any significant scientific equipment. While the number of physics students rose sharply after 1789, up until then there were fewer civil engineers in the private employment of mechanically knowledgeable entrepreneurs in France than in Britain. Indeed, there were more in Britain than in Continental Europe put together. Also, in 1793, all over France, *ancien régime* scientific academies were shut down by revolutionaries.[28] Hence, France's record up until around the turn of the century was highly checkered. That said, many pre-revolutionary scientific academies were scientifically at the forefront (Jacob 1997:136p; Kindleberger 1996:114pp).

Napoleon recognized that France was falling behind and saw the construction of a new education system as a remedy. A series of elite secondary schools were established (*lycées*) and from 1803 the *écoles d'arts et métiers* became the economically most relevant of the French education institutions. However, beyond this, Napoleon's vision was one of fostering discipline, respect for property, obedience to the social hierarchy, and loyalty to the nation. Hence, the curriculum of the *lycées* was classical rather than technical. Science and technology was reserved for the specialist technical schools. Thus, Napoleon's reorganization of higher education largely reestablished the old centralized structure of the *ancièn régime* and emphasized the training of *experts*, not researchers or creators. Hence, *école* trainees had a hard time finding relevant work experience in the industry. Most engineers instead entered military or government careers (Ahlström 1982:97; Chesnais 1993:197; Jacob 1997:182; Kindleberger 1996:114; Trebilcock 1981:127p).

---

28 True, the Paris Academy of Sciences was reopened two years later, but with only half of its pre-revolutionary faculty still intact. Many scientists were killed during the Terror (Jacob 1997:138).

Human Capital and the Cotton Textile Industry   Human capital, in the form of education, may not seem to have had much of an effect on the cotton textile industry. However, there is another argument to be made. While English education did not make any genuine strides forward few, if any, countries had a more literate, generally knowledgeable pool of people to draw upon. The skill level of the British labor force was undoubtedly higher than that of France (Crafts 1995b:767).

While literacy itself had little direct impact on the cotton textile industry, generally industrialization benefited from a more adaptable and literate workforce—but not until around the 1830s. The skill level required during the early years was low. While data is scarce and sometimes of dubious validity, Lancashire (home to much of the early cotton textile industry) even saw literacy drop (Graff 1987:321).[29] Literacy in textiles dropped from 80 per cent (1754–1784) to 61 (1785–1814), later rising to 84 per cent (1815–1844). Literacy rates in cotton textiles were actually lower than in most other industries (Mitch 1999:263). In France the evidence suggests that literacy did not matter much until the last few decades of the nineteenth century (Graff 1987:272). The findings are not conclusive. The fact that literacy declined with rapid industrialization could easily be due to the heavy influx of unskilled workers to these areas resulting from new employment opportunities. For example, Irish immigration into Scottish cities was the main reason why literacy rates dropped in central Scotland (Vincent 2000:68).

However, human capital may still have been important. Early nineteenth-century paper technology inventions[30] increased the availability of reading material. Hence, while literacy rates increased moderately at best, those that could in fact read gradually acquired greater access to written information. Britain rapidly acquired a comparative abundance of people with a high level of "technical literacy" (Mokyr 2002a:67pp).[31] While the role of the state was modest, the growth of cotton textiles still rested on technological breakthroughs. Crafts (1995b:752) finds that as much as

---

29 However, data is somewhat muddled, as the state did not require marriage registers to record the occupation of the groom and his father. Correcting for the fact that literacy rates usually refer either to children in school or to marriage registers, means pushing the years of declining literacy back in time to the late eighteenth century. And during the late eighteenth century, industrialization and the factory system was still very much in its infancy, and should hardly carry all the blame for declining literacy (Vincent 2000:68).

30 The Robert method of producing continuous paper was introduced in Britain in 1807 (invented in France in 1798) and improvements in printing, from cylindrical printing and inking using steam power, was invented by a German immigrant in 1812 (Mokyr 1999:19; 2002a:67).

31 There is also evidence that we have underestimated the skill levels involved in early Industrial Revolution factory work. According to Boot (1995:299p), the average skill level of British cotton textile factory workers in Lancashire was "surprisingly high, even by modern standards". Over their working lives, they received an income that was 70 per cent higher than that of unskilled workers.

26.5 per cent of the average percentage increase in national income between 1780 and 1831 can be accounted for by human capital, and that this contribution to overall economic growth was clearly expanding compared to 1760–1780.[32] With Brose (1998:45): "consensus is growing among economic historians that technical change in eighteenth-century England owed much more to science than was previously thought." While the technology of cotton manufacture was fairly simple, systematic thought went behind most innovations. Serendipity and chance may have played a part, but a minor one. Many inventions involved combining previously independent ideas. Crompton's mule united the jenny with spinning by rollers (Freeman and Louçã 2001:157; Hobsbawm 1969:59p). If it was all serendipity and chance, there is no reason why this should systematically have favored Britain over a France that was ahead in virtually any science, and even had a state that actively sought to diffuse and distribute useful knowledge for industrial and economic gain.

Joel Mokyr (1999:80) argues that the average level of scientific knowledge in Britain and France was approximately the same. But Britain and the Continent were good at different types of knowledge. Broadly speaking, Britain was good at knowledge of *how*, the Continent at knowledge of *what*. What happened in Western Europe, especially from the 1750s onwards, was a considerable broadening in the base of knowledge of *what*, something which made a stream of improvements and microinventions—in short, the Industrial Revolution—possible (ibid. 2002a:33). The body of knowledge that British tinkerers drew upon was to a large extent derived from the European Continent, in particular France. British sciences were experimental and technical, French sciences mathematical and deductive (ibid. 1990:241; 1999:36).

A major reason why Britain was better at making good use of scientific progress than France was the success of the informal English education sector. William Walker (1993:187) hails the early nineteenth-century British system for diffusion and dissemination of knowledge and technology as without a match in the world. Ties between scientists, inventors and entrepreneurs were much stronger in Britain than in France. Evans (1983:108) states that "the links between science, drawing heavily on the new European learning, and technology probably have never been closer." Personal interconnections, both between different layers of society and between metropolis and provinces, were strong (Ashton 1997:12pp [1948]; Mokyr 1990:241; Perkin 1969:68pp).

Learning happened outside the formal structure. Dissemination of technical knowledge through informal lectures, scientific societies and technical literature worked well, combined with a strong tradition for on-the-job training. Physicists and chemists were in intimate contact with leading figures of British industry. Among the members of The Royal Society of London, established in 1662, we find the names of instrument-makers, engineers, ironmasters and industrial chemists.[33] English

---

32 Human capital was responsible for an annual 0.1 per cent GDP growth between 1760 and 1780. This increased to 0.45 per cent for 1780–1831 (Crafts 1995b:752).

33 As early as 1665, The Royal Society of London started to publish the scientific journal *Philosophical Transactions*. This was probably the first periodical/scholarly journal

discoveries were the product of joint effort, and scientific societies, bringing people together, played a great role in the diffusion of knowledge (Brose 1998:27p; Crouzet 1990:30; Perkin 1969:69).

Hence, despite the obvious failings of English higher education, at the onset of the Industrial Revolution, Britain was endowed with a large number of technicians and craftsmen and a great variety of skilled artisans—far more so than France. These were not people that could perform great scientific feats, but they were a body of people well positioned with respect to tinkering and experimenting and with respect to applying knowledge developed elsewhere (Jacob 1997:165pp; Landes 1999:153; Mokyr 1990:240). By the late eighteenth century, the Royal Society was gradually declining into something of a gentlemen's social club, but scientific societies were popping up elsewhere. The most important ones were the Birmingham Lunar Society, the Manchester Philosophical and Literary Society, as well as societies in Liverpool, Hull, Bradford, Derby and Leeds. Lectures were paid for by the Royal Society or by aristocratic patrons, but also held ad hoc or by freelancers at coffeehouses and Masonic Lodges. The Society of Arts, founded in 1754, during its first 30 years gave out more than 6,200 awards for successful inventors. The 1799 Royal Institute was founded to communicate the findings of natural philosophy. The 1807 Geological Society of London sought to obtain practical information for the purpose of public improvement and utility. The 1818 Institution of Royal Engineers was a study association dedicated to the reading, discussion and publication of papers. By the mid-nineteenth century, approximately 1,020 such societies had a full 200,000 members, and more than 1,000 scientific and technical periodicals existed. There is evidence of informal learning communities playing an important role in the diffusion of innovation, especially within the cotton textile industry, where an ongoing process of improvement took place primarily through learning-by-doing. Well-developed cultural, technical and scientific communities existed, such as in the major cotton-textile producing city of Manchester (Armytage 1965:378pp; Freeman and Louçã 2001:180; Mitch 1999:271; Mokyr 2002a:43, 65p; Pyenson and Sheets-Pyenson 1999:225, 321). To paraphrase Joel Mokyr (2002a:65p): The crucial element of the Industrial Revolution was the formation of creative communities based on the exchange of knowledge, drawing on wider phenomena as literacy rates, improvements in schooling, copyright laws, easier access to texts and magazines in which technical information could be found. These communities consisted of a grand total of no more than a few thousand people, but played a crucial role in the circulation and diffusion of knowledge.

A greater tolerance for deviant ideas and modes of thinking also favored Britain. Religious intolerance on the European Continent led to a significant number of religious refugees ending up in Britain.[34] French industry lost some of its best people

---

in the world and played a considerable role in disseminating new scientific discoveries to an interested and knowledgeable readership (Britannica 1994:10/220).

34 By the eighteenth century, all French Protestants had been expelled from the country (Knutsen and Høibraaten 1998:247). A high percentage of these ended up in Britain.

and there are examples of British industry gaining directly from this inflow. The Belfast linen industry was developed by Huguenot refugees. Areas as different as paper mills and the atmospheric engine were products of French influence. The overall effect may not have been enormous, but it bears witness to an economic and political climate more conducive to competition and diffusion of ideas than in France. A conspicuous number of industrial champions were Dissenters (Quakers, Unitarians, Calvinists, Methodists, Baptists, etc.), having received their education at Dissenter academies. These academies were geared more toward the practical sciences and commercial arts and had much stronger links with industry (Evans 1983:108pp, 114). Dissenters were prominent within the Royal Society, and also formed their own nation-wide networks where knowledge was quickly disseminated. In other countries such activities might have been perceived as disruptive. True, in Britain, Dissenters were largely excluded from public office. But this meant that Dissenters instead often channeled their resources into innovation and industry. Also, they had their own non-conformist schools, ensuring that among the middle classes, they were the best-educated group (Ashton 1997 [1948]; Evans 1983:115; Freeman and Louçã 2001:170; Mokyr 1999:58; 2002a:274).

Despite Paris being the science capital of the world, it is doubtful that cotton textiles benefited. The *Ecole Polytechnique* came too late. At this time Britain was already dominant. Instead, French progress depended on (the belated) adoption of British inventions. Second, the French science effort started petering out during the first decades of the nineteenth century, because of a lack of funding. In terms of scientific journals, in the eighteenth century both France and Britain were laggards compared to the German states, where 61 per cent of all "substantive serials" were published. The French proportion was 10.7 per cent, the English less than seven. Third, education reform did not address the most pressing issue—the lack of mechanics and civil engineers. Post-1815, the most immediate problem for France was technical ignorance, not just in the shape of a lack of machines, but of skilled mechanics. These had to be imported from Britain, which was problematic considering that the emigration of British artisans was prohibited by law until 1825 (Chesnais 1993:194pp; Keck 1993:117; Landes 1969:147pp; Mokyr 1999:80).

No informal education sector played a role similar to that in Britain. The *Académie Royale des Sciences* had been founded as early as 1666 (only four years after the British Royal Society) with the explicit purpose of fostering scientific capacities and fitting them into machinery and government. However, the French *Académie* quickly turned into a closed academy limited to Parisian scholars and to the utilitarian concerns of the Colbertist administration. Like Britain, France experienced a plethora of new societies. But French societies were less influential than the British. Or; they had more influence on politics than on industry. The number of newspapers increased, salon societies discussed literature and politics, but very few people were actually involved in innovative work (Collins 1995:262; Roche 1998:441pp; 512).

It is not that the philosophical and scientific movement was weaker in France than in Britain. But in Britain, inventions seemed to have more direction. Leading manufacturers took a clear interest in applied sciences and perfected techniques developed elsewhere (often in France). Scientists and engineers had few problems finding commercially minded people for whom money was more interesting than politics or war. In France, scientists instead worked either *for* the political establishment or *against* it. State control of engineering hampered the development of civil engineering, fostering an elitist and statist approach to science. One would invent something, then get some academy or learned society to look at it. Intellectual activity had little practical application. Engineering knowledge was the property of the state, in the service of national interest, and with the clear political objective of catching up with Britain (Crouzet 1990:31; Evans 1983:108; Jacob 1997:139; Landes 1994:649; Mokyr 1999:79). Very few French inventors did well financially, despite government prizes and pensions used as incentives. Greenfeld (2001:144p) argues that nationalistic motives, patriotism and the desire for achievement and fame were far greater incentives than expectations of economic return. In contrast, in Britain engineers and scientists were normally exclusively industrially and commercially motivated, without any hidden political or military agenda. Equally important, the British state had no problems with this, was happy not to interfere with such interactions, and even encouraged them (Mokyr 1990:242pp; 2002a:74). To quote Crafts:

> … government policy recognized the importance of what would now be known as technology transfer encouraging technology inflows while seeking to prevent technology outflows. A striking feature of early nineteenth-century Great Britain was the mushrooming of associations that were designed to spread technological knowledge. (1996:199)

The irony is that the French state took a much more active role than the British. And still, the British system worked so much better. The French state actively sought to encourage the dissemination of technical knowledge, among other things because it recognized that diffusion was a much greater problem than in Britain. Much of French progress was not based on French innovation, but on the belated introduction of British machinery and techniques. This happened largely through personal connections, and despite a British prohibition on the export of most advanced machinery, as well as skilled artisans (law passed 1764–1765). Ever since the beginning of the eighteenth century, France had sent explorers and agents to Britain to spy on and to hire skilled British artisans. The spinning jenny arrived with John Holker in the 1770s, the water frame with James Milne in the 1780s. Britons were brought in as industrial advisers.[35] During the Napoleonic period, applied research was subsidized, industry given cheap credit and prizes awarded for useful inventions, with industrial expositions organized in order to emulate in a state-organized way

---

35 The systematic pursuit of British technicians resulted in Britain passing a law to prohibit the emigration of certain kinds of craftsmen, as well as the export of most advanced machinery. During the heydays of cotton, Britain restricted exports of both textile machinery and skilled workers. During the same period, French governments financed ventures to smuggle these into France (Magraw 1999:355). Heavy penalties would be exacted if caught.

the diffusion that the British seemed to accomplish by itself (Landes 1998:276pp; Mokyr 1990:253; 2002a:74; Wright 1995:70).

Where in Britain, *linkages* between science and industry characterized the sciences system, *divorce* is a term that better suits the French case. Despite formal institutions with the explicit purpose of creating linkages, these remained conspicuously absent.[36] The French educational impetus was not toward producing practical men. As Napoleon reestablished the centralized education structure of the *ancien régime*, he implicitly also persisted in giving primacy to the training of experts, as opposed to researchers and creators. True, French engineers were among the best in the world, but they played a larger part abroad than they did at home, performing for instance such spectacular engineering feats as the Suez Canal (Ahlström 1982:97; Brose 1998:49; Chesnais 1993:197).

With cotton textiles, Britain was the originator of every major invention. Hence, both the spinning jenny and the water frame were brought to France from Britain. With the outbreak of the French Revolution, followed by the Napoleonic Wars, such transfers came to an almost complete halt. By 1815, the modern sector of the French textiles industry employed equipment that had been obsolete in Britain for 30 years. The English education system cannot take credit for this. To the extent that higher education was important, it was so through the large influx of Scots, educated at intellectually stimulating schools and universities and because of Dissenter academies. But the success of British cotton textiles still depended on human capital. The informal education sector—scientific societies, public lectures, Dissenter academies—compensated for the flaws of the formal education system. And the system of knowledge diffusion was vastly superior to the French. The French system entailed state activism, but also state interference. And it was not thoroughly renovated until Napoleon (Crouzet 2003:234; Jacob 1997:178pp; Wright 1995:148). Joel Mokyr (2002a:82) makes a very plausible point when asserting that by focusing on formal science, we are bound to miss most of the action. The Industrial Revolution was a semidirected process of trial and error by skilled professionals with a vague, but gradually improving, comprehension of scientific and technological processes. This was something that Britain was far better at.

Wars (and Protectionism)

It may seem odd to include wars and protectionism under the same heading. They are both the result of activities undertaken by the state, but do not seem to have much in common otherwise. Still, wars undoubtedly have huge economic effects. With the Napoleonic Wars, the flow of technology slowly diffusing from Britain to the Continent

---

36 Jacob (1997:184p), looking at a handful of case studies of French engineering, finds that seldom or never did experts sent by the Crown, or otherwise just highly educated engineers, bother to collaborate with local entrepreneurs, or try to adapt their solution to local conditions, unlike what was the case in Britain, where local entrepreneurs would invariably meddle, and force expert engineers to interact.

came to a halt, stunting French industrial development. And both Britain and France sought to block the other party by shutting it out of important markets. The French Continental System sought to further French industry by shutting British exports out of the European continent, whereas the British Blockade prevented France from importing raw materials and selling its goods overseas. Hence, the economic effect in many ways was one of promoting domestic industries by preventing the enemy access to markets, in other words a crude and very unsubtle form of protectionism! Hence, wars, tariff protection and import restrictions suddenly belong to the same complex of economic factors.

Many accounts of the Industrial Revolution skip the Napoleonic Wars altogether. Wars are extra-systemic events that do not fit readily into economic models. Hence, scholars have been reluctant to give as much attention to the Napoleonic Wars as they have to technology, supply and demand, capital accumulation, infrastructure, education. Other scholars like historians and political scientists study wars, but are cautious about saying anything about the economic effects. However, it is impossible to overlook the turmoil in Europe produced by the French Revolution extending into the Napoleonic Wars. The consequences were huge. 1789–1815 was a lost generation with respect to French growth and development. Britain had a fairly small lead on France in 1789, both in terms of production figures and the technologies involved, and would probably have remained the dominant economic power regardless. However, what was a small gap in 1789 had grown to a chasm by 1815. The French Revolution and the Napoleonic Wars cemented and strengthened the developments that were already tilting the balance in favor of Britain (Magraw 1999:339; Mokyr 1990:252).

The Napoleonic Wars are often used as explanation for slow early growth during the Industrial Revolution. Greasly and Oxley (2000:103) speak of a trough in British aggregate industrial output during the wars, overall growth rates dropping to 1.5 per cent (then surging to 3.8 per cent in the 1820s). In absolute terms, 1789–1815 was an economic downturn. But in relative terms, compared to France, there is no doubt who suffered more. This was a case of British triumph and French defeat. The war enhanced Britain's economic advantage, derived from breakthroughs in cotton and iron. While consumer demand was probably reduced, this was countered by overseas demand for uniforms and supplies (Harley 1999:199; Hudson 1992:57pp; Mokyr 1999:56). By the end of the war, British industrial leadership was markedly stronger than it had been in the late 1780s, not only compared to France, but to the whole of Europe.

The 1786 Eden Treaty (often referred to as the Anglo-French Treaty) abolished prohibitions on British imports, reducing the level of customs duties and removing restrictions on exports of grain from France. The hope was that this would stimulate technology diffusion from Britain. With the wars, diffusion ground to a halt (Lyons 1994:270; Wright 1995:23).[37] However, this was also a boom period for French

---

37 There were still British technicians in France making huge amounts of money from helping to diffuse equipment that could be found in Britain. In the 1790s, Boyer-Fonfrède

cotton textiles, which enjoyed the absence of British competition. During the period of Consulate and Empire, cotton textiles, while losing out technologically, was the one French industry to undergo rapid mechanization and industrialization. Napoleon's Continental System, completed in 1806, was designed to keep all ports controlled by France closed to British trade. This meant new markets and a boom for French industry setting up in Italy and in the eastern parts of the Empire. Rouen increased its cotton production tenfold. Mulhouse became "the French Manchester", its number of cotton enterprises tripling. Even Paris for the first time saw modest industrialization. However, it soon became clear that the boom had been a product of the artificial economic and political context provided by the war. French industry had been sheltered for two decades, but Napoleon's industrial policies had not led to technological catch-up.[38] Hence, in terms of technology, the French cotton textile industry was decades behind the British. Between 1815 and 1818, before foreign (that is, British) yarn and cloth were banned, British textiles flooded the French market (Landes 1969:162; Lyons 1994:269pp; Magraw 1999:339; Trebilcock 1981:131; Wright 1995:145).[39]

What eventually created an independent French cotton textile industry was Continental protectionism post-1815. For all practical purposes, British imports were shut out (Amsden 2001:43). Import of cotton yarn, cloths and knitwear was prohibited. Other Continental countries followed suit, and British cotton textiles exports to the Continent declined post-1815.[40] Yet, French cottons continued to lag far behind. Except for certain outfits in Mulhouse, the French industry remained

---

adopted Crompton's mule and the flying shuttle, and also imported British workers to install and operate them. During times of war, this was difficult and dangerous, but it did happen (Landes 1969:145; Lyons 1994:270; Trebilcock 1981:116).

38 Even more serious than the failure to modernize was the geographical shift brought on by the war. As a consequence of the British naval blockade, French customs revenues decreased by 80 per cent. French external trade never recovered. By 1880, the value of French exports was still only 38 per cent of British export value. The economically most dynamic part of France—the Atlantic rim—was demolished. Bordeaux was destroyed, Nantes became a backwater, the entire southwest deindustrialized (Crouzet 2001:122; Cullen 1993:655; Freeman and Louçã 2001:182; Lyons 1994:260, 274; Pugh 1999:21; Trebilcock 1981:130p; Wright 1995:70). In contrast, Britain's cotton exports were *higher* during the Continental System than in 1802, which was the last peacetime year (Lyons 1994:215; Trebilcock 1981:131).

39 In the Seine-Inférieure region, the number of active spindles fell from almost 400,000 in 1808 to 98,000 in 1818. With prohibition of foreign yarn and cloth, it rose back to 960,000 in 1834 (Landes 1969:162).

40 Britain instead expanded by relying on colonial markets. In 1820, Europe and the US took more than 60 per cent of British cotton exports, with the underdeveloped world 31.8 per cent. By 1840, the figures were reversed—29.5 per cent vs. 66.7 per cent. This continued, as toward the end of the century, ever more countries developed domestic cotton textile industries. By 1900, only 7.1 per cent of cotton exports went to Europe and the US (Hobsbawm 1969:146).

high-cost, unable to compete abroad, with the exception of new overseas markets, like Algeria (Hudson 1992:185; Landes 1969:164).

The French Revolution, the Revolutionary and the Napoleonic Wars did not lead to Britain industrializing faster or acquiring a larger and more prosperous cotton textile industry, but it did further cement Britain's head start. War indemnities paid by France post-1815 and the drain on manpower and human capital had a definite and lasting impact on the economy (Crouzet 1990:235; Mokyr 1999:36). Obviously, there was no master plan by Britain to foster technological progress and industrial leadership by challenging and crushing its most powerful opponent. Hence, there were fortuitous components to British leadership. Thus, the economic effects of the Revolution and the subsequent wars can be thought of as a giant experiment of protectionism. Both parties blocked the other, protecting their industries, but Britain was better at it and had overseas markets that it could tap into. Hence, the outcome in terms of cotton textiles was a British hold on the market that was far stronger than before. The only way for French businesses to stay alive post-1815, was to rely on tariffs. Table 2.5 above shows that French imports of raw cotton increased from 8,000 metric tons in 1810 to 115,000 in 1860. Despite its slow start and the dominance of Britain, cotton textiles would still be one of the most important sectors in the eventual French industrialization. By this time, however, other industrial sectors (iron) had become more important for continued economic expansion.

Smithian Growth

This is a story of Schumpeterian growth, of technological progress, on knowledge and human capital, and on invention and innovation leading to industrial prowess. Why a subchapter on Smithian growth? The Industrial Revolution signals a new era, an era where growth and development to an ever greater extent hinges on technological progress. But at the *beginning* of the Industrial Revolution, the pace of technological progress was still only modest. Both qualitative accounts about how change was limited to a few revolutionary sectors (cotton textiles, iron), and quantitative accounts focusing on for instance TFP growth, reveal the very limited overall impact of technological progress in this early phase. GDP growth in Britain had probably been accelerating for some while already, starting with the institutional breakthroughs following the English Civil War and the Glorious Revolution (e.g. Clark 1999; Jones 1988; North and Weingast 1989; O'Brien, Griffiths and Hunt 1991). Without the prior acceleration of Smithian growth, the Industrial Revolution would probably not have occurred when it did.

Thus, the Industrial Revolution, and Britain's leadership in cotton textiles, also rested on a number of Smithian background conditions—infrastructure, property rights, transaction costs, capital accumulation, supply and demand, natural resources. The first three seem to have the most going for them. While distinctly laissez-faire on most issues, one area saw particular activity in late seventeenth- and eighteenth-century Britain, namely the building of canals and turnpikes. Britain was already blessed with a geography that made it particularly conducive to cheap and fast transport (coastline and rivers)—much more so than France. And despite French infrastructure efforts, improvements were far greater in Britain. Between 1700 and 1750, Parliament passed an average of eight Turnpike Acts a year, increasing to 40 annually in the 1760s and 1770s.[41] Canals cut the cost per ton between Liverpool and Manchester or Birmingham by 80 per cent. The cost of transporting coal routinely dropped by 50 per cent. By 1820, England and Wales had more than twice the internal waterways per square kilometer of France, where markets were fragmentary and scattered, with a transport system consisting only of a few canals and a cobweb of mediocre roads (Freeman and Louçã 2001:164pp; Hobsbawm 1969:46; Hudson 1992:102; Mokyr 1999:33; 2002a:56). 1760–1789 saw a French canal fever, but political and financial constraints meant that the only major canal built was the Saône–Loire canal. French roads improved considerably after 1660, but most roads were of greater political than economic importance, binding the provinces more closely to Paris rather than constructing a proper trade and communication network (Collins 1995:220; Trebilcock 1981:142).

However, while boosting the overall performance of the economy, cotton textiles were among the industries that benefited the least. Raw cotton was measured in million pounds rather than million tons. Movement of cotton was less of a problem than the movement of coal! Tellingly, the cotton industry did not contribute much in terms of financing infrastructure developments (Freeman and Louçã 2001:167). This gradually changed, as the cotton industry came to rely ever more on steam power (which requires coal), but not until later.

Regarding property rights, Britain was again ahead. Hudson (1992:109) and Mokyr (1990:246) refer to the British system as government of, by and for property owners. North and Weingast (1989) single out a limited English state, defending claims to property as the most important factor behind pre-industrial British growth. Mokyr (1999:57) describes the right to property in Britain as sacrosanct, contrasting it with the confiscations and conscriptions during the French Revolution and Napoleonic Wars. Late eighteenth-century French *parlamentaires* advocated a system of property rights based on the British concept. *Ancien regime* France had several different varieties of property, over which the propertied elites had only modest control. The Revolution abolished feudal rights and hailed the principle of property rights, attempting to introduce "rational" economic institutions, but for practical purposes the period instead came to represent confiscation of property, punitive taxation, terror and social anarchy. The 1804 Napoleonic Code introduced the modern conception of property with the individual having absolute rights of ownership. However, not until Louis-Philippe (1830–1848) did France get a king who seemed to finally be able to lay the Revolution to rest (Collins 1995:213, 246; Furet 1995:354; Pipes 1999:43; Price 1993:156pp).

---

41 Although this did not mean that the British state actually financed these projects (Mokyr 1999:47).

Britain was also ahead in intellectual property protection.[42] British patent law dates from 1624, French from 1791. Patenting was far more widespread in Britain, and increased markedly toward the end of the eighteenth century, with textiles being one of the industries that experienced the most dramatic increase. This might be a reflection of an increase in the propensity to innovate, or an increase in the propensity to patent innovations, and no proof *per se* of the patent system *causing* the innovation (Griffiths, Hunt and O'Brien 1992:896; Sullivan 1990:355pp). It could also be evidence that the British patent system worked better than the French, and thus contributed to British growth. Yet, the British system had numerous flaws. It did not encourage diffusion, but secrecy, small-scale, in-house technical improvement, which ultimately led to technological obsolescence, and was not reformed until 1852. Before then, patents were expensive, as well as yielding dubious defense against plagiarism (MacLeod 1992:288; Mokyr 1999:43). It could well be that the reason for the rapid rise of British cotton textiles was inefficient patent protection, rather than the opposite. Crompton did not have the money to take out a patent for his mule, and so the mule rapidly diffused. Arkwright's water frame spread rapidly, once a patent court *found against him* in 1785. Even before this, Arkwright's solutions had been used to solve technical problems without this being in breach of the patent (Cookson 1994:750; MacLeod 1988:78, 92). Deficient as patent laws may have been, the number of patents rose steadily for the entire period, consistently staying above France (Freeman and Soete 1999:50; Pugh 1999:29; Sullivan 1989:430; Webb 1911:449p).

Arguments about property rights flow directly into the transaction cost argument, made famous by Douglass C. North (1981; 1990). Transaction costs are costs of information and enforcement. Increased capital mobility, lowered information costs, improved enforcement of contracts and the spread of financial risk through banks, stock markets and insurance companies have all come about as a result of institutional innovations that have lowered transaction costs and ensured a smoother, more efficiently functioning economy (ibid. 1994:2).[43] While Britain had been one free trade area since 1707, in France, a load of timber sent from Lorraine to Sète

---

42 Intellectual property rights, as in patenting systems, could easily be considered Schumpeterian, which is how I treat it in the Chemicals chapter. The reason why it is included as a background variable here is that until 1852 no significant changes took place with respect to the British system. If Britain benefited from its patenting system, it did so by drawing upon a system that had long been in place. Still, the system was in continuous development, especially between 1717 and 1720. 1700–1749 saw a rise in patenting—a total of 216 patents—over 1660–1699 (52 patents). 1750–1799 saw a dramatic acceleration—1,596 patents altogether (MacLeod 1988:40, 126p). Still, it is difficult to know if this is part of a secular trend or actually caused by the 1717–1720 changes.

43 When Wallis and North (1986) attempted to measure the transactions sector in the American economy, their finding was that by 1970, transaction costs had risen to more than 45 per cent of national income, up from 25 per cent in 1870. While this suggests that transaction costs are a bigger problem today than during the Industrial Revolution, it also illustrates that no matter how much it has increased or decreased, it is bound to be a sizable problem.

in 1788, had to pay 34 different duties in 21 different places (Braudel 1991:491)! No single French economy existed, only a series of provincial ones. Eradication of internal tolls and tariffs had begun in the mid-1770s, but in essence, administrative unification, common institutions, a common language, common coinage and a common system of weights and measures had to wait until the French Revolution. Double-entry bookkeeping and a Central Treasury were not introduced until 1788 (Collins 1995:238; Trebilcock 1981:126; Weber 1989:172p). As Wright says:

> Royal institutions grew up gradually, haphazardly, with a barnaclelike encrustation of overlapping functions and useless sinecures ... the administrative structure resembled a palace that had been built piecemeal by adding rooms and wings without any renovation of the original structure or any attempt to harmonize the whole. (1995:8)

While the French economy steadily improved during the eighteenth century, it still lagged behind Britain. Also, despite improvements brought on by the Revolution, the long-term consequence was a reversal of the process of market integration, with credit markets suffering the worst. Markets functioned better during the *ancien régime* than during the Revolution (Hoffman and Rosenthal 2000:448p). Between 1789 and 1815, transaction costs actually rose.

There is little doubt that the British financial system was better than that of the French. This is one among several reasons that Britain managed to fight wars—primarily against France—throughout the eighteenth century without major problems, whereas France suffered ever more serious fiscal crises culminating in the Revolution. There is also little doubt that ready access to capital is crucial for entrepreneurs. And British capital markets improved during the Industrial Revolution. Still, the margin between Britain and the Continent was probably less than previously thought. And, while capital markets were important to the British economy in general, it is hard to make the link between these and cotton textiles. For most cotton enterprises, capital requirements were met by personal or family funds, industrialists struggling to raise enough capital for investments in machinery and mills, even if these investments were relatively small. At this stage of industrialization, fixed-costs of setting up a small firm were modest, and usually the increase in output generated by the factory could in a fairly short time cover the capital costs. TFP estimates also suggest that capital formation was relatively unimportant and contributing little to actual growth (Freeman and Louçã 2001:167; Kurth 1979:6; Mokyr 1999:95pp, 102; Pugh 1999:6; Rosenberg and Birdzell 1986).

The argument has been made that an increase in demand made Britain a more likely candidate for an industrial breakthrough, that a "consumer revolution" preceded the Industrial Revolution. Mokyr (1990:111; 1999:59p) asserts that the role of demand remained passive. The timing and location of the Industrial Revolution cannot be explained by exogenous change in consumer demand. If a consumer revolution took place, it was between 1680 and 1720, not later. To put it with Griffiths, Hunt and O'Brien (1992:897): "At no point in the eighteenth century did anything approaching a 'mass' market for textiles emerge in Britain. Production remained geared to the demands of polite society ..." At the same time, Greasley and Oxley

(1997:945) suggest that domestic market size did play an important role. Market opportunity raised the level of inventive activity. Export demand however, did not. Obviously, the cotton textile industry depended on imported raw materials, but there is no evidence that access to cotton *caused* the changes in the cotton textile industry. The growth of the cotton textile industry fueled a demand for more raw cotton, not the other way around (Greasley and Oxley 1997:945; Mokyr 1999:67pp).

Finally, there is the argument that Britain industrialized first because of its relative abundance of coal. However, access to coal was relatively unimportant in the early cotton textile industry, as the overwhelming majority of cotton textile factories were fueled by water power. Until 1850, the steam engine could only provide small gains over water power. Hence, the resource argument applies far less to cotton textiles than it does to iron (Landes 1999:156; Mokyr 1990:90; 1999:33; Trebilcock 1981:117, 168).

There is no doubt that Smithian growth was an important part of the Industrial Revolution. However, several of the Smithian arguments rest on shaky foundations. With infrastructure, property rights and transaction costs remain the most credible Smithian arguments. While there is no direct causal link with cotton textiles, well-established and secure property rights are the bedrock of economic development. It is also obvious that high transaction costs will seriously hamper the development of an economy. As will be seen later, while there was violent resistance against new technology in both Britain and France, the British government was more willing and more able to defend entrepreneurs, hence implicitly property rights. When modern property rights were finally established in France, they were so in a context of revolution and war, which meant that for all practical purposes, it was still an unsolved problem.

Vested Interests, Political Consensus, and Social Cohesion

Britain Clamps Down on Vested Interests, France Does Not   Vested interest groups have sought to resist the implementation of new technology in many different ways. In its simplest form, opposition has been one of sheer physical resistance, with workers and artisans destroying machinery and other physical equipment. In other cases, opposition has taken the form of laws and regulations, for instance through guild systems and state monopolies. In modern, industrialized societies, physical resistance is unusual, as institutional channels through which dissent can be voiced exist, without the physical destruction of equipment. However, as of the early Industrial Revolution, this was only to a limited extent the case. Large groups had no voice or representation, while at the same time being greatly affected by industrialization. Also, at a time when industrialization was still fragile and in its infancy, it was possible to wreak considerable havoc through simple means. Thus, the eagerness and resoluteness with which the state crushed popular physical resistance against the implementation of new technology, especially within cotton textiles, was important with respect to industrialization, and one reason why Britain's cotton textile industry was so successful.

To Knutsen (1999:107) eighteenth-century Britain was experiencing "a robust social consensus anchored in a distinct and relevant political mythology … forged on the anvil of large-scale war,…this consensus rendered England self-confident, productive and strong". Yet, as in France, resistance against new technology was commonplace. Industrialization had potentially grave implications, with workers and artisans, especially in skill-intensive industries, fearing that they would lose their jobs to machines. Hence, both Britain and France experienced assaults on physical equipment. In 1768, 500 sawyers attacked a mechanical sawmill in London. Spinning jennies were destroyed throughout Lancashire in 1769, and riots were commonplace in 1779. In Manchester in 1792, a firm was burnt to the ground for employing the power loom. In the English southwest, opposition in spinning and weaving of wool was very strong. Shearers made numerous attempts at blocking the introduction of gig mills. Probably the most serious wave of riots occurred between 1811 and 1816, when "Luddism"[44] arose in the Midlands, leading to the destruction of numerous machines. The 1819 Peterloo Massacre saw 60,000 rally in Manchester, with 11 killed by government troops and hundreds injured. Hand loom weavers in Lancashire rioted in 1826, and in the south the 1830–1832 "Captain Swing" saw riots against threshing machines (Hobsbawm 1969:67; Mokyr 1990:256pp; 2002a:265pp; Morgan 1999:46; Parente and Prescott 2002:95; Pugh 1999:40).

In France, there was consistent pressure on the nascent cotton textile industry. Collins (1995:256) tells us how political consensus had been shattered in the 1750s–1760s, and that things grew gradually worse from then on. Roche (1998:671) describes how the attitude toward authorities kept changing, manifesting itself in an increase in the number of strikes, plots, and work-related conflicts, especially after 1760. France saw widespread resistance against new technology and against industry, and it seems obvious that the increasing lack of popular cohesion led to riots that impeded the rate of industrial progress. Persistent rioting occurred between 1788 and 1791, as machinery was perceived as threatening the livelihood of workers.[45] Anti-machinery vandalism spread from Rouen in the summer of 1789 to Paris, St. Etienne and numerous other cities. These riots were not directed only against textile machinery in general, but also against Britain, as this was from where the machines had been imported. Weavers in Lyon resisted the Jacquard loom during the first decade of the nineteenth century, and the following decade saw opposition against wool-shearing equipment. Within other industries, armories employing interchangeable parts in their rifle production were violently and successfully resisted by artisans, merchants and officers, with the government refusing to come

---

44 Named after the mythical leader Ned Ludd. The Luddites were a secret group of workers in Nottinghamshire, Lancashire and Yorkshire. Nottinghamshire Luddites protested exclusively against the textile industry, whereas political motivations beyond this can be found with both Lancashire and Yorkshire Luddites (Morgan 1999:47).

45 Yet, because of endemic riots all over France, it is hard to know to what extent riots were directed against the introduction of new technology and physical equipment, or just against the regime.

to their rescue. Post-1815, workers and craftsmen gained in strength, as a result preventing new inventions from gaining a foothold. Resistance from weavers forced cotton entrepreneurs to withdraw mule jennies in the 1840s. The inventor of the sewing machine, Bartélemy Thimonnier, saw his factory destroyed—twice. As late as the 1860s, weavers fiercely resisted the power loom (Magraw 1999:346; Mokyr 1990:258pp; 1992:332; 2002a:270).

Hence, the point to be made is not that Britain faced less resistance against new technology than France, but that where the British state crushed any resistance with a conspicuous lack of tolerance, the French state vacillated. French policy toward technological change constantly shifted, with different parts of the government pulling in different directions (Mokyr 1992:330p).

The British state was unequivocally on the side of industry. To quote Mokyr (2002a:268): "When violence was resorted to, the government sent soldiers, who smothered the rebellions in a wave of executions and deportations and did all they could to prevent the organization of groups that could be hostile to the emerging industrial class." The 1779 Lancashire riots were suppressed by the army. The response against Luddism was particularly fierce, resulting in hangings and deportations. Government spies were used to infiltrate meetings. More troops (12,000) were sent to squash the Luddite riots of 1811–1813 than were originally enrolled in Wellington's 1808 peninsular army (Mokyr 1990:257; Morgan 1999:47; Parente and Prescott 2002:94p).[46]

In contrast, the French state to a great extent was too weak to assert itself. The old regime tried to reform in the 1770s, but unsuccessfully so. With the French Revolution, the attitude changed in favor of technology. However, it also brought major upheaval, diminishing the state's ability to stamp out resistance against new technology. Order was not restored until Napoleon, who consistently squashed all opposition to new technologies. Resistance against both Jacquard looms, and wool shearing a decade later, was suppressed. However, with the 1815 Restoration, the state once again weakened, to the advantage of workers and craftsmen. Once more, resistance against new technology would frequently succeed (Mokyr 1990:259p; 2002a:270; Price 1993:139; Wright 1995:34).

But resistance is not only about physical resistance. This is really a desperate measure, and the reason why such resistance was so widespread in Britain, was that the state was doing a good job at preventing vested interests from using legislation to hinder technological change. Physical resistance was the only means left! In 1769, Parliament made tampering with bridges and engines in mines a capital offense. It also rejected a 1776 petition by cotton spinners to forbid spinning jennies. Wool combers in 1794 petitioned against a wool-combing machine, but were denied. The Combination Acts of 1799 made attempts to band against new technologies illegal. Similar acts were used to limit the powers of trade unions. Labor organizations

---

46 The only successful attempt at Luddism in Britain was the 1830–1832 Captain Swing riots against steam threshers, which led to steam threshers vanishing from southern England until the 1850s (Mokyr 2002a:267).

were made illegal if perceived as threatening the advance of technology. The ban on gig mills in the wool-finishing trade was repealed in 1809.[47] Ancient statutes and regulations in the woolen industry were considered inimical to new technologies, and repealed between 1803 and 1809. The Statutes of Artificers and Apprentices[48] were removed in 1814. Finally, unlike on large parts of the Continent, the guilds lost their power as early as the 1688 Glorious Revolution (Freeman and Louçã 2001:178; Mokyr 1990:257p; 1999:49; 2002a:268; Morgan 1999:46).

In France, guilds had weakened since the 1750s. After 1776, remaining regulations were often not enforced. Yet, the guild structure was still powerful. A network of craft guilds and small producers supported by local authorities in general opposed technological innovation, and helped by local authorities, were often strong enough to resist labor-saving inventions. The regulations and restrictions presented by French guilds would have made it difficult for someone like Richard Arkwright to set up shop as a cotton spinner (Mokyr 1990:259). In textiles in particular, to get around guild regulations, manufacturing would move to the countryside, where wages were low and regulations non-existent. In some cases there were even alliances between guilds and merchants. Merchants would use guilds to regulate trade, to maintain inefficiency in production and uphold their monopolies. Hence, when in 1762 a royal edict gave rural areas the freedom to produce any type of cloth, merchants in Lille fought the edict for a decade and a half. Similar patterns could be found in Paris and Orléans. Also, noblemen and local authorities in the countryside would frequently go against the central government by supporting craft guilds and small producers (Mokyr 2002a:264, 270).

While guilds were formally abolished in 1791, the idea lingered on. Between 1805 and 1810, 13 *syndicats* were set up. Although these were at best pale imitations of the guilds, it still implied a high level of organization among French workers, with illicit unions continuing to fight against entrepreneurs introducing cost-cutting machinery. Often, small entrepreneurs would ally with workers to keep larger and technologically more efficient entrepreneurs out. Also, the demise of Napoleon and the 1815 return of the Bourbons meant a considerable weakening of the French state. This fueled a new debate about guilds, that did not die down until the 1830s (Bossenga 1988:694pp; Fairchilds 1988:690; Mokyr 2000:79; 2002a:269; Sewell, Jr. 1980:182; Sibalis 1988:726pp; Trebilcock 1981:116).

Beyond guilds, rent-seeking was a far more serious problem in pre-revolutionary France than in Britain, and hence resistance to change was more widespread there (Crafts 1995b:763; Jacob 1997:167; Mokyr 1992:331p; 2002c:16pp; Root 1991). In both countries, lobby groups sought to affect governmental regulations. However, in Britain, the role of Parliament led to rent-seeking by vested interests being a

---

47 This ban had been in place since 1551—a prime example of successful resistance against technological change!

48 Instituted in 1563, it specified that every worker undergo a formal apprenticeship before being employed in a trade. This was considered a nuisance, as it was perceived as unnecessary as common laborers would easily suffice (Mokyr 1999:50).

very slow and cumbersome process, with such activities to an ever greater extent belonging to the public sphere. In contrast, the French government did not have to face up to any parliament. Hence, secrecy shrouded the wheeling and dealing of pressure groups and government (Root 1991:338). The British government may have had less leverage with respect to implementing policy than the French King's Council, which could issue legislation by decree, and thus seem more inefficient.[49] However, the more direct French process was both opaque and top-heavy, with economic regulation the prerogative of bureaucratic discretion. To quote Root:

> The rationale underlying the administration and regulation of the nation's industrial expansion was simple: The government barred competition in exchange for a share of the monopoly rents generated. In other words, the mercantilist state granted regulations, subsidies, taxes and licenses to favored producers and consumers so that the government could take a share of the excess profits regulation created. (1991:340)

The process was governed by the French controller general, who was the head of the *Conseil royal des finances*—the most powerful of the individual councils forming the King's Council of State. His number one concern was the accumulation of royal revenues. But making the institution responsible for fiscal health also be in charge of economic development led to a preference for short-term revenues over long-term planning. Commercial and industrial profits were redistributed toward preferred clients. Getting royal patronage was a more likely path toward industrial success than working as an entrepreneur. Hence, there were strong incentives for competing for the King's ear, rather than spending time on productive activities. "Ministerial dirigism of the economy transformed France into a nation of self-centered clans and corporations, each fighting to maintain or expand its privileges" (Root 1991:364).

In contrast, the British parliamentary system made fighting for the King's approval less important.[50] A British lobbyist had to present a petition to Parliament, followed up by an MP presenting a formal request in Parliament. Then a committee would consider the proposal, implying witnesses, experts, and hearings. Not until then could the lobbyist present his case in the House of Commons. While slow and cumbersome, the practice of relatively open and public negotiation and compromise led to strong resentment against favoritism. Parliament could not easily be manipulated by vested interests seeking monopoly rights. Britain was corrupt—maybe more so than most countries—but this did not imply redistribution of income in favor of specific actors, nor monopoly rights (ibid.:351pp; Crafts 1995b:763; Mokyr 2002c:17p). The French process may have been faster, but it also resulted in French policies being a cobweb of favoritism and vested interests.

---

49 The King's Council actually issued more legislation in four years than the British Parliament during the entire 60-year reign of George III (Root 1991:355).

50 These were developments stemming from the English Civil War. Aghast with Stuart practices of awarding monopolies and sinecures to their favorites, post-Restoration Parliament sought to limit such practices (Root 1991:351p).

The cotton textile industry itself is valid proof that the British Parliament functioned as a better check on vested interests than the French controller general. The story of cotton textiles is among other things a story of lobbying and vested interests. One cannot credibly claim that the British state consciously promoted or encouraged cotton textiles. And yet, indirectly it still did so, by discontinuing industrial policies that were very clearly a product of vested interests. By ceasing its meddling in industrial politics, the British state removed the very explicit barriers that existed against cotton textiles. Add to this an odd fortuitous element: Banning Indian calicoes made it possible for domestic cotton weaving to gain a foothold in the market. Between 1696 and 1774, pressure group activity led to the passing of British laws conducive (sometimes by accident, sometimes not) to the development of the cotton industry.

During most of the eighteenth century, wool was the predominant British industry, favored by legal restrictions. Cotton, was just a by-product of colonial commerce. India produced the world's finest cotton yarn and textiles, which led to the English East India Company creating a market for cotton fabrics in Europe. Toward the end of the seventeenth century, this market was growing fast, as Indian cloth and calicoes made from cottons, were both cheaper, lighter, more decorative, and easier to wash and clean than European cloths made from wool (Hobsbawm 1969:57; Landes 1998:154).

The European wool, linen and silk industry was deeply worried by what they perceived as penetration by a foreign industry and strongly opposed calicoes. In England,[51] wool and silk forged an alliance to combat imported linens, silks and cotton, and sought to rally Parliament through lobbying. Hence, in order to stimulate consumption of domestic wool cloth, legislation of 1666 and 1678 proscribed that the dead should be buried in wool shrouds. The woolen industry was politically influential: Members of the House of Commons represented constituencies where wool, woolen yarn and woolen cloth were important industries. The peers in the Upper House collected rents that were closely connected with the prosperity of the woolen industry. In Scotland, in 1681 the parliament prohibited the wearing of calicoes and mixtures of cottons with other fibers. In England, merchant interests were strong, hence the English (and the Dutch) government was the only government in Europe to resist pressures from the woolen industry. However, manufacturing interests still prevailed, pushing through the 1721 Calico Act, which closed the market to Asian textiles. The act prohibited the import, sale and wearing of printed, stained or dyed calicoes (Landes 1969:82; 1998:207; Mokyr 1999:50; O'Brien, Griffiths and Hunt 1991:397pp).[52]

---

51 The seemingly random use of England or Great Britain is due to the fact that the union with Scotland did not occur until 1707. Some of the developments with calicoes and cottons started prior to 1707, hence England and not Britain.

52 The British state imposed a fine of £5, which may not sound all that punitive. However, the fine was not to be paid to the state, but to the "informer" (O'Brien, Griffiths and Hunt

However, the resistance that the British government put up against pressure from the woolen industry between 1696 and 1721 eventually became crucial for the growth of cotton textiles. First, even if finished Asian textiles were banned from England (1700), imperial markets were still open. Second, the Calico Act had important loopholes, effectively creating expanding market niches for Celtic linens and English fustians (O'Brien, Griffiths and Hunt 1991:414).[53] While the act explicitly extended to "any Stuff made of Cotton or mixed therewith …" (O'Brien, Griffiths and Hunt 1991:409), fustians, neckcloths and muslins, as well as linen cottons produced by domestic manufacturers, were exempt by the regulations, despite this being bitterly fought by wool and silk producers. Exemptions were also given for calicoes dyed blue.[54] [sic] The main reason for the exemptions was political, as Parliament acknowledged the importance of the linen industry for Scotland and Ireland as well as the importance of avoiding riots on the Celtic fringes of the only recently united kingdom of Great Britain.[55]

Against this, the wool industry lobbied in Parliament that fustians were indistinguishable from calicoes, and should be banned. However, the 1736 Manchester Act decisively rejected the wool industry, making it clear that linen yarn and cotton wool were a branch of fustians, and thus not unlawful. Hence, Parliament gave the go-ahead to spin, weave, dye, and print fustians consisting of a mix of linen and cotton fibers. Lancashire and Derbyshire fustians now replaced Indian calicoes as the main threat to woolens and silks (Landes 1969:82; O'Brien, Griffiths and Hunt 1991:409, 414p).[56]

Growth in Celtic linen production resulted in price hikes on yarn (prices almost doubled between 1746 and 1763), affecting the entire British textile industry. Moreover, the linen industry boom following from The Seven Years War (1755–1763) led Parliament support for linens to dwindle. Also, by now, the relationship between England and the Celtic kingdoms was less tenuous, making political concerns over linen support less important. In the meantime, the fustian industry had grown through technological progress. Richard Arkwright was bullish about

---

1991:409). In other words, if wearing calico, in theory you could be "informed upon" an infinite amount of times by private individuals.

53 A fustian is a fabric consisting of a mix of cotton and flax, or cotton and low-quality wool.

54 It is possible that the exemptions for calicoes dyed blue was on behalf of the infant cotton industry in Weymouth, which had made a petition to Parliament for protection (O'Brien, Griffiths and Hunt 1991:409).

55 It was acknowledged that linens were as important to Scotland and Ireland as woolens to England. Putting restrictions on linens would jeopardize the already tenuous relationship between England and "the Celtic kingdoms" (O'Brien, Griffiths and Hunt 1991:408). Also, in 1696 the Crown had officially encouraged the manufacture of linens in Ireland, hence completely omitting linens from the 1721 act, even though linens were as big of a threat to wool and silk as calicoes were.

56 At this stage fustians allied with wool to counter favoritism toward linen (O'Brien, Griffiths and Hunt 1991:410).

the prospects of the cotton industry after being granted a patent (1774) for his water frame, spinning machine. He successfully petitioned for the repeal of the Calico Act (Mokyr 1999:51; O'Brien, Griffiths and Hunt 1991:411p).

This had been about politics, not economics: Concern with riots in the Celtic lands made Parliament support the linen industry. The growth of linens created a loophole for domestic cotton manufacture, sheltered by the very same act against competition from Asia. While this was unintended, there is still much to be said for the role of the British state. To a much greater extent than France, the British state resisted pressure from the vested interests of woolens and silks—used to state support through tariffs and other legislation. By the dawn of the Industrial Revolution, Britain to a much larger extent than most had abandoned elaborately regulated government-sanctioned monopolies (DuPlessis 2003:78; O'Brien, Griffiths and Hunt 1991:412pp; Parente and Prescott 2002:134).

In contrast, the French state did not have the required autonomy to do this. The import of calicoes and Chinese silks (except silks for re-export), as well as the finishing or printing of plain Indian calicoes, were banned in 1686. French markets were completely closed to Asian textiles by 1701. Richelieu and Colbert had earlier tried to encourage French cotton manufacture, but Controller-General Louvois, prohibited the sale of printed linens and cottons. In France, no less than a total ban on the sale, wear or use of printed cloth would do. According to O'Brien, Griffiths and Hunt (1991:418): "Apparently the French government lacked the administrative capacity to placate native woolen, silk, and linen industries by weapons less than a total ban …"

Britain's success at preventing pressure groups from stifling the implementation of new technology was essential. But regional British differences are also instructive. Cotton did not have strong pressure groups, much unlike wool, which had a long tradition of organization and regulation. As a consequence of pressure groups resisting new technology, a major shift took place in British textiles production. The eighteenth century saw a 150 per cent increase in wool textiles. Of this, West Riding of Yorkshire increased its share of wool production from 20 to 60 per cent of the total. In Yorkshire, technological innovations like the spinning jenny were rapidly diffused and incorporated, without much local resistance. The West Country on the other hand, saw major worker opposition, with strong resistance against machinery, strengthened by traditions of solidarity and collective action among the workers from earlier industrial and food riots. The result was a West Country that faded into industrial irrelevance, whereas Yorkshire grew to become the center of British wool production. British regions that opposed new technology rapidly lost out to the regions that embraced it (Hudson 1992:116; Mokyr 2002a:261, 265).

Britain: Political Consensus through the Merging of Political Elites   Politics played a positive role in Britain, unlike in France. Obviously there are many reasons why the British state was better able to quell vested interest opposition than France, but much of it has to do with the *political consensus* of the ruling elites, with *social cohesion* in the populace also playing some part. In Britain, the ruling elites increased their prestige, and local government was dominated by landed interests favoring industrialization. They also converged in terms of political and economic interests. In comparison, in France, the Crown sought to encourage technological innovation and industrial progress through a number of different means—privileges, pensions, monopolies. But here, the ruling class effectively split the country in a policy-making stalemate. The countryside would frequently torpedo the central government, local authorities doing their best to support craft guilds and small producers and resisting technological innovation, and the lack of reform ultimately undermined the prestige of the Crown to such an extent that the outcome was revolution (Mokyr 2002a:264, 270; Pugh 1999:9).

In Britain, two crucial developments took place in the mid- to late eighteenth century. The first is what Colley (1992:155) describes as "the making of the British ruling class". The second half of the eighteenth century saw an increasingly hostile attitude toward the aristocracy. Colley (1992:152) writes: "… everyone in the British Establishment had his hand in the till, advanced his own male and female relations and was closely related by blood or marriage to everyone else in high office." The landed class was seen as parasitic, separate from the king. However, much of the reason why the ruling elites were increasingly singled out for criticism was their relative homogeneity. Most politicians had connections with land. The distinction between Tories and Whigs was unclear, with party loyalty often a matter of family tradition. Toward the end of the century, party lines became *less* clear (Pugh 1999:15pp; Root 1991). A very rapid fusing of English, Welsh, Scottish and Irish elites through marriage and inheritance[57] saw a convergence of perspectives that increased the cohesion of the British ruling class, be they Whigs or Tories, and which led to an overarching consensus on issues like industrialization. Also, faced with threats from the French Revolution it was possible for these elites to credibly redefine themselves as a patriotic and heroic, authentically and enthusiastically *British* ruling class.[58] While domestic social unrest did not cease altogether, the ruling class was no longer perceived as parasitic. It had managed to restore its authority and legitimacy, and in the process helped reshape a British identity (Colley 1992:177–93).[59]

---

57 As well as education: In the early 1700s, the ruling classes largely arranged private tutors for their children. By 1800, 70 per cent of all English peers received their education at Eton, Westminster, Winchester or Harrow (Colley 1992:167).

58 Colley (1992:164) asserts that this did not only happen from pure self-interest. Massive wars and empire-building, brought members of the landed classes from all over Great Britain together against Americans, French (both in Europe and in Asia), Indians, Africans, Australians and people from the West Indies. This made it far easier for the English, Welsh, Scottish and Irish to realize their common bonds, and to perceive themselves as genuinely British, united against an external other.

59 Change was not just a matter of appearance (Colley 1992:189). Where politics had once been something bordering on a landed leisure activity, by the late eighteenth century, politicians had become genuine workaholics. While during most of the eighteenth century, it had been possible for important politicians to be more or less openly promiscuous, the image of the nineteenth-century statesman was that of having an impeccable private life.

The second development is more directly linked to industrialization, and started a few decades earlier. Previous British governments had vacillated considerably on manufacturing, but this changed in the decades preceding the Industrial Revolution. In 1760, George III became king. Eager to be perceived as above politics, he included Tories in the government, despite the Whigs having dominated politics for half a century. Thus, the Tories largely gave up their previous position as the party of the country opposition. These were in many ways not very strong governments. However, it is conspicuous that controversies toward the end of the eighteenth century and into the early part of the nineteenth were mainly personal struggles, not political ones. The number of contested elections shrank, and political controversy receded. The political parties for all practical purposes instead merged into one single ruling class—unanimously and staunchly pro-industry. Unlike France, the fact that the locus of early British industry was the countryside was no disadvantage. Because of mining (being a less than mobile industry) and the easy access to water power, the landlord class had a direct stake in industrialization, for instance from mines on their land. Hence, the early phase of industrialization benefited the landlords, as technological change led to sharp increases in real estate values in the industrializing and mining regions, without there being much risk involved (Freeman and Louçã 2001:166; Mokyr 2002a:268p; Pugh 1999:17; Van Horn Melton 2001:33p).

Rivalry between landed and industrial interests would arise anew, but not until the end of the Napoleonic Wars. Pugh (1999:38) writes: "when peace suddenly returned in the summer of 1815, it took the British politicians by surprise." During the war, Britain had cultivated large areas of land in order to feed a population shut out from Continental grain by Napoleon's Continental System. However, since this land had now been cultivated, a vested interest had formed to keep it being farmed at a profit. Hence, in 1815, Corn Laws were imposed, whereby farmers and landowners received protection by the government banning the importation of corn until the domestic price reached £4 per quarter (Pugh 1999:38p).[60] Lord Liverpool's 1812–1827 Tory government was resented among manufacturers and workers for introducing such blatant class legislation. Lord Liverpool was not considered a strong PM (Disraeli dubbed him the "Arch Mediocrity"). Still, he provided law and order and stable government, clamping down on popular unrest and resistance against technology and industry—like the Luddite riots (Pugh 1999:38pp).

The French Revolution and the Napoleonic Wars most likely also had impacts on the cotton textile industry through social cohesion. Conspicuously, most cases of industrial unrest occurred either *prior to* or *after* this period. The 1780s saw a short-lived wave of radicalism and a movement for parliamentary reform and suffrage, as well as the anti-Catholic Gordon riots (Pugh 1999:22; Van Horn Melton 2001:40). Tilly (1995:92) provides us with a list of arrests and casualties in contentious gatherings in Great Britain, 1758–1834. Between 1789 and 1811, the number of arrests and casualties was negligible compared to the marked increase after 1819 (peaking between 1830 and 1832). For the years preceding 1781, the number of

---

60 During the war, wheat prices peaked at £5.

arrests and casualties was also considerably higher. Hence, the years 1789–1815 cemented the British lead in cotton textiles not only because France was cut off from British technology diffusion, but also because resistance against technology shrank markedly. Revolution and war provided for a period of greater cohesion.[61]

Colley (1992:1) asserts that British nationality was forged by war, primarily with France—almost continually from the end of the seventeenth century until the fall of Napoleon.[62] The French Revolution caused enormous stir and nervousness in the British ruling class, which was not convinced that the same could not happen in Britain. However, there is scant evidence of pro-Frenchness or revolutionary activity in Britain once the Revolution had occurred. Britain experienced few problems recruiting people for military duty against France. And social class had very little impact on volunteering. One might expect the down-and-outers and industrial poor to be more influenced by revolutionary ideals, but the ones most reluctant to volunteer were peasants from remote, rural areas, and not industrial workers.[63] Britain apparently had reservoirs of latent cohesion in its populace to draw upon (Best 1982:132p; Colley 1992:287; Evans 1983:81). Hence, again 1789–1815 was important for the cotton textile industry in the sense that the wars halted the resistance against new technology (Colley:293pp). While overall British growth fell between 1789 and 1815, cotton textiles flourished.[64]

---

61 However, the French Revolution also led to levels of repression not seen in Britain since the civil war. Hence, the absence of riots to some extent stems from this. In 1794, politically oriented movements inspired by the French Revolution were closed down. Mass-membership affiliations were perceived as dubious, and held under tight government control until the 1820s. A number of restrictions on individual freedom were introduced. 1792 saw the "Proclamation against Seditious Writings and Assemblies" restricting the freedom of the press. In 1793, people were prosecuted for circulating radical literature. The 1795 "Treasonable Practices Act and Seditious Meetings Act" greatly restricted the rights of speech, press and assembly: Meetings with more than 50 people were prohibited, and anyone speaking or writing in criticism of the constitution could be prosecuted. The restrictions on military and police intervention in riots were eased and *habeas corpus* temporarily suspended on numerous occasions. Still, nothing resembling any organized revolutionary movement ever arose. Compared to France, Britain was far from repressive, and it was politically stable (Pugh 1999:23p, 38pp; Tilly 1995:10, 419pp).

62 Wars against France: 1689–1697, 1702–1713, 1743–1748, 1756 1763, 1778 1783, 1793–1802, 1803–1815 (Colley 1992:1)!

63 In the seven predominantly rural English counties, 22 per cent of all men volunteered. The pattern was different in counties predominantly engaged in trade and industry. There were eleven such counties exhibiting an average volunteer rate of 35 per cent of the eligible male population (Colley 1992:298).

64 Modelski and Thompson's (1996:99) figures reveal that British raw cotton consumption increased from 3,000 metric tons in 1780 to 14,000 in 1790, 24,000 in 1800, and 56,000 in 1810. These are pretty good figures for an export industry in an economy at war! During the same period, France's raw cotton consumption increased from 4,000 metric tons in 1780 to 8,000 in 1810.

The French Revolution and the Napoleonic Wars at one and the same time became crisis point and salvation. Since the 1760s, reaching a temporary peak in the 1780s, the British ruling class was becoming ever more unpopular, with the number of riots increasing and the general level of dissent and resentment rising. 1789 gave the ruling class the break it needed, with respect to suppressing any potential opposition, and to reforming and legitimizing itself, which it duly did (Colley 1992). The result was a ruling class that headed a Britain much more stable in social and industrial terms, and with much more authority than the rest of Europe.

France: Fragmentation of Political Elites   In France, ruling elites blocked each other instead of merging.[65] Eighteenth century France was not at all static. Between 1750 and 1789, changes were taking place at a more rapid rate than ever before, especially with respect to the economy, the monarch seeking to bring the political system in line with ongoing economic and social changes (Collins 1995:224). However, no political consensus existed with respect to structural reform, with no major change taking place, with respect to physical resistance against new technology, financial politics, and guilds. One might think that an absolutist monarchy like France had an easier time implementing change than Britain. This was not the case, and the main reason was the lack of political consensus among French ruling elites. The king was reliant on power alliances that put very obvious confines on his political leverage.

The ever recurring problem of the late eighteenth century was that of budget deficits. France, being less able than Britain to finance its wars,[66] had run into a situation where expenses far exceeded income. By 1787–1788 the budget had a deficit of 25 per cent. More than 50 per cent of the expenses went to interest rate payments, the figure rising for each passing year. The problem was primarily one of low tax revenues. Tax reform was a recurring theme throughout the eighteenth century, but imposing a direct permanent tax proved impossible, primarily because of

---

65 France essentially had two categories of nobles, the sword nobility (*noblesse de l'epée*), and the robe nobility (*noblesse de robe*). The sword nobility was the traditional nobility, dating back to the medieval ages. The robe nobility was a service nobility, going back to 1644, founded on holding hereditary, ennobling titles, either through the purchase of an office that carried the prize of hereditary nobility, or through the direct ennoblement by the king. They were in the majority, accounting for roughly two-thirds of the nobility. There is a tentative consensus that the two types of nobility converged somewhat during the *first part* of the eighteenth century, but *drifting apart after 1750*. The sword nobility claimed social superiority, but positions in the *parlements* were held by the robe nobility. These were the nobles that the king clashed with over reform, eventually leading to revolution. However, it is not as simple as the nobility of the sword being *for* the king and the nobility of the robe *against* him. The nobility of the robe stemmed from the development of a modern state. The nobility of the sword were the ones that really had reason to feel under threat (Gwynne Lewis 2004:12, 68–74, 87p, 199–211).

66 The Seven Years War took a particular toll, delivering the French economy a shock that it never recovered from. Annual income would be in the range of 250–475 million livres. The war cost 1.5 *billion* livres (Collins 1995:227).

opposition from the privileged classes (Collins 1995:237pp; Hoffman and Rosenthal 2000:442pp; Price 1993:71; Wright 1995:9, 36).[67]

In many ways, French politics has been a centuries-long struggle by the king to wrest power away from the landed classes. The nobility's claim for a larger share in government in return for going along with royal reforms meant reclaiming lost feudal rights and privileges. This was not something that the king could look favorably upon. During earlier attempts to reform the tax base, Louis XV had repeatedly run into resistance from the vested interests of nobility, Church, and guilds. Thus, for reform to be implemented, the king would for all practical purposes have to side *against* the forces from which he derived most of his support, and *with* forces toward which the bulk of his traditional support would be extremely skeptical, if not downright hostile. Reforms affected the privileged classes enough to arouse their resistance, but not the bourgeoisie to such an extent that he could draw upon it for support. Ironically, the Crown's search for new revenues led it to empower groups that would then be able to resist its policies (Collins 1995:237pp; Hoffman and Rosenthal 2000:442pp; Price 1993:71; Wright 1995:9, 36).

Virtually every French controller-general in the second half of the eighteenth century was a reformist—Terray, Turgot, Necker, Calonne. As early as 1751, Louis XV had failed in his attempt to impose the *vingtieme*—a five per cent tax on income from land. *Parlements*,[68] nobility and clergy had fought this for three years, and won. In 1763–1764, the *parlement* of Paris claimed the right to verify taxation. By 1769, the budget was in complete disarray, two years' revenue having already been spent in advance. Maupeou, the chancellor of Louis XV, in 1771 exiled the Paris *parlement*, replacing it with salaried officials instead. The entire legal profession went on strike. In response, Maupeou reorganized the judicial system, abolishing the sale of official and judicial posts, instead appointing magistrates for life, salaried by the Crown. This was perceived as monarchical despotism, and by his death in 1774, Louis XV was genuinely unpopular even if this was because of moves that would have gone some way toward reforming the state. As the budget was almost back to

---

67 In its broad arrangements—hearth tax (*taille*), salt tax, sales tax—the fiscal system harked back to 1360 (Collins 1995:16).

68 There were 13 *parlements*. These were "sovereign" courts of law, going back to the thirteenth century, and serving as final courts of appeal. The one in Paris was the most important. Members of the courts could not be removed, and had a history of royal opposition. This would take the shape of *remonstrances*, that is, as criticisms of legislative proposals, or by the *parlements* refusing to register a law. If so, the law would become inoperable within the jurisdiction of that court. The king had the legal means to force registration, but this would seriously compromise his legitimacy and undermine the effective implementation of the edict. Historically, the *parlements* had been divided amongst themselves, but by 1750 this was changing. By 1780, the *parlements* constituted the most vocal expression of noble dissatisfaction with the monarchy, and a core component in what became a revolution (Price 1993:71p; Van Horn Melton 2001:48).

fiscal balance, reforms were being abandoned just as they were starting to come into effect (Furet 1995:17p; Price 1993:73; Wright 1995:12, 33).[69]

Louis XVI bought himself peace by reversing his predecessor's attempts at reform, while quietly aware of the need for change. In 1776, Controller-General Turgot proposed that the *corveé*[70] be replaced by a property tax applicable to all sections of the population, and that trade guilds be abolished. This created large-scale tension, with clergy, nobility, magistrates, craftsmen, merchants and urban people uniting against it. Turgot was dismissed (Furet 1995:26; Schama 1989:85p; Wright 1995:36).

A lack of political consensus, evident in the absence of trust and cooperation between French ruling elites, was the more or less direct reason why France was soon on the path to revolution. In 1786, Controller-General Calonne was trying to reform a France on the brink of financial collapse. He proposed to replace the *vingtieme* with a property tax on all lands without exception, proportional to income. In the same process, the *taille*[71] would be reduced, the *gabelle*[72] simplified and state debt gradually canceled through the transfer of royal domains. Also, internal customs would be abolished. In return, a hierarchy of consultative assemblies would give all property-owners a stake in government. Calonne knew that the *parlement* of Paris would never acquiesce. Instead, he proposed to call an Assembly of Notables— a handpicked body of aristocrats, clergy and bureaucrats—summoned to grant the king financial aid. But the Assembly refused, Calonne was dismissed and the proposals put in front of the *parlements* instead. The *parlements* also refused, and deadlock asserted that only an Estates-General—an institution which had not met since 1614—could sanction the king's decree.[73] By now it was 1788, and Louis XVI attempted to emulate his predecessor by stripping the *parlements* of their right to register royal edicts. The move was extremely unpopular, and he backed down, instead calling the Estates-General, which duly assembled in 1789 (Furet 1995:40; Price 1993:85; Schama 1989:227pp; Wright 1995:36pp). The following is well-known history. By July, the revolution was in full swing. A complete lack of political

---

69 The budget deficit was down from 100 million livres in 1769 to 30 million in 1774, the state's debt reduced from 400 million livres to 20 million (Furet 1995:19).

70 The corveé was the forced labor service, owed to the state by commoners. It was hated in the countryside for taking manpower away from the family during times of plowing or harvest (Schama 1989:85).

71 The *taille* was the main direct tax, going back to the fourteenth century. Nobles were exempt, as were the bourgeois of certain privileged towns (Collins 1995:xxxiii).

72 The *gabelle* was the salt tax, the king having a monopoly on salt in most of the country (Collins 1995:xxiv).

73 The Estates-General had been used by French kings between the fourteenth and the sixteenth century. It would assemble around the king a representative body for the kingdom of France. It did not have legislative authority, but it was common for kings to ask the Estates-General for advice about reforms and incorporate its suggestions in his final edict (Collins 1995:xxiv; Furet 1995:51).

consensus had made it impossible to push reform through, with no solution found short of full revolution (Furet 1995:51p; Wright 1995:38p).

Ancien régime governments had rather vacillating takes on technology and industry. Contributing to the unrest and turmoil leading up to the revolution was the 1786 Eden Treaty. It had been the intention of Calonne to put pressure on the French textile industry to modernize by forcing it to compete with British imports. He also suspected that this would enable France more easily to employ British technology and best-practices. Calonne had pushed the treaty through with virtually no consensus in the ruling classes or in the people lending support to it. When the immediate effect was France being flooded with British textiles and large parts of the industry driven out of business, the treaty was despised, attributing bad faith to the king.[74] In a cruel twist of fate, this coincided with consecutive bad harvests. As the country was in the midst of its most serious political crisis ever, grain prices rocketed and the textile industry suffered massive layoffs. Normally, this would not go beyond a major crisis, but by the 1780s consensus among the ruling elites was lower than at any time. Hence, the economic constraints of *ancien régime* France were crumbling at exactly the time that revolutionary political forces were taking control of the state (Collins 1995:266; Thompson 2000:132; Trebilcock 1981; 117). While the revolution had certain beneficial long-term effects, the short-term was a catastrophe, both in terms of the unrest that it caused, and in terms of the effects that subsequent wars had on technology imports from Britain.

Hence, levels of political consensus and social cohesion in France were altogether considerably lower than in Britain. France was definitely changing. There was a growing recognition that the nation was above the king. Enlightenment criticism emphasized individual rights. What had earlier been a conflict between the monarch and the *parlements* was being complicated by a growing public sphere, and of public opinion. Salons and literary societies sprang up from the 1770s onwards. 380 cafes in 1723 had grown to 2,000 by the 1770s. An increasing amount of newspapers, pamphlets and brochures transmitted news to ordinary people. For the period 1774–1786 there were a total of 312 such publications, increasing to well above 3,000 by 1789.[75] A fairly broad-based public sphere and a political society were developing. As the decades passed, discourse switched ever more toward national issues as taxes and the reforming of the state apparatus, the elites to an ever greater extent dissociating from the state (Collins 1995:223pp; Furet 1995:16; Roche 1998:441pp).

In France it was far harder to give grievances any clear institutional expression than in Britain, where, despite considerable discontent with Parliament, it would be very hard to find anyone of the opinion that Parliament should not on some level

---

74   The Eden treaty led to French cloth production dropping by 50 per cent between 1787 and 1789. In Amiens and Abbeville the number of looms was down from 5,672 (1785) to 2,204 (1789). 36,000 workers were put out of work (Fagan 2000:163). France denounced the treaty in 1793.

75   French periodicals, 1720–1799; 1720–1729:40; 1740–1749:90; 1770–1779:148; 1790–1799:167 (Van Horn Melton (2001:63).

be responsive to the nation. Public opinion had an institutional locus (Van Horn Melton 2001:62). In France, the absence of such a locus gave the term "public opinion" an elusiveness and vagueness that made it hard to pin down. Very few French eighteenth-century periodicals carried actual political news, maybe only four or five.[76] In contrast, as early as 1746, London alone had 18 newspapers.[77] France did not even have a daily newspaper until the last quarter of the eighteenth century (Colley 1992:41).[78] Britain also had a greater variety of outlooks. There were numerous middle-class journals and radical pamphlets, many of which were openly hostile toward the government. Some of the newspapers and journals intended for the growing working-class readership had a circulation of 40,000–50,000. By 1780, the weekly sale of British newspapers was 340,000, as opposed to 80,000–90,000 in France. In Britain in 1789, hundreds of popular demonstrations and addresses congratulated George III on his recovery from illness. Ten years earlier, British riots had reached a high, but now politics was calm and the monarchy more popular than ever. In contrast, France faced revolution, with the king only years away from being beheaded (Evans 1983:185; Knutsen 1999:110; Van Horn Melton 2001:61pp).

While the first phase of the French Revolution was characterized by reform (among other things breaking up the guilds) and a surprising amount of consensus between three estates on fiscal and judicial reform, more open access to office, and a semblance of representative government, from the execution of the king onwards, the Revolution became ever unrulier. The years between 1795 and 1802 were extremely bloody. Napoleon's 1799 coup, which made him First Consul for 10 years, was met with indifference. When the Conceil d'Etat in 1802 suggested a national plebiscite on whether Napoleon should become Consul for life, a large majority was produced, with Napoleon crowned and made Emperor in 1804. Without going into any detail, Napoleon achieved what French kings had struggled to do for centuries—relative autonomy. Law and order was largely restored, with the last royalist plot crushed in 1804. Revolution had been replaced by a conservative Emperor (Furet 1995:59pp; Price 1993:97pp, 131; Wright 1995:43pp, 67p).

---

76 Instead, much of what passed for journalism was court gossip and scandal, which if anything tended to undermine the monarchy. One should not underestimate the importance of slander and defamation in a world where personalities counted more than politics, and where politics took place almost solely at the royal court. In a world where censorship, police, and booksellers' guilds put strong constraints on what could be published, what the general public knew about politics was what it could divine from the shady underground literature specializing in court rumors, gossip, scandals and slander (Darnton 1982:vi, 203p). Hence, the rise of a French public sphere did not exactly boost the regime!

77 Its first newspaper was established as early as 1702. One of the reasons why we actually have data on British unrest was the growing abundance of newspapers in Britain reporting on such unrest, whereas it is much harder to find reliable data on France.

78 This was the *Journal de Paris*, established in 1777. With the French Revolution followed a temporary upsurge with a subsequent clampdown during Napoleon. Only a handful of dailies existed in the whole of France (Unwin, Soundy Unwin et al. 1994:432).

Unlike earlier monarchs, Napoleon's power did not rest upon a fragile alliance with the privileged classes or with a tacit understanding that attempts at reform would destroy the alliance. Rather, Napoleon rose from chaos, with the country desperate for someone to restore law and order. Many of the political problems that had proved lethal to Louis XVI had already been dealt with by the Revolution. Hence, Napoleon's task was not to reform the system from the bottom up, so dealing with the remnants of the aristocracy and with the lower classes was a simpler task than it had been for the king. Napoleon had a far greater degree of autonomy than Louis XVI, and could make and implement decisions far more easily than him.

In terms of domestic politics, Napoleon's reign was significant for being a period of comparative (if oppressive) calm and of industrial, educational and legal reform. Reforming the education system was high on his agenda, part of his grand design being to create a system of education that could churn out highly qualified experts for science and the industry. The *Ecole Polytechnique* had been established prior to his takeover. However, it was very much an institution that he approved of, and several schools followed, most notably a series of elite secondary schools (*lycées*). Among his achievements, we also find the Code Napoleon, including the 1807 Commercial Code, which essentially preserved the gains from the French Revolution, abolishing privilege, recognizing equality and individualism, and extracting the legal system from the old religious framework (Lyons 1994:102p). While it is hard to evaluate the performance of French industry, it is true that cotton textiles thrived. However, by 1815, most French cotton textile factories were technologically several decades behind Britain, suggesting that the boost during the reign of Napoleon, while to some extent resulting from law and order being reimposed, was mostly a result of peculiar wartime conditions. In general, Napoleon's reign was too short to have much substantive impact on industrial growth (Lyons 1994:260; Price 1993:133; Trebilcock 1981:125pp).

The argument about political consensus to some extent stands. Napoleon's ascendancy might seem a little like consensus by dictate. This has an obvious awkward ring to it. However, developments following his demise make it very evident how fragile France actually was. Political consensus during Napoleon's reign is something that can most easily be observed by comparing it to its total absence before him, and its reoccurring absence post-1815 (Furet 1995:280; Price 1993:157; Wright 1995:93). After France's capitulation in 1814, the Bourbons were restored to the throne by the victors, with Louis XVIII the new king. However, the monarchy started on extremely shaky foundations. Following his escape from Elba, Napoleon gathered enough support to overturn the newly installed monarchy. Defeat at Waterloo condemned him to St. Helena for the rest of his life, and left the nation more divided than ever. When Louis XVIII was reinstated in 1815, he was seriously weakened by the fact that large parts of the population had enthusiastically welcomed Napoleon's successful attempt at overthrowing him (Furet 1995:280; Price 1993:157; Wright 1995:93)!

Hence, the Bourbon monarchy was persistently low on political consensus. Louis's power rested on a very tenuous coalition. The hundred days of Napoleon had weakened his legitimacy, and radicalized both the right and the left wing. The new Chamber of Deputies had three major power blocks, right-wing ultras (even more reactionary than the king), moderates, and liberals. In the first election 78 per cent of the 402 elected deputies were on the extreme right. The king instead chose to balance power by leaning toward the moderate royalists, as with the ultras, there was always the suspicion that their real agenda was a return to a semi-feudal state with large autonomy for the nobility. Subsequent elections saw a drift toward the left and the electorate increased to around 100,000. However, in 1820 the heir to the throne was assassinated. The ultras regained control, which they kept until the 1830 revolution. Repression and censorship increased dramatically, and the liberal opposition was marginalized.[79] The accession to power in 1824 of Charles X increased tensions further, as he, unlike Louis XVIII, leant heavily toward the right. The electorate was reduced, and there was a general fear that a return to pre-revolutionary days was imminent. Elections in 1830 resulted in majorities hostile to the government.[80] Charles X invoked emergency decree powers, tightened censorship further, dissolved the Chamber, and reduced the electorate to 23,000. After three days of riots in Paris, the royal administration collapsed. The king abdicated in August 1830 (Furet 1995:284pp, 320pp; Price 1993:158pp; Tombs 1999:62p; Wright 1995:94pp).

Final remarks   In terms of consensus and cohesion, France was far weaker than Britain. However, since we are less well endowed with industrial data from early French industrialization than we are from Britain, it is more difficult to determine to what extent consensus and cohesion affected the progress of cotton textiles in France compared to in Britain. Still, there is no doubt that lack of consensus among the ruling classes made economic reform nigh impossible. A lack of consensus among the ruling classes, as well as a lack of cohesion in the people, was a major reason why the Estates-General escalated into full-blown revolution. And there is no doubt that the revolution affected not only cotton textiles negatively, but French industrialization in general. Following the revolution, social order deteriorated, making it far easier for workers and artisans to physically resist the introduction of new technologies and machinery. The lack of order made for a much more uncertain and unsafe business environment. On the political side, the revolution meant an end to technology diffusion from Britain.

With all the political turbulence, it is difficult to determine the impacts of subsequent governments. Napoleon restored social order, with business and industry experiencing a short-lived boom. He also contributed to long-term growth through the Commercial Code. With hindsight, the subsequent Bourbon regime looks very much like an intermezzo, its fragility and overall lack of cohesion taking away its ability to implement major policy change. To the extent that political consensus existed, it was a very conservative consensus, one about preserving the status quo rather

---

79 Down from 110 to 20 seats.
80 Opposition groups received 274 votes, the ministry only 143 (Wright 1995:103).

than fighting it. Social cohesion was low, both because of the regime's authoritarian nature, and because of the legitimacy issue.

The last few sentences of the previous paragraph talk about consensus and cohesion in France as being distinctly low. In contrast to this stands consensus and cohesion in Britain, which improved during the same period. This can be seen, amongst other things, through the merging of the ruling elites into one, decidedly pro-industry class. Both the cotton textile industry and British industrialization in general benefited from this, as the British government clamped down hard on physical resistance against new technology, as well as rejected all attempts at using institutional channels to curb technological progress. British governments, aided by a landed aristocracy with most of its assets in real estate and agriculture, showed no hesitation in supporting industrialization and coming down hard on those opposing it. The evidence from Yorkshire and the West Country suggests that these processes did not only happen between, but also within countries. British regions that opposed new technology very rapidly lost out to those that embraced it. The fact that vested interests could neither block industrialization in general nor the rise of cotton textiles in particular, was not the result of farsighted governmental industrial policies. Such hardly existed. As suggested earlier, political concerns were more important than economic ones. The fact that these concerns led to regulations that had economic benefits was somewhat fortuitous. Fortuity aside, what the British government had going for it to a far greater extent than foreign governments, was a willingness to abstain from meddling in industrial affairs with the exception of upholding law, order and the respect for private property. This probably was the number one British advantage at this stage of industrialization.

While revolution and war normally mark a time of crisis, this was only one of the sides to the French Revolution and the Napoleonic Wars. Earlier, I have stressed how this period cemented the advantage that Britain already had over France in cotton textiles. Here, I suggest that there were beneficial effects in terms of cohesion as well. The renewed focus on foreign policy, and the very genuine external threat of French dominance and invasion, directed the attention of the average Briton away from industrial and social unrest. Hence, because of extra-systemic events, a shift in social cohesion in the people took place at a time when Britain needed it the most. Hence, not only economically, but politically as well, 1789–1815 cemented the advantage that Britain already had, by drastically reducing the level of resistance against technology, and through a more legitimate and authoritative ruling class.

Conclusions

In both Britain and France, cotton textiles was the first sector to industrialize. Compared to the rest of the Continent, France did reasonably well, often considered the second European power to industrialize. Change was taking place, economically and politically, at a rate never seen before. And yet, the period stretching from roughly 1760 into the 1820s marks a time where a once modest British lead developed into hegemony. Britain was already ahead in cotton textiles by the 1780s, but only in per capita terms. French consumption of raw cotton actually surpassed that of Britain. Yet, by the end of the Napoleonic Wars, France had been relegated to a second-rate industrial power. Britain industrialized rapidly throughout the wars, but while French cotton textiles experienced a temporary upswing during the same period, the industry failed to modernize. While in a European context, both countries were early industrializers, in relative terms there was only one winner, and compared to this winner, everybody else looked like losers. This was the period of British industrialization, and the success of the British cotton textile industry. By the 1820s, no country was remotely close.

While the English education system can hardly explain the rise of cotton textiles, there is much to be said for human capital. In terms of higher education, the English performance was lamentable. Fewer people were channeled through higher education than in France, and the higher education provided was irrelevant for industrial pursuits. The English state preferred to stay out. This very much in contrast to the French higher education policy, where a great number of highly qualified experts were churned out by a system that considered education one of the most important components in securing industrial and military leadership through the implementation of new technology. Napoleon was very explicit with respect to the importance of education for a future dominant France, and around the turn of the century and for the early decades of the nineteenth century, France was the world's leading nation in terms of science. At the dawn of the Industrial Revolution France was ahead of Britain in nearly every science imaginable.

However, the breakthroughs leading to the industrialization of cotton textiles—spinning jenny, water frame, mule, power loom—were in many ways technologically fairly simple. In no way should the brilliance of the people behind these inventions be underestimated, and in no way should one deny that these were truly breakthrough inventions. Rather, the point is that as of yet, the sciences had not advanced to such a stage that they were incomprehensible to the able, intelligent and mechanically gifted layman. Revolutionary breakthroughs could still be accomplished by people of modest schooling. This is exactly where Britain had its advantage. The English primary school system was better than the French. English enrollment rates and literacy levels were among the highest in the world, and Britain had a larger pool of reasonably skilled men than probably any other country. More importantly, where France had its comparative advantage in the sciences, Britain had its advantage in the *application* of science, that is, in technology. Britain was a nation of mechanically skilled experimenters and tinkerers, of people that used whatever scientific and technological knowledge they possessed for the benefit of industry. Contemporary France had the world's best engineers. However, one would find these in government bureaucracies, in the military or abroad. The last place one would come across one would be in industry.

Britain's advantage—crucial to early industrialization—was in the application of technology and science to industry, and in the close links that existed between entrepreneurs and mechanically skilled experimenters and tinkerers. The human capital argument has often been downplayed, but it is obvious that human capital played a crucial role. The Industrial Revolution, while benefiting from a century of preceding Smithian growth, was Schumpeterian by nature, founded on technological progress, on human knowledge and on skills. At the same time, it is evident that the role of the state was only very modest. In fact, the state that actively tried to promote human capital failed! Britain's laissez-faire take on education worked well in a period where the sciences had not yet advanced very far. It became a distinct liability later on, but not for another half a century yet.

Hence, the role of the state may be framed in negative terms. Emphasizing the links between different sectors of the British economy and the closeness of the relationship between technology and entrepreneurial activity in Britain, unlike in France, did not imply much involvement by the state. The crucial difference between the British and the French state in this respect was that in Britain, the state was happy to stay out of these links. In contrast, the French state was activist, and it insisted on interfering, where a combination of activism and *non*-interference probably would have been more beneficial. In Britain, engineers and scientists rarely had any hidden political or military agenda. In France, engineering knowledge was the property of the state, in the service of national interest. As a scientist, you either worked *for* the political establishment, or *against* it. French scientists were dependent on personal relations with the political establishment, much unlike in laissez-faire Britain.

But Britain was far from laissez-faire in other areas. Structural change, as is often the consequence of revolutionary technological progress, will always meet with resistance from groups defending their vested interests. This was the case in both countries. It is hard to detect major substantive differences between the two with respect to the sheer level of physical resistance against new technology. However, the stance of the British and the French state was vastly different. France vacillated with respect to technology and industry. French governments were far from pro-technology, often more preoccupied with balancing a tenuous social status quo than with implementing decisions that might rock the boat. In contrast, the British state stifled any resistance, coming down on the side of manufacture and industry on every single occasion. This applied not only to sheer physical resistance, but also to attempts at using regulations to prevent change. Parliament rejected petitions going against the interests of new industry time and time again, and old regulations and artifices deemed to hamper the progress of industry were persistently repealed. Granted, the British ruling elite did not have much of a *conscious* industrial policy. Of the eighteenth-century political decisions that led to cotton textiles becoming the dominant industry, many had been made for political reasons—like the concern with avoiding unrest in the Celtic parts of the monarchy—and not from any economic foresight. Accidental or not, political outcomes still persistently went against old, vested interests and in favor of cotton textiles.

As with human capital, the role of the state almost becomes a negative one. The greatest virtue of the British state compared to France, was its willingness not to meddle. It did not cave in to vested interests (primarily wool, but also the outright physical resistance from workers and artisans), and it secured a glorious future for cotton textiles by letting the industry develop, devoid of constraints and regulations. There *were* regions primarily in the South, where resistance was not met with the same show of force from the state. Conspicuously, these regions were industrially and economically left behind, as industrial production rapidly shifted north. Lastly, it should be stressed that using the military to quell riots, introducing capital punishment for tampering with bridges and machinery, and removing statutes and regulations harmful to new industry, suggests that the British state was more active than it is sometimes given credit for.

The French Revolution and the Napoleonic Wars clearly influenced the outcome. In 1789, Britain's lead over France in terms of industrialization and cotton textiles was slender. By 1815, it was huge. The Revolution and subsequent wars cemented the British advantage. The breakthrough inventions had all occurred in Britain, thereafter diffusing slowly into France. With the Napoleonic Wars, diffusion came to an almost complete halt. French cotton textiles experienced a short-lived boom during the wars, but without modernizing. By the end of the Napoleonic Wars, France depended on technologies and machinery that in Britain had been obsolete since the 1780s–1790s. Post-1815, only steep tariffs could keep Britain from completely overrunning French cotton textiles.

Smithian factors were important too. There are good reasons for including Smithian factors with respect to this time period. The Industrial Revolution was really quite slow. There were revolutionary changes in certain sectors, but the impact of new technology on economic growth was at first very slight. The Industrial Revolution thus signals the beginning of persistent Schumpeterian growth, but not an immediate transition from a Smithian to a Schumpeterian economy. With developed countries, background conditions like property rights and infrastructure may not hold much promise, simply because the variation between developed countries is very small in this respect. But going back to the late eighteenth century, considerable differences between the world's leading economies still existed. Hence, while some of the typical Smithian approaches do not apply with respect to cotton textiles, France was behind Britain in virtually every Smithian respect. Most likely, property rights, infrastructure and transaction costs were areas of importance to industrialization and to cotton textiles, and these were areas where Britain had a clear head start.

Finally, this is a story about political consensus and social cohesion. While Europe would eventually have industrialized regardless, consensus and cohesion were important in explaining why Britain succeeded and France failed. Britain's success in implementing structural change was linked to its considerably higher level of consensus and cohesion than France. As British ruling elites merged, in France they split. From the 1750s–1760s onwards, British ruling elites fused into one ruling class, almost unanimously pro-technology and pro-industry. In France, French kings ever more desperately sought reform, realizing that they were stuck with a structure of government that perpetuated huge budget deficits and hampered economic progress and industrial growth. However, in absolutist France, kings were not strong enough to go against powerful vested interests. And because of the low level of cohesion in the people, French kings could not jeopardize the implicit power alliance they had with the privileged classes and instead seek support from reform-minded elements in the bourgeoisie and the lower classes. As social and economic change accelerated from the 1750s onwards, the structure of government became ever more inefficient and under ever more pressure. While, admittedly, social cohesion in the British population was also shrinking around 1750, this was countered by an unusual degree of political consensus in the ruling elites. Further, the dissent and resentment in France seems to have been of an altogether more fundamental nature than in Britain.

Again, the French Revolution and the Napoleonic Wars arrived at a fortuitous time for Britain, and an equally unfortunate one for France. From 1789 and until the last few years of the wars, the level of dissent in Britain fell radically, both dissent in general and resistance against new technology. While Britain probably did not gain in absolute terms from this period of turmoil, compared to the rest of the Continent it did so strongly. In France, turmoil, resistance and unrest increased correspondingly. The Revolution and the wars also gave the British ruling elite, which was coming in for ever more and hostile criticism from the lower classes, a chance to reform itself as heroic, patriotic and authentically British. Hence, in addition to removing the most important source of technology diffusion from France, 1789–1815 reduced the resistance against new technology and strengthened the legitimacy of the ruling classes. In contrast, France was in chaos, with law and order not reestablished until Napoleon. Post-Napoleon, a France weary after more than 25 years of turmoil, needed decades to return to normalcy, fears of a return either to an arch conservative *ancien régime* or a radical revolutionary regime not easily extinguished. By 1815, Britain had opened up a huge lead in cotton textiles, as France's own cotton textile industry could only survive behind trade barriers.

Chapter 3

The Iron Industry

Introduction: The Age of Iron and Steam

The second most important industry of the early Industrial Revolution was iron. While the Industrial Revolution was always about more than just cotton, after the Napoleonic Wars, the British economy drifted toward something resembling a crisis of structural adjustment, as cotton textiles could no longer carry the economy forward. The growth of the iron industry started as early as the 1780s, only a decade or two after cotton. However, it was not until after the Napoleonic Wars that it became the driver of the economy. British post-Napoleonic growth was fueled by an iron industry that stood head and shoulders above that of Europe, and came to symbolize the high-water mark of British economic and industrial dominance. By 1850, Britain produced more than 50 per cent of the world's iron, but also two-thirds of the world's coal, as well as generating a quarter of the world's trade and still maintaining a share of 50 per cent of world cloth production (Greasley and Oxley 2000:114p; Hoppen 1998:155; Landes 1969:124).

The breakthroughs in the iron industry were not as spectacular as those of the late eighteenth and early nineteenth century. The main macroinventions had occurred essentially during the same time period as for cotton textiles, preceding by several decades the industry's predominance. The rate of path-breaking invention dropped after 1825, but subsequent microinventions steadily improved the efficiency of the industry. Its influence came from being a carrier industry, economically crucial by being a vital input to other industries. Freeman and Louçã (2001:163) mention only a few of the applications depending on iron: rails, gears for water wheels, ships anchors, munitions and weapons, vessels and pipes for the chemical industry, hammers and tools for the metallurgical industry, nail, iron ploughs, shovels and picks for mines and construction, steam engines, pumps and gears for mines, blowing cylinders, cutlery, clocks and instruments, bridges, grates and stoves, textile machinery, iron frames for cotton mills and warehouses, water pipes and tanks, cooking utensils, furniture, and ornamental objects.

Probably the most crucial of the iron industry's linkages to other industries was with railroad construction, which for periods consumed most of Britain's iron production. Hence, it was not only the steady microinventions that made iron a carrier industry. Rather, it was the stream of microinventions *converging* on each other from several industries. Improvements in steam engines, combined with the innocuous, but groundbreaking idea of combining steam with iron rails, which transformed transportation and provided an enormous boost to the demand for iron.

But railroads also had an important feedback mechanism into the industry. Britain already had a well-developed canal and turnpike system, but transportation still was a far more obvious problem with iron than with cotton, just because of the sheer weight of the product. Also, iron smelting depends on fuel for heat. In the early industry, this was provided by charcoal. Technological innovation allowed the industry to switch to coal-based fuels. But out in the nature, coal and iron are often not located very closely to each other. In France, where both resources were scarce, only a transportation system linking the two might possibly solve the problem. Hence, railroads provided the iron industry with the coal without which the iron industry would not itself be able to produce the iron products required for large-scale railroad construction! The link between iron production and railroad construction was crucial to mid-nineteenth-century growth. This also meant that to a much greater extent than with cotton textiles, the iron industry was closely intertwined with infrastructure development and with resource endowments.

The previous chapter made the point that the contribution of new technology to overall economic growth in the late eighteenth century was modest at best. By the 1830s, the initial progress made by industrialization had started to mature. To paraphrase Joel Mokyr (1990); the astonishing thing about the Industrial Revolution was not that it happened—periods of technological progress have happened before as well—but that it persisted. By the 1830s, technological progress had become a permanent feature of European economies. It had become self-sustaining. TFP figures show that technology was becoming more important as a driver of growth. Typically, TFP estimates for Britain for the period 1830–1860 range between 0.8 and 1.0 per cent,[1] as compared to the far more modest 0.1 per cent for the early Industrial Revolution (e.g. Crafts and Harley 1992; Crafts 1996; Harley 1999; Hoppen 1998). For practical purposes, this means that the contribution of technology to overall GDP growth for this interval was somewhere between 31 and 40 per cent, up from 8–10 per cent for the early Industrial Revolution.

There is some overlap between cotton textiles and iron in terms of the time periods. Many of the causes of British preeminence in iron are strongly related to the causes found in the Cotton Textiles chapter, and they stem from the same period. Hence, many of the reasons for British success are to be found in a time period preceding the one highlighted here. To the extent that there is a clear overlap with cotton textiles, I will refer to the relevant passages in that chapter. The story presented in the following is that of British success and French failure. France might be considered a partial success in the sense that when industrialization finally occurred, it was driven more by heavy industries like iron than by cotton textiles. Yet, by 1860, the French iron industry was not only far behind that of Britain, but also falling behind other European countries (Belgium, Germany), despite originally having been far ahead. As with cotton textiles, a human capital advantage explains the far higher level of technological sophistication in the British iron industry than in the French. This gave

---

1   Antràs and Voth's (2003:63) figure of only 0.33 per cent is a clear outlier in this respect.

the British industry opportunities for growth that did not exist in France. And as with cotton textiles, the Revolution and the Napoleonic Wars prevented technology diffusion, cementing the lead. The British industry expanded greatly between 1789 and 1815. The French did not, despite demand from the armaments sector. Hence, some of the main reasons for British success far precede 1830. Gradual French catch-up would take place behind tariff barriers, but catch-up was slow, and overall Britain was most capable of preserving its lead.

But resource endowments, for all practical purposes in coal, are also important. France never fully overcame its factor endowment problem. France's inability to work around its disadvantage by producing a railroad network to link its scarce resources of iron and coal was more crucial than the scarcity itself, and highly politically related. In contrast, in Britain a railroad network provided the necessary infrastructure for bringing coal to the iron ores, and iron efficiently to the market. Hence, the following story is also one of how politics can be of crucial importance to the development of industry. In France, vested interests succeeded in blocking structural change. No one could wrest control over railroad construction away from the French bureaucracy. French railroads were the finest, fastest and most sophisticatedly constructed in the entire world. But this also led to French railroad construction being slow, expensive and dominated by prestige projects of little relevance to the economy, the iron industry in particular, unlike in Britain. Tariff policies were a hodgepodge, awarded to whichever interest could make the most fuss and became an attempt at maintaining an obsolete industrial structure rather than providing incentives for modernization and change. Finally, France was cursed with weak governments—the period saw two revolutions and a *coup d'état*—that were often distinctly conservative and anti-industry. Not until Louis-Napoleon's (later Napoleon III) 1851 *coup d'état* did France have an administration with any noteworthy level of relative autonomy, and only for the first decade of his reign. Not until then did France have a government both willing and able to pursue pro-industrial policies.

Britain also faced problems, but solved them. Problems with unrest and low social cohesion were countered among other things by franchise extensions. The repeal of the Corn Laws symbolized the final victory of manufacturing interests over agriculture, and only came about when political consensus over the future of the monarchy had materialized to such an extent that not even the Conservative Party would anymore block repeal. In Britain, vested interests were countered, and not allowed to block structural economic change.

History

The Early Years

Compared to cotton textiles, change in iron was gradual, incremental, and spread out over a longer period of time. Hence, "early years" is a somewhat arbitrary term. Still, a shift did take place in Britain in the 1780s–1790s, marking the start of the "modern" iron industry, based on Cort's puddling-and-rolling technique, and on coal and coke as the fuel of the iron-smelting process. This, as opposed to the charcoal based processes employed prior to this.

The precursor of an iron industry came to Britain from France in the sixteenth century, when Henry VIII imported 500 French furnace workers. The following centuries saw steady, but unspectacular growth, until reaching a plateau of 28,000 tons in 1750. Production was small and expensive, and Britain was forced to import iron from abroad.[2] Lack of fuel was the main problem. Converting iron ore into pig iron requires fuel for the smelting process, and the early iron industry was wholly dependent on charcoal (from wood) for this, smelting the ore at a blast furnace (Evans and Rydén 1998:188, 195; Landes 1969:94; Morgan 1999:51pp).[3]

The increasing demand for iron depleted traditional sources of fuel (charcoal), resulting in a dramatic increase in charcoal prices. Also, in terms of transport, the dependence on charcoal put severe constraints on the industry. Charcoal would crumble to dust if transported more than 5–10 miles, and access to a nearby forest was therefore essential. Technology and resource endowments thus effectively put an upper limit on British iron production. Contrary to this, France was abundant in timber, facing no immediate problems with respect to the supply of charcoal. While Britain produced more iron per person than France, during the mid- to late eighteenth century, France was ahead in overall production of pig iron (Landes 1969:94; Mokyr 1990:93; Morgan 1999:54; Trebilcock 1981:117, 168).[4]

The solution to Britain's resource problem was to find a different fuel for iron smelting, coke. Coke is purified bituminous coal, that is, coal that has been roasted in ovens in order to burn away its impurities. The first to use coke as fuel in blast furnaces was Quaker ironmaster Abraham Darby in 1709, but his method did not diffuse. From the 1730s onwards, British forgemasters spent considerable effort looking for a replacement for charcoal. But until the 1750s, Darby was the only ironmaster to use this technique—partly because prices for charcoal had still not gone through the roof, and partly because his coked pig iron was of low quality. This was because the fuel would be in direct contact with the ore. Since fuels contain substances that react with the ore, the final product is contaminated from impurities in the fuel. These impurities are far more serious in coal than in wood. Hence coking resulted in pig iron significantly more brittle than pig iron from charcoal. While

---

2   Imports, primarily from Sweden and Russia, doubled between 1711–1715 and 1751 1755. In 1750, more than 65 per cent of the British bar iron supply was imported (Fremdling 2000:197).

3   The resulting *pig iron* is brittle, and hence has to undergo additional processing at a forge to transform it into *wrought*, or malleable, *iron*, before it can be of any industrial use.

4   Although it is hard to find reliable figures for eighteenth-century French iron production. Modelski and Thompson's (1996) 1780 figure is considerably lower than their figure for Britain. Other scholars post far higher figures for France, which fit better with qualitative assessments of France having a higher overall iron production than Britain. Crouzet (1990:23p) claims that in 1789, French iron production was twice the size of what it was in Britain.

coking processes improved, charcoaled pig iron was qualitatively superior until well into the nineteenth century. The advantage of coke lay in the much lower price. Hence, coke iron would be reserved for castings where thickness could compensate for the inferiority of the iron—vats, pipes, cannons, bridges and building components (Brose 1998:41; Landes 1969:89pp; Mokyr 1990:93).

In 1762, John Smeaton improved upon Darby's methods by using water-driven bellows to raise the temperature of the blast furnace, improving the efficiency of combustion, hence reducing the amount of impurities. Pig iron still remained brittle and unsuited, and conversion to wrought iron time-consuming and expensive. Another development of the 1760s was the potting and stamping process, whereby silicon was removed by melting coke pigs with coal and eradicating sulfur by breaking the cold iron into small pieces, put them into clay pots and onto a coal-fired furnace (Freeman and Louçã 2001:160; Landes 1969:89pp; Morgan 1999:55).

These inventions were important. Iron production rose between 1760 and 1790. By 1788, less than one-third of the English and Welsh furnaces still used charcoal. By 1785, Britain produced almost 48,000 tons of coked pig iron, against only 14,000 tons of charcoaled pig. But not until Henry Cort's puddling and rolling, combined with coke, patented in 1783 and 1784, did iron production, including wrought iron, sharply accelerate.[5] In comparison, no French coke blast furnace was set up until 1785,[6] and no puddling-and-rolling works until 1818. As late as the mid-1850s, charcoaled pig iron was still produced in larger numbers than coked pig (Brose 1998:41; Freeman and Louçã 2001:160; Landes 1969:140; Trebilcock 1981:142).

The "Modern" Iron Industry

The iconic invention of the iron industry, economically the most conspicuous, and the one signaling the start of the "modern" industry—Cort's *puddling-and-rolling* process—was anything but a radical departure from the past. And it was made as early as the 1780s, during the early phase of industrialization. The substitution of coke for charcoal, and Cort's puddling and rolling brought the British iron industry from high-cost laggard to world leader. For puddling, Cort used a reverberatory furnace to decarburize the pig iron. The coke was separated from the pig iron by a wall that allowed heat to rise over the divider and convert the pig into wrought iron. The oxidation of carbon was accelerated by having a worker stir into the iron mass with a metal bar.[7] Afterwards, the heated metal would be rolled, using grooved rollers,

---

5   This process significantly reduced the amount of impurities, as the metal would never come in direct contact with the fuel (Lewis 1976:23).

6   In Le Creusot on the initiative of the French government, which brought the ironmaster Wilkinson over from Britain for guidance (Landes 1969:140). Along with de Wendel, these were France's only two ironworks to employ coke smelting.

7   Puddling considerably improved the fuel efficiency of refining. Using charcoal had required 2.5–3 tons per ton of crude iron produced. Puddling (using coke) brought this down to 1.5, and with further refinements to around 0.75 by the mid-nineteenth century (Landes 1969:93).

replacing the costly and laborious process of hammering and beating by instead squeezing out the dross. The rolling worked 15 times as fast and had the additional advantage of making it possible to turn out a near unlimited range of standardized crude shapes, like beams, bars and rails (Brose 1998:43; Landes 1969:91, 95; Mokyr 1990:93; 1999:22).

Puddling and rolling made for rapid acceleration of British iron output. Wrought iron increased by 500 per cent between 1788 and 1815. Exports increased from 57,000 tons in 1814 to 1,036,000 in 1852. In 1789, French iron production had been greater than that of Britain (Crouzet 1990:23p), but by 1848 Britain produced more than the rest of the world put together. Prices dropped from £22 in 1801 to £13 in 1815 and £5 by 1842. While some of the British increase was due to war-time demand, it should be noted that France saw no great increase during the wars. French iron makers expanded along traditional lines. Coke was rejected both on grounds of quality and expense (Brose 1998:50; Freeman and Louçã 2001:160; Landes 1969:95, 143).

The first three decades of the nineteenth century saw relatively few breakthroughs. Essentially, James Neilson's hot blast, patented in 1828, was the only major invention before 1850. It caused a surge in Scottish iron production (England and Wales were considerably slower), which now became the leading British region in terms of iron production, soaring from 29,000 tons in 1829 to 825,000 in 1855 (pig iron). Between 1791 and 1830, changes in the blast and in the shape and size of furnaces had reduced coal consumption from eight tons per ton of pig to one and a half ton by 1850. Neilson used the waste gases produced by the blast furnace to preheat the inside air. This provided for a more complete combustion and for temperatures hot enough for other fuels than coke, such as anthracite. The hot blast represented a further saving of one-third in terms of coke consumption. As a result, between 1828 and 1840, Scottish producers cut their costs by two-thirds. Also, reduced fuel consumption meant that less sulfur had to be used, improving the quality of iron by reducing the amount of impurities. Improvements resulted in major reductions to the amount of pig iron drawn off in the slag. In early puddling furnaces, slag could result in a loss of half the pig. By the late 1830s, waste was down to eight per cent, by the end of the century only five (Brose 1998:53pp; Cameron and Neal 2003:198; Landes 1969:92p; Mokyr 1990:95; Morgan 1999:56; Pugh 1999:29).

After the Napoleonic Wars, French iron was hit hard by British imports. Le Creusot—one of only two ironworks to produce coked iron prior to the wars—went bankrupt in 1818.[8] By 1820, a mere 20 French ironworks employed refining and rolling techniques. Only five of these survived the 1830s. The French industry saw no transformation, only a slow diffusion of new methods. While overall output increased, this arose from traditional modes of production, not from the erection of

---

8   Among the reasons that puddling and rolling was not employed by French ironworks until around 1820 was the unsuitability of the local coal and iron ore to the process of coke smelting. It was not until around 1820 that the technical difficulties associated with low quality coal and ore were overcome (Landes 1969:175).

modern ironworks. The number of charcoal blast furnaces kept increasing until mid-century, with charcoal production rising until 1856.[9] Charcoal was more common than coke all the way up until the mid-1850s. Still, by 1826 40 per cent of French wrought iron came from coal-fired furnaces. However, of the 150 puddling furnaces fueled by coke, only about one-third utilized puddling and rolling (Brose 1998:50; Fremdling 2000:211; Landes 1969:175pp; Trebilcock 1981:143).[10]

Despite French catch-up,[11] Britain would dominate until the end of the century, when it was caught up with and surpassed, not by France, but by the US. In 1870, British manufacturers produced half the world's iron, five times more than France, four times more than Germany and three and a half times more than the US. Continuous improvements allowed British furnaces to grow considerably. The average French blast furnace (1846) would smelt 18 tons a week, the average coke-blast furnace 66 tons. The average 1840s British furnace could smelt 89 tons a week, with the biggest Welsh ones reaching 120. By the 1870s, the *average* British unit was capable of smelting 183 tons, with the most powerful furnaces reaching 450–550 tons of pig per week (Landes 1969:180p, 219; Trebilcock 1981:151).

Table 3.1 Output of Pig Iron (in 1,000 metric tons)[12]

	Great Britain	France
c1700	10	
1740	17	
1750	28	
1780	45*	26
1790	80	36
1800	171	54

9   By which time it hit 335,000 tons (Landes 1969:175).

10   By 1845 this had increased to nearly 90 per cent, with coke-based furnaces accounting for two thirds of wrought iron output. However, the multitude of tiny charcoal-based producers still managed to produce half of all pig iron (Landes 1969:176; Trebilcock 1981:145).

11   French growth rates in iron production were high, averaging 3–6 per cent a year: Landes (1969:219), 6.7 per cent a year, 1850–1869; Trebilcock (1981:159) 5.2 per cent, 1851–1873. Some of the discrepancy refers to the fact that France lost 80 per cent of its known iron-ore deposits with the 1870–1871 German annexation of Alsace-Lorraine. British growth rates in iron—5.2 per cent a year (1848–1870)—very respectable indeed for a country that was already on top.

12   1700, 1750 Morgan (1999); 1740, 1790, 1830 Landes (1969); 1790 Freeman and Louçã (2001). The remaining figures are from Modelski and Thompson (1996). The French figures are from Mitchell (1998b), with the exception of the 1800 and 1820 figures, which are from Modelski and Thompson (1996).

	Great Britain	France
1810	225	77
1820	320	130
1830	678	266
1840	1,400	348
1850	2,250	406
1870	6,059	1,178

Sources: Freeman and Louçã (2001:159); Landes (1969:96); Mitchell (1998b:456pp), Modelski and Thompson (1996:99); Morgan (1999:51).

*   These figures suggest that British iron production was well above the French by the dawn of the French Revolution. As mentioned before, reliable sources claim this not to be the case. Landes (1969:95) states that French iron output was greater than British output in 1780, but that this was offset by French production not being much higher in 1815 than in 1789 (ibid.:143). Crouzet (1990) estimates French output of pig iron at 130–140,000 tons by 1789 against 60,000 tons for Britain. While the French figure seems excessive compared to other sources, it does indicate that Modelski and Thompson's estimates may be on the low side.

British pig iron production was far superior to that of France. In Britain, iron peaked in 1871 with a gross output of 11.6 per cent of gross national product (Deane and Cole 1962:226). In France, at the same time the value of iron *and* steel products only amounted to 7.4 per cent of gross *industrial* product (Marczewski 1960:380).[13] However, it is unfair to judge the French industry solely by the standards of Britain. While charcoal persisted, technological progress considerably improved the productivity also of charcoaled iron between the 1820s and the 1850s, for instance by fueling puddling furnaces by coal and using charcoal only for the blast furnace. The hot blast increased the productivity of *both* coke and charcoal smelting, and actually diffused more rapidly in France than in England and Wales. By 1846, 43 out of 55 active French furnaces were equipped with hot blasts (Fremdling 2000:213pp; Landes 1969:180). From 1880 onwards, a marked slowdown occurred, primarily due to a substantial drop in steel prices. From now on steel became the number one raw material of industrial growth (Hobsbawm 1969:117).

A difference between cotton textiles and iron should be noted. As a percentage of national income, the total value of the textile industry in Britain was larger than that of iron until as late as 1865. In terms of exports, cotton was always more important. Iron and steel (together) never reached export figures of more than 18 per cent of total exports (1850–1859) (see tables in the Cotton Textiles chapter). Whereas more than 50 per cent of cotton textiles output was exported, during the 1830s, the iron

---

13   There is no way of comparing British national product with French industrial product, but clearly a national product is far bigger than an industrial product, further emphasizing the gap between British and French figures.

industry only exported around 23 per cent of its output, rising to 39 per cent by 1851. Hence, the importance of iron stems less from exports and more from its widespread industrial application (Freeman and Louçã 2001:201; Hudson 1992:183; Morgan 1999:57).

Steam and Coal

The main reason for the economic impact of iron was the interaction with other economic sectors. First, the steam engine had only a very modest impact on early cotton textiles, but iron would not have been such a success if not for the considerable improvements occurring in steam power. Second, to break free of the production ceiling that charcoal for all practical purposes put on iron output, the iron industry had to find alternate sources of fuel, namely coal-based coke. Without a healthy supply of good and cheap coal, iron would only have had a limited impact on the economy. And third, the iron industry cannot be seen in isolation from the railroad. Railroads provided a huge demand for iron products, primarily rails. And they provided a transport network for freight of heavy goods. In some areas iron ores and coalfields were fortuitously located in close proximity to each other. Where this was not the case, the absence of a proper railway network would make it slow, cumbersome and expensive to transport tons of coal to the ironworks. Hence, developments in these areas were of major importance.

Table 3.2 Coal Output (1,000 metric tons)[14]

	Great Britain	France
1800	10,000	
1815	22,300	900
1830	30,500	1,900
1850	62,500	4,400
1860	87,900	8,300
1870	115,000	13,300
1880	149,000	19,400

Source: Marks (2002:108), Mitchell (2003b:428pp).

In terms of access to coal, Britain had a huge advantage. France was scarce in coal, and what coalfields it had, contained coal of a quality that was not good for coking. The above figures hide the fact that France also consumed far less coal than

---

14 Britain 1800: Marks (2002). The rest is from Mitchell (2003b).

Britain. In 1850, 40 per cent of the consumed coal had been imported, down to around 30 per cent by 1869. As late as 1912, 50 per cent of French coke came from abroad, 82 per cent of it from Germany. The French coal industry persisted as an industry of small, private producers. In 1924, 90 per cent of the output in the Ruhr came from 12 coalmines. 715 small coal pits produced 98 per cent of French coal (Cameron and Neal 2003:198; Landes 1969:174, 194; Trebilcock 1981:167pp).

Technologically, breakthroughs in steam were all-important. The first working steam engine had been built by Savery in 1698, and perfected by Newcomen in 1712. This was also the first year that a steam engine was installed in a coal mine. It was inefficient, slow and expensive, but yielded three to five times as much power as water wheels and pumped four times more water than a team of horses. Four hundred Newcomen engines had been installed by 1775. However, the engine was prone to overheating, with subsequent explosions when the steam pressure was too great. James Watt's steam engine, patented in 1769, was a great improvement, propelling Watt to heroic status in contemporary Britain as the originator of the Industrial Revolution and British industrial supremacy (Brose 1998:38; MacLeod 1998; Morgan 1999:52). Watt's engine reduced fuel requirements and increased thermal efficiency (from one per cent to four and a half per cent), and a reduction in steam pressure made it far less prone to explosions. By the 1790s, 500 Watt engines were employed in British coalmines, and a few dozen on the Continent. (Brose 1998:54; Cameron and Neal 2003:195; Mokyr 1990:85; Morgan 1999:52).[15]

Watt engines were useful for mining, but too big for transport. Hence, Trevithick's 1802 high-pressure steam engine was a necessary breakthrough in order for a future railroad revolution to be possible. It was simpler than the Watt engine, and could deliver the same amount of power with a smaller piston, requiring only 30–50 per cent of the amount of coal per hour per horsepower of the Watt engine. Lighter, cheaper and using far less water, the high-pressure engine made it practically feasible to mount steam engines onto moving vehicles. Yet, it took another two decades and technological improvements to the engine placement, axles, brakes, springs, couplings etc. before Stephenson's famous *Rocket* in 1829 demonstrated the potential of the railroad (Freeman and Louçã 2001:202; Landes 1969:102; Mokyr 1990:126pp). With the exception of the high-pressure engine, which was also developed independently in the US by Oliver Evans,[16] the breakthroughs were all British. Hence, Britain remained far in front of its Continental counterparts in terms of the total amount of horsepower. In 1840, British steam engines had a total of three times the amount of horsepower of French, Belgian, German, Austrian and Italian

---

15 The only main improvement to the Watt engine came in 1845, when John McNaught built on Arthur Woolf's 1803 compound engine, adding a second high-pressure cylinder, boosting the amount of horsepower from 10–20 in the first Watt engines to around 60, and thermal efficiency to 7.5 per cent (Mokyr 1990:88).

16 It was extremely fuel *in*efficient compared to British high-pressure engines, consuming five times as much fuel. But fuel was cheap in the US relative to labor and capital, and the machine proved a great success (Atack and Passell 1994:200; Cowan 1997:73).

steam engines put together (Atack and Passell 1994:200; Brose 1998:56; Cowan 1997:73).[17]

Table 3.3 Capacity of Steam Engines (in 1,000 horsepower)

	Great Britain	France
1840	620	90
1850	1,290	370
1860	2,450	1,120
1870	4,040	1,850
1880	7,600	3,070
1888	9,200	4,520

Source: Landes (1969:221).

The Role of the State

Human Capital

While formal education only had a modest impact on the success or failure of early industrialization, human capital was still crucial. Despite poor higher education, Britain had far more mechanically skilled people than France, and was far better at making good use of them.

Since many of the breakthroughs in the iron industry occurred in more or less the same time period as for cotton textiles, much the same story can be told with respect to iron as to cotton textiles. Britain gained a lead that was slender in terms of production figures (although as with cotton textiles, rapidly increasing between 1789 and 1815), but considerable in terms of production *technology*. This section to a certain extent overlaps the corresponding part of the Cotton Textiles chapter. Hence, for general characteristics of the education systems of the period up until around 1815, I refer the reader to the previous chapter. However, the overlap is not complete. Both in terms of human capital and in its diffusion, there were differences between cotton and iron.

As with cotton textiles, many of the breakthroughs within iron were of less than revolutionary nature, not requiring expert knowledge of the natural sciences, or a lengthy formal education. Brose (1998:45) refers to eighteenth-century metallurgical innovations as "technological artistry". It would take another century before scientists were able to explain the chemical reactions of the iron furnace. Maybe the best

---

17 Although it is true that the US had passed Britain in terms of steam engine horsepower as early as 1840.

evidence for this was the absence of cheap steel. As early as 1786, French scientists discovered that the difference between cast iron, wrought iron and steel is in the carbon content. Steel is really just a special case of iron. However, the discovery had no effect on steel making (Mokyr 2002a:86), and the science of metallurgy had very little impact on the practice and development of the metal industry. While the role of formal education was less than obvious, advances were made in numerous areas, as in the physics of heat, and in the understanding of the locations of mineral deposits. To an ever greater extent these advances resulted from deliberate and scientific search for solutions to problems (Mokyr 2002a:84).

Figures indicate that literacy dropped in cotton textiles between 1785 and 1814, and the same applies to metal (including iron). Illiteracy rates *increased* to 29 per cent for the period 1785–1814 (up from 22 per cent), and then decreased to 19 per cent for 1815–1844 (Mitch 1999:263). Hence, literacy does not seem to have been a necessary skill. However, there is evidence indicating that on a more overarching level, education had positive effects during the first half of the nineteenth century. Vincent (2000:83) suggests that literacy became a direct cause once the economy had reached a certain level of sophistication in terms of its communication infrastructure, which for a number of European countries meant somewhere around the 1850s. In fact, by the 1840s, the rate of return on literacy was high, and much higher than for instance for capital (Mitch 1984:560pp).

In both England and France schooling changed little in the mid-nineteenth century. England was not among the leaders, with an education system that remained essentially unaltered between 1800 and 1850 (Cipolla 1969:78).[18] Education was still considered potentially damaging by landlord and Tory opposition perceiving of mass schooling as seditious, dangerous, unnecessary and above all, expensive. But also, Parliament had a strong hold on local finance, preventing local taxation and local funding of schools. A stubborn dependence on a combination of central government financing and private sources prevented funding for mass schooling (Lindert 2001; Vincent 2000:31).[19]

With the exception of the years during Napoleon, the French state was indifferent toward elementary schooling until the 1830s, when a gradual centralization occurred. However, France was deeply split between secular revolutionaries and a

---

18 Education reform was implemented in 1833, when the Whig government devoted annual government grants of £20,000 to voluntary societies offering elementary education. However, these grants were more important as symbolic acts that the role of government was changing, than for the impact they had on education. Grants remained low. Moreover, the grants were provided by the state to religious organizations, hence for practical purposes subsidizing Church schools. This created huge complications for future governments (Evans 1983:324; Hoppen 1998:95pp; Pugh 1999:51; Vincent 2000:31).

19 In 1830, the proportion of government expenditure devoted to (all kinds of) education in England was 0.1 per cent. By 1841 it had risen to 0.5 per cent. In comparison, the 1832 French figure (which was also quite low) was 1.0 per cent, rising to 2.3 per cent in the 1870s, but then quadrupling up to World War I. France was spending five times as much on maintaining law and order as it was on education, Britain 11 times (Vincent 2000:36p).

very conservative and anti-revolutionary Catholic Church. Education reform had to be slow and cautious. The school law of 1833 had a Protestant bent, and was a reaction against the Bourbon Restoration and an attempt to free education from the supervision of the Church, but from the 1840s onwards, state funding dried out. The 1850 law restored the role of the Catholic Church and suppressed the schools founded since the 1833 reform. The revolution of 1848 could have brought renewed government interest for education, but the educational policies of Napoleon III were ambivalent and erratic, and to a considerable extent a result of a balancing of interests between secular and democratic reformers on the one hand and conservative Church and university officials on the other.

In 1863, he made the liberal and strongly anticlerical history professor Victor Duruy Minister of Public Education. Duruy immediately embarked on a program to create free and compulsory primary education. However, he was heavily attacked by the Church and by other conservatives, and in 1867 Napoleon III repudiated his own government's plan for universal primary education, despite in 1865 pompously declaring that "in the country of universal suffrage, every citizen should be able to read and write". Instead, a feeble law was passed, freeing communes to raise more local taxes if they wished, creating more schools for girls, and liberalizing the curriculum. Only after the shock of Prussian invasion in 1870 did French attitudes change (Birnbaum 1998:123; Chambliss 2003; Crouzet 1993:xv; Furet 1995:334p; Lindert 2001; Vincent 2000:54, 133). In general, the French state was not actively concerned with education until the 1880s, with human capital not positively affecting economic growth until 1885 (Hage, Garnier and Fuller 1988:825, 833).

Formal education was probably even less important in iron than in cotton textiles. While in Britain, guilds belonged to the past, the position of forgeman, where for all practical purposes the knowledge behind successful iron smelting rested, was usually reserved for kin, with the knowledge guarded as a trade secret. The secrets and techniques of iron smelting remained within this very select group of no more than a thousand people.[20] Forgemen did not allow recruitment from people not raised as forgemen from birth. Technological progress took place through the forgemen, and not the ironmasters, and very little technical literature on iron smelting existed. The best early description of puddling was actually found in France (Evans and Rydén 1998:190pp).[21]

This monopoly on knowledge caused a reaction. When the technique of iron puddling was invented in the 1780s and 1790s, it had been sponsored by one of the greatest ironmasters of the day (Richard Crawshay) with the explicit purpose of breaking the crafts monopoly of the forgemen. He decided to have the new methods

---

20 These were the descendants of the furnace workers imported by Henry VIII. There is little written information about their migrations or their networking, but what is conspicuous is the regularity with which French family names occur in British iron districts.

21 According to Evans and Rydén (1998:199) little of substance was written on iron before David Mushet's 1841 *Papers on Iron and Steel*. Attempts at forming technical discussion groups (late eighteenth century) were a conspicuous failure.

taught to locally recruited novices, with no ties to the forgemen. Hence, cost was not the only reason for coke-fired forges. Part of the attraction was also a break with kinship as the organizing principle of the industry. The massive expansion in the iron industry resulting from techniques utilizing coke opened the industry to an influx of skilled labor without kinship ties, and broke the forgeman monopoly (Evans and Rydén 1998:196pp). Hence, it took a decisive technological breakthrough *before* the iron industry could start utilizing the general human capital advantage that Britain had. Up until then, the monopoly of the forgemen was perceived as constraining, prompting central actors to try to outmaneuver them by promoting new technologies, thus rendering their skills obsolete.[22]

This suggests that diffusion was slower than in cotton textiles. In cotton textiles, one of Britain's advantages lay in its ability to utilize its pool of knowledge, whether produced in universities or not, very much in contrast to France. But this seems to have been less the case in iron. Secrecy was the name of the game, and entry-barriers formidable. Abraham Darby's 1709 coke-fired iron furnace for instance remained the sole ironworks to produce coked pig iron for half a century (Landes 1969:89; Morgan 1999:54).

On the other hand, technological change in iron did occur in Britain to a much greater extent than in France. There is evidence that human capital was an important comparative British advantage, as men like Smeaton, Wilkinson (both John and William), Watt and Trevithick, responsible for some of the most important breakthroughs of the era, were all very well connected with the network of scientific societies. This was also the case with Matthew Boulton, who financed the activities of Watt. While these were people without much formal education, they were well-read in technical matters, and possessed in abundance what Mokyr (2002a) labels "technical literacy". The Newcomen steam engine, to mention just one famous example, would have been impossible without the theoretical ideas of Boyle, Torricelli and others. Watt derived much of his knowledge from close interaction with scientists in Glasgow (Brose 1998:45p; Landes 1969:104; Mokyr 2002a:72). Still, it is probably also true that many of the advances within steam engines were accomplished through a combination of experimenting and good mechanical intuition, without much of an epistemic base. However, James Neilson's hot blast was informed by courses in chemistry that he took at the university in Glasgow, where he learnt about the expansion of gases, ironically discovered through the work of the French chemist, Gay-Lussac (Mokyr 2002a:84pp).[23]

---

22 Landes (1969:216) makes the same point for the Continent. Much of the iron industry was in the hands of small, technically ignorant furnacemasters. While technological ignorance was not the only problem—they were constrained by tariffs, costly transport, and the avoidance of price competition—it was definitely among the reasons why the Continent failed to modernize sooner. And on the Continent, no impetus from resource scarcity in wood provided individual ironmasters with incentives to come up with alternative methods.

23 At the same time, the steam engine example, hailed as an example of interaction and cooperation, incorporating the collaboration of Black, Watt, Boulton and Wilkinson may well

In the previous chapter, I mentioned the role played by Dissenters and by Scottish universities. The impetus to both scientific inquiry and its practical application came from Scotland, which at the time may have had the best education system in Europe. The universities of Glasgow and Edinburgh far surpassed Oxford and Cambridge. In England, Dissenter academies provided a much more scientific and practical education than the English higher education system. Iron manufacturers like the Darbys, Lloyds and Crowleys were all Dissenters, and so were Watt, Boulton and Neilson. Both Watt and Neilson were connected with Scottish universities, and Watt and Boulton played prominent roles within the Royal Society of London (Evans 1983:108pp, 114; Freeman and Louçã 2001:170; Mokyr 2002a:84).

In this way, Britain distinguished itself. Numerous French governments perceived of the need for technological catch-up, and took active steps to accomplish this. However, first, scientific knowledge was particularly deficient in machinery, which clearly hampered industrialization. Technological change was stifled by the contrasting scientific culture of France, and by France's lack of Britain's scientific and technological knowledge. Aristotelian physics prevailed in 60 per cent of early eighteenth-century French liberal art colleges. The *Grandes Ecoles* produced some of the world's best engineers, but they did not provide industrial education. This was left to the lesser *écoles*, like the *Ecoles d'Arts et Métier*. These institutions were very theoretical and produced few graduates. In 1871, such *écoles* were limited to a mere three schools and a total of only 900 students. Furthermore, their impact on industry was extremely limited. Industrial positions were reserved for people of status and kin (Brose 1998:46; Trebilcock 1981:194p).

Second, linkages between science and industry were more or less absent. True, there were prizes for the emulation of British technology, special societies to encourage technological progress and large industrial fairs to promote technology and industry. However, these were not a success. Scientific literature produced in France, like Carnot's book (1824) on heat and efficiency, was ignored, whereas second-hand translations soon found their way to Britain, where they attracted much interest. Instead, diffusion took place by way of British experts traveling across the Channel. Coke-fired ironworks did not exist in France until ironmaster William Wilkinson was brought over as technical adviser. On his specification, in 1785 Le Creusot was chosen as the site of France's first coke blast furnace. However, the ironworks did not employ Cort's recently invented puddling-and-rolling process, which with the coke furnace were the two inventions that enabled Britain to accelerate its pig iron output over the next decades. In comparison, between 1789 and 1815 French output grew in capacity, but little in terms of technological sophistication. Coke smelting did not spread beyond Le Creusot and de Wendel, and no puddling and rolling found its way to France until after the Napoleonic Wars, when Welsh puddlers went to Belgium, France and Germany (Freeman and Louçã 2001:160; Landes 1969:91, 140pp; Mokyr 1999:22; 2002a:88). Attempts in the late eighteenth century to import

---

have exaggerated the linkages among them (Crouzet 1990:30). Another example; Stephenson, best known for the Stephenson locomotive, was a scientific illiterate.

Watt steam engines were persistently frustrated and delayed by indifferent and haughty academic scientists (Brose 1998:49; Jacob 1997).

Finally, the government mining bureaucracy, the *Corps des Mines*, to which French mining activities were subjected, was extremely conservative and discouraging with respect to industrial activity. The *Ecoles des Mines* provided graduates at the highest theoretical level, but often had to back out because of a lack of necessary skills to solve practical problems (Trebilcock 1981:171, 185, 196).

While the human capital argument should not be stretched too thin, France was clearly suffering from a human capital lag—in particular its shortage of engineers with skills in machinery—which affected the development of its iron industry. It had some of the finest scientists in the world, but their impact on industry was limited. Hence, the technological sophistication of the French iron industry remained far below that of the British. In contrast, Britain had a large pool of mechanically skilled men. This went together with the superior access (and seemingly also; interest) that British entrepreneurs and engineers had to scientific and technical journals, far more rapidly diffusing scientific knowledge that could be useful for industrial purposes.

Protection: Wars and Tariffs

With cotton textiles, a small advantage by the onset of the French Revolution had grown to a large gap by 1815. The same story applies here. Britain was slightly ahead by the start of the French Revolution, (although in production technologies rather than production figures), but between 1789 and 1815 British output soared, while French output stagnated. As with cotton textiles, one of the reasons why 1789–1815 was so important was that French technological improvements to a great extent depended on technology diffusion from Britain. Granted, resource endowments made French success in iron less likely than in cottons, but this does not change the fact that Britain greatly increased its gap over France during this period. And it does not change the fact that technology diffusion came to a halt, just as France was trying to introduce coke-fired forges.

British demand for iron soared as a consequence of the Napoleonic Wars. However, demand accelerated further once the war was over (exports rising by a factor of 20, 1814–1852). Also, in France, war stimulated neither expansion nor innovation. Despite increased demand for arms, moderate increases in iron production occurred, but nothing resembling the cotton textiles boom. In fact, the adoption of new metallurgical techniques actually slowed down during the wars. The attempts of Honoré Blanc at machine-tooling muskets were thwarted by conservative forces within the army and the government, which cut off its contracts with him. British ironmasters improved the design of artillery and developed new methods of cannon boring, even leading to civilian spinoffs, as in methods for producing accurate cylinders for steam engines. In contrast, the technology of French armories did not change. Once peace arrived and iron could no longer hide behind the Continental System, wartime gains were wiped away (Brose 1998:50; Landes 1969:95; Lyons 1994:275; Mokyr 1990:185; Pugh 1999:31; Trebilcock 1981:132).

Moreover, France's post-war reparations were among the largest successfully coerced money transfers in history. With additional payments and interest, France ended up paying a grand total of 1,863.5 million francs, or around 20 per cent of one year's GDP. Reparations constituted a large shock to the economy and were among the reasons for slow French growth in the 1820s.[24] The long-term effects may not have been major, but the drop in lending and investments would almost necessarily be more of a drag on capital-intensive industry like iron than on other industries. Conspicuously, after 1815 iron struggled, and it was not until France imposed an almost prohibitive tariff on iron imports that production started accelerating (Fremdling 2000:204; White 2001:340pp, 351, 361).

It is easy to overlook that the British iron industry had once been young and vulnerable. In the eighteenth century, British iron was high-cost, and apart from a small coke-based portion, not particularly sophisticated. In 1750, more than 65 per cent of British bar iron was imported. While tariffs were most useful during these early years of the industry, for a host of goods they lasted much longer than they had to from the perspective of industrial competitiveness. At a time when Britain produced 45 per cent of all European iron (1830s), the average level of British duties was still almost 50 per cent, coming down somewhat in 1825 and 1833, and falling to 12–20 per cent in PM Peel's 1842 budget.[25] Following the repeal of the Corn Laws, for practical purposes free trade was implemented in the 1850s (Fremdling 2000:197pp; Bairoch 1993:20; Chang 2002:23; Lloyd-Jones and Lewis 1998:50; McKeown 1989:364).

The end of the Napoleonic Wars also meant an end to the Continental System, and the opening up of the Continent to British exports. The resulting British onslaught on European iron led to lobbying on the part of French interest groups—iron, textiles and farming. A new tariff was introduced in 1822, effectively doubling the price of British bar iron. The duty on iron goods eventually reached 120 per cent. Between 1821 and 1822 British bar iron exports to France fell from 13,800 to 5,100 tons. British bar iron had accounted for 80 per cent of French imports, but was now down to less than 20. Following the 1822 tariff, a number of ironworks based on coke fuel were erected. However, these ironworks found it hard to compete domestically with charcoaled French pig iron. By 1830, there were still only 10 coke furnaces in France—all small and inefficient. Economic success in coked pig could not start improving until the early 1830s (Fremdling 2000:204p, 213; Wright 1995:146).

However, there were also less beneficial effects from the tariffs. The 1860 Anglo-French Cobden–Chevalier treaty for all practical purposes introduced free trade between Britain and France. Increased competition following from the treaty now

---

24 White (2001:361) suggests that the direct cost came to an annual loss of 1.7 per cent of GNP for a period of 5 years. The effects were smoothed out by some borrowing.

25 While this means that duties went down, 12–20 per cent is hardly negligible. In fact, since tariffs were set at a fixed rate rather than *ad valorem*, and since the price level had fallen since the 1820s, for practical purposes the effective rate of protection had increased since the Napoleonic Wars, despite tariff reductions (McKeown 1989:364).

made it clear that tariffs had allowed a number of inefficient French ironworks to survive. The archives of firms like Le Creusot and de Wendel bear witness to major restructuring as a response to international competition. Charcoal furnaces had actually increased in terms of total production since the 1820s. The low 1860 tariffs, combined with much improved transportation, radically increased competition, and rapidly killed off charcoal-fueled pig iron. Hence, coked French iron doubled in production between 1860 and 1870, while charcoaled production by 1870 shrank to a third of what it had been a decade before (Landes 1969:201, 216; Trebilcock 1981:170).[26]

Protection is an area in which the role of the state is obvious. Britain and France were affected differently. France suffered from war, Britain benefited. The argument is essentially the same as for cotton textiles. The major breakthroughs in iron diffused to France from Britain. With revolution and war, this came to a halt, with the result that France was technologically far behind by 1815. For both countries, tariffs were important at different stages. However, tariff protection also harbors a danger, namely that it unduly shelters an industry, removing its incentives to modernize. In Britain, tariffs remained high until the late 1840s, despite strong industrial dominance. While useful in the eighteenth century, now Britain was probably the country where tariffs were the least beneficial. In France, they were necessary in order not to be destroyed by British competition, but remained in force for too long, allowing inefficient producers, particularly those employing charcoal, to stay in business.

Resource Endowments

One argument stands out as significantly more important with respect to iron than to cotton textiles. For cotton textiles, steam engines did not become important until the nineteenth century. With iron, the energy problem was larger from the outset. Most early British steam engines were used in mines, and when the iron industry grew into the dominant industry of the mid-nineteenth century, this was to a large extent because of the railroad, where steam power was utilized not for mining, but for locomotives. Hence, in the iron industry, being behind in coal was a much bigger drawback than in cotton textiles.

Britain was abundant in coal, and in the right kind of coal. Often, coal fields would even be conveniently placed near iron ores, reducing the need for expensive transportation infrastructure. Not so France. Coal was far less abundant, it was rarely located close to the iron ore, and it was often of a quality that made it less amenable to coking (Landes 1969; Trebilcock 1981:116p).

But the resource endowment argument can easily be turned on its head. Is it scarcity or is it abundance that drives innovation and industrial growth? True, Britain was well-endowed with coal and benefited from it, but what made Britain turn toward

---

26 Coked production increased from 582,000 tons in 1860 to 1,262,000 in 1869. Charcoaled production fell from 316,000 tons in 1860 to 119,000 tons in 1869, 55,000 in 1880 and 12,000 tons in 1890 (Landes 1969:217).

coal in the first place was not the abundance of coal, but the scarcity of charcoal. Britain was scarce in timber. An increasing demand for iron, and bottlenecks in iron production as Britain was exhausting its timber, caused British ironmasters to search for production methods that did not involve charcoal. Similarly with respect to France: Being well-endowed in charcoal, early French iron production did not suffer bottlenecks. In Britain, excess demand was met by imports. In 1740, Britain consumed well over twice the amount of wrought iron per person that France did. Eyewitness accounts tell of French wagon wheels shod with wood when iron had long been utilized for such purposes in Britain. Hence, consumption and utilization of iron was considerably greater in Britain already before the widespread introduction of coking. The early British iron industry kept growing *in the face of* resource constraints, and despite iron being neither abundant nor cheap.[27] During the 1770s and 1780s France started to experience competition from British iron, especially with the 1786 Eden Treaty, which removed prohibitions on trade and drastically lowered tariffs. This led to pressures for technological change in French iron production, despite labor being cheap and timber plentiful. Again, with the Revolution, this process came to a halt. Hence, not only did France not enjoy diffusion from Britain, but ironminers were also relieved of competitive pressures to modernize production. Resource endowments can tell us something about why France did not make a transition toward new methods of production earlier, but *not* why demand for iron, and the willingness to use it despite it being an expensive material, was so much higher in Britain (Fremdling 2000:213pp; Landes 1969:94p; Trebilcock 1981:116p).

France, with its abundance of timber and scarcity of coal, saw less of an incentive to research new methods of production. But, natural resources are a given, and to the extent that they hamper a country's industrial and economic development, the obvious task for the state is to try to work around these obstacles. This was a role that the French state filled only hesitantly. France was lacking in coal and in transportation infrastructure. Both with respect to locating new strikes of coal and providing a railroad network to link coal, iron and markets, the French state was a drag rather than a stimulus (Fremdling 2000; Trebilcock 1981; Smith 1990). Hence, while resource endowments played a larger role in iron than in cotton textiles, blaming the French lag on the lack of natural resources is wrong. Britain suffered scarcities, but managed to invent itself out of the problems. France refused to do so.

---

27 By 1815, only 5–10 per cent of Britain was still covered by forests. This could not have yielded charcoal enough to produce more than roughly 100,000 tons of pig iron. Britain broke the 100,000 barrier as early as the 1790s, and was by 1815 producing 3–4 times that amount (Marks 2002:110).

Railroads[28]

The railroad revolution started in Britain and was of tremendous importance to the iron industry. Iron was needed for locomotives, rolling stock, track, nails, etc., in addition to the railroads providing the means by which coal was transported to the ironworks. In 1750 it took three days to travel from London to Liverpool, by 1855 only six hours. The 10–12 days it took from London to Glasgow had dropped to 13–14 hours (Hobsbawm 1969:337). Britain benefited greatly not only from being lucky enough to have high quality iron ore and coal fields located in close proximity to each other, but from being the first country to develop a transportation infrastructure tying iron and coal together.

The first locomotive-driven railroad line was opened in 1825 in the midst of the northeast coalfields, with the main purpose of linking coal-producing areas to existing transport links, primarily canals. For some of the early railroads, like the 1830 Liverpool–Manchester line, profits were huge. However, many of the later lines did not see great profits at all. They were created in a few frantic spurts, most notably during the years 1834–1837 and 1844–1847—outbursts of "railway mania". No pretensions of creating a national network existed. Construction was piecemeal, with many gaps, whereas in other areas different railroad companies duplicated each other's work by laying down separate sets of tracks in the same area. The role of the state was modest. Most railroads were privately financed. Governments essentially restricted themselves to passing Railway Acts. Between 1844 and 1846, the annual number of such acts passed rose from 48 to 270. While this does not provide for a very activist role, it gave Britain distinct advantages over France. While the absence of central planning had certain negative effects, like the absence of unified standards for gauges, it also meant that the railroad network was at its densest where it was needed the most, as in the industrial areas, unlike the centralized French system, where Paris served as the hub for virtually every railroad line. French governments up until Napoleon III regulated and centralized railroad construction to such an extent that it severely hampered construction (Freeman and Louçã 2001:190pp; Hobsbawm 1962:45; Morgan 1999:86pp; Nairn 2002:8; Schonhardt-Bailey 1991:553p).

28　In the previous chapter, infrastructure (roads and canals) was one of several *Smithian* growth factors. Here, it to a very great extent means railroads, and I have instead presented it as a component to *Schumpeterian* growth. A few comments may be useful. First, boundaries between different types of growth, like Schumpeterian and Smithian, are fluent. Most growth processes comprise both Schumpeterian and Smithian features. Second, the infrastructure argument can be both Schumpeterian and Smithian, depending on how it is framed. An infrastructure argument focusing on how railroads led to the enlargement of markets would be Smithian. On the other hand, if infrastructure implies improvements to diffusion and the dissemination of ideas, through greater ease of communications, then the argument is about knowledge and innovation rather than markets, and hence Schumpeterian. This chapter falls somewhat in-between. Railroads had a direct impact on iron. They enabled the substitution of coke for charcoal, which is Schumpeterian, and they brought iron goods more efficiently to the markets, which is Smithian.

Since the British state restricted itself to passing Railway Acts, and since railroad undertakings were decidedly capital-intensive, private investors must have been fairly abundant in capital. The country *was* abundant in capital, but financial reform had made large-scale investment easier. Up until the mid-1820s, The London Stock Exchange had for all practical purposes been limited to London, and with the market largely confined to trading in government securities. Now, a capital market was developing. Despite the 1825 repeal of the Bubble Act having only minor general effects (Mokyr 1999:51),[29] there is evidence that railroads benefited. Numerous members of the political and economic elites perceived of joint-stock companies as a form of business organization for the future, especially with respect to capital-intensive projects like canals, docks and other infrastructures. In fact, one of the major issues in 1825, driving the process of repeal, was the debate over the Liverpool–Manchester railroad line (Harris 1997:681pp; Schonhardt-Bailey 1991:552p). The repeal also led to a boom in overall share trade as previously unchartered joint-stock companies could now sell their shares on the stock exchange. The opening of the Liverpool–Manchester line led to a surge in railroad stocks. Railroad companies only had to advertise the availability of stocks before being flooded with applications.[30] In 1846–1848 half of total British investments went to the railroads, despite profits often being distinctly modest (Freeman and Louçã 2001:165; Harris 1997:675p; Schonhardt-Bailey 1991:552pp).

Between 1830 and 1850, output of coal and iron trebled, mostly because of the railroad (Hobsbawm 1962:45).[31] Each mile of railroad required 300 tons of iron just for the tracks. Between 1837 and 1842 Britain went through its most serious economic crisis since the start of the Industrial Revolution, hitting the iron industry particularly hard. Soaring demand from railroad construction was one of the main reasons why the iron industry recovered. In the early 1840s, roughly 25 per cent of domestic sales went to railroad construction. At one stage (1845–1847), railroads accounted for somewhere between 40 and 50 per cent of the entire domestic consumption of iron. In the 1850s, when this started to decline, British iron benefited from railroad booms abroad (Freeman and Louçã 2001:199; Greasley and Oxley 2000; Landes 1969:153; Marks 2002:109).

Much of the inspiration for the French railroad system came from Britain. The size and shape of rails was influenced by Britain, and early locomotive technology directly based on British models. However, by the late 1840s onwards, the French industry was producing its own locomotives, and while one early line, Paris–Rouen,

---

29 Further restrictions on incorporation were lifted in 1834 and 1837 with completely free incorporation secured through the 1844 General Incorporation Act and the 1855–1856 Limited Liability Acts (Harris 1997:675p; Schonhardt-Bailey 1991:552p).

30 In 1836, the New Gravesend Railway made 30,000 stocks available, and received 80,000 applications. Other examples: 400,000 applications for 120,000 shares for the Direct London–Exeter, 1,400,000 applications for 120,000 shares in the Direct Western Railway (Schonhardt-Bailey 1991:553).

31 Hobsbawm (1969:114) suggests that railroad construction alone was responsible for a doubling of British iron production between the mid-1830s and the mid-1840s.

was designed and constructed by British engineers, this was the one exception to the overall rule (Caron 1998:280; Smith 1990:672).

In France, the emphasis was on passenger transport (Braudel 1991:492), and it was state financed, regulated and centralized. In a country far less abundant in capital than Britain, the more activist attitude of the state should have been an advantage. However, whereas state financing might have been beneficial, government regulation and centralization were not. The dominant institution through which the French state controlled railroad construction was the *Corps des Ponts et Chaussées*. During the Bourbon Restoration (1815–1830), the *Corps* developed a grand plan for "the canalization of France" (Smith 1990:661). Railroads were looked into, as a substitute for canals in terrain where canal building was too difficult. The 1830 Revolution led to a reshuffle. The new director General, Simon Bérard, scrapped canal building in favor of railroads. However, the government fell in 1832 and under Victor Legrand's new leadership, Bérard's plans for privatization, for cheap and unplanned railroads, and the death of canals, were thrown out. Railroads were deemed too important to be left to profit-hungry businessmen (ibid.:665pp).

While building to a high standard may seem useful, in France it seriously reduced the speed of construction. Private proposals to build rail lines, as the 1833 Paris–Orléans line, were defeated. Until 1837, only three short lines out of Paris were entrusted to private companies. By 1840, only one line was longer than 100 kilometers (Strasbourg–Mulhouse). Applying much more exacting standards than in Britain meant that costs were astronomical. And by focusing on speed and the time of travel, the *Corps* would often choose the most direct line (to Paris), circumnavigating important population and industrial centers.[32] The centralized nature of the French state enabled one corps of engineers to impose a uniformly costly design that not only encompassed railroads but also the notion of complementarity—railroads would be complemented by canals, further increasing the costs.[33] The 1848 Revolution led to another short-lived liberal revival, but the *Corps* survived, and even the canals were kept intact (Mitchell 1997:21; Smith 1990:670pp; Trebilcock 1981:144).

One of the major problems with the French transportation network was its centralization. Railroads were not constructed to connect coal and iron, but resembled more a number of railroad spokes all converging on the hub of Paris. Mine-owners lobbied for improved water connections, but were rebuffed. After 40 years of lobbying, the first section of the Canal du Nord was finally finished in 1908 (the entire waterway in 1960). Until the 1840s, the main source of fuel supplies to Paris was water-borne coal from St Etienne. Paris was not connected by rails to

---

32 The Paris Chamber of Commerce had requested for the Paris–Channel railroad to be constructed in the Seine valley. The *Corps* instead decided to go the direct route across the plateaus, straight to Le Havre and Dieppe. The Paris–Strasbourg railroad crossed the Brie plateau instead of following the populous Marne valley. This meant that traffic would be much less, as the plateaus were scarcely populated, and construction ended up being far more expensive (Smith 1990:670).

33 The idea was for passenger traffic to use rails and freight to use canals.

major sources of fuel until 1860. By 1850, coal still traveled to Mulhouse by road. The Alsatian industry was far closer to German railroad lines than to French lines! Still, while conspicuously slow with respect to providing a transportation network benefiting iron, by 1870, transport costs for fuel had decreased to one-seventh of what they were in 1840 (Trebilcock 1981:169p). Yet it suggests that while facing resource constraints, France could have worked around these to a much greater extent by constructing a well-functioning transportation network for the benefit of industry.

Another reason for the slow construction of French railroads was the fact that the French iron industry was not able to produce a metal that was able to stand up to the loads and shocks that railroad iron would have to endure. Amazingly, this problem persisted, and was never really solved until steel took over as the primary raw material. Some of the iron rails, at least in the beginning, had to be imported from Britain, which was excessively expensive, especially considering the heavy tariff that France had imposed on the import of iron goods (Caron 1998:278, 284; Wright 1995:148).

In Britain, railroad construction was the most important stimulus to the economy during the 1840s. In France, railroads cannot have had much effect until around 1855. Total investments in railroads averaged no more than 34 million francs per year between 1835 and 1844. During Napoleon III, this rose to 487 million a year (1855–1864). Railroad investments peaked at 7.2 per cent of French gross industrial production (1855–1865)—proportionately slightly more than in Britain. In contrast, for the period 1835–1844, the corresponding figure was 0.85 per cent. Louis-Philippe's 1842 railroad law had included large-scale government aid to railroad construction, but the scale of construction was modest. Instead, the major upsurge in railroad construction had to wait until 1855, and lasting for three decades thereafter. Between 1850 and 1860, the amount of railroad kilometers more than tripled (Caron 1988:81, 101; Mitchell 1997:21; Smith 1990:677pp; Trebilcock 1981:144p, 151p, 186; Wright 1995:150pp).

In France, the state made an effort to construct a national network, but failed. True, abundant in capital and with natural resources favorably located, Britain had numerous advantages. However, it is conspicuous that the French state, through the *Corps des Ponts et Chaussées*, regulated construction to such an extent that construction critically slowed down. The French state failed to provide a railroad network that could contribute to connecting its relatively scarce and scattered resources of coal and iron. The decentralized network of Britain did much better, channeling resources to where it would benefit industry, with iron and coal the main beneficiaries. It is hard to escape the conclusion that in terms of the role of the state, laissez-faire Britain was far more successful than activist France. Although this should be tempered by evidence from the second Empire: While still hampered by numerous problems from the past, activist policies by Napoleon III did accelerate French railroad construction greatly. Activism *per se* was not the problem. Rather, it was one of creating a useful framework for activism. In this respect, the British approach worked better in the sense that the state at least shied away from making decisions that affected railroad construction in decidedly negative ways, unlike France.

Table 3.4 Length of Railway Line Open (in kilometers)

	Great Britain	France
1825	43	17
1830	157	31
1835	544	141
1840	2,390	410
1850	9,797	2,915
1860	14,603	9,167
1870	21,558	15,544
1880	25,060	23,089

Sources: Cameron and Neal (2003:201); Freeman and Louçã (2001:193); Mitchell (1998b:673pp).

Vested Interests, Political Consensus, and Social Cohesion

Britain: Cohesion and Consensus arises from Crisis   One of the central propositions of this book is that long-term economic success through technological innovation and industrial prowess requires a state that has sufficient relative autonomy to withstand the pressures of vested interests. In this respect, France performed far worse than Britain.[34] During both the Bourbon Restoration (1815–1830) and the July Monarchy (1830–1848), French kings struggled with only limited autonomy. Change had to wait until Napoleon III. The first decade of the reign of Napoleon III was a clear improvement compared to previous decades. Since Napoleon Bonaparte, the 1850s were probably the years in which the French state was at its strongest, with the greatest degree of autonomy relative to vested interests. However, on the whole, vested interests hampered the French iron industry, both directly, and indirectly through the transportation network. In Britain, this was a period of turmoil, but at the same time a period where the British state, dominated by landed interests, actually went against these very same interests, both with respect to the repeal of the Corn Laws and the extension of the franchise. On other issues as well, as in the matter of

---

34 I also refer the reader to the corresponding section of the Cotton Textiles chapter. There is no reason repeating what is already mentioned there. The vested interests section of this chapter hence focuses on the early to mid-nineteenth century.

canals vs. railroads, the British state came down on the side of the newcomer, and not canals.

The most contentious economic policy issue of the day was the Corn Laws, imposed in 1815. This was a classic case of landed vs. manufacturing interests, with landed interests controlling the state, hence blocking structural change for all practical purposes by putting a steep tax on workers and manufacturers. However, within a few decades, the British state pushed vested interests aside to give way to the demands of industry. Repealing the Corn Laws was important for several reasons. For most people, the immediate benefit was the provision of abundant and inexpensive food to a rapidly expanding population, alleviating hunger and preventing dissent from arising. This also yielded the added bonus of providing industry with fit and healthy workers,[35] hence boosting industrial growth. From an industrial point of view, putting a minimum price tag on wheat for all practical purposes also put a rather steep tax on manufacturers. The political battle over the Corn Laws was the main manifestation of the growing tension between landed and manufacturing interests. Repeal implied a transition from protectionism toward free trade (Hobsbawm 1969:120; Judd 1996:58pp, 65; Pugh 1999:101).

Repeal strongly divided Parliament. Maybe repeal would have happened sooner or later regardless, since manufacturing grew ever more important. In 1810, agriculture's share of GNP exceeded that of manufacture by 70 per cent. By 1840, *industry* exceeded agriculture by 60 per cent. Lord Liverpool's Tory government had been highly ambivalent about trade and industry. Some concessions to free trade interests were made by reducing a number of duties in 1825 and in 1833, but calls for a repeal of the Corn Laws were flatly rejected. In the 1830s, Parliament was dominated by (pro-industry) Whigs. But Whig dominance would also not do away with the Corn Laws. Britain struggled with unprecedented levels of popular discontent, and political polarization put the Whigs in a position where they could not utilize their majority. The decade was marred by a clear lack of political consensus, with strong conservative fears of further radicalization resulting in a rallying of support around the Tories. Thus, Whig majorities declined following 1832, as Whig governments failed to satisfy the reform eagerness of their own supporters, while at the same time driving vested interests into the arms of the Tories (Bairoch 1993:21;

---

35 Regression analyses suggest that for the period 1820–1845, workers' living costs were raised by 8–14 per cent by the Corn Laws (Lindert 2003:329). Other estimates indicate that in the 1830s, repeal would have led to an increase in real wages by as much as between 12.3 and 23.3 per cent (O'Rourke 1994:133). Also, in the nineteenth century a much bigger proportion of the average person's income was spent on food than is the case today. Figures for 1688 suggest that almost 40 per cent of the income was spent on food and beverages, as opposed to around 11 per cent today (1996) (Maddison 2003:18). Income certainly increased between 1688 and 1840, but there is little doubt that the 1840 figure resembles the 1688 much more than the 1996 figure.

Chang 2002:23; Lloyd-Jones 1990:598; Lloyd-Jones and Lewis 1998:49p; Pugh 1999:52).[36]

Hence, what might seem paradoxical really is not: The biggest economic reform of the first half of the nineteenth century—the 1846 repeal—would not result from parliamentary Whig majorities. With persistent tension in Parliament, only a Conservative government, itself usually seen as part of vested agricultural interest, would be strong enough to go against those same interests. Repeal thus had to wait until the Conservative government of Sir Robert Peel (1841–1846), and his willingness to go against the grain of his own party (Bairoch 1993:21; Pugh 1999:38p, 91). Peel established an agenda in which repeal seemed the next logical step, after lowering import duties in 1842 and 1845, the 1844 Bank Act, and the 1842 reintroduction of the income tax. Further, the 1845–1846 Irish potato famine made the consequences of artificially high grain prices extremely obvious, and provided him with an immediate excuse for repeal (Bairoch 1993:21; Hoppen 1998:93, 127pp; McKeown 1989:365; Pugh 1999:38p, 69, 91).

For Peel, the repeal was politically risky, as it went against the interests of landowners. The economic boom following the Napoleonic Wars meant that issues of free trade and the Corn Laws had been low on the political agenda. The mid-1830s economic crisis changed this. Cotton textiles could no longer serve as the engine of the economy. At the same time, vested interests were blocking new industries from taking over. Iron was growing too fast for an economy where government policies had placed artificial restrictions on the expansion of markets. Both within iron, coal and cotton, the crisis of 1837–1842 brought falling profits and rising unemployment.[37] To the landed classes, this meant that industrialization must be progressing too rapidly, requiring production cuts in order to restore the natural balance of the economy. To free-traders it was a crisis of underconsumption and of artificial trade barriers, thus connected with the Corn Laws. The Corn Laws reduced the disposable income of the working class, and hence of the economy as a whole. And, they prevented commercial intercourse with other nations (Lloyd-Jones 1990:599; Lloyd-Jones and Lewis 1998:51pp; McLean 1990:280; Pugh 1999:63).

Peel saw the crisis as structural, caused by underconsumption and artificial trade barriers. This pushed him toward the conclusion that free trade had to be implemented and the Corn Laws repealed. However, Parliament remained heavily dominated by the landed classes. Roughly 80 per cent of the MPs (1841–1847) belonged to the landowning aristocracy. Hence, by voting as a group, landowners could easily block repeal (Lloyd-Jones 1990:603; Schonhardt-Bailey 1991:547). However, the repeal

---

36 From 483 MPs (to 175 Tories) in 1832, to 385 in 1835 and 345 in 1837. The 1841 election was a disaster, Whigs losing their majority outright, only returning 291 MPs, with the Conservatives (up until then referring to themselves as Tories) winning 367 seats (Pugh 1999:50pp).

37 Unemployment among iron founders rose from 11.1 per cent in 1839 to 18.5 in 1841 (Lloyd-Jones 1990:600). As production kept increasing, the price of pig iron fell from £10.50 per ton (1839) to £5.50 (1842) (Lloyd-Jones and Lewis 1998:53).

passed by 348 votes to 251. 241 Tory MPs voted against it. Those Tories voting for it joined Peel in leaving the party.[38] The Whigs were almost unanimously in favor. Hence, the astonishing part is not that numerous Tories voted against Peel, but that a full third of them actually voted for a repeal that they had been massively against as recently as 1842 (Hoppen 1998:127; McKeown 1989:356; Pugh 1999:69p).

Two basic arguments have been advanced. The first focuses on the changing structure of the economy, and how the struggle between land and capital ever more favored capital. However, this does not explain the large changes in voting between 1842 and 1846, during which no election had been held. A second explanation emphasizes how the governing class was gradually converted to liberal ideology (McKeown 1989).[39] The truth is found somewhere in-between. McKeown (1989:353) rejects the ideology argument, but still argues for the importance of a "more congenial political environment that had arisen due to the changes induced by British economic development." Other concerns than personal or class economic gain, were important. For instance, it was widely perceived that repeal would lead to a cheaper and more abundant supply of food for the lower classes, thereby reducing social tension (McKeown 1989:365; McLean 1990:280). Further, Peel framed repeal in almost moralistic terms, as in showing the masses that in a time where tension was strong there was a moral core to the state, receptive to the needs of the masses (Hoppen 1998:129). There is also something to be said for the land vs. capital argument. The landed classes to an ever greater extent diversified their holdings and invested returns from land into nonagricultural ventures, especially such ventures that were closely tied to the land, as heavy industry and railroads.[40] Landowners were longtime investors in industries like coal, iron and steel. These were the industries where exports had increased the most over the previous decades, and where Britain had more to benefit from free trade than protection.[41] Hence, "diversified landowners" were more likely to vote for repeal than landowners that remained tied to the land (Schonhardt-Bailey 1990:557).

The repeal of the Corn Laws was the most conspicuous mid-nineteenth-century economic policy decision made in Britain, and the one that most clearly symbolized the transformation from agriculture to industry. To some extent it reflected different

---

38 Peel resigned later that same year, and in the 1847 election, Whigs and Liberals won 336 seats, Tories 201 and Peelites 117 seats (Pugh 1999:91). The Conservatives did not win an election outright again until 1874.

39 Or maybe rather, how organizations like the Board of Trade and the Anti-Corn-Law League were leading a new movement of opinion rather than just expressing an already prevailing political and economic mood (McKeown 1989).

40 For the period 1820–1844, a full 28 per cent of the capital invested in railroads, came from "peers, gentry and gentlemen", up from 22 per cent during the "early years" of the railway era (Freeman and Louçã 2001:165).

41 Schonhardt-Bailey (1991:551) makes the point that nineteenth-century industrialization differed from eighteenth century industrialization by being led by exports rather than increasing domestic demand. Hence, landowners diversifying in the nineteenth century would be more likely to favor free trade than landowners of a century earlier.

economic and class interests of Tories and Whigs, and the fact that these interests had again started to converge. However, what cannot be disputed is that a Parliament where 80 per cent of the members were part of the landed classes, voted for repeal. Peel was well aware that this might lead to the split of the Conservative Party and to his own resignation (he was right on both accounts). Also, the impact of the strong pro-trade lobby should not be underestimated. Politician Robert Cobden and Board of Trade member John Bowring argued that agricultural protection had made the factory system viable in countries like the US, Germany and France, where it would not have flourished if not for Britain depriving itself of competitiveness by over-protecting agriculture (Bairoch 1993:18; Chang 2002:23).

There was something peculiarly British about the whole process. This was a country where contentious issues like repeal were resolved peacefully within the existing system. In France, consoling different interests usually led to stalemates, to tense and uneasy status quos, or even revolution! In Britain, a parliament dominated by landowners moved toward free trade, suspended the combination acts, and incorporated the middle classes into the power structure. While clearly in disagreement over particular issues, they were settled within the confines of the institutional structure, autonomously, with Parliament not falling prey to pressures from vested interests.

Parliament also went against old, established interests on other occasions—as with the repeal of the Bubble Act.[42] One of the cases that brought this about was the 1824–1825 debate over the projected Liverpool–Manchester railroad line. Cabinet minister and President of the Board of Trade, William Huskisson, promoted the Liverpool–Manchester Railway Bill on the grounds that cotton took longer to get from Liverpool to Manchester than from New Orleans to Liverpool, and that canals thus held merchants and manufacturers to ransom. It was opposed by the shareholders of the Liverpool–Manchester *canals*, as well as local landowners, using experts to testify that canals could accommodate all future transport and that railroads were inefficient. Even the Archbishop of York involved himself for canals, against railroads! The bill eventually went through, and the Liverpool–Manchester line set a pattern for things to come. The point to be made is not one of political consensus around new and promising industries—to quote Harris (1997:686), this was "a straightforward confrontation between long established vested interests and newcomers". However, it is worth noting that with very powerful vested interests fighting against the railroad at a time when the railroad was still unproven, even administrations otherwise ambivalent toward industry (Lord Liverpool, the Duke of

---

42 The Bubble Act had been imposed in 1720, prohibiting the free and spontaneous formation of joint-stock companies (Harris 1997:675; Mokyr 1999:51). The repeal made it considerably easier to form joint-stock companies, but no rush to create such corporations actually arose. It is unclear to what extent repeal stimulated iron. In theory, it made it easier to channel funds into capital-intensive industries (like iron). For practical purposes, the 1856 Limited Liability Act and the 1861 Bankruptcy Act were more important (Harris 1997; Hoppen 1998:201; Mokyr 1999:51). However, as the previous subchapter suggests, the Act benefited railroad construction, which definitely benefited iron.

Wellington) came down on the side of the newcomer (Freeman and Louçã 2001:194; Harris 1997:685p). Conservative governments failed to side with what would normally be considered conservative interests, very much opposed to in France, where the inherent conservatism of the state apparatus allowed canals to be backed and lobbied from inside—by the bureaucracy.

However, the 1830s–1840s was no period of peace and tranquility. If cohesion was down, how does this square with 1830–1860 being the period in which Britain reached its strongest industrial dominance ever? Britain never came closer to a social revolution than it did between 1830 and 1832 (Evans 1983:207; Hobsbawm 1969:72; Pugh 1999:48; Tilly 1995:50). Pugh (1999:48) suggests that if election reform had not been passed in 1832, the result would have been popular armed resistance. Quoting Hobsbawm (1969:72): "At no other period in modern UK history have the common people been so persistently, profoundly and desperately dissatisfied." For most manual laborers, the early nineteenth century was a time of hardship. Real wages did not point decidedly upwards until the 1840s. The average annual rate of increase in real earnings for the period 1790–1840 was a measly 0.1 per cent (Feinstein 1995:32; Hobsbawm 1969:77, 93p).[43]

Unrest lasted throughout the 1840s, with the Chartist movement mobilizing hundreds of thousands in bitter and violent protests, demanding universal suffrage, abolition of property qualifications on MPs, annual parliaments, and the secret ballot. In 1839, 3,000 colliers and ironworkers were met by troops dispersing the protests, killing 24 Chartists. Parliament flatly rejected petitions from Chartists, despite these on one occasion (1842) bearing as many as 3.3 million signatures. Chartist protests would not subside until 1848, when the government countered a mass rally by recruiting 100,000 volunteers to repel the threat (Pugh 1999:59pp).

However, by mid-century, Britain was again a calmer place, and so the best way to approach the question of social cohesion may be by looking at the extent to which Britain was able to deal with its problems. Conflicts were gradually being resolved and protest channeled into institutionalized forms. The 1832 extension of the electorate was a key reform in this respect (Evans 1983:218). Occasional unrest would still flare up, but after 1850, all explicitly working-class revolutionary organizations faltered while the implicitly revolutionary ones went legal, working within the system rather than trying to bring it down (Perkin 1969:393; Tilly 1995:12). By 1860, Great Britain was far less turbulent than it had been in 1830. Compared to leading Continental powers, it was downright calm. In 1848, as revolutionary rebellions plagued the rest of Europe, Britain saw no upsurge in unrest. Strikes were few and far between, lock-outs in 1852 and 1859 being the two largest conflicts of the period (Tilly 1995: 396p).

The transformation of protest was striking. It shows how social cohesion grew stronger and how the country was molded into a more homogenous unit. The right to

---

43 This compares to a far more impressive 1.5 per cent a year between 1840 and 1873 (Feinstein 1995:32).

form associations had become a routine affair (ibid.:12).[44] Parliamentary reform was one of the reasons. The 1832 Reform Act effectively doubled the size of the franchise, to roughly 20 per cent of all adult males.[45] It enfranchised the middle classes, but not the numerous workers who had also fought for the extension. Ironically, as Chartism threatened the political system, the middle class would now instead come down on the side of the traditional elites, for social and political stability, against anything resembling revolution. In France, the absence of middle-class support at crucial instances led to revolution. In Britain the middle class would play a crucial role in maintaining social and political stability, providing the regime with a legitimacy sorely lacking across the Channel (Hobsbawm 1969:77; Pugh 1999:48pp, 71pp; Tilly 2004:163).

The Reform Act did not pass easily. The Duke of Wellington (Tory) replaced Lord Liverpool in 1827, but refused to consider parliamentary reform. This coincided with the revolution in France (1830), making a number of prominent Tories, among others future PM Peel (at the time Home Secretary), aware of the potential of the masses. It also coincided with the industrial Swing Riots (see previous chapter) in southeast England, initiated by agricultural laborers rebelling against low wages and poor conditions (and threshing machines!). Incapable of restoring order, Wellington's government fell. The subsequent Whig government, headed by Earl Grey, came to power on a platform of reforming to avoid revolution. In 1831, his reform bill passed by *one* single vote, but was rejected in the House of Lords. The reaction to the rejection was widespread popular violence, especially against houses of peers and bishops that had voted against the bill. The problem was not solved until 1832, when King William IV appointed a number of new peers to the House of Lords, so as to secure majority for reform (Lloyd-Jones 1990:591; Pugh 1999:48pp; Quinault 1993:197).

Beyond extending the franchise, the Reform Act redistributed a number of constituencies. The old system of representation unduly favored the southern, agricultural regions. The changes were fairly small, but went in favor of manufacturing, with seven industrialized counties gaining seats. Eighty-six boroughs, mostly rural with very small electorates, were wholly or partially disenfranchised. Forty-two new boroughs were created, more than half of these from industrial areas. However, large cities were still grossly underrepresented, with industrial cities like Birmingham and

---

44 Tilly (1995:341pp) admits that his data are scattered and filled with holes. Still, he concludes quite assertively that there was a substantial change in the nature of "contentious gatherings" between 1789 and 1833. The proportion of non-violent interactions increased dramatically. The public meeting was almost instituted as an official political instrument, as a way for those not being part of the electorate (i.e., most people) to be heard.

45 Or to be exact, 17.8 per cent of all adult males, as all male householders occupying property worth at least £10 a year in rent. In absolute figures, the extension increased the electorate to 650,000–700,000 voters out of an adult male population of 3.5 million, at a time when the French electorate was less than 200,000 out of a male population more than twice as large. Further reforms followed in 1866, 1869 and 1884 (Evans 1983:352; Justman and Gradstein 1999:119; Price 1993:166; Pugh 1999:48p).

Manchester having the same representation as small rural towns. Parliament was still dominated by landed interests, and doubling the franchise did not greatly alter this (Pugh 1999:49; Quinault 1993:198p).

While extending the franchise and redistributing constituencies had minor consequences for the political balance, they were important. They were reforms aimed at preventing revolution, and they were successful. First, they included large parts of the middle class, securing its support for the basic institutions of government. Second, it catered to manufacturing by redistributing constituencies. The changes brought increased legitimacy for the ruling elites. Despite a number of economic slumps from the 1850s onwards, support in the system of government kept increasing, Britain avoiding the constant threat of revolutionary change that plagued France. Post-1832 British regimes could rely on a groundswell of cohesion in the populace. Hence, British governments had far more autonomy to pursue independent policies than did their counterparts in France (Hobsbawm 1969:77; Pugh 1999:48pp, 71pp; Tilly 2004:163).

Consensus and cohesion may have been less important than with cotton textiles. The 1830s and 1840s were turbulent, with social cohesion at a temporary low, and with political consensus a thing of the past. Still, conflicts were dealt with relatively smoothly and peacefully. A parliament dominated by landowners moved toward free trade, and incorporated the middle classes into the system of government. This could not have happened in France! Clearly, a number of these actions were taken because the ruling elites felt pressured, choosing reform over revolution. Still, it meant that the ruling elites had to confront strong vested interests that they were themselves part of. For such to be conceivable in the first place, Britain must have been characterized by substantially greater levels of consensus and cohesion than France. While not as consensual as earlier, a growing consensus as to the political, economic and industrial future of Britain was starting to materialize. Hence, political consensus and social cohesion are still significant with respect to explaining the success of British industry, in particular iron, during the nineteenth century.

France: Fragility and Weak Government—with the Exception of Napoleon III
In France, it is far easier to find examples of vested interests blocking structural change. First, while heavy tariff protection for iron following the Napoleonic Wars was necessary in order to avoid being driven out of business by British exports, more surprisingly farm producers joined industry in demanding tariffs. Even wine-growers received protection! During the Bourbons vested interests were simply too numerous and strong. A government commission even expressed the view that lower tariffs would unjustly harm those that had entered into business with the expectation that tariffs would be upheld. In other words, tariffs should be understood solely in terms of protection, and not as a means by which vulnerable industries could modernize and regain competitiveness, and tariffs were eventually lifted. To quote Wright (1995:147): "Here was a classic example of special privilege crystallizing promptly into vested interest."

In Britain, turmoil and unrest had not led to revolution. Britain reformed, growing socially and politically stronger. France did not. The Bourbon monarchy headed by Charles X, was overthrown in 1830. It was replaced by the July Monarchy of Louis-Philippe, head of the House of Orléans, which lasted until 1848, also overthrown by revolution. The second Republic that replaced it only lasted until 1851, when its president, Louis-Napoleon—a nephew of Napoleon Bonaparte—seized power in a *coup d'état* and created the second Empire. This was acknowledged by the population in a plebiscite the following year. Louis-Napoleon renamed himself Napoleon III, taking the title of Emperor, which he kept until 1870, when he was captured and deposed during the Franco-Prussian war. Most of the period was characterized by weak government and by regimes of dubious legitimacy. Ironically, the least legitimate of them all, that of Napoleon III, was the strongest, ushering in growth and industrial expansion.

No major change occurred during the Bourbons. Vested interests prevented the state from implementing any major initiatives on education, science or industry. The regime rested on a very tenuous power balance in the Chamber of Deputies, and the state did not show much interest in promoting economic change in any case. In many ways, this was also the case during the July Monarchy. Louis-Philippe wisely carried on sheltering the iron industry, which would otherwise have been forced into extinction by British iron. But while this tariff was useful and necessary, vested interests within both the advanced and the reactionary sectors of metallurgy imposed contradicting pressures on the state. Thus, while encouraging modern methods of metal production, the French state simultaneously promoted the use of wood for iron smelting in order not to go against the interests of charcoal iron producers. And he upheld protection for farming, raising the food costs for the entire country. Tariffs were applied on an ad-hoc basis, dependent more on the strength of the vested interest crying out for protection than the actual need for it (Trebilcock 1981:186p; Wright 1995:147p).

Even less logically, Louis-Philippe upheld tariffs on coal. One of France's major resource problems was a lack of coal. But the response was not to increase imports, or intensify the search for new sources of coal. Rather, responding to pressure from coalminers, in a situation where France was dependent on importing coal from other countries for iron smelting, French mining interests managed to push through tariff *restrictions* on coal imports! Thus, a tax on coal was imposed by maybe *the* European great power most desperately in need for such fuel (Trebilcock 1981:187). This is only one example of France being very slow to comprehend the need for integration between iron, coal and transportation infrastructure. Coalmining persisted as an industry of small private producers, exhibiting "egocentricity, commercial timidity, and conservatism … of an exceptional order" (Trebilcock 1981:170). Coal producers did not interact closely with other branches of industry. Iron ores were far removed from coal deposits, and unlike Britain, communication between coal producers and ironmasters was minimal. Coal producers did not diversify into metals, and had no interest in keeping the costs of fuel down. Again, unlike Britain, coal and iron lobbies had differing, often competing, interests. Weak governments sought to reconcile all these different business interests by imposing tariffs on a various number of goods. Put together, this made for inconsistent policies.

Another reason why governments were too weak to deal with vested interests was that on many occasions, vested interest was located deep inside the state apparatus. The case of coalminers was bolstered by the conservative and powerful *Corps des Mines*. The government's mining bureaucracy subjected mining to the control, regulation and almost military discipline of the *Corps des Mines* (ibid.:185). On numerous occasions, discouraging assessments by the *Corps* would prevent mining from going ahead. At Briey, later found to be the richest source of iron ore in Europe, the *Corps'* first denied the existence of the strike, then doubted that it could be mined. It discouraged industrial attempts at extraction, and finally parceled out the ore-fields in undersized lots, thus preventing an efficient scale of exploitation. The recommendations of the *Corps des Mines* also extended to the coal industry, making poor, but influential decisions about the availability of raw materials. The glaring problem of nineteenth-century France was not one of resource endowments, but rather one of poor exploitation of essentially adequate resources (ibid.:171pp).

Part of the reason for the lack of integration between coal and iron had to do with a transportation policy that was highly conservative, favoring vested interests. Here, vested interests were again entrenched in the state apparatus. Among the most important reasons for the hesitant construction of French railroads, as well as the fact that they were constructed for speed and transportation (to and from Paris), and not for industry, was the control exerted over policy-making by the *Corps des Ponts et Chaussées*. The *Corps'* authority came under threat only during short-lived periods of reform—typically after revolutions—with new regimes seeking to exploit the newfound political consensus to get rid of old vested interests.

The 1830 Revolution undermined the *Corps*, with new leadership, both in the *Corps* and in the Chamber of Deputies, insisting that infrastructure policies be reshuffled along British lines. This was an attempt of a new, liberal regime to end the wasteful commitment to canals and instead accelerate the construction of cheap, private railways. The liberal moment ended when in 1831 a cholera epidemic killed PM Casimir Périer, one of the few strong and outstanding leaders of the July Monarchy.[46] His government fell the following year, and with it the willingness to resist the *Corps*. For two years, the *Corps* had struggled against privatization efforts, which would have led to a multitude of cheap and unplanned railroads, and a breakup of its monopoly. Now it was back in control, rejecting all attempts by private investors to build railroad lines, instead favoring its own prestigious and extremely well-engineered projects, that were however of little relevance for industry. Also, the *Corps* kept pushing for more canals, at a time when the canal era had really long ended (Smith 1990:665pp, 674p; Trebilcock 1981:169).

As the only remotely strong and long-lasting government of the July Monarchy, the Guizot administration (1840–1848) had some leverage. Hence, in 1844 for the

---

46 To the tacit delight of Louis-Philippe, who was deeply skeptical of the liberal ideas and plans for large-scale reform advocated by the Périer administration (Wright 1995).

first time, the *Corps'* doctrine of canal building was rejected. However, the 1842 railroad law which had sought to rationalize the structure of railroad construction, reserved for the *Corps* the rights to regulate the layout, location and the civil engineering of every railroad project, no matter whether capital stemmed from private or from government sources. Hence, any railroad project for all practical purposes was subject to the *Corps'* standards. An attempt to make railroads both cheaper and looking more like a true network than a series of spokes emanating from the hub of Paris was thwarted when the Corps allied with military engineers to defeat the idea of constructing intermediary railway hubs, so as to prevent national bottlenecks around Paris and save costs. The result was a France that was extremely slow to produce an infrastructure network benefiting industry, as in linking iron and coal (Smith 1990:665pp, 674p; Trebilcock 1981:169).[47]

Discontent with the *Corps* and cries for change and for British-style industrial liberty, were far louder after the 1848 revolution. Foreign minister Alphonse de Lamartine presented a bill to convert the uncompleted railroad system into a public works project, employing workers from workshops set up after the Revolution in order to deal with unemployment and economic crisis. However, the proposal was rejected by the Constituent Assembly and calls for privatization and the dissolution of the *Corps* successfully fought by the *Corps*. Moreover, in 1849, it even managed to preserve the emphasis on canals (Smith 1990:670pp). The weakness of the second Republic meant that no strong lobbying was necessary on the part of the *Corps*. Weak governments allowed vested interests to pursue a policy of railroad construction that was not at all beneficial to the country.

When push came to shove, the parliament would never go with manufacturing and merchant interests against those of the *Corps*. Not until Napoleon III did France have a government strong enough to go against it. Hence, during the time of Napoleon III, the structure of railroad companies was rationalized and capital inflow secured through government guarantees. As seen earlier, Napoleon III also initiated a strong acceleration of railroad construction (Smith 1990; Trebilcock 1981:152p, 186).

His influence was felt in other areas as well, like tariffs (where the 1860 Cobden–Chevalier treaty introduced free trade between Britain and France, much against the voices of both agricultural and manufacturing interests), and in finance: The growth industries of the era were capital-intensive—iron, coal, railroad construction. In a distinctly capital-scarce France, financial reform was essential. Here, the old banking structure persisted, governments adhering to the interests of the Bank of France, and of conservative banking houses resisting innovation. Existing banks were small,

---

47 The army emphasized the strategic necessity of having fast and direct routes from Paris to the eastern frontier. Ironically, during the Franco-Prussian war, this proved a disaster. True, those that arrived at the Prussian border arrived there faster than the Germans. However, as most soldiers had to travel by Paris no matter where they started from, the net effect was increasing rather than decreasing traveling times. It meant that the Paris–Strasbourg line, being the only main line to the front, did not have the capacity to deal with traffic. Once Paris was captured, the system broke down anyway (Smith 1990).

conservative, exclusive credit clubs owned by family or a small-knit group, lending money only to the most low-risk customers. Capital for more risky activities, like business ventures had to be borrowed at excessive interest. Hence, up until 1848, 60 per cent of the capital raised for French railroads came from abroad, mostly Britain. Credit liberalization began 1848–1849. Most important was the foundation of the first investment bank, *Crédit Mobilier*, whereby surpluses were redistributed as investment capital for business, providing a source of risk capital that the old *haute banques* would not. The *Crédit Mobilier* was crucial to railroad construction, and hence to the iron industry as during the second Empire, railroad construction finally began creating an infrastructure network integrating iron and coal. Still, it was disliked and resisted by strong forces within the old *haute banque* system, as well as from the political establishment (Smith 1990:675pp; Trebilcock 1981:150pp, 184pp; Wright 1995:128, 150pp).[48] Financial reform was not a consequence of any political consensus among the ruling classes. Rather, during the second Republic, it survived because it was the brainchild of president Louis-Napoleon, against the resistance of the Bank of France. Major policy change would have to wait until the second Empire (Trebilcock 1981:144p, 151p).[49]

On the matter of education, the second Republic was not strong enough to uphold the reforms of Louis-Philippe, who in 1833 had implemented a new education law wresting power away from the Catholic Church. The Catholic Church would not regain its influence until 1850, when Louis-Napoleon, reluctantly and in the hope of being able to extract concessions on other issues, signed a bill by the Legislative Assembly to increase Catholic Church influence in the supervision of state primary schools, and giving it the right to operate secondary schools (Furet 1995:335; Wright 1995:113, 132).

Both Bourbon and July Monarchy governments were generally weak. Staying in power without triggering revolution was hard enough in the first place, without having to challenge vested interests as well. Also, the ruling elites often had interests that overlapped closely with those of the most powerful vested interests. Things were complicated further by the fact that in many instances, the most powerful vested interest was entrenched in the state apparatus through the bureaucracy, and by the fact that one-third of the members of the Chamber of Deputies were at the same time holding positions in the civil service bureaucracy.

The biggest problem of the July Monarchy was always its lack of legitimacy, perceived by the right as betraying the monarchy and by the left as betraying the revolution. Being the head of the House of Orléans, Louis-Philippe was a princely

---

48   Although it is true that many representatives of the *haute banque* had themselves been experimenting with ideas along the lines of the *Crédit Mobilier* (Wright 1995:153).

49   When Napoleon III further contributed to the modernization of the financial sector by the overseeing of modern financial institutions like the *Crédit Foncier* and the *Crédit Lyonnais*. By 1870, the entire credit system had been revamped. The government would increase public spending, but the encouragement of private speculation and investment may actually have been more important for the overall capital flow in an economy that up until then had been distinctly scarce in capital (Chang 2002:37; Smith 1990:677; Trebilcock 1981:143).

cousin of the Bourbons. In the words of Furet (1995:341) neither elected nor chosen, but "a prince luckily found near the broken throne, whom necessity made king." Hence, he started his reign on even shakier foundations than Louis XVIII. There were ongoing riots throughout the 1830s, and 10 assassination attempts against Louis-Philippe between 1830 and 1840 (some of these extremely near misses), most of these stemming from a feeling that not much had changed since 1830. The years up until 1834 were especially turbulent (Furet 1995:353; Price 1993:168; Weber 1989:158; Wright 1995:106, 112).[50]

It is also clear that the power balance among the ruling elites was tenuous. 1830–1840 was a period of permanent instability in government, with most ministries averaging less than a year, and the Chamber of Deputies torn by conflict (Wright 1995:109p). Very few governments were both strong enough, and willing, to go against major vested interests. To the extent that the king could garner support, he did it by leaning toward the right, in other words to those that were the least interested in change. The Guizot administration of 1840–1848 was relatively strong, but at the same time ideologically committed to *not* rocking the boat. Hence, in terms of political decisions going against vested interests, the political consensus exhibited during the Guizot period would *not* lead to controversial decisions. While stable, prosperous and peaceful, much of this stability derived from the government's increased willingness and ability to curb unrest (Price 1993:168). Hence, with stability went the erosion of public support. Guizot was obsessed with order, distinctly right of center, hostile to the sovereignty of the people, against the expansion of the franchise and social reform. Assassination attempts on the king meant harsh measures against the opposition, with opposition leaders denied the right to hold public political meetings.[51] While gaining leverage in terms of policy-making by taking advantage of a weak and divided opposition, Guizot lost support both from the ruling elites and from the people at large (Furet 1995:351, 380pp; Kale 1997; Price 1993:168p; Wright 1995:109p).[52]

The one major legitimizing feature of the regime was its ability to produce prosperity. Louis-Philippe's regime was pro-business, although largely restricting its role to leaving business and industry alone. Still, certain governmental concessions and financial guarantees were given and considerable sums spent on public works like canals, roads, and railways. However, the regime's number one priority was

---

50   The 1831 Lyon insurrection led to 600 casualties, as the National Guard was called up to counter a total of 15,000 workers (Wright 1995:110).

51   This was avoided by instead arranging banquets, where the participants were allowed to speak between the courses! Toward the end of the regime, banqueting had become widespread (Wright 1995:120).

52   He very extensively employed personal side-payments to secure support from the Chamber, among other things by offering Deputies in the Chamber positions as government bureaucrats while still being Deputies. Hence, at the most extreme, a third of all the Deputies had salaried government posts on the side. Without the support of these, he would never have stayed in power for eight years. Bills to deny bureaucrats sitting as Deputies were proposed— and defeated—no less than 18 times (Wright 1995:113).

always harmony, order and stability, rather than structural change (which has a habit of upsetting order). Thus, the July Monarchy was characterized more by growth than change. And so, business and industry were supported only to the extent that this did not upset the somewhat precarious political and economic balance (Furet 1995:351pp; Price 1993:167p; Tombs 1999:64; Wright 1995:148pp).

Windows of opportunity for structural change were few and short-lived. The lack of general legitimacy of the July Monarchy, and the absence of social cohesion in the people, made it very difficult to go against the interests of business, bureaucracy and finance, as these were essentially the interests that kept the regime alive. Until the boat *was* actually rocked by economic crisis in 1846, the regime was stable. The regime drew most of its support from various shades of property owners. The crisis in industry combined with financial crisis eroded the support of the bourgeoisie, which now joined the lower classes in demands for large-scale reform and the abdication of the king. Urban workers turned against the regime when the price of wheat (helped by the same weather that also produced the Irish potato famine) rose by 250 per cent. Mines and factories shut down, railroad companies went bankrupt and unemployment soared (Furet 1995:351, 380pp; Price 1993:168p; Wright 1995:109pp).

The second Republic came into being in February 1848, with the explicit ambition to end the elitist rule of earlier regimes. Universal suffrage increased the electorate from 250,000 to more than 9.5 million voters overnight. However, already by June the same year, the country was on the brink of civil war.[53] The new constitution, finalized in November 1848, further complicated matters. It specified a presidential system, with the president elected in separate elections, but being an obvious compromise, the constitution left the relationship between the president and the legislature very vague. Some deputies expected the executive and legislature to balance each other out, others were afraid that the outcome would be a president overrunning the legislature. Thus, one of the reasons why many deputies supported Louis-Napoleon's candidature (apart from the obvious name-recognition factor) for president was their suspicion that he would prove weak and manipulable, easily dealt with by the Assembly.[54] This turned out not to be the case. Louis-Napoleon

---

53 40,000–50,000 turned to the streets in an attempt to overthrow the regime. The immediate reason was the abolition of workshops established in February. The workshops were a mix of unemployment benefits and public works labor projects offering low-paid manual work in the biggest cities. At the most, 80,000 people were enrolled (Price 1993:173; Wright 1995:128).

54 There were definite reasons for believing so. In 1831, he had been expelled from France for associating with republican subversives. In 1836 and 1840 he had staged spectacularly unsuccessful attempts at invading and taking over the country. After the first attempt, he had been exiled to the US, after the second sentenced to life imprisonment, of which he spent six years before escaping. He fled to Britain, but returned to France after the 1848 Revolution, where he was elected to the Constituent Assembly in a by-election. He seemed an utter political adventurer, and not even a very successful one at that (Wright 1995).

was elected president with 74 per cent of the vote,[55] and from now, politics was a three-way struggle: The parliamentary majority consisting of moderate republicans, the party of order dominated by former Orléanists, and Louis-Napoleon (Furet 1995:402pp; Price 1993:174pp; Wright 1995:125pp, 151).

The republic was further undermined by the 1848–1851 economic crisis. France suffered a "shock-like decline in industrial production in 1848" (Berger and Spoerer 2001:293p, 319). It not only paralyzed railroad construction, but also wreaked havoc with coal and iron. Coal production dropped 20 per cent overnight, iron production declined more slowly, but by 1850 it was only 70 per cent of what it had been in 1847 (Cameron and Neal 2003:234). Riots prolonged and intensified the crisis (Price 1993:176; Wright 1995:126pp, 151). This created the backdrop against which Louis-Napoleon could overthrow the Republic in a *coup d'état*.

Hence, French governments were considerably less secure than British governments. The lack of social cohesion meant that the prevention of revolution was always an overriding concern. While for considerable periods of time French administrations looked stable and secure, when crisis occurred, there was no groundswell of social cohesion in the populace to support and uphold them. Among French citizens, there existed no broadly shared vision that disagreements were to be resolved through peaceful means and through institutional channels. There was no widespread acknowledgment that the regime was legitimate, or any trust that the leadership had much concern for the interests of the people. Unlike in Britain, institutional compromises held no legitimacy (Furet 1995:386). Whenever famine occurred, there was always suspicion of government involvement, and that food shortages had been deliberately created for the personal enrichment of particular ministers or the state. While famines engendered suspicion in Britain as well, it was never directed against the central government (Van Horn Melton 2001:71p). Social cohesion in the British people may not always have been strong, but there is little doubt that in France, trust in the ruling elites was considerably less. Consequently, governments were left with little leverage in policy-making. As long as the economy did well, France was reasonably stable, but any famine or economic downturn would lead to political crisis, and fears of impending revolution (Price 1993:160pp; Wright 1995:147).

Hence, economic crises were instrumental in bringing down the Bourbon Monarchy, the July Monarchy and the second Republic. The 1830 Revolution was preceded by the economic crisis of 1826–1829, the Bourbon regime collapsing more or less by itself. The hostility against Louis-Philippe in 1848 was considerably less. He was unpopular, but overthrowing the regime seemed far out of proportion— very little talk of revolution circulated prior to 1848 (Furet 1995:351, 380pp; Price 1993:168p; Wright 1995:109pp). As Wright (1995:122) puts it: "No other regime in modern French history missed so good an opportunity to perpetuate itself as a durable political system." Still, it demonstrates how a regime deficient in perceived

---

55 Louis-Napoleon Bonaparte 5,434,000 votes; Cavaignac 1,448,000; Ledru-Rollin 370,000; Raspail 37,000; and Lamartine 17,000 (Furet 1995:415; Wright 1995:130).

legitimacy has little leverage. To the extent that the July Monarchy shaped politics, it did so by adhering to the interests of the groups from which it derived its support. When the support of these groups was withdrawn, the regime did not have any reserves of social cohesion to fall back on. This rendered it vulnerable during crisis. When Louis-Napoleon in 1851 brought down the second Republic, there was very little resistance. Not even a democratic republic could mobilize any more support than previous authoritarian regimes.[56] During economic crisis, the tenuous balance otherwise holding French governments and regimes in place, ceased to exist. The regime would have to rely on a backdrop of cohesion, legitimacy and trust to survive, and it simply was not there (Cameron and Neal 2003:234; Furet 1995:351, 380pp; Price 1993:168p; Wright 1995:109p).

One might be forgiven for thinking that Louis-Napoleon, rising to power through a *coup d'état*, legitimized by rigged plebiscites, and overall resting his legitimacy on a very dubious foundation, would be vulnerable to a lack of social cohesion. His regime was authoritarian, it tightened institutional controls, increased press censorship, curtailed the rights to free association, and ruthlessly removed political opponents. He even pondered closing down the universities, and his relationship with the Church was highly conflictual (Furet 1995:445; Nord 1995:11pp). A legislative body would still exist, but performing only a very minor role. But paradoxically, at least during his first decade, this most illegitimate of regimes brought something that previous French regimes had lacked—legitimacy! Social cohesion is illusive, and it is clearly often hard to predict what appeals to the people. Wright (1995:119) makes the point that a main problem of the July Monarchy was that it did not trigger enthusiasm. It was healthy and stable as long as it could produce growth, but distinctly unglamorous, and insisted on very cautious foreign policies in order not to raise fears that France was back on the warpath. France was bored! The prime virtues of the regime suggested cowardice and stagnation!

True, Louis-Napoleon had more than 26,000 people arrested and the rule of law for practical purposes suspended.[57] Despite this, he did bring something to French politics that had been sorely lacking, at least in the perceptions of a multitude of people. In the 1849 presidential election (second Republic), he won by a landslide. In December 1851, immediately following the *coup*, he asked a plebiscite to approve the changes, changing the term of the presidency from four to 10 years and significantly reducing the power of the legislature. Ninety-two per cent voted in favor. In November 1852, the Senate (appointed by Louis-Napoleon) proposed the institutional transformation from republic to empire, voted on by full suffrage

---

56 Some of this undoubtedly had to do with the fact that after a first few months of reforms, the second Republic succeeded in abandoning virtually all of these reforms as time progressed, among other things even revoking the right to vote for the one-third of the poorest voters (Price 1993:176).

57 Furet (1995:445) says 28,000. Of these, roughly 10,000 were deported to Algeria, as the left and the leadership of the second Republic were cut off from politics.

in a plebiscite. This time, 97 per cent voted in favor.[58] While there is suspicion that elections were rigged, there is little doubt that the majority would nevertheless have been massive. This was a leader who brought France a vision, who promised to restore the nation's glory and pride, not through conquests, but by redefining national glory in terms of dynamic change, technological progress and economic expansion, urging the importance of rural roads, canals and railroads. Under the name Napoleon III, Louis-Napoleon would play the role of "legislator-hero", drawing upon powerful images from the French Revolution (Furet 1995:448pp; Price 1993:173pp; Charles Tilly 1986:305p; Wright 1995:131).

Napoleon III is the best example that social cohesion is important. The regime enjoyed considerable popularity, which gave him more leverage in policy-making than any French leader since Napoleon Bonaparte. This enabled him to shape policy without fearing that controversial political decisions would lead to political crisis and revolution. Thus, unlike for previous regimes, Napoleon's political program was one of state activism, strongly pro-business, industry and technology. No regime between 1789 and 1914 was more favorably predisposed toward industrialism (Trebilcock 1981:152). While he was fortunate to benefit from economic recession yielding to economic boom (1852–1857), something which had little to do with economic policy, there is no doubt that industrialization in general, and coal and iron in particular, benefited enormously from the program of railroad construction initiated almost at the inception of the second Empire. With the 1852 reorganization, Napoleon III granted railroad companies the most generous subsidies in Europe. The structure of railroad companies was rationalized and capital inflow secured through government guarantees, whereby the state guaranteed stockholders a minimum return. Liberalization of credit and the growth of banking continued, and while the government increased public spending, the encouragement of private speculation and investment was probably more important for the overall capital flow. Consequently, 90 per cent of the rail investment during the second Empire was private. Napoleon III should not be seen as the savior of France. He was a mysterious character even to his closest relatives, and various motives have been ascribed to his actions and initiatives, some onerous and visionary, some far less so. He kept the National Assembly, but stripped it of its powers. Ministers were responsible to him only, and plebiscites used to give the illusion of popular accountability. However, what is also beyond doubt is that this was a watershed period for France, the country undergoing its most rapid economic change ever (Furet 1995:451; Smith 1990:677; Trebilcock 1981:143; Wright 1995:152).

But ruling France was still a balancing act. Part of the reason for the lack of social reform during the 1848 second Republic was the need for business support (Price

---

58 However, in addition to the 7.8 million in favor and only 250,000 against, there were over 2 million abstentions (Furet 1995:448). In the 1851 election there had been 1.5 million abstentions, 7.5 million voting yes, and 640,000 no. It should also be noted that Louis-Napoleon had made it very clear to all officials that their continued employment hinged upon their enthusiastic campaigning for the president (Price 1993:178).

1993:173p; Wright 1995:163). While business had been favorably predisposed to Napoleon's coup, the cities were skeptical. Hence, while the Emperor, by creating a strong and (in his own mind) non-political executive, sought to modernize France economically and socially, the tacit support that he depended upon came from groups with very different perspectives.

The large majority of his popular support was drawn from the peasantry (much of it from simple name-recognition), but in terms of actual policy-making he depended on support derived from an alliance with the Catholic Church—carefully cultivated since 1848 (and which would last until 1859)—and from business interests (Price 1993:179). He satisfied the right by providing staunch protection against revolution and of private property, and appeased the left by guaranteeing against a return to the old order of privilege and aristocratic elitism (Furet 1995:452pp; Wright 1995:137pp). The leverage gained from these alliances did not begin to unravel until changes in his foreign policy and education policy affected his relationship with the Catholic Church.[59] Also, changes to tariff policy (the Cobden–Chevalier treaty) led to deteriorating relations with business.[60] Hence, from 1859 onwards, policy-making became a far more tenuous balancing act. He could have chosen to be more authoritarian. Instead, as he ran into political problems, he turned toward the left, and started liberalizing by taking steps toward a more parliamentary regime, and by relaxing repressive legislation. Political exiles were amnestied in 1859. Strikes were legalized in 1864 and 1868 saw concessions made with respect to public meetings, as well as greater tolerance shown toward the press (Furet 1995:467pp; Hobsbawm 1975:125p; Price 1993; Weber 1989:158; Wright 1995).

This failed. Concessions with respect to strikes and union activity undermined conservative support, but failed to win the left over. Napoleon's support base had always been the countryside, not the cities. Hence, allowing strikes and union activity did not increase support for the regime, it merely accelerated industrial conflict and strike activity. Plebiscites and elections for the national assembly saw opposition candidates receive ever more votes, suggesting that the regime was

---

59 In 1859, France involved itself in the wars over Italian unification—which was hugely popular with the public, but not with the Catholic Church. Napoleon III sponsored unification, against compensation in the form of territory. As part of the unification process, the Vatican lost most of its territory, now being limited to a small area within the city of Rome, with French troops stationed in Rome, not leaving until 1866. The Church never forgave him. Also, the Church heavily attacked Napoleon III when in 1863 Minister of Public Education Victor Duruy set out to create free and compulsory primary education.

60 The effects of the Cobden–Chevalier treaty are disputed. It exposed French industry to foreign competition. Some industries gained, some lost, and it did force many French industrialists to modernize and to enlarge. The immediate impact was an economic down-turn. However, chances are this was more because of the American Civil War than because of any independent effect from free trade (Chang 2002:38; Furet 1995:464; Trebilcock 1981:153; Wright 1995:154).

having a harder time raising support.[61] Thus, he to an ever greater extent pursued policies that antagonized the groups that he had relied on for support, while not winning over those whose rights he had violated during the coup. Yielding to pressure, a new constitution was drafted in 1870, turning the regime into a semi-parliamentary monarchy, bringing him considerable public support. A plebiscite on the new constitution was overwhelmingly favorable.[62] While this looked like something that the nation could live with, foreign policy again made life difficult. The semi-parliamentarian nature of the new regime meant that politics was now to a much greater extent out of his hands. Fueled by the ambitious, impulsive and extremely nationalistic and anti-German foreign minister Agenor Gramont, France was getting embroiled in a conflict with Prussia over the rightful heir to the Spanish throne.[63] Napoleon III was ill and sidelined, which was exploited by Gramont and by PM Emile Ollivier. At a stage when the conflict was all but solved, Gramont insisted on a personal apology from Wilhelm I of Prussia. This would not happen. Prussian Chancellor Otto von Bismarck, who had also been ill and incapacitated, opportunistically escalated the crisis by cutting and pasting a telegram from Wilhelm I to the French government. The rest is history. France declared war—against the will and instincts of a severely weakened Napoleon III. The Franco–Prussian war determined the fate of the Empire. Napoleon III was captured by Prussian troops on September 2. On September 4, the second Empire collapsed and gave way to the third Republic (Furet 1995:454pp, 467pp; Hobsbawm 1975:125p; Price 1993:174pp; Weber 1989:158; Wetzel 2001; Wright 1995:163pp).

It is obvious that the lack of political consensus and popular cohesion played a large part in explaining how vested interests could block structural economic

---

61 In 1852, government candidates received 5,248,000 votes, opposition candidates only 810,000 (although there were a full 3,613,000 abstentions). In 1869 government candidates only received 4,438,000 votes against 3,355,000 for the opposition (Price1993:185).

62 7,350,000 voted 'yes', 1,538,000 'no'. The cities still voted against it (Price 1993:188).

63 The Spanish Revolution of 1868 meant the end to the Bourbon queen Isabella II. The war between France and Prussia arose over disagreements as to who would replace her. In Isabella, France had a friendly neighbor. Bourbons had ruled France for centuries, including as recently as 1815–1830. When France very heavy-handedly blocked all potential heirs to the Spanish throne, the most likely remaining candidate was the Sigmaringen Prince Leopold from the house of Hohernzollern, from which the Prussian king also traced his bloodline. France thus faced the possibility of losing a pro-French Spanish monarch for a pro-Prussian, which was perceived of as a grave threat. One of the main mistakes made by Gramont (although Ollivier was also culpable) was to assume that this was a plot instigated by the Prussian king. However, Wilhelm I was highly uncomfortable with the situation and genuinely just wanted the problem to go away. He did what he could to placate France, but refused to behave in a way that made him look as if he accepted any responsibility for what had happened. To Wilhelm I, the Spanish throne had been offered to Leopold, and he had accepted the offer. If Leopold wanted to renounce the throne, that would be his choice. Gramont was the one pushing for a crisis, and for him to ask Wilhelm I for something resembling a personal apology, was to Wilhelm downright insulting (Wetzel 2001).

change in France. Both in the populace and among the ruling elites, cohesion was far weaker than in Britain. For sustained periods of time, weak and fragile governments played balancing acts in order to survive. Not only did they struggle from a lack of perceived legitimacy, resulting in every major economic crisis leading to a revolutionary situation. Also, most governments were short-lived, without the autonomy required for independent policy-making. French parliaments were fragmented and characterized by a fundamental lack of consensus even as to basic rules of the political game. There were a few notable exceptions. However, these were governments that were more interested in preserving the status quo than in change, the reason for their longevity being their support for the king. In other words, the governments that had the greater capacity for change lacked the willingness! The main exception to this pattern occurred during the first decade of the second Empire. Napoleon III was the strongest leader in France since his more illustrious forebear and uncle. While blatantly authoritarian, his popular base of support was broader than that of previous regimes, and he faced fewer constraints on his power from other potential decision-makers in the French elite. This gained him leverage in policy-making that he used to among other things accelerate infrastructure developments, greatly benefiting the iron industry by among other things finally integrating iron and coal in one railroad network. Consequently, from the 1850s onwards, France rapidly changed from charcoal- to coke-fueled iron smelting. The second Empire did face ever greater problems toward the end of its life-span. But unlike previous regimes, it was not brought down by internal strife, but by war—indication that social cohesion had increased considerably since the early century. True, Napoleon III was pushed toward a hysterically strong stance against Prussia by conservative forces. Also, he refused to make the one strategic military move that might have saved him—slowly retreating to Paris and making a stand outside the walls of the capital—because he feared political repercussions from conservatives interpreting this as weakness. But still, the second Empire was overthrown only months after its most resounding victory in a plebiscite ever. Hence, it is very unlikely that Napoleon III would have been overthrown by anything resembling popular uprising. While less stable than during his first decade in power, the problems that Napoleon III faced maneuvering his way through French politics should not be exaggerated. France had developed over the past half a century and one of the consequences was that protest was to an ever greater extent channeled into semi-institutional forms, like strikes, demonstrations and mass meetings instead of invasions of fields, destruction of machinery and tollgates, and riots and uprisings (Furet 1995:493; Charles Tilly 1986:307). To quote Trebilcock:

> ... French policy achieved its best results whenever the executive could secure sufficient independence of economic action ... whenever the executive was subordinated to democratic processes, it tended merely to replicate the irrationalities of the business community, pulled hither and thither like a wayward planet. (1981:187)

Conclusions

It is harder to make a strong case for the role of the state and for political consensus and social cohesion for the iron industry than for cotton textiles. One of the reasons for this is that Britain's advantage over France between 1830 and 1860 was as much a consequence of developments taking place during earlier decades than it was of any involvement on the part of the state. Many of the crucial developments in iron occurred during the same time period as the breakthroughs in cotton textiles. Hence, as with cotton textiles, because of technological progress Britain had eased ahead of France by the time of the French Revolution. And as with cotton textiles, French technological progress largely stemmed from diffusion of technology across the Channel. Hence, with the Revolution and the Napoleonic Wars, diffusion ground to a halt. Consequently, by 1815 France found itself far behind Britain. Puddling and rolling was introduced in Britain in the 1780s, but did not diffuse to France until after the wars. In other words, benefiting from its human capital superiority, the foundations for Britain's dominance in iron were already in place before the 1830s. Iron was an industry where formal schooling was less important than mechanical skills and a talent for tinkering and experimenting. For now, these were the kinds of skills that were relevant for industrial development. Again, this means that the post-1830 variation in performance between Britain and France is explained by earlier events as much as by events in the mid-nineteenth century.

A second reason is that the case for political consensus and social cohesion is harder to make than for cotton textiles. That France was distinctly low on consensus and cohesion is beyond doubt. This had strong negative effects on infrastructure policies and most certainly harmed the French iron industry. It is not at all hard to find examples of harmful influence on the part of French administrations. But with Britain, the case for political consensus and social cohesion seems weaker than during the initial phases of the Industrial Revolution. In the Cotton Textiles chapter, ruling elites developed converging interests during the period that cotton textiles broke onto the industrial scene. But the period following the Napoleonic Wars saw a reverse pattern. Politics became a fight between landed and manufacturing interests, and in the populace, tension was greater than at any time since the seventeenth century. Hence, Britain's mid-nineteenth-century dominance does not seem to follow easily from social cohesion!

The counterargument, and a valid one at that, is that in Britain, things improved. By 1860, Britain was far more at peace with itself than it had been in 1830. Britain had become a more peaceful country because the political establishment had dared to go against vested interests, among other things through the 1832 franchise extension. In terms of politics and economics, the repeal of the Corn Laws had tremendous symbolic importance. The repeal is also important in that it was an example of aristocratic interests in Parliament going against vested agrarian interests, securing a majority for a momentous political decision by voting with manufacturing interests. However, the repeal did not take place until 1846, and free trade had to wait for another decade, which brings us very close to the end of the time period analyzed in this chapter. However, what is still beyond doubt is that the Corn Laws channeled major resources away from productive and into non-productive sectors. In as capital-intensive an industry as iron, this was bound to have an effect, and there is no doubt that the Corn Laws had detrimental effects for the overall economy. The argument has been made, probably most forcefully so by Lloyd-Jones and Lewis (1998), that in the 1830s and 1840s, Britain was headed toward political and economic crisis. Just building on the advantage deriving from victory in the Napoleonic Wars would not suffice for continued economic and industrial progress. Depression and structural crisis coincided with political turmoil, and the role of the British state should be hailed rather than derided, as neither crisis could have been resolved without the intervention of the state. The complex of decisions that made the crises boil off involved including the middle classes in the political process. With the demise of the Liverpool and Wellington Cabinets and the rise of Whig and pro-industry Tory Cabinets, it also involved a definite shift in favor of industry. An 1840s structural economic crisis affecting in particular iron, and government policies artificially restricting the expansion of markets, especially foreign markets, was not resolved until the Peel cabinet of the early 1840s began reducing and abolishing customs duties, culminating in Corn Law repeal. Hence, the case for the British state having had a crucial influence on industrial development is stronger than what it may at first glance seem. What resolved a very serious complex of crises was the combination of renewed consensus and cohesion. While British ruling elites were not always enthusiastic about structural change, the prevailing mood was one of reform, and one of a far greater receptiveness to the demands of both people and industry than in France. While the importance of consensus and cohesion may have been more obvious in cotton textiles, it does apply for iron too.

A third reason why it is easier to make a case for cotton textiles has to do with the importance of resource endowments, more specifically the abundance vs. scarcity of coal. With iron, this argument makes sense. Coal was essential, both as fuel for smelting iron, and because of the strong complentarities between the iron industry and steam power. Britain was far better endowed in coal than France. It had more coal, coal deposits were often in fairly close proximity to iron ores, unlike in France, and coal deposits were of a kind that made them amenable to coke smelting, whereas known French coal deposits generally contained coal of inferior quality.

However, there are numerous reasons why we should be tentative about resource endowment arguments. First, we are not at all sure whether technological innovation, growth and prosperity are caused by scarcity or by abundance. Britain benefited from its abundance in coal, but had managed to get itself into such a privileged position in the first place because of problems of resource *scarcity*. Iron smelting traditionally employed charcoal for fuel, as technologies utilizing coke without this leading to poor quality iron had not yet been invented. A charcoal shortage would have produced a crisis in British iron production unless new methods had been invented. Britain innovated its way around a problem that would otherwise have been debilitating to its iron industry. If Britain could, surely France could work its way around its coal scarcity?

Moreover, in France, there is much evidence that other factors, particularly in the political sphere, were more important. Even though it would always be hard to innovate around the lack of such a basic resource as coal, there were obvious avenues that could have been pursued. In a France scarce in iron and coal, political authorities should have seen it as an important task to tie these resources together in an integrated infrastructure network, especially considering the French penchant for government planning. Instead, France was a distinct European laggard in this respect. It took a long time before French metallurgic industries were able to benefit from railroad construction. While not rejecting the resource argument altogether, what is conspicuous is how little effort France spent finding a solution to its resource problem. Centralized political decisions instead actually accentuated the problem.

Finally, to what extent was iron important for mid-nineteenth-century economic development? Britain, beyond a shadow of a doubt, was the big success story. Its iron industry was the largest and the most modern in the world, and Britain was the country that to the greatest extent managed to exploit the complementarities that existed between iron and coal. Granted, Britain had natural resource advantages, but the country also rapidly developed a network of railroads that tied iron and coal together and made it easier to efficiently transport iron goods to cities and markets abroad. There is broad consensus that the iron industry provided Britain with a tremendous economic boost at almost exactly the time when cotton was running out of steam. France was much slower to realize the complementarities between iron and coal. France was a leading power that failed to perform. When France did eventually industrialize, iron was the core economic engine of this process. But in terms of both production figures and technological sophistication, it continued to lag far behind Britain.

Chapter 4

The Chemical Industry

Introduction: The First Science-Based Industry

Often, when technical revolutions are discussed, chemicals slip quietly away where cotton textiles, railroads, and information and communication technologies get all the attention. But the chemical industry is actually a particularly interesting case of technological and industrial leadership. It is widely held as the world's first science-based, high-technology industry. In the synthetic dye industry, scientific progress led more or less directly to industrial success. Also, the chemical industry is at heart a very generic technology, and has given rise to a number of breakthroughs in other areas. The chemical industry today ranges across more than 70,000 products, comprising paints, pharmaceuticals, soaps, cosmetics, plastics, dyestuffs, explosives. Moreover, chemical industry has had spillover effects into other industries: Automobiles, rubber, textiles, consumer products, agriculture, petroleum refining, pulp and paper, health services, construction, publishing, entertainment, metals, some of this war-related, like rubber and fertilizers (Arora, Landau and Rosenberg 1998a; 1998b). Finally, the rise of the chemical industry signaled a shift both economically and in international relations, as it represented a transfer of technological and industrial leadership from Great Britain to Germany.[1] Britain had been reigning supreme, but was now overtaken in terms of industrial performance, also giving impetus to German great power aspirations in world politics. The chemical industry is an important reason why industrially, by World War I, Germany was Europe's number one power.

The boundaries of "chemical industry" are often somewhat confused. Also, statistics regularly lump together very different kinds of products, such as inexpensive sulfuric acids and expensive dyes or fibers (Standen 2003). The main raw materials used are air, water, limestone, sulfur, phosphates and fluorspar. These raw materials are converted into intermediate and finished products.

---

1 Since no German state existed until 1871, for the pre-1871 era the following will have a clear Prussian bias, as Prussia was the most powerful of the German states (with the exception of Austria). However, the bias is somewhat unfortunate in the sense that Prussia was economically more conservative and pro-agrarian than other German states, and also because the chemical industry largely sprang up outside of Prussia. Still, most of the available evidence stems from Prussia. Also, the smaller German states were dependent on tariff revenues collected and distributed by Prussia. And the 1840s and 1850s saw German states ever more tightly knit together in a railroad network, tying together industrial districts and cities (Tipton 2003:117; Trebilcock 1981:56). Hence, the links between Prussia and the other states were strong, and growing stronger.

Inorganic chemistry takes as its focus compounds taken from the earth, primarily salt and minerals, which are then processed into useful products like alkalis (lime, soda ash, caustic soda) and acids (sulfuric, nitric). Inorganic chemistry is often referred to as *heavy* chemicals (although today organic chemistry is more typical of heavy chemicals), and *sulfuric acid* most often the unit of measurement for statistical comparisons. Historically, inorganic (heavy) chemical industry was not particularly research-intensive, and in many ways more similar to mining than to the science-based industries of today (Arora, Landau and Rosenberg 1998a:10; Standen 2003).

Organic chemistry is based on hydrocarbons, as coal, oil, natural gas, and has generally been more important since 1856, as organic compounds are more diverse and pervasive than inorganic. In the subsequent processing, chemicals like chlorine and oxygen are added, giving rise to a variety of final products, like nylon, polyester fiber, plastic and pharmaceutical products. The typical unit for statistical measurement has been *dyestuffs*. Historically, organic chemistry used to be referred to as light chemicals, although this does no longer hold. Today, organic chemicals like ethylene, benzene, and propylene are more typical examples of heavy chemicals (Arora, Landau and Rosenberg 1998a:10; Standen 2003).

Not politically unified until 1871, and with a turbulent history, Germany was no early leader in chemicals. But from scarcely even *having* a chemical industry in the 1860s (Cameron and Neal 2003:241), Germany grew to become totally dominant within a few decades. By 1870, Germany controlled roughly 50 per cent of the global synthetic dye market, 85 per cent by 1900, even 90 by the start of World War I (Arora and Gambardella 1998:389; Murmann 2003).

There are numerous reasons for the industrial rise of Germany and the stagnation and fall of Britain. As late as the early 1860s, it seemed unlikely that Britain would surrender its number one position, blessed as it was with first-mover advantage, access to a huge home market, colonies and dominions, and endowed with an aura of industrial infallibility. It had a huge heavy chemical industry producing alkalis, acids and salt, and all the ingredients required for carbon-based manufacture. No country produced more coal-tar, or did it more cheaply. It had the world's biggest market for textile dyes, and the demand from what was by far the world's largest textile industry for goods like bleaches, soda, sulfuric acid etc., meant that Britain had the world's number one chemical industry as well (Landes 1998:288). Only a few decades later a complete turnaround had taken place.

This was a period in which Britain was not only losing its edge in chemicals, but where productivity figures in general were pointing downwards. Some figures deny that there was *any* TFP growth between 1873 and 1913 (Hoppen 1998:310). Others point to a very modest increase: Crafts (1995b:752) reports 0.05 per cent for the interval 1899–1913, and a somewhat more respectable 0.4 per cent for 1873–1913 (ibid. 1996:198). While no comparable TFP figures for Germany exist, the industrial growth figures in Table 4.1 below (while not saying anything about technological progress *per se*) bear witness to a British economy that was stagnating compared to Germany and the US. The British industrial sector actually experienced an outright decline in productivity per man-hour during the same period (Brose 1998:84).

In aggregate industrial potential, Germany passed Britain in 1913, and was also well ahead in terms of GNP per capita growth (Horstmeyer 1998:249; Stürmer 2002:87).[2]

Table 4.1 Annual Industrial Growth, 1870–1913

Annual industrial growth	Great Britain	Germany
1870–1913	1.9%	4.9%

Sources: Brose (1998:83); Gilbert and Large (2002:38).

The following demonstrates how educational shortcomings made Britain unsuited for success in chemicals, and how Germany benefited from having the world's best system of higher education. However, the fact that so many gifted German chemists went to work in Britain during the early years of the industry, strongly suggests that education was not the reason for the rise of German chemicals *per se*. The German chemical industry benefited strongly from German human capital, but mostly so from the 1870s–1880s onwards, at a time when the German industry was already ahead. Beyond human capital, patent regimes provide some of the explanation for the rise of German chemicals. However, on a more general and overarching level, this is a story about vested interests. In Britain, structural change was blocked by old industries (cotton textiles) and by conservative and religious forces, and by a lack of understanding as to the requirements of new industries. In Germany, no strong vested interests existed, and despite German governments not being particularly strong or consensual, structural change could not be blocked.

History

Early Years

William H. Perkin's 1856 discovery of the first synthetic dye (mauve) signals the origins of the modern chemical industry. Until then, Britain and France had been the dominant nations, and chemical industry more or less exclusively about inorganic chemistry. France was ahead of Britain in science and research, but Britain was the power that benefited from it. Sulfuric acid (H_2SO_4) was obtained by a process invented in France in 1666, but not made much of before being adopted in Britain in 1740.[3] The discovery of chlorine gas for bleaching by the French chemist Claude

2   Britain 1.3 per cent, Germany 1.8 per cent (Horstmeyer 1998:249).
3   The process obtained sulfuric acid by essentially adding saltpeter to sulfur in large glass vessels. Joshua Ward perfected the technique, managing to lower the price of sulfuric acid from £9 to 10s per pound. John Roebuck, in partnership with the industrialist Samuel

Berthollet, was put to industrial use by Scottish firms in the 1790 (Standen 2003; Cameron and Neal 2003:179; Mokyr 1990:107).

Another group of chemicals important for industrial use was alkalis (caustic soda (NaOH), potash (K_2CO_3)). As these were previously produced by burning vegetable matter, in 1775 the French Academy of Sciences offered an award of 100,000 francs to anyone who could invent a chemical process by which common salt could be converted into sodium carbonate (NA_2CO_3), needed for soap and glass manufacture. French surgeon Nicolas Leblanc solved the problem in 1787, and the process became known as the Leblanc process. Despite this, Britain became the early Leblanc leader. The process (sulfuric acid reacting with salt to create sodium carbonate[4]) was made commercially viable in the 1820s (Cameron and Neal 2003:179p; Brose 1998:79; Fox 1998:87; Mokyr 1990:107).

Hence, from the 1830s, Britain had the world's dominant chemical industry, based on the production of heavy inorganic chemicals. It was technologically simple, largely mechanical, relying on the same kinds of skills that had sufficed half a century earlier, in other words the practical ability to tinker and experiment in order to come up with basic inventions and gradual improvements. Theory improved only slowly.

The leaders of industry were self-taught chemists, working in makeshift, private laboratories with inexpensive apparatus, and without support from a laissez-faire British government. They had at best some basic skills in academic chemistry, and on-the-job training was the prevalent mode of education (Fox 1998:88p; Freeman and Soete 1999:88; Horstmeyer 1998:234). Still, as early as 1850, more than 10,000 people worked in the chemical industry (primarily producing soda through the Leblanc process).[5] British soda production was three times that of France, and its chemical industry as a whole the largest in the world—primarily because of the tremendous demand of the enormous British textile industry for essential goods like bleaches, mordants, detergents, soda, sulfuric acid and heavy chemicals (Horstmeyer 1998:235; Mokyr 1990:107; Rosenberg 1998:193).

1830–1850 saw an array of new natural dyes. Still, the scientific contribution was modest. When Perkin in 1856 invented mauve, his discovery was serendipitous. He was actually, by trial-and-error, instead seeking a medicine for malaria, by synthesizing quinine (Murmann 2003:2).

Garbett began production of sulfuric acid on a commercial scale in 1746 (Cameron and Neal 2003:179; Mokyr 1990:107).

4   Salt (sodium chloride (NaCl)) is treated with sulfuric acid to yield sodium sulfate, which is reduced to carbon to give sodium sulfide. Sodium carbonate (soda ash) results from a reaction between sodium sulfide and limestone (calcium carbonate).

5   In comparison, textiles employed roughly 400,000 (1862) (Landes 1969:271).

The Rise of the Modern Chemical Industry

In order to capitalize on his discovery, Perkin in 1857 set up a factory for the production of aniline purple and remained the world's only producer until a few months later similar discoveries were made elsewhere. The French chemist Verguin discovered aniline red, also called magenta or fuchsine in 1858–1859, and the German dyestuffs industry started off with Jäger entering the industry in 1858 (Mokyr 1990:119; Murmann 2003; Murmann and Landau 1998:30). Most subsequent inventions were German. The last British invention was that of synthetic alizarin, by Perkin in 1869, although German chemists Carl Graebe and Carl Lieberman, pooling their resources with Heinrich Caro of BASF, beat him to the patent office by one day (Mokyr 1990:119). This was the last of the British trial-and-error individual brilliance type inventions, and the first in a long line of German laboratory discoveries, whereby alizarin was the conscious result of a clear and focused research effort (Landes 1969:274; Mokyr 1990:119p; Murmann and Landau 1998:39).[6] Kekulé's work on the benzole molecule (the benzene ring theory, 1865) laid the theoretical foundations for advances in coal-tar chemistry. Before this breakthrough, chemists had scant knowledge about how a particular molecule would create a particular color. The theory did not have an immediate impact, but when it did, German dyestuffs advanced rapidly. Still, the process leading up to synthetic indigo took 17 years and cost over 20 million Marks: In 1880, Professor Baeyer at the University of Munich produced indigo at his laboratory. However, it took a second process by Baeyer (1882), a third synthesis by Swiss chemist Heumann (1890) and a laboratory accident involving a broken thermometer and spilt mercury, before a commercial process was found in 1897. The contact process was developed by BASF in the 1880s, based on theoretical work in physical chemistry at the University of Leipzig. The Haber–Bosch process for synthetic nitrogenous fertilizers was a result of the work of Fritz Haber at the Karlsruhe Technische Hochschule in 1908 (Freeman and Soete 1999:89pp).

During the first years of synthetic dye production, Britain was ahead, with France, and not Germany, challenging for industrial leadership. However, from the mid-1860s, Britain was rapidly challenged by Germany (Landes 1969:275; Murmann and Homburg 2001). Already by 1870, German firms controlled 50 per cent of world production, persistently rising, and eventually reaching a maximum of 85–90 per cent.

---

6   It may be hard to understand all the fuss stemming from something as innocuous as colors. However, certain natural dyes were prohibitively expensive. One of the reasons why purple and blue became archetypal royal colors, was that these were by far the most expensive pigments. Red and yellow were relatively inexpensive in Europe, extracted from the roots of the madder plant. In contrast, Tyrian purple could only be extracted from a gland on the body of a mollusk. One gram of Tyrian purple required 12,000 mollusks! Beyond kings, very few could afford purple clothes (Murmann 2003:67, 121, 241). Hence, synthetic dyeing presented the industry with huge potential savings and new business opportunities.

Between 1873 and 1879 Germany was hit especially hard by worldwide recession (Stürmer 2002:38; Wehler 1985:33).[7] The dyestuffs companies that survived grew to become strong, eventually developing into giants—firms like Bayer, BASF, Hoechst. Alongside electricity, chemicals was Germany's most dynamic industry, and rapid growth of the overall German economy created demand for industrial chemicals. By 1913, Germany produced 140,000 tons of dyestuffs, out of a world total of 162,000. In comparison, Great Britain produced 4,400 tons and the US 3,000 (Arora, Landau and Rosenberg 1998a:10; Cameron and Neal 2003:242; Murmann 2003:25; Rosenberg 1998:198). In 1871, world total dyestuffs production had been a meager 3,500 tons—an expansion in production of more than 4000 per cent (Murmann and Landau 1998:30; Murmann 2003:25)!

In the technologically far less complicated *inorganic* chemicals sector, British preeminence was also waning, but far more slowly. This was a sector where Britain had a solid lead due to demand from its huge textile industry, and because of access to large and sheltered colonial markets. Britain was the undisputed leader until the 1880s, and managed to preserve a respectable market share up until World War I. By then, it had been overtaken by Germany in the production of sulfuric acids, but was still dominant in technically less sophisticated fields, like soap, heavy chemicals, coal-tar intermediates and explosives, and in soda production.

Table 4.2 Soda production (1,000 tons)

	1867	1910
Great Britain	304	1,150
Germany	33	500

Source: Murmann and Landau (1998:29)

A reason for Britain's early hold on the market, but also for its eventual decline, was the Leblanc process (employed among other things for soda ash). As British firms had perfected this process, it effectively prevented other countries from making inroads in sulfuric acid. A look at Table 4.3 below, makes it abundantly clear how far ahead Britain initially was in terms of production, and how long it took for others to catch up (Eichengreen 1998:270; Hoppen 1998:292p).

The one momentous change that created new opportunities for non-British manufacturers occurred in 1872, when Belgian Ernest Solvay patented a new process for producing sodium carbonate (or soda ash), based on ammonia-soda (NH_3)

---

7   There is disagreement as to how seriously dyestuffs were affected. Murmann and Homburg (2001:188p) contend that only a few firms were forced out of the industry, whereas Horstmeyer (1998:247) speaks of scores of young dyestuffs companies being hit hard.

(Rosenberg 1998:199).[8] British firms had already invested heavily in the Leblanc process. Hence, the British attempted to modernize the Leblanc process rather than investing in new equipment. In contrast, Germany faced no such constraints, and had no problems adjusting to the Solvay process. Germany started off slowly, but accelerated rapidly. In 1878, 19 per cent of German alkalis were produced by Solvay methods, 75 per cent by 1887 and over 90 per cent by 1900 (Brose 1998:79; Freeman and Soete 1999:88p; Kindleberger 2000:147; Landes 1969:271pp).

By modernizing (and through intense competition from the Continent), British industry had by 1890 squeezed the price of Leblanc alkalis down to one-third of the 1872 price level (Landes 1969:272p). Yet, Leblanc production was a lost cause. In 1891, to counter the pressure from Solvay producers, the industry merged, founding the United Alkali Company (UAC), consisting of 48 out of 50 British Leblanc producers.[9] However, by 1900 it was clear that even the UAC was unable to breathe life into the Leblanc soda industry. This became abundantly clear as British companies were now not only competing against Solvay producers, but against an even more efficient process that gradually replaced Solvay, namely the contact process, made commercially viable by BASF in the 1890s.[10] These were electrolytic methods that hit directly at those areas where the Leblanc based industry remained profitable, and Britain lagged here as well: By 1904, only 18 per cent of the British industry had switched to electrolytic processes. Germany was far ahead with 65 per cent (Arora and Rosenberg 1998:77; Eichengreen 1998:269; Landes 1969:272p; Mokyr 1990:120; Murmann and Landau 1998:35p).

Sulfuric acid is often used as a rough measure of overall production in the chemical industry (e.g. Landes 1969; Modelski and Thompson 1996; Rostow 1978). However, this is an indicator that considerably biases the overall picture of chemical production. This is the inorganic, simple kind of chemical production that Britain was good at. Hence, Table 4.3 gives the impression that Britain remained the number one country in chemicals until the turn of the century. The same goes for soda production—another inorganic chemical, which was relatively easy to produce. It is harder to find reliable figures for the dye industry. However, it is overwhelmingly obvious that in organic chemicals, Germany was miles ahead. And that in both organic and inorganic chemicals, Britain was rapidly waning.

---

8   Solvay had started Solvay and Cie, using the Solvay process, as early as 1863. However, it took him almost 10 years to perfect the process. Hence, it was not patented until 1872. The process produced sodium carbonate from salt and limestone, using ammonia.

9   Murmann and Landau (1998:35): 45 out of 50 firms.

10   The original breakthrough was pursued in both Britain and Germany. Thus, Squire of England and Winkler at BASF developed the catalytic process in 1875, but the Germans came to dominate it. Here, as in the technologically more advanced organic sector, British inability to perform compares with the more resource-intensive German chemical industry and more skilled German chemists (Arora and Rosenberg 1998:77; Mokyr 1990:120; Murmann and Landau 1998:36).

Table 4.3 Sulfuric Acid Production (in 1,000 metric tons)[11]

	1780s	1840s	1870	1880	1890	1900	1910
Great Britain	1	300	590	900	870	1,010	1,065
Germany			51	130	420	703	1,381

Source: Modelski and Thompson (1996:101).

The Role of the State

Human Capital

Links between science and industry were at best weak until the mid-nineteenth century. This changed as greater theoretical understanding was required in order to successfully grasp the potential of the new technologies of the day. To paraphrase Lindert (2003:317): Whereas so far, growth had largely been a case of property rights and contract enforcement, from the early nineteenth century onwards, the human investment policy channel played an ever greater role. Nowhere was this more obvious than in chemicals, often considered the first science-based industry. The final decades preceding World War I signaled an era of transformation—a process of divorcing science and intuition (Hobsbawm 1987:243pp). Breakthroughs in chemicals gave rise to a chemical industry where success depended upon firms' ability to master existing technologies as well as innovate on a regular basis, and where having the edge in the production of skilled experts was key. For the first time, government-sponsored research and science–industry relations became important. For the first time did a country's ability to promote industrial progress by producing highly qualified specialists become a crucial aspect of industrial and economic growth. These were areas in which Germany excelled.

In terms of literacy and enrollment, by the late nineteenth century most Western countries had made significant progress. However, England had fallen behind. By 1850, English literacy rates were well below those of Germany. Anecdotal evidence suggests that in industrial centers, school attendance was lower in 1860 than a generation earlier (Landes 1969:341). Not until the very end of the century did England catch up. The school system had endured basically unaltered. The middle classes could afford to send their offspring to private schools, but the masses remained illiterate. Educational facilities greatly expanded during the nineteenth century as new schools were founded, but average attendance was short and schooling still highly stratified (Lindert 2001:13; Schofield 1968:316pp).

---

11 Different sources provide somewhat different estimates. Landes' (1969:273) 1900 figure for Germany is somewhat low, with 550,000 tons, Arora, Landau and Rosenberg (1999:220) slightly high, with 830,000 tons.

Table 4.4 Adult Literacy Rates (1750–1915)

	1851[*]	ca. 1865	1880	ca. 1900
Great Britain[**]	67–70[***]	69–76[†]		96–97[††]
Germany[†††]	80		95	88

Sources: Cameron (1994:23); Cameron and Neal (2003:215); Cipolla (1969:115pp, 127); Graff (1987:232, 318); Tortella (1994:11); Vincent (2000).

[*] Estimates from Cipolla (1969:115). Figures have an upward bias as they refer only to reading, not reading and writing.

[**] England and Wales.

[***] Scotland: 80 per cent (Cipolla 1969:115).

[†] Estimate from Tortella (1994:11). The interval's lowest rate denotes 1860, the highest 1870.

[††] Estimates from Cameron (1994:23) (lowest) and Tortella (1994:11) (highest).

[†††] Prussia. Figures from Cameron and Neal (2003:215). 1880 figure from Vincent (2000).

Table 4.5 Estimated Primary School Enrollment Rate, 1850–1900 (per 10,000 population)[12]

	1850	1882	1900
Great Britain[*]	1,045	1,107	1,407
Germany	1,600	1,547	1,576

Source: Easterlin (1981:18p).

[*] 1850: England and Wales. 1882: England and Wales, Scotland and Ireland.

The view that a good mass education might constitute a national advantage was lost on Parliament. Rather, it was perceived as expensive and unnecessary as well as potentially seditious and dangerous. Not until 1870, after long and heated debates, did Parliament pass the Elementary Education Act, stating that schools should be provided in such locations that no one should lack the geographical opportunity to attend school. Still, this did *not* make elementary schooling either compulsory or free. This was left to each and every local school board. Also, the act did not aim to find talent for science or industry. Rather, it drew on teachers who were inferior, and it was primarily an institution meant to "discipline a growing mass of disaffected proletarians and integrate them into British society…[and to] civilize the barbarians" (Landes 1969:341p). Thus, elementary education became *universal*

12 Easterlin (1998:59) considers rates above 1,200 synonymous with complete enrollment.

in 1870, *compulsory* in 1880 and *free* with the Fees Act of 1891 (Chambliss 2003; Evans 1983:324; Lindert 2001; Murmann and Landau 1998:36; Vincent 2000:31).

Amateurism remained the central characteristic of the British system (Kindleberger 1996:143pp). The state took little interest in revising a system that had brought industrialization and economic preeminence. But while this had earlier sufficed, it was no longer adequate, as new industries, requiring scientific knowledge to develop and service, professional skills to maintain and manage came to the fore. Hence, the education system was incapable of providing the chemical industry with skilled chemists. Both in terms of numbers of chemists produced, and their skill level, Germany was far ahead. British industry was constantly hampered by not having access to trained managerial and technical personnel. Higher education almost seemed designed to keep clever students as far away from the worldly pursuits of engineering and applied sciences as possible. Even in the late nineteenth century, the notion that universities should pursue scientific research, or engineering, was alien. When government-appointed commissions on scientific and technical instruction along with the expansion of examinations in mathematics, chemistry and metallurgy started to appear, it was already late nineteenth century. And several of these commissions were decidedly conservative. In 1882, the Samuelson Commission, maintained that it was "pure" science that was important, and that applied research was clearly subordinate (Donnelly 1986:204p; Hobsbawm 1975:59). Laboratories at Oxford and Cambridge were not established until 1871 and 1880, and at the same two universities, the grand total of Bachelor of Science honors degrees between 1880 and 1900, was a measly 56 students (Murmann 2003:55).

Earlier industrial success had provided a template that suggested that industrialization did not depend on large-scale educational or scientific backing. This applied to the chemical industry as well.[13] What had grown up instead of formal schooling, very much in line with the ideal of "gentleman science" as an *avocation* rather than a profession, was scientific societies. But with the 1870s and 1880s, the scientific societies were marginalized, as amateur science could not cope with new and more complex technologies, and with government-supported university-based models of science, research and technical training (Donnelly 1986:207; Hoppen 1998:308; Landes 1998:283; Murmann and Landau 1998:37p; Pyenson and Sheets-Pyenson 1999:321pp).

There was no lack of warnings that the system was failing, but criticism of the classical education fell on deaf ears, and aristocrats and intellectuals frowned upon initiatives that might make the curriculum more conducive to industrial progress, and were appalled by the ugly social consequences of industrialization (Brose 1998:85p; Freeman and Louçã 2001:252). Cameron and Neal (2003:223) speak of a tardy, half-hearted introduction of new, high-technology industries, and blame it on the backwardness of the education system. Hoppen (1998:307p) qualifies this

---

13 Donnelly (1986:208) quoting his contemporary John Dunn, states that in the 1860s, the least important man in a chemical works was the chemist. His salary was low, his status and working conditions poor.

by emphasizing that Britain was improving. The system was less focused than the German, and British universities were in decay. But in 1856, the Department of Science and Art had started a substantial state-aid system of technical training. From 1850 onward, numerous provincial colleges were formed, and from the mid-1870s, institutions of higher education gradually tried to accommodate industry and include industrial knowledge on their curricula, following pressure from industry. 1880–1914 was a period where the relationship between civic university technology departments and industrial firms was closer than ever. True, the number of graduates was small, but then, the industry did not ask for more (Crouzet 2001:135; Donnelly 1986:214; Hoppen 1998:308).

The Royal College of Chemistry was formed as early as 1845 with the German chemist August Wilhelm Hofmann (later Perkin's teacher) hired to bring the teaching and laboratory techniques of the renowned German chemist Justus von Liebig to Britain. But as much as this shows a genuine early interest and concern with new scientific and technological developments, the fragility of the system also shines through, witnessed by the fact that when Hofmann in 1865 decided to leave London for Berlin, the college folded (Murmann and Landau 1998:30, 37; Pacey 1990:169).

Other initiatives were the Select Committee on Scientific Instruction (1868), the Royal Commission on Scientific Instruction and the Advancement of Science (1870–1875), the reorganization of the Royal School of Mines (1882), the Royal Commission on Technical Instruction (1883), and the Technical Instruction Act (1889). And in response to the government committees, seven civic universities were set up in the 1870s. It is not that competition from Germany was simply overlooked. However, where Germany's effort was systematic, the British effort was fragile and half-hearted. Typically, British initiatives were insular and eventually ran into problems from the lack of funding and support from the surrounding political and economic environment. Hence, attempts were made to teach "chemical technology" at Owens College in the 1850s, but the course regularly failed, at least until the program was restructured in 1857. An attempt at setting up a department of chemical technology was made at the University College of London in 1879. Courses were offered on a number of subjects, but came close to a halt in 1889, and finally ended in 1894. Henry Roscoe, who was the prime force behind organizing interactions between science and industry, set up a course in Technological Chemistry around 1880, but most courses were discontinued in 1889. Roscoe was also behind the foundation of the 1907 Imperial College, merging the Royal School of Mines, the Royal College of Science and the City and Guilds College. Unfortunately, it did not enjoy close connections with local industry (Donnelly 1986:216p; Kindleberger 2000:154; Murmann 2003:175; Murmann and Landau 1998:38).

Scientific and technical training expanded considerably between 1857 and 1914. However, while British universities were financed locally with private grants and tuition fees, German universities were funded by the central government. By the end of the nineteenth century, the British government spent £26,000 on universities for all purposes.[14] Prussia alone spent £476,000. The corresponding figures for 1911–1912 were £123,000 and £700,000 (Murmann 2003:59, 176; Murmann and Landau 1998:40). Between 1900 and 1913, the British student population increased by 20 per cent, the German 60 per cent (Murmann and Landau 1998:38). In 1872, the University of Munich alone produced more trained chemists than the entire Great Britain (Brose 1998:86)! In organic chemistry research, Germany in 1882 produced 574 scientific abstracts, Britain 59 (Horstmeyer 1998:246). By 1913 Britain was outnumbered ten to one by Germany with respect to engineering students,[15] and in terms of overall students, Britain had 9,000,[16] Germany 60,000 (Berghoff and Möller 1994:269pp; Keck 1993:119; Murmann and Landau 1998:38; Schulze 1998:182; Walker 1993:158; Wehler 1985:124).

Against the mediocre performance of Britain, the Prussian (and German) education system was the standard of the day, both in primary and in higher education. While Britain did not make free, compulsory primary education universal until 1891, Prussia in 1772 was the first European country to do so (Crouzet 2001:137; Keck 1993:121; Murmann and Landau 1998:36).[17] Even though instruction was often poor, already by the early nineteenth century, the Prussian system was famed throughout Europe. The system was reorganized after the loss at the 1806 Battle of Jena, where Prussia was routed. Strong voices argued that the education system should be turned around, so as to cultivate a spirit of nationalism and patriotism. Schooling was also important for social order. The humiliation at Jena led to widespread reform, modernizing both funding and administration. Lindert (2003:332) stresses that the absolutist Prussian government ceded control of education to local government. Hence, the system flourished where demand for education was strong. The consequence was a primary education that created a much larger pool of students for higher education than the British system (Chambliss 2003; Hage, Garnier and Fuller 1988:827; Keck 1993:122; Landes 1969:342; Lindert 2001; Murmann and Homburg 2001:36).

Academies of science had existed in several German states since the eighteenth century. Already at this stage the research orientation was stronger than elsewhere. In 1780, 11 laboratories performed chemical research. Universities were poorly

14 Keep in mind that not even Oxford and Cambridge were funded by the state at this time (Murmann 2003:55).

15 Germany produced 3,000 graduate engineers per year, against 350 in England and Wales—for all branches of science, technology and mathematics (Hobsbawm 1969:182).

16 Excluding Oxford and Cambridge. Murmann and Landau's (1998:38) figures for engineering students (1911) are Britain 2,700 vs. Germany 11,000, not including those engineering students at regular German universities. Germany had matched Britain as early as 1870, with 2,759 full-time students. Berghoff and Möller (1994:269pp) report 6,000 British "full-time students" in 1913. Hobsbawm's figure (1969:182) is 9,000 ("university students"). The point remains the same: British efforts were negligible.

17 Although as early as 1717 Frederick Wilhelm I had ordered children to attend schools if such existed (Chambliss 2003).

funded and in decay,[18] but the first decades of the nineteenth century marked a turnaround. Universities were formed, or reformed,[19] with an emphasis on research and with autonomy for those university professors that wanted to devote themselves to science (Chambliss 2003; Keck 1993:117p). In addition, technical schools, like the Gewerbeschule (School of Trade and Industry) (Berlin 1821), provided basic education in among other things chemical–technical subjects. The 1830s signaled the start of the polytechnical school, which was at least as important as the universities with respect to educating engineers and craftsmen.[20] Still, early nineteenth century reforms were modest compared to what would follow. They did not include laboratory training, and science curricula had little practical relevance. Famous chemists, like Justus von Liebig, were brushed off by both the faculty and the Prussian state. Liebig represented an ideal that was still considered antithetical to the university–technical training, lust after discoveries to attract more students, practical applications of knowledge.[21] Still, beyond doubt is the fact that even before the birth of the chemical industry, German states hosted an excellent research and teaching system in organic chemistry (Keck 1993:119; Landes 1998:283; Lenoir 1998:23; Murmann 2003:51pp; Murmann and Landau 1998:37).

Germany was very much at the forefront with respect to diffusion as well. German fragmentation may actually have been beneficial. Leading German states were competing against each other. Hence, several German states set up competing palatial chemical institutes in the 1860s, and competition also applied to faculty, which gave professors leverage with respect to laboratory space, assistants and equipment. This provided Germany with a far deeper pool of talent and resources than other countries. Prussia's realization that it had fallen behind the other German states, triggered the attempt to lure Hofmann to Berlin by agreeing to fund and build a large chemical institute, including laboratories. Hofmann left London in 1865, and the British chemical industry never recovered (Lenoir 1998:23p; Murmann 2003:76; Rocke 1993:54p).

Still, the real expansion occurred later,[22] particularly from the 1870s onwards, when the Franco-Prussian war (at least to contemporaries) made the benefits of science, technology and industry apparent, even to anti-business and anti-industry

---

18 Even as late as 1859, a once-proud university like Marburg had only 216 students (Rocke 1993:57)!

19 New universities in Berlin (1810), Breslau (1811), Bonn (1818), Munich (1826).

20 The 1825 Technische Hochschule of Karlsruhe was the first (Landes 1998:283). Schools were also set up in Saxony (1826), Bavaria (1827), Württemberg (1829), Hanover (1831), Brunswick (1835), Hesse–Darmstadt (1836). By 1850, these schools hosted a total of 5,000 students a year, representing almost half the students in higher education at the time, and twice the amount of British engineering students more than half a century later (Brose 1998:63; Murmann and Landau 1998:38; Schulze 1998:182).

21 Liebig's laboratory attracted many foreigners. Between 1830 and 1850, 12 per cent of his students were British. These students went on to become the leaders of British academic chemistry, proof of how far ahead Germany was already (Murmann 2003:54).

22 Twelve new universities were set up between 1870 and 1918 (Wehler 1985:125).

Junkers (Kindleberger 2000:124). Thus, in the 1870s, the polytechnics were upgraded to technical universities, with enrollment rapidly expanding (from 14,000 in 1870 to 60,000 in 1914). Government funding increased even more rapidly, up by a factor of five from 1860 to 1910 (Freeman and Louçã 2001:252; Keck 1993:119; Murmann and Landau 1998:38).

Knowledge and the Chemical Industry   The German education system has been credited with the success of the German chemical industry, the British system with the failure of the British industry. Beyond the simple facts that the British system was in a state of decay, and that Germany actively promoted education as a source both of nation-building and industrial prowess, it seems obvious that the state *did* play a part, and that human capital *was* important, although not in a simple linear fashion. For instance; during the early years of the industry, Germany produced far more chemists than its industry had use for, hence we should not blindly accept that the superior higher education system of Germany was all-important in explaining German success.

When Britain was still a leader in chemicals, this was due to a huge textiles industry requiring bleach, detergents and other chemicals, to sheltered export markets in the colonies and dominions, and to a tradition of experimenting, tinkering and innovation based on trial-and-error within a context of close relationships between business and science. This was conducive to breakthroughs as long as sciences and technologies were at a fairly basic and intuitive level.

Thus, it is no surprise that Perkin (and Britain) was the originator of the first major breakthrough in organic chemistry. It is also no surprise that the early British lead could not be sustained. Both Perkin's discovery of aniline purple and his 1869 discovery of alizarin were small-scale efforts based on tinkering and experimenting rather than theoretical understanding. But from 1869, Germans were behind every major discovery and invention. Thus, it is also no coincidence that Perkin discovered purple while a student of the German Hofmann. The early British chemical industry to a considerable extent depended on an influx of German chemists.[23] This was a great benefit and a blessing to British chemicals, but also made abundantly clear Britain's inability to produce people with similar expertise. As the German chemical industry grew, most of the Germans returned to jobs in Germany, leaving Britain without enough skilled chemists for its industry (Landes 1998:290; Mokyr 1990:199; Murmann and Landau 1998:37).

It may be true that the British system was not a failure in the sense that there is little evidence that the British industry had any desire for more graduates. In other words, the problem was not one of under-supply of chemists, but of under-*demand*. Schooling did not drive the process; markets did (Hoppen 1998:308pp). However, it is also true that the government's inability and unwillingness to invest in R & D provided British firms with a different optimization solution than German

---

23 Also, early British chemists often had experience from German universities (Donnelly 1986:196).

firms, making it much less profitable for British firms to invest in R & D than for German firms. Instead, the British maximized profits by spending as little on R & D as possible (Murmann and Landau 1998:43). The lack of state involvement made it irrational to demand a large number of skilled experts. By the 1880s, changes were happening. By now, most British chemical firms had chemists among their employees. However, compared to Germany, this was too little too late (Donnelly 1986:212p).

Clearly, much was wrong with late nineteenth-century British industry. British businessmen seem to have been both technologically conservative and risk-averse.[24] And equally damaging, the willingness to share information was virtually non-existent (Coleman and MacLeod 1986:601; Kindleberger 2000:147). Britain's host of small-scale businesses took pride in producing a variety of goods totally lacking in standardization. Whereas Britain earlier had initiated technical change and diffusion, it now let others invent, without emulating these inventions or adapting them to British conditions (Phillips 1989:395). Early British success had convinced industrialists that educational or scientific backing was not needed. And while German firms staffed huge R & D laboratories with chemists and engineers, British firms were only reluctantly hiring university graduates. It was a widespread belief of the age that Britain had grown complacent and tired, locked in old technologies, without the will or ability to reform (Hoppen 1998:308; Landes 1969:337; Murmann 2003:176).

The above suggests that this was not just a demand problem. British industry lived largely off its German experts, and experienced ever greater problems when these started leaving. There were voices in Britain warning that foreign manufacturers were much more willing than Britain to employ chemically educated personnel in order to come up with new processes and improve upon the existing ones, and that this would be the undoing of the British industry (Donnelly 1986:208p; Murmann and Landau 1998:37). Thus, while some of the problems may be ascribed to demand issues, some to the lack of government-funded R & D, and some to a more conservative outlook on the part of businesses, it is evident that the absence of highly skilled British chemists was a huge problem, and a growing one at that. As the industry became more resource-intensive and required ever larger investments in physical equipment, this deficiency became ever more serious.

This became a vicious circle, whereby small domestic demand for organic chemists meant no incentive for British universities in setting up programs in organic chemistry. Thus, progressive firms could not find British chemists of the required quality, and instead had to hire from abroad. This led to British firms losing market

---

24 Still, Berghoff and Möller (1994:282) conclude that there were far more convergences than discrepancies between English and German businessmen. But they also show that almost twice as many German as British businessmen had studied at technical and commercial colleges (24 vs. 13 per cent). The figure probably underestimates the discrepancy regarding the chemical industry as this was a highly research-intensive sector with a disproportionate amount of highly educated experts.

share, and further diminished their ability to lobby for reforms in the British education system. Like German firms, British firms interacted with academic institutions for advice and recruitment. The Society of Chemical Industry was formed in 1881 among other things in order to facilitate exactly such interactions. But because the British university system was so inferior to the German, British firms could not draw even nearly as much help and expertise from the universities that German firms could from theirs (Murmann 2003:57, 176).

While the state should not take all the blame, it clearly could have done more. However, it seems appropriate to portion out the blame among several actors, recognizing that the interactions between them were of a kind that was not conducive to continuous success. Both government and industry persisted with the old system of patronage, personal connections and the networks of scientific societies (Murmann 2003; Perkin 1969:70). But new industries like chemicals required greater involvement by the state. An observation by Landes (1969:347) may serve as illustration: In the eighteenth century, foreign observers to Britain had noted that recruitment happened largely through talent. There was social equality to the acquisition of knowledge, and social mobility was, for its day and age, great. A century later, this is exactly the same observation made by British observers visiting Germany at a time when this seemed to be less true of Britain.

The German system both encompassed solid funding of a university system that already emphasized technical education and close connections between science and industry. However, since German chemists went to Britain in large numbers, to take up employment in the British industry, it is hard to say to what extent the early growth of *German* chemicals drew on education. This did not change until the growth in German textiles in the 1860s–1870s led to increased demand for chemists in the coal-tar dye industry. At the same time, it is also true that in Germany there was a larger number of start-up firms than in other countries, which suggests that chemical firms in Germany could more easily than elsewhere gain access to qualified personnel. The larger number of German chemists made for a larger number of start-ups (Freeman and Soete 1999:89; Keck 1993:122; Murmann and Landau 1998:37; Rosenberg 1998:208p).

If the industry did not need chemists, it is probably true that human capital initially had limited effects. It was important, but in a sense that resembled the British model, namely through chemist-entrepreneurs who started their own firms, bridging the gap between theory and practice through their own personal knowledge. A firm like Bayer built laboratories as early as the 1860s, but these were small and poorly equipped, with a very limited amount of chemists employed. The relationship between science and industry changed, but primarily from the 1880s onward. Up until then, chemical formulae were not familiar, the constitutions of most dyestuffs unknown, financial risks incalculable, and the general idea that systematic research could yield commercially important dyestuffs not yet very strong. Before industrial research could become important, academic research needed to provide the necessary theoretical preconditions for successful R & D. As this happened, the relationship between different actors—government, academia, industry—grew close. R & D laboratories retained close links with university-based research. The industry supplied universities with materials, equipment and with students, whereas universities offered trained graduates, prospects for scientific cooperation and consulting work (Chandler, Hikino and Mowery 1998:433; McClellan and Dorn 1999:311p; Meyer-Thurow 1982:364pp; Murmann and Landau 1998:40; Schulze 1998:183).

It is still partly true that the R & D laboratories sprang out of a feeling that universities did not respond to the needs of industry. The first R & D laboratory was set up in the late 1870s, and before the end of the 1880s, all major German manufacturers had their own in-house laboratory with permanently employed academically trained chemists. Also, from the mid-1880s, the chemical industry started sponsoring reform at German universities and technical universities because of its dissatisfaction with German chemical education. Consequently, the academic curriculum was reshaped to reflect the demands of the chemical industry. Furthermore, the industry formed alliances with German academics to form special research institutes (with government funding and support). Also the government stepped in by subsidizing R & D laboratories and by sponsoring industry research institutes. Thus, in 1887, the Imperial Institute for Physics and Technology was created, and 1911–1914 saw the foundation of the Kaiser Wilhelm Institute for Chemistry, the Kaiser Wilhelm Institute for Physical Chemistry and the Kaiser Wilhelm Institute for Coal Research (Lenoir 1998:25; Meyer-Thurow 1982:376; Murmann and Homburg 2001:199; Murmann and Landau 1998:38pp).

Still, as late as the 1870s–1880s, the relationship between university and industry was strained, with polytechnics considered inferior from a university point of view, and with universities concerned with theoretical science, not its application. Thus, for a while the German system was characterized by strife between universities and polytechnics, and at times with the industry, which perceived the universities as too theoretical (Keck 1993:120). Tensions between academia and industry petered out, as the barriers to technical education decreased, and by the late nineteenth century, connections between universities, technical universities and industry were close— the result of an acute awareness of the importance of academic science for industry, and of the importance of industry to the German state. The increase in chemists employed was exponential between 1880 and 1900, and firms now primarily recruited from the universities. Connections were formed with academic research chemists and formalized through contracts, newly graduated Ph.D.s were given one-year assignments in the industry, and then sent to university or technical university laboratories working on projects relevant to the firm. By the late nineteenth century the knowledge flow between universities and technical universities was better than anywhere else, as were the flows between the universities and industry. Professors taught at both universities and technical universities, and took on consultancy work for industrial firms, often moving back and forth between academia and industry

(Horstmeyer 1998:246; Keck 1993:120pp; Lenoir 1998:25; Meyer-Thurow 1982:368pp; Murmann 2003:5p; Rosenberg 1998:209).[25]

Even if the process of technical innovation was often less than linear, links between science and industry were strong. It is absolutely implausible that the progress eventually made in chemicals could have been achieved *without* the ever more solid theoretical foundation provided by the best higher education sector in the world. That the early phase of the German chemical industry did not owe much to the education system does not mean that it was not crucial later on. From the 1880s, higher education was crucial, as universities received greater funding, as the industry hired more chemists, and as further progress was ever more linked to a combination of theoretical understanding and technological progress. And from the 1880s, cooperation between the higher education and industry research grew much stronger. As a consequence, the German dyestuffs sector expanded enormously, and developed a complete lock on the market.

Human capital was clearly important for the growth of the chemical industry. A lagging British education system with only a weak and belated emphasis on primary education failed to produce a large pool of people for higher education to provide any strong impetus to a science-based industry like chemicals. Britain slowly caught up, but too late to have any impact on the chemical industry, as the race was already well and truly lost. Previous industries had been scientifically relatively simple. This had suited Britain well. Now, Britain fell behind, witnessed among other things by its thirst for German chemists. That Britain had been ahead in the early phase of the chemical industry was largely due to demand from its textile industry and the large influx of German chemists. Hence, Germany held a clear human capital advantage. But Germany produced far more experts than its industry could employ. There was little use for them in Germany, and thus they had to seek employment elsewhere. This suggests that in addition to the Schumpeterian story, there is also room for Smithian elements, at least during the early phase. Then again, the far larger number of dyestuffs start-ups in Germany than in Britain suggests that the wealth of German chemical talent did have a very tangible effect on the German industry. And once German dyestuffs started expanding, the industry actively (and successfully) lobbied for an academic system that could churn out even larger numbers of organic chemists. But Germany also benefited from an education system that was the best in Europe— producing the largest number as well as the most skilled chemists in the world. By the mid- to late nineteenth century, the German state(s) was funding science ever more generously, and the system vastly outperformed Britain with respect to the amount of students it produced. Moreover, during the late nineteenth century, the government's receptiveness toward the needs of the industry, and the relationship

---

25 As always a note of caution is appropriate: The status and prestige of research scientists remained ambiguous. Research was a dead-end career, as all the outlets for promotion were in management. Thus, most scientists that worked in the industry went into production, not research (Meyer-Thurow 1982:379)!

between industry and science, improved. Not only did the sciences receive very generous funding, but R & D facilities within chemical firms were in part funded by the state.

Patenting

Among the most important prerequisities for technological progress is a well-developed system of intellectual property rights protection. In this area Britain was far ahead, with a patent law dating all the way back to 1624. Germany did not have a patent law until 1877 (Mokyr 1990:247). Advantage Britain? However, patenting systems of earlier years were often highly imperfect, and this affected the chemical industry more than other industries, because of the knowledge-intensiveness of chemical industry compared to traditional industries. The patent systems that had benefited Britain in the past turned into an institutional rigidity with respect to chemicals. The new industrial context was one in which distinguishing between *product* and *process* became crucial The British system was unable to do this. Hence, paradoxically, Germany benefited from *not* having a patenting system.[26] When a patenting system was finally established, the German state accommodated the needs of chemicals by inserting a special clause, following lobbying activity by the dye industry. This enabled Germany to extend its lead dramatically. The British patenting system coped well with the interests of old, established industries like textiles, to the detriment of chemicals. The German system favored chemicals.

One of the problems of the old British patent law was uncertainty about what a patent really covered. Did it cover the rights to produce one specific color? Did it provide the rights to the process used to produce that color? How broadly did it extend? Since the 1852 patent law had not foreseen developments in future industries like chemicals, no consensus existed as to what constituted a valid dye patent. When Perkin filed for a patent for aniline purple, numerous other British firms emerged, exploiting essentially the same techniques. Between 1861 and 1865 this resulted in extensive litigation over which firms had the rights to produce what colors. Entry into the industry was severely restricted as a consequence of several synthetic dyes being under patent protection.[27] The firm Maule, Simpson and Spiller managed to obtain a patent for the color magenta, thereby forcing other magenta producing firms out of business by way of law. Workable rules for the interpretation of patenting rules in the chemical industry were not in place until 1865, when this patent was declared void. However, by this time, British firms were already losing out to

---

26 That is, 29 of the 39 German states had patent laws of some sort, but Prussia gave out patents very rarely due to an anti-patent bureaucracy, and an 1842 article in the Zollverein forbade members of the Zollverein to *prevent* other German states from selling a product in all member states. For all practical purposes, no patent protection existed for the entire nation (Murmann 2003:87).

27 Murmann and Homburg's (2001:188) data make it very clear that the entry rate into the industry was much lower in Britain than in Germany.

German competition. German firms, not subject to any patent law, as none existed, had learnt how to produce magenta far more cheaply, and were now flooding the British market. During the early years of the industry, British firms spent more time in the court than they did coming up with novel processes and practices! The patent system gave Germany a head-start from day one (Murmann 2003:87pp; Murmann and Landau 1998:41).[28]

One of the demands of the British chemical industry was the insertion of a patent clause mandating patent holders to operate their patents from within Britain within four years of the patent being issued. This was countered by interests outside of the chemical industry, particularly from traders, who would lose business if foreign production would have to be moved to Britain. In 1883, this clause was actually inserted into British patent law, but it was viewed as unenforceable. The wording was so vague that German dye firms continued to hold the overwhelming majority of British patents, while manufacturing everything in Germany. Not until 1907 did the chemical industry get a patent law that required the patentee to work his patent from British soil.[29] Two years later, the law was watered down again (Murmann 2003:187pp).

Instead of favoring chemicals, the British patenting system was strongly biased toward capital-intensive activities, like textile machinery and steam engines. Whereas other patenting systems favored technical novelties, the British system favored those that had enough money to make something of their ideas, as applying for a patent was very expensive (Khan and Sokoloff 1998:294pp; MacLeod 1992:288). While the chemical industry eventually developed into a high-value, capital-intensive industry (although in Germany rather than in Britain), it most certainly was not so from the outset.

The lack of a German patent law meant that German firms could borrow and steal, freely copying British ideas for production in the domestic German market, while its competition abroad was embroiled in costly and time-consuming litigation. The lack of entry-barriers created enormous competition. Not only did huge amounts of firms enter the market, but the ones that survived had to develop skills unbeknownst to sheltered British firms. Since Britain *did* offer patent protection, German firms could patent their products there, thereby locking out the competition from the British domestic markets, without Germany providing the same rights to British firms in Germany. When court litigation ended in Britain, Germany was ready to patent a wide range of products in Britain, preventing British firms from establishing a viable national industry (Horstmeyer 1998:239; Murmann and Homburg 2001:194pp;

---

28 Murmann (2003:87) quotes Aitken: "A British patent conveyed little more than the right to bring suit. When claims to property rights came into conflict, the courts would decide." Only the courts could decide whether a patent was valid or not, not the patent office. The consequence was that any patent dispute would involve a drawn-out and costly legal process. In Germany, only the patent office could rule a patent invalid (ibid.).

29 Although the predictable result was that now, German dyefirms would instead set up plants in Britain, and thus outcompete the British dyestuffs industry from inside Britain instead of from the outside (Murmann 2003:190)!

Wehler 1985:32). Quoting Murmann (2003:29): "Had the German patent law arrived in 1858, it is doubtful that as many German firms would have developed into such strong competitors. Fewer firms would have entered into the industry and efficient firms would have been more likely to survive, as was the case in Britain". The German industry got its patent law at a time when German firms were finished imitating and had started innovating. They now needed a patent law preventing other countries from doing exactly what they had done!

Hence, with respect to the timing, Germany got lucky. In 1877, when the patent system arrived, it proved highly advantageous. By now, German firms were ahead. Hence, patent protection against the copying by other countries was necessary. The chemical industry was actually split over the idea of a nationwide patenting system, and was not a driving force behind the process. After all, things had worked pretty well so far. But when the dye industry, through the German Chemical Society, finally did decide to get involved, it managed to secure for itself what was an absolutely crucial clause.[30] The clause applied to chemicals, pharmaceuticals, and food products and for these specific industries allowed *process patents only*, not product patents. In other words, it made it impossible to patent something along the lines of "the color red", but at the same time gave German firms the incentive to invest in different and ever more advanced processes by which to come up with new and different dyes. Thus, the patent law also entailed an incentive for more intense scientific research (Freeman and Soete 1999:90; Kindleberger 2000:127; Murmann 2003:91; Murmann and Homburg 2001:199).[31]

Because of the lack of patent protection, the early years of the German industry had seen underinvestment in R & D. With patent protection, the institutional arrangements necessary for Germany to take advantage of its superior human capital potential was in place, resulting in an increase in the amount of chemists hired by German companies. None of the intra-firm industrial research laboratories that Germany became so famous for, were set up before a patenting system was in place, but within ten years of the patenting system, all major German dyestuffs firms had their own R & D laboratories. The laboratory strategy enabled German firms to "carpet patent" large amounts of dyes, for practical purposes preempting foreign firms from entering the industry. Also, lobbying efforts were made in order to prevent entry for foreign firms. Swiss firms typically copied patented German dyes, and then marketed these same dyestuffs on the German market. In 1891, a successful lobbying effort by the German industry meant that from now on, in patent infringement suits, the burden of proof was reversed, so that if a German firm accused a Swiss firm of infringing, the Swiss firm would have to prove that it produced the dye using a different process (Chandler, Hikino and Mowery 1998:433; Horstmeyer

---

30 BASF actually actively helped formulate the new patent law (Freeman and Soete 1999:90).

31 The German Chemical Society also managed to make parliament include a provision saying that the patent office need to seek expert advice at every stage of the patent process. One of the four experts appointed was Hofmann (Murmann 2003:183).

1998:239; Murmann 2003:89, 184; Murmann and Homburg 2001:199; Murmann and Landau 1998:42).

The timing of the German patenting system was fortuitous. German firms could free-ride on foreign patenting systems that were not well adapted to a modern knowledge-intensive industry. When Germany finally got its patenting system, it differed from the British system by explicitly taking heed of the special needs of chemicals. Upon lobbying from the dyestuffs industry, the German parliament allowed for an exception in the patenting system that provided incentives to the industry rather than stifling it. The outcome was a system that enabled German dyestuffs to benefit further from its human capital advantage, and to strengthen an industry that already controlled 75 per cent of the market. True, Germany might have outperformed the British dye industry even without a patent system, but, as Murmann (2003:179) asserts: "… without patents in Germany and in other large dye markets, the German dye industry would not have been able to acquire a virtual monopoly."

Tariffs (and War)

Tariffs probably played some part in the rise of German chemicals, but were far less important than patents and schooling. Still, the pattern is the same as for the other sections; the old industries were far stronger in Britain, leading to a lack of recognition of the interests of new industries like chemicals. While tariffs were not used to any great extent in Germany, the chemical industry was influential enough to get the regulations that it wanted, whereas in Britain, it was ignored. Instead, the textile industry, not really requiring protection and without much further growth potential, was able to use the state to block changes to tariff policy.

By 1860, Britain had undergone a full transformation from protectionism to free trade (Bairoch 1993:22; Chang 2002:23p). However, as Britain stayed with free trade, the rest of the world was shifting toward protectionism. During the 1870s, British exports to Europe and the US declined. The British chemical industry preferred tariffs. However, the textile industry, which wanted access to cheap and high-quality German dyes, lobbied heavily for free trade. As it was about 100 times bigger than the dyestuffs industry, dyestuffs did not stand much of a chance. They were also lobbied against by dyers and colorists (Murmann 2003:193). Protectionist voices arose in the 1880s, but on the whole, no strong British protectionist movement existed until the early twentieth century (Bairoch 1993:27; Brose 1998:81). Hence, no tariff was imposed until far too late. Instead, Britain suffered from the tariffs of other countries. The German Zollverein had admitted Britain's most favored nation status in 1865, and the British soda industry, which at the time was the world's largest, had subsequently taken over a large share of the German market. However, British inorganic alkalis suffered when Germany, following recession and lobbying from soda manufacturers, put tariffs on soda in 1879, and raising them in 1882. British alkali exports to the US, which had been its largest export-market, came to an almost complete halt, when the US in 1897 raised its duties on soda ash, caustic and bicarbonate soda by 50 per cent, and placed a tariff on bleaching powder (Eichengreen 1998:272; Horstmeyer 1998:239; Murmann and Landau 1998:42).[32] However, quantitative evidence suggests that the industry's reluctance to shift away from the obsolete Leblanc process and toward the more modern Solvay and contact processes was more important (Krause and Puffert 2000).

Tariff policies essentially remained unaltered, and changes were not implemented until, and because of, World War I. Hence, when protectionism arrived, it did so for political and military reasons, not economic. The state took control of the chemical industry and reorganized it, so as to enable it to supply the chemical compounds needed for waging war. The high degree of wartime government intervention set the stage for a more active role for the state post-war, and the scarcity of dyes convinced the government of the necessity to establish a national dyestuffs industry. Hence, Britain finally introduced tariffs during the interwar years (Eichengreen 1998:277; Murmann and Landau 1998:44pp).

It is common to think of German industrialization as having taken place behind a veil of tariffs. However, Germany was never very protectionist. More important than tariffs was the 1833 erection of a German Zollverein (customs union) that abandoned internal tariffs between German states. Generally, external tariffs were low, although for political and not economic reasons. Prussia sought to become the leading German power, by wresting the hegemony away from Austria, which had historically been the dominant power. To achieve this, Austria was refused entry into the Zollverein by external tariffs set so low that the traditionally protectionist power would not see fit to join. Even though certain tariffs were raised, as on iron (1844) and cotton yarn (1846), tariffs were still moderate. Primarily for reasons of shutting out Austria, German tariffs were kept low until the 1870s, despite strong competition from British imports (Cameron and Neal 2003:239; Chang 2002:32p; Kindleberger 2000:118p, 131; Wehler 1985:19). Hence, in the period leading up to the breakthrough of the chemical industry, tariffs played no part in German industrial success.

It is also the case that despite raising tariffs after the German unification, this did not primarily affect the chemical industry. There had been moderate duties on imported chemicals during the years of the Zollverein, but the 1865 treaty with Britain removed these. Tariffs were enacted among other goods, on soda in 1879,[33] and raised in 1882. The 1878 elections brought a protectionist majority to the Reichstag, establishing a grand conservative coalition between the landed elite, peasants, industrialists, military, and higher civil servants, primarily over iron and rye. However, no tariffs were enacted on dyestuffs. The dye industry was internationally competitive, and had more to lose from retaliation against German tariffs than it had to gain from tariffs. Thus, after lobbying from dyestuffs, dyes and intermediates

---

32 The 1897 Dingley tariff resulted in total British soda exports falling from 312,400 to 188,500 tons (Landes 1969:273).

33 These tariffs were still lower than in for instance the US, France and Russia (Eichengreen 1998:270).

were excluded from the general tariffs enacted in 1879 and 1882. However, tariffs did provide some temporary help for the considerably more fragile soda industry, as it regained control of the German home market. During the 1880s, alkali imports fell to zero. Still, most of this advantage had to do with the decline in local raw material prices[34] and the adoption of the Solvay process (Krause and Puffert 2000). Yet, the flagship of the German chemical industry was the far more sophisticated organic chemicals sector, in particular dyestuffs. Here, no protection was necessary (Bairoch 1993:24; Eichengreen 1998:270p; Fulbrook 1992:132; Horstmeyer 1998:239, 249; Murmann and Landau 1998:42). To the extent that the tariff argument has validity, it is primarily because it shows how the dyestuffs industry faced a state that was willing to listen to the needs of the industry and to make exceptions for it, unlike in Britain.

Vested Interests, Political Consensus, and Social Cohesion

Britain: Vested Interests Firmly Blocking Structural Change   Politically, Britain was calm and stable. The mid-Victorian period ushered in economic growth and social stability. Problems of national identity were long resolved, Ireland being the only problem. No strong class consciousness existed. Strikes were few and unsuccessful. Organized workers favored radical Liberalism rather than revolutionary movements. The middle class was healthy. All classes took part in economic growth and no particular class seemed to dominate (Colley 1992:12pp; Landes 1998:219; Pugh 1999:71pp, 103). True, there were seeds of a revolutionary working-class movement, and urbanization and industrialization did put strains on British society, but these were fairly minor problems.

In 1867, as electoral reform took place, following an economic slump that led to discontent and to people flooding onto the streets, it was the Conservative Party that promoted the franchise extension.[35] This could be done because the working class was no longer considered revolutionary. In fact, the Conservatives felt that what they needed to do was to appeal to the lower classes in order to regain political initiative. Hence, from the 1860s, the Conservative Party mixed a distinctly imperial, patriotic and increasingly racial rhetoric with arguments about protecting private property and the lower and middle classes against heartless laissez-faire liberalism. The ideological justification for this was that a true conservative party was a party where the ruling elites showed compassion and responsibility for those less fortunate (Hobsbawm 1969:126; Pugh 1999:98pp; Thompson 1999:27p). Further reform

---

34 Because of supply shortages, during the 1870s German soda production faced far higher input prices than the British soda industry (Krause and Puffert 2000:288).

35 A very cautious bill was in 1866 proposed by the Liberal party under William Gladstone, for practical purposes extending the franchise by some 100,000 people. It was turned down, resulting in a minority Conservative government by Benjamin Disraeli the following year pushing through a bill increasing the electorate from 1.3 to 2.45 million, or roughly 30 per cent of all male adults.

followed, with the Secret Ballot introduced in 1872 and the 1885 Third Reform Act (also promoted by a Conservative cabinet) extending the franchise to 5.7 million, or roughly 60 per cent of all adult males (Hobsbawm 1969:126; Pugh 1999:98pp; Thompson 1999:27p). With exception for the decade leading up to World War I, social cohesion was on the rise, and politics reflected the fact that the ruling class was fairly homogeneous. The leadership of both Liberals and Conservatives consisted of aristocrats with industrial and financial connections, all with the same classical education from Oxford or Cambridge.

At the same time, the ability of British decision-makers to resist vested interests had declined markedly compared to only a few decades earlier. The preceding half century had been marked by a struggle between agricultural and industrial interests. By the time of the rise of the chemical industry, cotton textiles controlled the state.

Mancur Olson's insight that over time vested interests will grow powerful and resist change, leading to rigidities and economic stagnation is highly relevant for the chemical industry. Resistance by vested industries against technological change and new industries goes a long way toward explaining the failure of Britain and the success of Germany. One of the areas where the German chemical industry stood out was in its ability to affect important government decisions. To a large extent, this relationship between the industry and the state explains the German success. The German chemical industry did not have to fight strong vested interests, and was better able to extract resources from the state than the industries of Britain. German firms successfully engaged in collective action to shape tariffs, patent laws and university policies. In comparison, in Britain there was little or no interest in supporting new and upcoming industry. Instead, different vested interests had fought a long battle over the dominance of the state apparatus and were not about to let new interests interfere.

There was already a huge British infrastructure in support of the natural dye industry. In India, 2,800 British indigo firms had sunk huge investments in indigo plantations. These firms considered synthetic dyes a threat rather than an opportunity, and would go on to create considerable obstacles and inertia with respect to developing institutions supporting the synthetic dye industry. In Germany, institutions could be built from scratch, as no natural dye industry existed. The other powerful vested interest was cotton textiles. Unlike in Germany, the British chemical industry had no clear, unified voice, and no presence in Parliament. Consequently, lobbying by the British dye industry fell on deaf ears. While a cotton textile industry existed in Germany as well, it was not particularly strong. Here, lobbying proved highly effective.

> In the battles between the domestic dye industry and domestic textile industry, the power equation in Britain and the U.S. was always heavily tilted toward the textile firms, and as a result textile firms typically obtained tariff regimes they favored. In Germany—where the textile industry was not nearly as large as in Britain or the U.S. when the synthetic dye industry appeared on the scene—the dye industry was able to achieve tariff regimes that were in its favor. (Murmann and Homburg 2001:201)

Britain's patent laws favored the old industries. High patenting fees ensured that patenting favored capital over invention (Khan and Sokoloff 1998:298pp). With the chemical industry, the patenting system led to firms at a crucial stage of the industry being embroiled in years of complex litigation rather than expanding abroad and spending on R & D, as it did not distinguish between process and product patents. In contrast, when the German patenting system arrived in 1877, it benefited the chemical industry, as through lobbying, the dyestuffs industry managed to acquire for itself an exception, so that only processes, and not final products could be patented.

The German dye industry could get the patent law that it wanted. Britain could not. And where British firms failed to speak with one voice, German manufacturers ironed out their differences within the Chemical Industry Association. In Britain, the lack of prestigious and skilled experts and the presence of a powerful textile industry went together with a lack of organization in the chemical industry to make for an industry unable to credibly push for an adequate patent system. When the new patent law finally went through, the wording had been made so vague that foreign (German) patentees for all practical purposes could keep doing what they had already been doing—preempt the British industry by "carpet patenting". When in 1907 the British chemical industry succeed in changing the patenting system in the favored direction, two years later British courts watered the law down, again leaving British chemicals with a patent system it had *not* wanted (Murmann 2003:187pp).

British education policies catered to the needs of the old industries, where formal schooling was less important. On-the-job training had been the prevailing method of providing skills, and only half-hearted measures were taken in order to reform the education system. Compulsory elementary education came very late, not until 1870, as aristocratic interests torpedoed reform, failing to grasp its importance. First they could not see why it mattered. After all, during previous waves of industrialization, it had not. Second, they were afraid of the consequences of awakening the masses. Education might lead to revolt or even revolution. Third, it would cost massive amounts of money.[36] Even if this could be raised locally, there were all sorts of hurdles, as for practical purposes the local initiative to Parliament had to come from local landed interests (as a high minimum property ownership was required to have any local vote). Thus, the British education system was dependent more or less solely on the central government or on wholly private funding. Finally, aristocratic interests consistently considered technology to be beneath the universities. Scientific pursuit was a noble and gentlemanly activity, not something with the aim of benefiting industry, and not something that should be pursued full-time as a profession. Moreover, there was no real pressure for education reform from industrialists, the working classes or the Liberal Party either. The Liberal Party, including PM Gladstone, wavered,

---

36 Indeed, the result of the 1870 Elementary Education Act was a rapid increase in expenditure on education, from £1.6 million in 1870 to £5.1 million in 1885, or from 4.1 to 8.6 per cent of government expenditures. Local spending rose from £2.2 million in 1875 to £3.2 million in 1885. Add what was spent locally in Scotland and Ireland, and the 1885 figure is very close to what was spent on the Royal Navy (Hoppen 1998:600)!

among other things very hesitantly forcing reform on Oxford and Cambridge. This is surprising, considering how Gladstone was personally convinced that German success during the Franco-Prussian war at least in part was a fruit of the German education system (Evans 1983:324; Hobsbawm 1962:30; Hoppen 1998:597pp; Landes 1969:344p; 1998:290; Lindert 2001; 2003:330; Mokyr 1990:199).

However, British governments also enjoyed a lack of autonomy because of the need to balance against religious interests. These were important, as much of the elementary education had been previously been taken care of by different churches. The Anglicans of the Church of England opposed the spending of tax money on secular elementary education altogether, but primarily what complicated things, was that the Church of England and the Nonconformists were both largely Liberals, and that the Liberal Party thus had to satisfy very divergent religious interests in order to provide support for reform.[37] Hence, any reform bill had to be cautious (and for cost reasons, cheap). The bill that eventually passed managed to provoke both Anglicans and Nonconformists.[38] Anglicans disliked it for its godlessness. Nonconformists greatly resented the fact that Anglican schools would still receive state funding (Hoppen 1998:598p; Lindert 2003:330; Pugh 1999:101).

Conservative and religious opposition did not yield until after the Third Reform Act (1884–1885) again extended the franchise. But even as late as 1902, religion was a problem. The 1902 Education Act, promoted by the Conservative–Liberal Unionist Cabinet of Arthur Balfour, placed all elementary schools under county and town control, with the purpose of ensuring a minimum amount of standardization. While this improved elementary education, it again provoked Nonconformists, as it implied tax money for Anglican and Roman Catholic schools (Gilbert and Large 2002:46; Judd 1996:189; Lindert 2001). No overarching political consensus existed, and because of previous economic success, more so than elsewhere, in Britain it was difficult to forcefully make the point that changes were necessary. Hence, education reform could relatively easily be blocked, as Britain fell behind in terms of human capital. Its chemical industry would suffer dearly as a result.

Within tariffs, Britain had committed itself to free trade, and stubbornly stuck with this. Industries like cotton textiles, long competitive, lobbied hard for free trade. Cotton textiles blocking tariffs for chemicals for all practical purposes amounted to old vested interests preventing new industries from rising (Chang 2002:38; Horstmeyer 1998:235). After the Corn Law repeal, free trade had more or less become British official doctrine. The Conservatives made a few futile attempts at re-introducing tariffs, but in a remarkably short time, protectionism became synonymous with political suicide. Protectionism was associated with high food prices, starvation and the selfish interests of the aristocracy. The major new groups to receive voting rights

---

37 Other interests that had to be placated were those of the newly founded (1869) National Education Union (pro-religion, favoring the original system) and the National Education League (secular and pro-universal).

38 Which became obvious when the Liberals lost a lot of Nonconformist votes in an 1874 by-elections (Hoppen 1998:599).

in 1867 were strongly pro-free trade. A strong alliance reigned between Liberals and the organized working class, supported by most of the manufacturing industry (Hobsbawm 1969:120; Judd 1996:58pp, 65; Pugh 1999:101). At large, socialist organizations were weak, as can be said for the trade unions, whose membership numbers actually *decreased*, down to 750,000 in 1888 (from around a million in 1874), or 15 per cent of manual workers, despite the fact that union membership did not suffer any legal repression. Most workers enthusiastically supported free trade (Evans 1983:351; Gilbert and Large 2002:39; Hobsbawm 1969:238; Hoppen 1998:649; Pugh 1999; 123pp).

As Britain's industrial power waned, one might have expected protectionism to become a contested domestic issues. Conservative MP Benjamin Disraeli (PM 1868, 1874–1880) had raised the issue as early as 1872. Also, a Fair Trade League arose in the 1880s, advocating retaliatory tariffs against foreign protectionism. However, trade did not become a hot topic until the very end of the century, when it was obvious that Britain was struggling, and when even the traditional industries were having a hard time. MP and Cabinet member for the Liberal Unionists, Joseph Chamberlain, made the abandonment of free trade his number one issue in 1903, tearing the Unionist–Conservative government apart, and leading to his own resignation that same year. Chamberlain also succeeded in making free trade the major issue in the 1906 election, with the Conservatives and Liberal Unionists supporting reform. But even as late as in 1906, tariff reform was not a winner. The Liberals scored a landslide win, for practical purposes postponing any notion of tariff reform into an indefinite future (Judd 1996:150, 187pp; Klug 2001:221; Pugh 1999:115, 145). While different groups of the electorate voted largely according to their own economic interests, Klug (2001:238) shows that there was also a large constant of pro-trade sentiment among occupational groups for which no pattern should be expected. In other words, the "neutrals", with no strong economic interest for or against, considered free trade a good thing.

In other words, for political rather than economic reasons, the tariff issue could and would not be raised. A combination of strong anti-protectionist sentiment amongst the voters and the political dominance of the pro-free trade Liberal Party made any tariff increases impossible. The Conservatives could have raised the issue, but chose not to, as it would have been political ruin. This can be clearly seen in their political strategies.

By the 1860s, British politics was centering around a fairly radical Liberal party under the leadership of William Gladstone.[39] The Conservatives, under Disraeli, had only to a very moderate extent managed to adjust to mass politics and had been out of power for 20 years. Extending the franchise would only worsen this, unless something drastic was done. Hence, the Conservative Party consciously sought to win the vote of the lower classes by casting itself as the party of traditional values, benevolent paternalism and protection against brutal laissez-faire. Against a radical

---

39 Taking over the mantle from Lord Palmerston, who had headed Liberal cabinets in 1855–1858 and 1859–1865 (Pugh 1999:96).

Liberal Party, the Conservatives put up a staunch defense of private property, and as the century progressed, against radicalism, Irish nationalism and socialism. They also courted the trade unions, and they rejected the puritanism and asceticism of the Liberals with respect to among other things alcohol. Above all, it became the party of patriotism, of Imperial ambition and pride, and of British superiority. While this did not bring the Conservatives back in power immediately, in 1874, with a far larger franchise, Disraeli could form a Conservative cabinet that lasted until 1880. From 1886, under the leadership of Lord Salisbury,[40] the Conservative Party would go on to dominate British politics for 20 years, even through a third franchise extension in 1884–1885, granting more than 60 per cent of the male population the right to vote (Hoppen 1998:645; Pugh 1999:98pp; Thompson 1999:27p).

1886 signaled a shift in British politics. Previous decades had been decades of domestic politics; free trade, peace, retrenchment and reform. But defending traditional causes like the Union with Ireland, the monarchy, the Empire, the Church of England, religious education and private property had brought the Conservatives significant amounts of voters. Thus, the following decades would be dominated by fears of external threats—colonial rivalry, naval race, the fear of invasion. Conservatives actively pushed domestic issues off the agenda, pushing foreign policy, and staying away from thorny issues like free trade and schooling. Both Gladstone and Salisbury were deeply reluctant over colonial issues. Still, the increased enthusiasm shown for the Empire by ordinary citizens was striking, and late nineteenth-century British politics would to a great extent focus on Imperial triumphs and fiascoes, as on the prospect for new colonies, rather than free trade and protectionism (Hoppen 1998:649; Pugh 1999:107pp, 129pp).

While this seems to indicate a healthy level of cohesion in the British population, after the turn of the century, Britain experienced problems on an ever larger scale. From now and until World War I, wages stagnated or even fell.[41] Harmony, stability and prosperity gave way to uneasiness and tension. This went together with stronger unions (membership increased to 1.9 million in 1900, and 4.1 million in 1914 (Pugh 1999:125)), labor unrest, strikes, the radicalization of the socialist left and general political breakdown. The number of strikes increased from 300–400 a year in 1902–1906 to 800–900 in 1911–1914, Britain no longer being more peaceful than other European countries. When World War I arrived, it was met almost with relief, as a respite from crisis (Gilbert and Large 2002:41; Hobsbawm 1969:193; Perkin 1969:173; Pugh 1999:127, 147; Shorter and Tilly 1974:309).

> ... they were the only years when the stable and flexible mechanism of British political adjustment ceased to function, and when the naked bones of power emerged from the

---

40 Lord Salisbury led three Conservative governments: 1885–1886, 1886–1892, and 1895–1902.

41 The period prior to the downturn had seen the so-called Great Depression. However, impoverishment of British workers was *not* one of the consequences—counterintuitively, the last quarter of the nineteenth century was the period in which the situation of British workers improved the most rapidly (in particular 1880–1895).

accumulations of tissue which normally concealed them. These were the years when the Lords defied the Commons, when an extreme right, not merely ultra-conservative but nationalist, vitriolic, demagogic and anti-Semitic, looked like emerging into the open, when scandals of financial corruption racked governments, when—most serious of all— army officers with the backing of the Conservative Party mutinied against laws passed by Parliament. They were the years when wisps of violence hung in the English air ... (Hobsbawm 1969:193)

For most of the period British politics was calm and stable, certainly compared to what had been the case in the 1830s and 1840s. And with the exception of short spells, and notably immediately preceding World War I, social cohesion also seems to have been at an altogether higher level than during the 1830s and 1840s. How then do we explain the failure of the chemical industry? Yet, even if politics was stable, it was close to impossible for British governments to actively pursue industrial policies, even when it became clear that British industry was falling visibly behind. While British society was cohesive in the sense that there was no impending threat of revolution, franchise extensions also meant that going against the grain of popular opinion would lead to electoral defeat. The Conservatives, otherwise sympathetic toward policies of protectionism, de-emphasized domestic politics and focused on foreign politics instead. The Liberals were not interested in industrial policies in the first place, supporting the free trade interests of traditional manufacturing industries like cotton textiles. Hence, to the extent that cohesion and consensus surrounded British politics, it was cohesion and consensus about the wrong policies, about policies of status quo rather than change! As British industries grew weaker, the interest and ability of politicians to push through reform weakened. To this should be added the inability of the British chemical industry to speak with one voice, also having no one to speak for it in Parliament (Horstmeyer 1998:235), as well as the fact that it had a much less powerful social network than the German industry, and consequently faced much bigger problems with respect to lobbying and collective action in general (Murmann 2003:7p). This was a political environment that found it exceedingly difficult to make decisions that went against the status quo. The necessary political consensus for industrial policies that would have increased the chances of new industries to flourish never stood much of a chance of rising.

Germany: No Strong Established Vested Interests   In contrast to Britain, Germany provided its chemical industry with the world's best education system, for its day generously funded by the government, and with an orientation much more toward the technical than in other countries. When the industry was still not happy, lobbying prompted government funding of R & D laboratories, as well as facilities and resources for the training of chemists. Through business–government cooperation, even industry research institutes were set up, and experts went back and forth between universities, technical universities and the chemical industry (Keck 1993:120pp; Murmann and Homburg 2001:199; Schulze 1998:183).

However, for the 1860s, which was the formative period for the new chemical industry, the Prussian state (no Germany existed yet) was for all practical purposes too weak to take any strong economic action. The same government inefficiencies that made economic interventionism impossible in Britain—where chemicals failed—plagued Prussia, too.

Hence, in one sense, crediting the state with the rise of the German chemical industry seems dubious. But the fact is that German states never faced similar problems with religion and education as did Britain. No such vested interest constraints hindered the development of primary or higher education. Instead, the education impulse had been extra-systemic. Napoleon in 1806 routing Prussian troops at Jena had had a profound effect on Prussia (and on other German states). Elitist and conservative Junkers would generally loathe the idea of mass schooling. However, they had been resoundingly beaten, and so, policy-making of potentially great importance to technological and industrial progress was pursued not for economic reasons, but for the purpose of preventing future military defeat. A window of opportunity arose in which broad political consensus existed with respect to modernizing the funding and administration of education. Much of the control was transferred to local authorities. Thus, education flourished where demand was strong, whereas in the eastern parts of rural Prussia—the core Junker area—considerably less was spent than in the more developed west.[42] It implied an education system that was flexible and responsive to local demand, and a system robust against the arbitrary intrusion from conservative backlashes of the Prussian state. In higher education, the state was more active, again partly stemming from the fear of military defeat. But as mentioned before, the fragmented structure of the German Confederation also introduced an element of competition. Various sovereign German states used the sponsoring of higher education in order to challenge for future German leadership. Baden and Saxony both directly sponsored chemistry research. To smaller states that could otherwise not compete, this was a way of stimulating future growth. Hence, prior to the unification, nearly every German university had at least one small institute of chemistry (Kindleberger 2000:122; Landes 1969; Lenoir 1998:23p; Lindert 2001; 2003:332p).

With tariffs, unlike Britain, when the soda industry lobbied for a tariff (with numerous other industries, it should be admitted), it got it. However, as the tariff was enacted, the dyestuffs industry simultaneously lobbied for an exception, as it was already competitive. Thus, what is significant is not that a tariff was enacted *per se*, but that on the behest of one specific group, an exception was made for this group.

Prior to the Napoleonic Wars, roughly 300 separate German principalities had all had the right to levy tolls.[43] Following the wars, a loose German Confederation was set up, with the number of states reduced to 39. Attempts at creating a German

---

42 In 1876, on average, the Prussian state only accounted for 8.9 per cent of the budgets of public primary schools, as opposed to 72.8 per cent being raised through local taxes (Lindert 2001).

43 Resulting in 1,800 customs frontiers and 30 customs houses on the Strasbourg–Dutch frontier alone (Kindleberger 2000:113p).

state followed the uprisings in 1848–1849 failed, but a German Confederation and a National Parliament was set up in Frankfurt, although without the power to pursue economic policies, including imposing or collecting taxes. Military power rested solely on the member states, for all practical purposes Prussia and Austria. The Confederation continued to exist until 1866, but was impotent, with no practical policy-making power (Fulbrook 1992:117; Horstmeyer 1998:243; Kindleberger 2000:113; Tipton 2003:52, 90).

A parallel and more effective power structure had existed since 1818, when Prussia abolished tariff differences between town and country. Other German states joined Prussia in what effectively became a North German customs union dominated by Prussia. Prussia resisted persistent pressure from industry for higher tariffs. In fact, this probably held early German industrialization back, despite the 1840s and 1850s otherwise routinely being considered the take-off years of German industry. Early German chemical industry found it hard to compete with British imports, as duties on imported chemicals were low. However, prior to the unification, complaints from industrialists that low tariffs were hurting them against competition from abroad, were not taken seriously. When the German chemical industry eventually rose, this was not because of tariffs. Prussia (and subsequently Germany) remained wedded to low tariffs until the mid-1870s. As with education policies, it is conspicuous that decisions about economic policies were routinely not taken from any desire to promote infant industries, but for foreign policy reasons. In Prussia, tariff policies of the early to mid-nineteenth century were not about economics. Obviously, it helped that Prussia was land abundant, exporting grain, with powerful Junker landowners both being pro-trade and in control of the Prussian Landtag. Thus, the issue of tariffs was not much of a battle, as it united the landed aristocracy and the workers. However, the low external tariff set by Prussia for the Zollverein was set for the purely political goal of preventing Austria from joining (Eichengreen 1998:270; Fulbrook 1992:114p; Greenfeld 2001:209; Kindleberger 2000:118p, 131; Rogowski 1989:39; Tipton 2003:117).[44]

On a purely economic level, the exuberance of the unification gave way to the Great Depression, with major recession lasting from 1873 to 1880. The reaction to the crisis was a conservative one, as established industries cried out for protection. As industrialists were becoming increasingly influential, and as American grain producers were now undercutting Junker grain prices, an alliance between the landed aristocracy and heavy industrialists (primarily iron and steel manufacturers) formed—the so-called marriage of iron and rye. This resulted in a series of tariff increases. However, infant industry arguments were never part of the discourse surrounding these tariffs. This was not the German administration consciously boosting vulnerable, but prosperous industries like chemicals. Rather, the tariffs

---

44 Prussia signed a most favored nation treaty with France in 1861–1862. This made the Austro-Prussian commercial treaty of 1853 giving preferential status to Austrian goods null and void. Prussia knew this full well, and subsequently did its best to reject Austrian attempts at finding a solution (Tipton 2003:117).

reflected a Germany that was in the pockets of industrialists and Junkers, either incapable or unwilling (Bismarck himself was a Junker, and proud of it) to pursue independent policies. Bismarck had pursued free trade more by habit than by conviction, and now began cooperating with the protectionists in the belief that this would enable him to raise more money independently of the Reichstag, as well as release him from his dependence on the National Liberals. Elections in 1877 and 1878 greatly increased the representation of conservative parties, and made this possible.[45] While the elections have been interpreted as the voters choosing between free trade and protectionism, it should not be forgotten that Emperor Wilhelm in 1878 suffered two assassination attempts. This increased the support for the conservatives.[46] The assassination attempts came as a welcome opportunity for Bismarck to dissolve the Reichstag. He could now blow off the National Liberals, and forge alliances elsewhere (Fulbrook 1992:132; Klug 2001:225; Rogowski 1989:39p; Stürmer 2002:39; Tipton 2003:175; Trebilcock 1981:84).

The first powerful lobbying organizations were founded in the 1870s, all in favor of protective tariffs: Langnamverein (1871), Verein Deutscher Eisen- und Stahlindustrieller (1874), Centralverband deutscher Industrieller (CdI) (1876). The CdI, founded by the iron and steel concerns, rapidly came to embrace most of German industry (cotton, linen and woolen manufacturers, iron and steel). The close relationship between interest groups and the government—in particular the Ministerium für Handel und Gewerbe—gave large firms a powerful position with respect to influencing tariff rates. Iron and steel drew advantage from this in its campaign for protective tariffs in 1878–1879. However, what is curious in this respect is that the chemical industry was *not* interested. This was in part because it depended on imported raw materials, and did not want tariffs on these, but also because dyestuffs was already competitive. The main concern of this industry was to avoid retaliatory tariffs by other countries. Hence, in 1895, chemical and textile firms formed their own organization, the *Bund der Industriellen* (BdI)—free trade and a counterweight to the CdI (Born 1976:19, 31; Klug 2001:224; Webb 1980:313; Wehler 1985:83pp).

The tariff had little to do with promoting growth, and was all about protecting vested interests. For the economy at large, it is doubtful that it was of much benefit. The dye industry violently opposed it. Alkalis were not competitive and were in favor. Hence, to the extent that tariff policies were beneficial, they were so because dyestuffs, following strong lobbying action, was given an exemption from the general tariff regime. The alkali industry benefited, resulting in German soda manufacturers gaining a foothold in Britain, and reducing alkali imports from abroad to virtually

---

45 In the 1877 election, the Conservative Party increased its representation from 22 to 40. The National Liberals lost—down from 155 to 128 seats. Still, the liberal and pro-free trade majority was such that Bismarck's attempted tariff legislation did not go through in 1878, but had to wait until 1879 (Klug 2001:225; Tipton 2003:163).

46 Conservative parties boosted their representation from 78 to 116, with the National Liberals losing 29 seats to 99.

zero by the 1880s. Unlike in Britain, where established industries were far stronger than in Germany, no great conflict of interest existed in Germany. This made it easier for the chemical industry to find support in the government, and it made it possible for chemicals to get the exemption. This was also made easier by the fact that the German chemical industry could rely on a much stronger industrial and academic network—including the state—than in the industrially atomistic Britain. Hence, collective action on the part of the chemical industry was far more successful in German. Still, the tariffs of 1879–1887 were intended for the already established industries, not for infant industry protection (Eichengreen 1998:270; Murmann 2003:5pp; Murmann and Landau 1998:42; Trebilcock 1981:84).

A similar pattern can be discerned with respect to patenting. When German industries began pushing for a patenting system, what is conspicuous is how the interests of the chemical industry were taken into consideration, even though these were different from much of the rest of German industry. In this area, the chemical industry was highly vocal. Lobbying groups like the Verband deutscher Ingenieure (VdI)[47] was instrumental in convincing the Reichstag to enact a patent law. The dye industry managed to obtain a special clause for chemicals, pharmaceuticals and food products through a united lobbying effort. The clause allowed only *process*, as opposed to *product* patents, and hence encouraged a research focus with German firms by refusing them the opportunity to file large and vague patents for specific colors, and instead only allowed patents for the chemical process by which such colors could be created. The firm BASF was even involved in the actual formulation of the new law. On this point, it is worth noting how education policies, patenting policies and the lack of vested interests blocking dyestuffs all came together. The education system made it far easier for the German industry to make itself heard. German dyestuffs could forge alliances with a vast number of expert scientists and engineers with the ability to back it up. Moreover, the state bureaucracy was manned by highly educated people and to a much greater extent than in Britain, conducive to the needs of industry (Freeman and Soete 1999:90; Murmann 2003:187; Murmann and Homburg 2001:199; Murmann and Landau 1998:42).

Unlike Britain, rather than being blocked, the chemical industry enjoyed easy access both to the bureaucracy and to politicians. While Bismarck himself was not particularly interested in the economy, the bureaucracy was filled with experts supportive of science and industry. Murmann (2003:167) attributes particular significance to Friedrich Althoff, who between 1882 and 1907 was the bureaucrat who handled all appointments at Prussian universities and technical universities, and whose beliefs that scientific and technological research and education was essential for future growth and prosperity made him an invaluable ally to the dye industry whenever it lobbied to expand educational facilities. The relationship between Althoff and the Verein deutscher Chemiker was close and long-lasting. The dye industry also had excellent access to the Prussian Landtag. One of the directors of

---

47   Where Heinrich Caro, the chief chemist at BASF, was one of the founding members (Freeman and Soete 1999:89).

Bayer, Henry Böttinger, had a seat in the Landtag and used this to fight for higher education spending and for the dye industry in general. He was also a close friend of both the Prussian finance minister and Althoff, and could easily coordinate initiatives with key players in the Prussian government.

Thus, the German state (and prior to unification, Prussia) did not suffer the same constraints as Britain regarding education and tariffs. However, in both areas, policies that turned out to be beneficial to industrial growth were implemented for military rather than economic reasons. Furthermore, it is not obvious that these policies stemmed from any ability of the state to use political consensus to counter vested interests. On the contrary, the German state was not particularly strong, and German nineteenth-century history was characterized by far more turmoil than that of Britain.

When in 1862 the new Prussian regent, Wilhelm, appointed Bismarck Prussian Minister-President, he faced a very hostile Landtag. Bismarck started his relationship with the Landtag by making his famous blood and iron speech, but the Landtag was neither amused nor impressed. Thus, he did not waste time on the assembly, now delaring that this was a matter, not of constitutional rights, but of power! The authoritarian structure of the ruling apparatus made him invulnerable as long as he had the confidence of the king. However, politics became ever more complicated as the Liberals won the 1863 election, and for several years, the Landtag refused even to approve a budget. Instead, Bismarck was saved by a succession of foreign policy crises (1863 Schleswig-Holstein, 1866 Austria, 1870–1871 France).[48] Victory made him popular and allowed him some leverage in policy-making after 1866.[49] However, for large parts of the 1860s, the Prussian state was in crisis, not even with a proper budget. Perkin invented mauve in 1856 and Verguin aniline red in 1858–

---

48 Prussia went to war *with* Austria *against* Denmark in 1863, resulting in the occupation of Holstein. The next year, Schleswig was invaded, and Schleswig-Holstein put under Prussian and Austrian administration respectively. Friction over the administration of Holstein gave Bismarck an opportunity to attack Austria. In 1866, Austria attempted to use the German Confederation against Prussia for violating federal territory in Holstein. Thus Prussia declared the Federal constitution violated, and the Confederation to have come to an end. In the ensuing war, Prussia won, even if most German states sided with Austria. Consequently, Prussia annexed Schleswig-Holstein as well as territories from the German states that had allied against it. The German Confederation fragmented, and in its place, Prussia overwhelmingly dominated a newly founded North German Confederation. The Franco-Prussian war—the proximate cause in creating the German Empire—came when Bismarck exploited a disagreement with France over Spain. Prussian troops routed France, and annexed Alsace and Lorraine. The 1871 peace treaty with France simultaneously created the German Empire, where the southern German states that had not been part of the North German Confederation, but allied with Prussia against France, joined the new federal Empire. The Prussian king was crowned Emperor of Germany (Fulbrook 1992:128p; Schulze 1998:136p; Tipton 2003:118pp).

49 Bismarck in 1866 "apologized" to the Landtag by admitting that taxes had been collected illegally, and asked it to approve it retroactively—which it duly did (Tipton 2003:123).

1859. During these first years of the modern chemical industry, Prussia was in limbo, the state not being a positive factor (Kindleberger 2000:132; Schulze 1998:136p; Tipton 2003:119pp).

While Bismarck was skillful in manufacturing temporary alliances in the Landtag, and later the German Reichstag, it is fairly obvious that much of his political maneuvering was essentially that: Maneuvering! He had no intention of relying for support on any one party. Without any legal provisions he had seen to it that he as Minister-President of Prussia would also became German Chancellor after the unification. Hence, if he encountered resistance in the Prussian Landtag, he could get around it by repeating the process at the national level. He had insisted on male suffrage for both the North German Bundestag and the German Reichstag, as he was confident that the masses would be on his side. When this turned out not to be true, he very seriously considered a *coup d'état*. He was not ideologically opposed to modernization, industrialization and the demands of industry. But also, he had no commitment to it. Bismarck's commitment was to himself, to the Junkers and to the Kaiser. His success consisted of striking a precarious balance between powerful social forces, seeking to preserve some sort of a status quo, while the social and political consequences of industrialization at the same time became ever more evident.

His reaction to the 1873 recession reflects the fact that he had a hard time holding the country together. In the Reichstag, he was allied to the National Liberals. However, high on the liberal agenda was the so-called *Kulturkampf*, for practical purposes an anti-Catholic crusade.[50] This led to laws against religious (read: Catholic) influence on education (1871–1872), and the breaking off of diplomatic relations with the Vatican (1872).[51] Hence, from the mid-1870s onwards, the Catholic Center Party comprised a hostile and resentful permanent minority of around 20 per cent of the seats in the Reichstag (Schulze 1998:160p; Tipton 2003:164p). After 1878, Bismarck instead allied with the conservative parties to pass the anti-Socialist Laws, banning organizations supporting "activities designed to subvert the existing political and social order in ways that threaten the public order and particularly the harmony of the social classes" (Tipton 2003:167). He tried to counter the growing socialist influence by implementing social insurance legislation in the 1880s (Born 1976:28; Fulbrook 1992:134; Klug 2001:225; Schulze 1998:163pp; Tipton 2003:167pp; Wehler

---

50 In 1871, Bismarck dissolved the Catholic section of the Prussian Ministry of Ecclesiastical and Educational Affairs, and in 1872 the Prussian Landtag produced legislation abolishing supervision of schools by clerics (for all practical purposes implying Catholic school inspectors). It went so far that discussion of matters of state by clerics "in a manner endangering the public peace" was deemed a criminal offense. However, unlike Britain, at this stage Germany already had an education system widely held to be the best in the world. Hence, the Kulturkampf did not present a problem with respect to education policies (Tipton 2003:164).

51 The first steps to reestablish relations did not take place until Leo XIII became Pope in 1878 (Tipton 2003:169).

1985:132).[52] However, the combination of socialist parties growing in strength and influence and the ascendancy of a new and more hostile Kaiser (Wilhelm II), meant too many interests to balance. In 1890, he was retired by the Kaiser. While this does not deny the fact that Bismarck was successful in preserving for himself a certain amount of independence, it is indicative of a Germany where Bismarck's political survival consistently depended on his ability to strike a precarious balance between often wildly diverging interests. Bismarck never cared to build political consensus or formal political alliances. As the socialists rose in popularity, the lack of political consensus became ever more obvious (Rogowski 1989:40; Tipton 2003:159pp; Wehler 1985:57pp).

The post-Bismarck period (the Wilhelmine era) saw tensions rise further. Generally, chancellors were weak, their power resting on short-lived compromises and alliances. Pressure groups became ever more important. In order to counter socialism, the Kaiser and his nearest circle of government pursued the so-called Weltpolitik. While the shift in policy undoubtedly reflected the Emperor's personal preferences and delusions of grandeur, it was also a deliberate attempt to draw attention away from social unrest, an ever more powerful Social Democratic Party, and a growing working class.[53] It worked in part, but primarily by winning over the anti-aristocratic forces of the bourgeoisie.[54] The middle classes identified themselves with the nation and took pride in adventurous foreign policies. It proved a partial success even with the working classes, although several authors argue that the contradictions and tensions in the German Empire could only keep growing, and that the main reason why no revolution occurred, was because World War I came to the rescue. This reveals some of the problems that German chancellors faced. It was not only the matter of securing political majorities in the Reichstag, but the whole empire rested on weak social foundations. In order to engender social cohesion and take the focus off domestic problems, foreign policy diversions had to be manufactured. Still, by this time, Germany had become the industrial leader of Europe, surpassing Britain. The only power that could check it in industrial terms, was the US (Fulbrook 1992:117, 140pp; Greenfeld 2001:154, 218; Rogowski 1989:40; Schulze 1998:118pp, 173pp; Stürmer 2002:45; Tipton 2003:90, 159pp; 186; Wehler 1985:57pp, 89p, 102pp, 137, 177).

There were a number of differences between Germany and Britain. In Germany, dyestuffs did not find itself blocked by vested interests like textiles and agriculture.

---

52 Bismarck and Germany pioneered this kind of legislation: Sickness insurance legislation (1883), accident insurance (1884), and old age and disability insurance (1889) (Fulbrook 1992:134).

53 The popularity of the socialists kept rising after the 1890 abolition of the anti-Socialist Laws—from 1.4 million votes in 1890 to 4.2 million in 1912. With this went union growth from 680,000 members in 1900 to 2.5 million in 1913.

54 Wilhelm II was never more popular than when in 1896 he (stupidly …) defied Britain and sent a congratulatory telegram to the newly elected Boer president Paul Kruger of Transvaal in southern Africa, after Kruger's forces had defeated an invasion attempt by British raiders in Rhodesia (Pakenham 1991:490; Tipton 2003:246).

Instead, chemicals in general, and dyestuffs in particular, was able to speak with one voice. Within dyestuffs in particular, the industry–academia–government network was large and close-knit, giving the industry a much greater chance to succeed with collective action than was the case elsewhere. But as we have seen, for considerable periods of time, organizations lobbied a weak state, caught up in shifting alliances of day-to-day politics in a country where modernization and industrialization made stable government a challenge. Hence, the reason why tariffs and patent policies went in favor of the chemical industry was not that the government exploited any wealth of social cohesion to pursue potentially unpopular decisions going against major vested interests. Neither was it because of any strong political consensus about the direction of German industrial policies. Rather, the government catered to vested interests, including the lobbying efforts by the dyestuffs industry. This also applied to patents. Patent laws in other countries did not distinguish between product and process innovations. In Germany, institutional rigidities like an old patenting system did not put constraints on new industries, and the patent law that was created in 1877 took account of the process vs. product distinction emphasized by a united chemical industry.

With respect to education, German success was also *not* primarily a result of economic foresight. Rather, it was a reaction to military defeat. Policies beneficial to technology and industry were the side effect of military concerns. Still, German governments spent far more money on education, and took a more activist approach to knowledge diffusion than Britain. And it continued to spend more money, in particular on higher education, with a syllabus that was more practical and relevant to industry than in Britain. Problems with the Catholic Church were relatively minor compared to other countries. It also had a bureaucracy favorably predisposed toward both education and industry. Still, at least some of the success of the German state in terms of promoting industry and technology stemmed, not from conscious efforts by the state, but from military concerns.[55]

Conclusions

The chemical industry, dyestuffs in particular, was the world's first truly science-based industry. For the first time, success was intrinsically connected with the ability to systematically pursue scientific research, and to apply the subsequent results

---

55 One area of government intervention that has not been mentioned, but which often figures among the explanations for German rise, is a banking system more willing and able to finance capital-intensive industries like chemicals. In particular, a contrast has been made with British banks, which were more unwilling to provide capital for long-term risky operations (e.g. Horstmeyer 1998:239; Tilly 1999; Eichengreen 1998). However, while banking may have considerable leverage with respect to German industrialization in general, it makes less sense for the chemical industry. This is somewhat surprising as the chemical industry was fairly capital-intensive. Yet, it did not depend on capital from banks, instead preferring to finance its operations from within (Tilly 1986:128; Trebilcock 1981:96).

of this research. The methods of the first Industrial Revolution, of tinkering and experimenting by skillful, practical men without much formal training, did no longer suffice. Hence, human capital was crucial. Britain found itself seriously short of skilled chemists. Brilliant individuals still came up with the odd breakthrough, but by the 1880s, the industry had progressed to a level of sophistication that required more than just individual brilliance. From the 1880s, Germany very clearly benefited both from its superior higher education system and from the fact that the links between the education system and the chemical industry was far stronger than in Britain. The development of industrial research laboratories, pioneered by German firms, and supported by the government, is but one example of the much closer links between knowledge and industry, growing out of the needs of this era.

However, prior to the 1880s, there had been a surplus of chemists in the German chemical industry, to such an extent that the early prowess of British chemicals owed much to a surplus of German chemists traveling across the Channel to find employment elsewhere. Hence, while knowledge was undoubtedly important, during the early years demand problems were as great as supply problems. The industry had to mature before it could make good use of scientific expertise. Hence, the contribution of higher education to the early phase of the German chemical industry may well have been scant, even if from the 1880s, it consolidated and extended the advantage that Germany had already. Thus, the most developed market economy with the largest domestic market of the day—Britain—was able to absorb more chemists than Germany. That the British chemical industry to a large part depended on German experts is a clear indication that even in this early phase, human capital was key.

Two other areas of state intervention were patent systems and tariffs. Within patents, the German success was somewhat fortuitous. Normally, a patenting system should be an advantage, and this should have benefited Britain. However, the chemical industry brought new demands to the patenting systems. Hence, Germany, *without* a patent law did *not* suffer the institutional constraints provided by an obsolete system. During the early years of the chemical industry, Britain saw endless patent litigation, as the system could not cope. Was a patent simply to be given to the synthetic production of the color red? During this period, German firms could copy and imitate, not themselves constrained by similar laws. When in 1877 a German patent law finally arrived, it took account of the special needs of the chemical industry by including a distinction between product and process patents. Instead of excessively broad patents, like in Britain, only *process* patents were allowed, giving the industry a strong incentive for large-scale research in different production methods. The patent law thus contributed to the research-intensiveness of the German dyestuffs industry, further extending the German lead.

With tariffs, the evidence is more ambiguous. Britain was committed to free trade at the time of German take off in chemicals. Vested interests, primarily in cotton textiles and agriculture, made industrial protection virtually impossible. Infant industry arguments were not heard, and the British chemical industry had no unified voice with which it could gain access to the ruling elites. Thus, vested interests managed to control the state for its own purposes. When tariffs arrived, it was too late, and when they were introduced, they were not introduced as infant industry protection, but because vested interests had changed their minds. They were tariffs that strove to protect stagnant established industries, and that sought to prevent structural change rather than promote it. Tariffs from both Germany and the US were successful in shutting out British exports from these two very important markets for British industry, and in both instances, Britain declined to respond by imposing retaliatory tariffs of its own.

However, the tariff argument is problematic for the main reason that the German chemical industry rose to prominence virtually without protection. The tariffs of the Zollverein had been low for the political reason of shutting Austria out, and until 1878, free trade was the name of the German game, not protectionism. When protectionism arrived, it was only moderate, and more importantly, the dyestuffs industry went against it. Inorganic chemicals benefited somewhat from tariffs, shutting out British exports, but the success of the (organic) dyestuffs industry was one of being able to lobby the German Reichstag for an exemption from the overall tariff, which it was duly given. As German dyestuffs were already competitive, their primary priority was one of preventing retaliatory tariffs from other countries, not one of seeking tariffs for itself.

In Britain, major constraints prevented governments from pursuing industrial policies independently of strong vested interests. There were constraints against reforming the education system, both because of religious opposition and because landowning aristocratic elites did not see universal primary education as beneficial, and at worst as a potential threat. The symbolic importance of free trade, as well as the fact that strong industrial interests were heavily in favor of it, made raising the tariff issue political suicide. Hence, a lack of both consensus and cohesion deprived British governments of the opportunity to go against these vested interests.

The German situation was more complex. Success did not arrive from strong, enlightened and independent government decision-making favoring infant industry over old vested interests. Rather, the German state played along with vested interests. Success had to do with the chemical industry being strong and well-enough organized to lobby alongside other interest groups, and with traditional industries being weaker than in Britain, thus being less able to block the chemical industry than in Britain. The strength of German chemicals is linked with a system of higher education that was vastly better than in Britain in terms of the amount of people that graduated and with respect to the relevance of the education. It took time for the German system to adapt to the skill needs of industry, but the link between education and industry was always much closer than elsewhere.

The consequence of German chemicals being able to push its collective interests through was a patenting system adapted to the needs of chemicals, and exemptions from the overall tariff regulations. However, education reforms took place as a response to Prussian military losses during the Napoleonic Wars. Hence, as in other areas, reforms were routinely carried out not for economic, but for *political* benefits. Junkers would support education reform in order to avoid another military defeat, even if they would otherwise have opposed it. Thus, part of Germany's success was the side effect of a militaristic take on politics. With respect to tariffs and patents, Bismarck's economic policies had more to do with manipulating the surroundings in order to stay in power, than with any strong desire to industrialize. He shifted from free trade to protectionism, not from economic conviction, but because of a perceived need for new political allies in the Reichstag. Industrialization, a rapidly more popular Socialist party, and a growing working class, made Bismarck's balancing act ever more difficult. The success of German chemicals thus was one of being strong enough to prevent vested interests from going against it, and not one of the state being strong enough to resist these same interests. Both consensus and cohesion were low for much of the period.

The chemical industry neatly illustrates how difficult it was for new and fragile, but potentially prosperous industries to make their interests heard against the might of old and established vested interests. It illustrates how it is very possible for countries that are industrially ahead to get stuck in patterns that make structural change difficult. It illustrates how old institutional structures and vested interests can create formidable obstacles to change, and how change can be delayed for decades because a lack of political consensus removes any leverage a government might have with respect to making such decisions. However, the chemical industry also makes it clear that success sometimes come about in peculiar ways. Some of the reasons for success were fortuitous, and some of the German economic policies were more about politics than economics. The chemical industry did benefit from government policies, but not from a conscious attempt to protect it on the expense of established industries. The German government was receptive to the needs and demands of its chemical industry and much more so than the British government. Therein lies its greatest contribution to the success of the German chemical industry.

Chapter 5

The Automobile Industry

Introduction: The Dawn of Mass Production

The twentieth century saw the US move toward industrial supremacy. US population was growing rapidly—without impeding economic growth. Within the first decade of the twentieth century, the US surpassed Britain in terms of GDP per capita, and was even further ahead in terms of wages. World War I accentuated this, as European countries ravaged by war, struggled to rebuild. Before the war, the US had been a debtor, now it was a creditor. For the major European economies, the opposite was true. They were now debtor economies, crying out for US investment. Demand for consumption goods was far higher in the US than in Europe, and the US was the first economy to become one of both mass production and mass consumption. The US was number one, not only in car manufacturing, but in most consumer durables.

However, the world economy was stagnating as the old and mature industries were growing ever more slowly. At no time did this become more obvious than during the Depression. Germany produced less steel in 1930 than in 1910, Britain less than in 1920. Total world steel production in 1936 was just marginally above what it had been in 1918. World iron production was lower in 1936 than in 1914. Coal and brown coal production had been unchanged for three decades, and cotton consumption had stagnated (Freeman and Louçã 2001:266; Modelski and Thompson 1996:101). Yet, there were new industries ready to take over as engines of the world economy. And while the Depression was a time of crisis, it also symbolized the end of the old and the rise to economic predominance of the new. There was rapid growth in new industries like petrol, aluminum and nitrogen. But more commonly, we know this as the era of mass production, symbolized first and foremost by the growth of the automobile industry.

While the automobile industry is an obvious choice, it also entails a few problems. This book looks at economic growth stemming from technological progress, but an automobile is not in itself a technology. What were the groundbreaking technologies going into manufacturing cars? This chapter primarily focuses on the interwar years. By that time, the car was no longer technologically revolutionary. True, the combustion engine was, but it was invented all the way back in the early 1860s, when the Otto engine was conceived, with the first car produced in 1886. Yet, at that stage, the car was a curiosity, based more on craftswork by skilled artisans and technicians than being an actual high-technology industry. Its impact on economic growth was marginal.

By the interwar years, the automobile industry had become economically more influential, although not rapidly so. What changed the nature of car production was Henry Ford's mass manufacturing of Model Ts, with the 1913–1914 changeover to complete assembly line mass production. Mass manufacturing was what made the industry economically influential. The Model T itself was crude and unsophisticated, with virtually any other car on offer qualitatively superior. And so, the technology which revolutionized contemporary industry was not a product technology, but a *process* technology, namely the technology of mass production.

Furthermore, not only was this revolution carried out producing distinctly low-tech cars. Also, mass production technologies took the skill content out of the workplace. Where product technologies normally imply a higher skill base, new process technology allowed the company to produce the same goods using labor with *less* human capital. Car production now became about performing simple assembly line operations as fast and efficiently as possible. These were not technologies that one would need a doctorate in physics to comprehend. They were technologies that led to revolutionary change without themselves being revolutionary.[1] Also, they were not without historical precedent. The idea of producing a great number of similar products by using interchangeable parts and routinized processes goes back at least to the American Civil War, maybe even the Napoleonic Wars, the notion of standardized parts even further.

Why the interwar years? The major inventions and breakthroughs constituting what we think of as a "car", were made in the nineteenth century, but by the early twentieth century, car manufacturing was still peripheral. All the early inventions were made in Europe, with the US a relative latecomer. But only decades into the twentieth century, more than 90 per cent of the world's automobiles were produced in North America (Modelski and Thompson 1996:102; Ruttan 2001:437). European cars remained technologically superior, strongly suggesting that the advantage provided to Europe from being the first-mover and from being technological superior, were minor compared to the advantages from producing at a more efficient scale. Hence, the late nineteenth century cannot be the proper starting point.

If the focus were on growth *per se*, and not on the rise of a specific industry, the postwar era may have made more sense. Europe was economically broken following World War I, and mass production failed to have the impact that it had in the US until after World War II. However, the mass production revolution was an American one, and it began during the interwar years. In 1900, the US automobile industry was classified under "miscellaneous" industries by the US Census Bureau. By 1925, it was ranked first by value added. In 1929, the industry accounted for 12.7 per cent

---

1   This obviously does not imply that there was no product improvement in the automobile industry. Product improvements were at times extremely rapid, which is an important reason for the rapid growth of the industry. However, at the same time, diffusion has been extremely rapid. It has not regularly been the case that car manufacturers have been able to sustain prolonged and persistent technological advantages. Rather, success has been contingent on bringing a decent product to the market as cheaply and efficiently as possible.

of US manufacturing output, and General Motors had become the third largest US industrial corporation (by the end of World War II second only behind Standard Oil) (Atack and Passell 1994:578; Ferguson 1984:71; Mowery and Rosenberg 1998:49p; Parrish 1994:40). Hence, mass production was having an impact on the US economy at least as early as the 1920s.

Why the automobile industry? The more generic a technology is, the bigger its impact on the overall economy. In a literal sense the car industry is not generic, but it did have effects akin to the generic. It provided new demand for the production of raw materials such as steel.[2] It was the most important purchaser of rubber, plate glass, machine tools, nickel, lead and petroleum products (e.g. Kurth 1979:27; Leuchtenburg 1993:186 [1958]; Miller 2003:174). And it triggered large-scale infrastructure investments from the federal government for roads, telegraphs, telephone lines, and other public utilities. Accompanying this was a rapid expansion of service and supply centers and of oil refining (Freeman and Loucã 2001:261). This created jobs for people working on these projects, but also had effects on the overall economy by lowering transportation costs, improving the ease of communication, increasing the size of markets, increasing mobility, etc. Also, the combination of cars, refrigerators and supermarkets greatly enhanced the productivity of retailing. In a decade, car manufacture created one and a half million jobs, and was directly or indirectly responsible for the employment of four million people (Krugman 1994:60p; Miller 2003:174; Moss 1995:138).

Moreover, car manufacturing has had one crucially important complementarity of permanent nature—with the oil industry. Without technological breakthroughs in oil drilling and refining, the car industry would have had to look for alternative fuels.[3] Without car manufacturing, oil companies would have lost much of their demand.

Hence, the generic technology in question is not car manufacturing, but mass production. The carrier industry is not cars, but consumer durables. In 1920, eight per cent of all US families owned washing machines, nine per cent a vacuum cleaner. By 1960, the corresponding figures were 73 per cent for either item. Hence, the mass production era can just as well be thought of as the mass *consumption* era. Automobile production is an obvious choice because it was so conspicuous, because car manufacturers grew to become economic giants, employing vast numbers of people, and probably also because symbolically it represents so much—independence, wealth, happiness.

The four other industry chapters compare one successful country with one that was not. In this chapter it is easy to pick the winner—the US. It is far more difficult to pick a loser. It was not the case that one country moved ahead and stayed there because of an advantage that no other country could compete with. Rather, this is a case of delayed European development rather than failure. Technologically, Europe was never behind. Once Europe embraced mass production, catch-up was immediate. By 1960, Western Europe's share of world automobile production was almost 40 per cent. Even a

---

2   By the mid-1920s, 30 per cent of US steel went into car manufacture (Kurth 1979:27).

3   World crude oil production increased from three million barrels in 1862 to 2.1 *billion* barrels in 1939 and 22.6 billion barrels by 1991 (Freeman and Loucã 2001:281).

latecomer like Japan could catch up almost overnight, going from 0.3 per cent of world production in 1950 to 40 per cent in 1980 (Freeman and Louçã 2001:279; Modelski and Thompson 1996:102). While this is half a century away from the interwar years, it suggests that diffusion was fast, that monopoly benefits were hard to reap, and that when dominance is not linked to a science advantage, manufacturers in other countries can become competitive fairly quickly.

Hence, this chapter looks exclusively at the US, only adding illustrative evidence from other countries. But what we know with considerable certainty is that the US was ahead of other countries not just in terms of mass production. Comparing TFP growth rates suggests that the US was moving ahead of other countries. For the period 1913–1950, US TFP growth rates were an impressive 1.99 per cent. (This is even more than for 1950–1973 (1.85 per cent) and further indication that the interwar years is the right focus.) Of the major industrial powers, France came closest, at 1.42 per cent, with Britain (1.15 per cent) and Germany (0.87 per cent) languishing behind (Dow 199:82). In Sachs and Larrain (1993:558), TFP growth is considered to have contributed to more than 80 per cent of overall growth between 1929 and 1948.[4]

Growth rates and labor productivity figures (see Table 5.1 and Table 5.2 below) support this. Where other powers experienced a slowdown, US labor productivity growth improved between 1913 and 1950. Overall growth slowed in both Europe and the US, but US figures declined from a much higher level, and remained far higher than in Europe, where growth would not increase until the postwar diffusion of mass production.

Table 5.1 Average Annual Labor Productivity Growth Rates (GDP per man-hour)

	1870–1913	1913–1950	1950–1960	1960–1970	1970–1980
US	2.1	2.5	2.4	2.4	1.5
Germany*	1.9	1.2	6.6	5.2	3.6
Great Britain	1.1	1.5	2.3	3.2	2.4
France	1.8	1.7	4.3	5.1	3.8
Japan	1.8	1.4	5.7	9.6	4.3

Source: Freeman and Louçã (2001:297).
*   Figures for West Germany from 1945 onwards. The same goes for all other tables unless specified otherwise.

---

4   The figures are not undisputed, and broken down into its different components, the residual instead stands at only 40 per cent of total growth (Sachs and Larrain 1993:558). Yet, even this most conservative figure reveals a very handsome improvement over previous decades. Atack and Passell (1994:19) value technological progress (that is, the residual) for 1840–1860 at 15 per cent of overall growth, rising to 27 per cent for the period 1870–1930.

Table 5.2 Average Annual Growth Rates of GDP (%)

	1870–1913	1913–1950	1950–1960	1960–1970	1970–1980
US	4.1	2.8	3.2	3.2	2.9
Germany	2.8	1.3	8.1	4.8	2.8
Great Britain	1.9	1.3	2.7	2.7	1.8
France	1.7	1.0	4.7	5.6	3.5
Japan	2.5	1.8	8.6	10.3	4.7

Source: Freeman and Louçã (2001:297).

There were a number of reasons for US preeminence in mass production. One thing that distinguishes this time period from the others is the importance of Smithian growth. US dominance was very much a consequence of demand factors. The relatively wealthy working class made it economically conceivable to build something along the lines of a people's car in the first place. Also, finance and management skills were important, as automobile companies grew to become economic giants. Human capital was of relatively less importance than for most other industries. Rather, the primary role played by the state came through the construction of infrastructure. Here, the federal government took on a more active role than European governments which, impoverished after World War I, had no resolve or ability to do the same. The chapter also shows that vested interests were a problem: The Republican pro-industry tariff coalition, dominant since the Civil War, was coming under pressure from industry itself. This was because tariffs benefited labor-intensive industries instead of the rapidly growing capital-intensive industries (like car manufacturing). Labor-intensive industry needed tariffs because of high US worker wages. This was less of a problem in the capital-intensive industries, which preferred free trade. However, it took until the 1930s before capital-intensive industry finally won this battle, which is somewhat late for it to have much explanatory power with respect to the rise of the car industry. Thus, we are left with an account of the car industry that emphasizes Smithian rather than Schumpeterian growth.

Considering that this is a book about Schumpeterian growth, it may seem ironic that the period with the strongest and geographically most widespread growth (at least when we include the years following 1945 in Western Europe and Japan) came about through fairly unsophisticated technologies and through Smithian growth. On the other hand, if the new technologies are not very sophisticated, easily replicated by other countries, it should not be surprising if the majority of growth is Smithian since Smithian growth is about the expansion of markets rather than technological progress.

History

Early Years

Europe dominated the early years of car manufacturing. The first engine-driven vehicle was probably the French engineer Nicholas Cugnot's steam-powered wagon in 1769. In parallel with steam locomotives, huge steam-powered diligences were produced in limited numbers. The culmination of these was Frenchman Amédée Bollée's 1873 4.5 and 2.5 ton machines, reaching speeds of 35 kilometers per hour. Some lightweight wagons could even reach speeds of 60 km/h (Ruiz 1984:10pp).

However, there was a growing realization of the limitations of steam engines. Thus, numerous inventors worked on internal combustion engines. Belgian Jean-Etienne Lenoir built a working model of a gas engine in 1859, with the German Nicolaus Otto (hence, the Otto engine) picking up on his ideas to produce the first gasoline powered engine in 1861. The following year, Frenchman Beau de Rochas became the first to patent a four-stroke engine. The precursor to the modern four-stroke engine was invented, again by Otto, in 1876.[5] Another German—Rudolf Diesel—in 1892 invented the diesel engine (Cowan 1997:226; Freeman and Louçã 2001:272; Mokyr 1990:131p; Ruiz 1984:14).

The first car was developed virtually simultaneously by two Germans. In 1886 Gottlieb Daimler and Karl Benz independently of each other installed four-stroke petrol engines in a small carriage. Neither met with immediate commercial success. Instead the industry's first growth spurt occurred in France, as present survivors like Peugeot (1889) and Renault (1898) did some of the early running (Mokyr 1990:132; Nairn 2002:181p).

The US was a latecomer, but experienced rapid growth. The first US automobile occurred when the Duryea brothers in 1893 copied a Benz design, but already by the end of the century, US car production had outgrown Europe. Oldsmobile, founded in 1896, was the world's top seller, with a total of 425 sales of its Curved Dash in 1900, increasing to 2,500 in 1902. Generally, car production was primitive and experimental. In the US, a total of 57 manufacturers produced a total output worth less than $5 million. Other early US runners were Cadillac (1902) and Buick (1903) (Brinkley 2003:34, 43; Cowan 1997:226pp; Mowery and Rosenberg 1998:49pp).

None of this vaguely resembled mass production, which would have to wait until the Model T. However, at this stage, Henry Ford was not yet in business, as the Ford Motor Company was not founded until 1903.[6] The Model T was not introduced until 1908, and mass production only gradually introduced until the finished assembly line

---

5   Although because of de Rochas' 1862 patent, in 1886 Otto's patent for the four-stroke was revoked. This proved a blessing in disguise for potential German manufacturers. Now, they were free to make use of the four-stroke technology, as Otto could not use the courts to prevent them (Freeman and Louçã 2001:272; Nairn 2002:179p)!

6   However, Henry Ford had made earlier attempts. He produced a "quadricycle", in 1896, and in 1899 was one of the founders of the Detroit Automobile Company, which folded two years later (Brinkley 2003:32pp).

was in place by 1914 (Cowan 1997:228; Freeman and Louçã 2001:273; Hounshell 1984:218).

Mass Production

Henry Ford was the first to realize the vision of mass-produced cars at a price that was affordable to at least the middle classes. The Ford Motor Company produced the Model A as its first car, at $750 sturdier, heavier and more expensive than the Curved Dash.[7] With two more models introduced in 1905 and six more to follow over the next couple of years, Ford was a major success, having a hard time keeping up with demand, but not exactly mass-manufacturing. Still, by 1906 sales were up to 8,500 (Brinkley 2003:66, 87; Hounshell 1984:218).

With the Model T, introduced in 1908 at $850, Ford presented a car that was simple, but robust and sturdy. Still, as can be seen from Table 5.3 below, despite the T being an immediate success, mass production was introduced only gradually. In 1909, the Model T only accounted for 10 per cent of overall US sales (Brinkley 2003:121; Cowan 1997:228pp; Freeman and Soete 1999:141; Rae 1984:35).

Table 5.3 Manufacturing and Marketing of Model T Fords

	Retail Price (touring car), $	Total Model T Production
1908	850[*]	5,986[**]
1909	950	13,840
1910	780	20,727
1911	690	53,488
1912	600	82,388
1913	550	189,088
1914	490	230,788
1915	440	394,788
1916	360	585,388
...	...	...
1923	290	2,055,309

Source: Cars (1987:36); Hounshell (1984:224); Ruiz (1984:32).

[*]   The $850 sticker price is somewhat misleading, as it did not include the top, the windshields or the headlights. This would add an extra $135 to the price. Hence, the 1909

---

7   At the time, the "average car" cost more than $2,000 (Brinkley 2003:88).

model, which included these items in the fixed price, was essentially actually $35 cheaper (Brinkley 2003:111).

    ** Sales, not production. Production figures are not available for this year (Hounshell 1984:224).

The assembly line had been conceived of by Ford engineers as early as 1908, but unsure that it would work effectively, it was introduced piecemeal until 1914. Production was increased by a mix of means, drawing on traditional US strengths in interchangeable parts and specialized machine tools. The potential for mass production increased as Ford opened its new Highland Park factory in 1910. During the following years, conveyor belts were installed for the transport of the heavier items. Each worker performed a single operation, requiring little skill, moving the work to the worker as opposed to the other way around. The final step was made in late 1913. Magnetos were the first components to be mass produced, but final assembly could not keep up, and it was decided to convert final assembly to an assembly line process, reducing the overall time of assembly from 12 hours 30 minutes to 2 hours 40 minutes. When a new line for assembly of dashboards, front axles and body was completed in early 1914, total assembly time was cut further to a little over an hour and a half (see Table 5.4 below) (Brinkley 2003:153; Cowan 1997:228; Hounshell 1984:225pp; Rae 1984:36p).

Table 5.4 Craft Production vs. Mass Production, Model T Ford Assembly 1913 vs. 1914[8]

	Late craft production, fall 1913	Early mass production, spring 1914	Percentage reduction in effort
Engine	594	226.0	62
Magneto	20	5.0	75
Axle	150	26.5	83
Major components going into a complete vehicle	750	93.0	88

Source: Freeman and Louçã (2001:275).

Production rocketed and prices fell. As a consequence, Ford grew to become the world's foremost car producer by far. It produced and sold more cars than the next 10 US car manufacturers put together. By 1921, Ford controlled 60 per cent of

---

8   Minutes of effort to assemble various products and percentage reduction in effort.

the market, producing well in advance of a million cars a year, with prices falling (despite inflation), hitting $290 in 1927.[9] Model T number 10 million was produced in 1924 (Brinkley 2003:181, 273; Cowan 1997:229; Rae 1984:37p).

However, whoever refuses to adapt will most likely be left behind, no matter how big the initial lead. This happened as Ford refused to introduce models to replace or complement the Model T.[10] The General Motors Company was formed in 1908, as the brainchild of William Crapo Durant. He purchased Buick in 1907, and formed GM in 1908 buying Cadillac, Oldsmobile, Oakland (later renamed Pontiac) to make one multi-brand corporation. The first years were unspectacular, and it was not until after the 1920–1921 depression, when Durant resigned in favor of Alfred P. Sloan that the corporation became successful. Sloan adopted the idea of mass production and combined it with dividing GM into divisions producing cars for different market segments. Hence, GM took advantage of being able to offer a far wider range of models than Ford, with frequent new models, steady incremental improvements and styling changes (Freeman and Louçã 2001:277; Hounshell 1984:264; Nairn 2002:216p; Rae 1984:45, 51p).

Ford had acquired Lincoln, but otherwise continued to produce only the Model T. Hence, in 1927 GM surpassed Ford as the world's number one car manufacturer, and has remained so since 1932. In 1925, GM controlled 19 per cent of the market. This increased to 43 per cent by 1929 (Brinkley 2003:339pp; Freeman and Louçã 2001:264; Hounshell 1984:264p; Miller 2003:187; Rae 1984:51p).

While Ford was losing out to GM in the US, as a country, the US was extremely far ahead of the rest. France had been the European leader, but was caught up with by Britain, with Germany falling behind, but Europe taken as a whole was struggling even to match 10 per cent of US production (see Table 5.5 below). In 1935, in Britain there were 20 persons per car, in France 25, in Germany 100. In the US, the corresponding figure was one car per five persons, or almost one car per household (Kurth 1979:28; Leuchtenburg 1993:185 [1958]).

An obvious reason for this was the lack of genuine interest in mass production technologies, as the European industry to a much greater degree than the US relied on luxury car production. Still, several European pioneers went to Detroit to study mass-production techniques: In Britain, William Morris started something akin to mass production of the Morris Cowley in 1922, accounting for 40 per cent of British production. Morris was joined by Austin in 1922, which started production of its Austin Seven, an extremely light (only 365 kg!) and simple car, which was produced in a number of 350,000 up until 1939 (Cars 1988a:256pp; 1988b:1952). But the honor of "first mass produced European car" usually goes to France, where Citroën in 1919 began production of its 5CV at a rate of 100 vehicles per day. In Germany, Opel in

---

9   The 1925 T Runabout was only $260, which is the least that has ever been charged for a new US car, roughly the equivalent of three months' wages for a factory worker (Brinkley 2003:273; Heilbroner and Singer 1994:131).

10   He kept producing the T until 1927, by which time a grand total of 15,007,003 cars had been built (Rae 1984:63).

1924 plagiarized the 5CV design piece by piece, painting it bright green (whereas the Citroën could only be had in bright yellow), and calling it the Laubfrosch (leaf frog).[11] However, mass production at an American scale did not arrive until after World War II, as new people's cars were built by manufacturers in most major countries. In West Germany, the Volkswagen Type I[12] (or the "Beetle") went on to become the most sold car in the history of the automobile. In Italy, Fiat produced the Topolino (the "little mouse"). In France, Renault produced the 4CV, and in Britain, Austin produced the 35 and Morris introduced the Minor. Consequently, Europe had caught up with US production figures by the 1960s. Japan caught up too, among other things based on production techniques going beyond mass production—the so-called lean production, made famous by Toyota, but on a general level applied by the entire Japanese automobile industry (Ruiz 1984:46, 51; Womack, Jones and Roos 1990).

Table 5.5 Motor Vehicle Production

	US	Germany	Great Britain	France	Japan
1900	4,100	2,000	2,000	3,000	
1910	187,000	13,000	14,000	38,000	
1920	2,228,000	18,000	55,000	40,000	
1921	1,616,000		95,000*	55,000	
1929	5,337,000	128,000	239,000	254,000	400
1932	1,332,000	51,000	232,000	164,000	900
1937	4,820,000	331,000	504,000	202,000	17,800
1938	2,509,000	338,000	445,000	227,000	25,000
1940	4,472,000	72,000	134,000	119,000	46,000
1946	3,090,000	23,000	365,000	95,000	15,000
1950	8,003,000	301,000	784,000	357,000	32,000
1960	7,869,000	2,047,000	1,811,000	1,370,000	760,000

11 A German court responded to a law suit by Citroën for plagiarism by stating that the green color of the Opel clearly distinguished it from the bright yellow of the Citroën (Cars 1988c:2059).

12 In all fairness, mass production started prior to World War II, but only just, as Hitler's brainchild could only barely get going (1938) before it was time to engage the world in war.

	US	Germany	Great Britain	France	Japan
1970	8,239,000	3,825,000	2,099,000	2,750,000	5,288,000
1980	8,067,000	3,847,000	1,313,000	3,993,000	11,032,000
1990	9,784,000	4,949,000	1,576,000	3,847,000	13,475,000

Sources: Mitchell (2003a:479p; 2003b:550pp; 2003c:395p); Modelski and Thompson (1996:102).
*   1923.

A number of European attempts at mass production were actually spearheaded by US corporations, as Ford and GM invested heavily in Europe during the interwar years. In Germany, Ford and GM accounted for more than 70 per cent of overall car production. GM bought Opel in 1929, Ford set up a separate factory in 1931. In Britain, GM in 1925 bought Vauxhall, while Ford set up a separate production facility in 1929, and at the same time announced subsidiaries in France, Belgium, Italy, Spain, the Netherlands, Sweden and Finland (Brinkley 2003:371p; Keck 1993:131).

As a capital-intensive industry with economies of scale crucial, the industry has been marked by waves of consolidation. In the US, between 1900 and 1908, 500 new manufacturers entered the industry. Most failed. Fifty per cent of all new companies survived for less than six years. The two most important phases of consolidation occurred during the depression of 1920–1921 and after the 1929 Crash. More than 150 active firms were reduced to 90 during the 1920s, and to 42 by 1929. This was the period that saw the term the "Big Three"—GM, Ford, Chrysler—coined. The second face of consolidation took place after the Crash, with just 30 firms remaining by 1940 and the Big Three sharing 85–90 per cent of the market. However, the US position as the world number one was unrivalled (Miller 2003:179; Mowery and Rosenberg 1998:55; Nairn 2002:204pp, 228; Rae 1984:61p, 74).

The Role of the State

Human Capital

With the car industry the case for human capital is not as obvious as for the other technologies, industries and time periods in this book. Granted, human capital, in one form or another, did play a part, but the onus was on the application and diffusion of knowledge rather than knowledge and education itself. It is hard to see how human capital can explain how the US leapt so far ahead of Europe. Furthermore, if the US had an obvious knowledge advantage, US cars ought to have been unambiguously better than European car. However, European cars remained technologically more sophisticated. Also, the automobile industry was not a high-tech industry. Assembly line mass production did not require advanced scientific understanding. It was an organizational and managerial rather than a science and technology revolution. Hence, maybe we should not expect education and human capital to have provided the US with any decisive advantage. To a certain extent the US did benefit from an education system that provided it with engineers rather than scientists. Rapid diffusion, as well as the emphasis on practical skills no doubt worked in its favor. One of the reasons why Ford lost out to General Motors was because Henry Ford refused to spend money on R & D. Also, Detroit attracted skilled engineers from the entire world. Still, attributing US predominance to R & D expenditures would be as wrong as attributing it to the education system. The emphasis on engineering and on educating a large pool of people with good mechanical skills had a certain effect, but other variables have greater explanatory power. Smithian factors, like market size, capital and resource access, combined with path-dependencies and government infrastructure initiatives, were more important.

In terms of primary education, by the early twentieth century there were no major differences in literacy rates between the US and Europe. In enrollment, the US was ahead of most countries. In a number of US states, primary education was more comprehensive than in Europe, even if the South was still behind and the African-American population rarely included in official literacy figure estimates.

Table 5.6 Adult Literacy Rates, ca. 1900 (%)

	US	Germany*	Great Britain	France
1900	94	88	96–97**	83

Source: Cameron and Neal (2003:215).

*   Prussia.

**   The figures probably have an upward bias (Cameron and Neal 2003:215).

Table 5.7 Estimated Primary School Enrollment Rate, 1910 (per 10,000)[13]

	US	Germany	Great Britain	France
1910	1,828	1,570	1,648	1,414

Source: Easterlin (1981:18p).

US education efforts were persistently improving. By the 1930s, the US was three to four decades ahead of Britain and France in terms of post-elementary

---

13 Easterlin (1998:59) interprets rates above 1,200 as synonymous with complete enrollment.

education (Goldin 2001:267).[14] The US pioneered the publicly funded, academic secondary school for the masses. In 1929, 30 per cent of all 17-year-olds were in high school—up from two per cent in 1865. Goldin (2001:276) suggests that this system of academic yet practical education fitted the US well, as geographic mobility was vastly greater than in Europe. Young Americans needed general skills that could be applied in a number of jobs all over the country, whereas in Europe, where life-time employment was more common, it made sense to acquire skills through an apprenticeship system. The outcome was a system that produced a substantially larger pool of educated workers than in European countries. Still, the expansion of the secondary system was largely funded locally, and many of the industrial states lagged, with large parts of the population finding jobs in low-skill industries (Goldin 2001; Heilbroner and Singer 1994:131).

The ICT chapter reveals how the US remained largely low-tech until World War II. However, in terms of government expenditures, the change in trend happened with World War I. Up until World War I, government expenditures as a percentage of GNP had increased only very slowly—from 2.5 to five per cent between 1790 and 1920. From 1920 onwards, government expenditures rose rapidly, to 15 per cent by 1940 (Atack and Passell 1994:652). The same developments can be seen with respect to higher education. By the dawn of World War I, US universities had budgets twice as large as the top German universities, and with faster growth rates (Mowery and Rosenberg 1993:35).

Funding increased after World War I, but throughout the interwar years, industry accounted for two-thirds of total US R & D expenditures, with the federal government contributing no more than 12–20 per cent. Still, despite the modest federal contribution, public funding meant that US higher education was far better financed than similar European institutions. The number of scientists and engineers in industrial US research laboratories increased from 2,775 in 1921 to 27,777 in 1940. Still, European higher education was qualitatively superior, and most "serious" US scientists completed their studies in Europe. US higher education had a distinctly practical bent, geared more toward commercial opportunities than in Europe, with a greater emphasis on engineers than scientists (Mowery and Rosenberg 1993:35p; 1998:21p; Ruttan 2001:437).

Human Capital in the Automobile Industry?   But did the above improvements to the US education system actually matter with respect to the automobile industry? The higher education system was characterized by for its day very strong links between universities and industry. Public universities had to demonstrate the practical benefits of their education and research in order for funding to increase (Ruttan 2001:437). Mowery and Rosenberg (1998:23pp) stress how the decentralized structure and funding of higher education strengthened the links between academic and industrial research. Scientists and engineers trained at public universities would provide

---

14 By 1940, outside of the South, more than 60 per cent of US 18-year-olds had graduated from high school (Goldin 2001:267).

important links to industrial research, as Ph.D.s from public universities greatly contributed to the expansion of industrial research employment. The emphasis on state funding meant that the curriculum and research efforts of these local public universities would initiate programs so as to aid and benefit from local economic requirements. The large pool of skilled engineers greatly aided this, compared to in Europe, where the general emphasis was on fewer, but more highly educated experts and scientists. Hence, the US education system produced many of the same benefits as the English system during the early Industrial Revolution, depending on close links with industry, and on a large pool of skilled people. Goldin (2001:284) makes the point that in the US a new economy was emerging, increasing the demand for skilled workers. Mowery and Rosenberg (1993:36) conclude that even if US higher education did not advance the knowledge frontier, it was "an important instrument for scientific and engineering 'catch-up' in the United States during the early twentieth century."

However, it is more doubtful as to what extent the automobile industry *per se* gained from it. Car manufacture was drawing only lightly on advances made in the sciences. The combination of Fordism and Taylorism instead meant work processes stressing narrow, unskilled tasks performed repeatedly by workers under strict supervision. In the 1920s, car manufacture was one of the industries with the lowest number of scientists and engineers per worker. When the US research effort increased during the interwar years, most of this could be accounted for by very few industries. Most of the federal R & D funding went to agricultural research. Forty per cent of the laboratories founded between 1899 and 1946 were in chemicals, glass, rubber, and petroleum. These also accounted for 40 per cent of total research scientists and engineers in manufacturing (1921) (Mowery and Rosenberg 1998:20; O'Brien 1997:201; Ruttan 2001:436).

Not even in Europe was this a high-technology sector. Nicolaus Otto, who invented the Otto engine, had been a traveling salesman with no formal technical training. There were technological breakthroughs that relied heavily on scientific input—Rudolf Diesel was a brilliant academic at the Munich polytechnic. However, for the most part, progress was derived from learning-by-doing and learning-by-using. Advances made in machine tools, processes and in systems of production were first and foremost based on principles derived from practice. The US benefited from having a system that emphasized engineering and the wide diffusion of mechanical skills. Hence, the machine tools employed by Ford for mass production were created by very highly skilled mechanics, but not by people with anything resembling Ph.D.s (Cowan 1997:228; Freeman and Louçã 2001:272, 283; Mokyr 1990:131; Ruttan 2001:436).

However, the research intensity of car manufacturing[15] increased considerably between 1920 and World War II. In 1921, the US car industry employed 0.2 engineers

---

15 "Transportation equipment". Which means that these figures also incorporate the very substantial progress made in the aircraft industry, and hence probably overestimate the figures for car manufacturing (Mowery and Rosenberg 1993:34).

and scientists per 1,000 production workers. By 1940, this had risen to 3.2, and by 1946 to 4.6, making it the fifth most research-intensive manufacturing industry in the US.[16] Part of the reason for GM permanently overtaking Ford had to do with Ford's reluctance to innovate. GM adopted Fordist mass production technologies, but combined these process innovations with product innovation as well. Henry Ford opposed the idea of R & D facilities; GM embraced it. A number of people tired with Ford's reluctance to renew his model lineup led to some of his best engineers being lured away by GM. Offering a whole range of products at different levels of price and sophistication, GM established central agencies for research, advertising and product planning. During the 1920s, Detroit attracted industrialists and engineers from all over the world to study US techniques and to seek employment with US car manufacturers. Clearly, US car production was technologically sophisticated enough to attract brilliant engineers from abroad. And clearly, the car industry benefited from an increased level of skills primarily among engineers (Freeman and Louçã 2001:277; Mowery and Rosenberg 1993:33p; Rae 1984:52).

However, this is not what gave the US car industry its lead in the first place. General Motors surpassed Ford in the late 1920s, but at this time, the US already produced 90 per cent of the world's motor vehicles. Rather, while technologically ahead of Ford, GM was not a technological leader, simply because there was no need to be. In the words of its president, Alfred P. Sloan, GM existed, "not to make motor cars [but] to make money" (Farber 2002:59). As long as the Big Three controlled 85 per cent of the market, truly radical innovation could only upset the status quo, and thus threaten the dominance of the Big Three. Hence, caution took precedence over innovation, as in as capital-intensive an industry as automobiles, the price of failure is enormous. While this worked well as long as there was no serious competition from abroad, this changed with World War II. European manufacturers scaled up production, tariff barriers fell, and competition increased. It soon became obvious that competition between European manufacturers led to a level of technological sophistication well surpassing that of the US. This became even more obvious with the rise of Japanese car manufacturing (Freeman and Louçã 2001:278; Womack, Jones and Roos 1990).

In the final analysis, human capital did have some impact on US car manufacturing. The strongest way to put the case for the state in the sense of providing education comes from a focus on the kind of education provided compared to Europe. US education was practically oriented, focusing on skills useful for industrial success. Half a century earlier, this had left the US behind in dyestuffs. Car manufacture required different skills. In the initial phase, when car production was essentially a backdoor operation, good mechanical skills and intuition were crucial. As the industry grew in scale, fixed costs and development costs increased enormously. What became more important in this phase was capital to undertake the huge investments

---

16 To put these figures in perspective, between 1921 and 1946, the *chemical industry* increased numbers of engineers and scientists from 5.2 to more than 30 per 1,000 workers (Mowery and Rosenberg 1993).

required in order to stay competitive. In either case, the skill requirements would be along the lines of people with technical and mechanical skills and intuition. But mass production processes in themselves required very little of each and every worker, and so it is unlikely that the education system played much of a role with respect to the workers. And it is most likely that overall, other variables were more important.

Path-Dependencies

Path-dependencies are "spillover effects from previous technologies, which were themselves environmentally determined, thus combining geography and history" (Mokyr 1990:162p). In the other chapters, innovation has marked a radical break with the past. New technologies have been genuine macroinventions, and hence, path-dependencies have been minor. However, mass production has definite predecessor technologies and historical path-dependencies. A US advantage can be traced back to before the Civil War and to advantages in machine tools, precision engineering and interchangeable parts. Over the last part of the nineteenth century, the US developed another crucial competency, namely large-scale production, which benefited US producers in capital-intensive industries like car manufacturing.

Mass production consists of five components; precision, standardization, interchangeability, synchronization and continuity. Standardization and interchangeability can be traced back to the early nineteenth century (Harper's Ferry, Springfield arsenals) (Rae 1984:35). Continuous flow production (whereby workers remain stationary while the tasks are moved to them) goes back even further, to the Oliver Evans grist mill of 1787 (Cowan 1997:78p; Mokyr 1990:136).[17] All of these components existed well before the introduction of the automobile. Some had already been introduced in the auto industry. However, Ford was the first to put them all together.

The term "the American System of manufactures"—defined as the assembly of complex products from mass produced individual components—was a term that most likely arose during the 1850s from British reports on interchangeable parts in American manufacturing practices.[18] In 1854, the British Parliament established a committee with the purpose of finding the "Cheapest, most Expeditious, and most Efficient Mode of providing *Small Arms* for *Her Majesty's Service*" (Hounshell 1984:17).[19] British gun production was a handicraft industry, precisely fitting individual components together, through a process that required considerable

---

17 The first documented case of assembly line production occurred in Britain in 1804 (Mokyr 1990:137).

18 Not to be confused with the term American System as in the political program originating with Alexander Hamilton and propagated by Henry Clay (early nineteenth century), with the purpose of protecting infant industries in order to build a solid industrial base before opening up to competition and free trade.

19 The obvious context with respect to the timing of the committee, was the Crimean War that Britain was entangled in, and the fact that prior to the war, the British Board of Ordnance had had problems procuring sufficient muskets for the army.

skill and craftsmanship. In contrast, the US system required little skill and little maintenance. Armies no longer required large amounts of armorers for the repair of broken guns, as a new, standardized part could easily replace the broken one (Mokyr 1990:137; Ruttan 2001:426).[20]

Rather than interchangeable parts, the American System was about the application of high-quality, specialized machine tools to a sequence of operations (Mokyr 1990:136). The system had been created in the image of the Napoleonic Wars, with the failed efforts of Honoré Blanc as one of the main influences. In the US, a similar program was implemented, whereas in France it had been thwarted by conservative forces in the Army. Hence, as early as 1798, Eli Whitney received an $800,000 contract with the War Department for 10,000 muskets. The US government also took an interest in mechanized production. Thus, government armories and private arms factories received major government contracts in the first half of the nineteenth century. The first of these armories were established in 1794 at Springfield, Massachusetts (Cowan 1997:78; Hounshell 1984:27p, 32).

The British committee was impressed with the degree of uniformity achieved, with the scale of production, and the extent to which it was mechanized. Interchangeability of parts had largely been accomplished, and the technology had started spilling over into the civilian sector through machinists moving from arms factories to other industries. Hence, in the second half of the nineteenth century, mass production of sewing machines rapidly became the first industry to adopt armory practices. Invented by Elias Howe (probably) in 1846, it was transformed into a growth industry by Isaac Singer (who raised productivity by at least 500 per cent), and which led to annual production of sewing machines increasing from 810 in 1853 to roughly 500,000 by 1880. Bicycles was another transitional technology between the American System and mass production, bicycle sales reaching 1.2 million in 1896. This was the first industry in which armory practices were widely diffused. Also, bicycle manufacturers abandoned old metal-working techniques and introduced entirely new developments, like sheet metal stamping and electric resistance welding techniques. It led to the application of interchangeable parts to an array of areas where it had previously been deemed impractical, spreading the techniques and increasing the awareness of them in the manufacturing industries (Hounshell 1984:4pp, 70, 89, 329; Mokyr 1990:142; Ruttan 2001:426p).

Ford's obsession with interchangeability and precision tooling followed straight from developments in the bicycle industry, adopting the best of armory practice along with the technique of sheet steel punch and pressed steel work. Hence, by 1913— before finalizing the transition to mass production—problems of interchangeable parts had been solved. Still, it is important to stress how the use of interchangeable parts does not imply mechanized mass production. The idea of the moving assembly

---

20 The British had considerable doubts as to whether the quality of machine-made muskets could ever compete with man-made ones. Thus, the committee only cautiously recommended that manufacturing of small arms "should be tried to a limited extent" (Hounshell 1984:19pp).

line was probably inspired instead by the meatpacking industry (Gordon 1998; Hounshell 1984:6pp, 329).

In one more area did the US have path-dependency advantages. The US was more used to dealing with issues of large-scale production than were European manufacturers. Combined with the US comparative advantage in the education of engineers, US engineers could draw on a tradition of machine-building and machine-design well suited to economies of scale like in the chemical industry, where large-scale plants offered great potential productivity improvements. One example is BASF of Germany and the US General Chemical who were in litigation over the rights to employ the contact process in the US, with the rights held by BASF. Upon settling, the Germans realized that the relatively unsophisticated American plants outperformed German plants due to their enormous size. At 20,000 tons, the General Chemical plants were four times the size of the largest existing German plant (Arora and Rosenberg 1998:77; Rosenberg 1998:198). Scale advantages were inherent to US industrial thinking, both because of a huge domestic market, and because of the bias in the education system toward scale.

Unlike in nineteenth-century industries, in true Fordist mass production there would be no fitters, no crafts workers. Everything was mechanized, with workers performing only the simplest of tasks. Previous US industries represent a clear and obvious movement in the direction of mass production. However, the machine tool industry of the nineteenth century would never have been able to meet the standard that Ford set in 1913. But Henry Ford could build not only on a tradition of interchangeability, but on production of scale as well. US automobile production to a far larger extent than automobile production in other countries could draw upon path-dependencies from other sectors. This is a large part of the reason why the US rapidly seized the advantage over European car manufacturers.

Smithian Growth: Demand, Capital, and Markets

Mass production is a breakthrough somewhat akin to a microinvention, as opposed to Schumpeterian growth, which is all about macroinventions. Hence, almost by default, the growth processes of this period contain a strong Smithian component. Moreover, because the mass production era also signals the start of a mass *consumption* era, it makes sense that overall demand was an important factor. Finally, car manufacturers developed into giant corporations, spending billions on development costs and on production facilities. In industries with large economies of scale, availability of capital is crucial. On all these points, the US had a decisive advantage.

In terms of GDP per capita, the US passed Britain in 1901. It was hit hard by the 1929 crash, so that toward World War II, Britain actually caught up, but by 1946, the US was again clearly ahead. France and Germany kept lagging for the entire period (see Table 5.8, below).

Table 5.8 Per Capita GDP, 1900–1946 (1990 international Geary–Khamis dollars)

	1900	1909	1919	1929	1939	1946
USA	4,091	5,017	5,680	6,899	6,561	9,197
Great Britain	4,492	4,511	4,870	5,503	6,262	6,745
France	2,876	3,167	2,811	4,710	4,793	3,855
Germany	2,985	3,275	2,586	4,051	5,406	2,217

Source: Maddison (2003:60pp, 88).

However, wage differences were greater than suggested by aggregate statistics. Average US worker wages were more than twice that of British wages, with French and German wages 70–80 per cent of British wages (Zamagni 1989:116pp).[21] While both France and Germany had been catching up with Britain in terms of wage levels, by the turn of the century, no strong consumer goods sector had yet developed, and consequently no car industry of any significance. Losing World War I accentuated this. The most successful European car manufacturers were the two countries with the most consumer-oriented economies. Hence, with the most consumer-oriented economy and the highest per capita income in Europe, it was Britain, which had the world's second largest car industry, followed by France (Kurth 1979:22; Ruiz 1984:18; Trebilcock 1981:162; Wehler 1985:44).[22]

However, they all fell far short of the US. US average worker real income increased by 30 per cent between 1921 and 1929. The US was the world's most consumer-oriented economy, had the highest per capita income in the world, significantly higher wages and better productivity. Compared to Europe, the US was scarce in labor, which drove up wages and overall demand for consumer goods, and provided US manufacturers with incentives for mechanization. Wages increased to such an extent that when General Motors purchased manufacturers like Opel and Vauxhall, Alfred P. Sloan came under attack by US politicians for selling out, moving jobs out of the country by producing cars in countries where workers were paid 40 per cent of US wages (Cowan 1997:90; Dow 1998:146;

---

21 Britain, France, Germany: 1905 figures; US 1909. Adjusting for purchasing power, the US industrial wages were 20 per cent above Britain, rising to around 30 per cent by the start of World War I, and roughly the double of French and German industrial wages (Zamagni 1989:116pp).

22 Index figures from Zamagni (1989:117) show that French engineering wages amounted to 42 per cent of British wages in 1856, rising to 78 per cent by 1905. German engineering wages were higher, at 89 per cent of British wages, but had increased far more rapidly. Hence, the German middle class was a far more recent invention than that in both Britain and France.

Farber 2002:137; Kurth 1979:26; Maddison 2001:351; Miller 2003:173; Parrish 1994:31; Rogowski 1989:47p).

Capital was not particularly important in the early years, as car manufacture was not yet very capital-intensive. Hence, the early years saw the rise (and fall) of hundreds of manufacturers in both Europe and the US. However, in a few decades, the automobile industry had become among the most capital-intensive in the world. First, economies of scale could only be effectively exploited through mass production techniques, which meant enormous factories and huge machine tools expenditures. Second, it meant greater development costs. Hence, the industry went through major consolidation phases following World War I and then the crash.

The mass production facilities of Henry Ford changed the industry for all time. True, the US was more abundant in capital than Europe. And Britain and France were far more abundant than Germany. But also, the dawn of mass production converged with World War I, which hit Europe infinitely harder than the US. The US entered World War I with total European debts of $3.5 billions. By the end of the war, Europe owed the US $12.5 billion. The car industry became vastly more capital-intensive at the same time as European economies were strapped for cash (Heilbroner and Singer 1994:132; Parrish 1994:56).

The above to a considerable extent explains why Europe could not compete following World War I. Particularly in Germany, car manufacture was a strong reflection of the difficulties German firms had in raising capital for mass production, with more than 70 per cent of German car production accounted for by firms owned by US corporations. Hence, when mass production finally broke through in Europe, it was after World War II, when a combination of repressed wages and a large inflow of foreign funds (primarily through the Marshall Plan, but also through US direct investment) provided the capital (Keck 1993:131; Kurth 1979:28p; Wehler 1985:44).

That said, the US financial system was fragile, and massive bank failures one of the most important reasons for the Great Depression. This combined with a sudden fall in demand caused bankruptcies on an enormous scale. Purchasing power failed to keep up with productivity increase. When the bubble burst, over-production in a series of industries, not the least the car industry, combined with stock market crash, credit squeeze and liquidity crisis to create the most serious economic depression in modern history (Dow 1998:177pp; Parrish 1994:218).

In this complex of Smithian explanations, the best argument in favor of Schumpeterian growth might be found in the financial sector, which was more fragile than similar sectors in Europe, and which went through considerable institutional reform, among other things in 1935, mandating that all banks be part of the Federal Reserve System. Restoring confidence in the banking system was among the most important measures taken by President Franklin D. Roosevelt in order to get the economy back on its feet. However, the strong fluctuations of the US economy suggest that government policies were neither particularly growth-inducing nor stabilizing. Demand continued to play a major role throughout the depression. In 1937, Roosevelt was largely responsible for triggering a new serious depression by slashing federal expenditures and raising taxes. Thus, the economy was extremely sensitive to changes in overall demand (Moss 1995:240). The point has been made that if war had not finally arrived, economic stagnation might have lasted well into the 1940s (Kindleberger 1986:271p; Moss 1995:217, 231, 244).

Finally, in an industry reliant on scale, the size of the market is important. In a period of increasing protectionism, the US benefited greatly from its huge domestic market. The 1930 Smoot–Hawley tariff is widely seen to have provoked a tariff war, although it only increased the degree of protectionism in the US economy marginally, as US tariffs were already high. The 1909 Payne–Aldrich tariff had put a 45 per cent *ad valorem* tariff on European cars (and other industrial goods), and post-1930, tariffs on passenger cars actually fell to 10 per cent. Still, US automobile exports hardly exceeded 10 per cent of overall US production (1929) in any case, and so the extent to which European tariffs could harm US producers was limited (Freeman and Louçã 2001:279). Still, because of European tariffs, both Ford and GM set up their own European affiliates or purchased local car manufacturers in order to circumvent tariff regulations. Tariffs meant that the European market had become highly fragmented into a number of small, national car markets. At the time when mass production technologies were available, there was no huge integrated European market to produce such a car for. Tariffs for practical purposes made it impossible for European manufacturers to mass produce at such a scale as to make cars inexpensive enough for the average European worker. In the US, the market was already large enough for mass production technologies to be effectively exploited. European small cars remained far more expensive than in the US. The 1928 average price of a US car was $600, in Europe $1,430 (Brinkley 2003:369; Chang 2002:29; Farber 2002:135p; Freeman and Louçã 2001:263; Nairn 2002:204; Ruttan 2001:460).

Table 5.9 Tariffs on Passenger Cars, 1913–1937 (% of Customs Value)

	USA	Great Britain	France	Germany	Italy
1913	45	0	9–14	3	4–6
1924	25–50*	33.3	45–180	13	6–11
1929	10**	33.3	45	20	6–11
1932	10	33.3	45–70	25	18–123
1937	10	33.3	47–74	40	11–101

Source: Freeman and Louçã (2001:263).
*   1922. The 25–50 range reflects how the tariff varied in order to equal the tariff in the country of origin (Freeman and Louçã 2001:263).
**   1930 (Freeman and Louçã 2001:263).

In three typically Smithian areas—demand, capital, and market size—the US possessed significant advantages. Moreover, Europe was hit far harder by World War I, leading to a scarcity of capital, stagnant demand and tariff barriers effectively reducing the size of the market. As the car industry grew radically more capital-intensive, Europe became *less* able to compete in capital-intensive industries, unlike the US.

Infrastructure Developments

In one important respect governmental efforts were crucial for the expansion of automobile production. Infrastructure developments not only benefited the car industry, but the entire economy, as new industries and businesses flourished along new roads and highways—petrol filling stations, supply centers, oil refining industry—and as new land was opened up for settlement and business (Dow 1998:167; Leuchtenburg 1993:186 [1958]). Moss (1995:138) suggests that the automobile was to the 1920s what the railroads had been to the nineteenth century.

However, as Allen (1961:108) underlines, the car did not abruptly transform the US. First, the public needed access to reliable and cheap cars. Second, good roads would have to be built. And third, there would have to be garages and filling stations in such a multitude as to make long-distance travel feasible. The Model T satisfied the first condition. The second and third would have to wait a little longer. After the end of the Civil War, road construction in the US had faltered. It took until 1893 for the first paved road to appear (Bellefontaine, Ohio). In the same year, the federal government created the Office of Road Inquiry, and the pressure for better roads grew from the popularity of the bicycle. The AAA was founded in 1905, among other things with the purpose of pressuring local, state and federal government into improving existing roads and building new, paved highways. Still, by 1906, 96 per cent of all highway funds were appropriated by local government, and as late as 1914, the US had only 750 miles of concrete highway (Cowan 1997:233; Leuchtenburg 1993:184 [1958]; Miller 2003:189; Rae 1984:8).

The 1916 Federal Highway Act was supposed to address the road infrastructure problem, but because of World War I, federal efforts were meager. The act set aside money to states that would organize their own highway departments, matching federal grants. However, from 1916 to the 1921 arrival of the Second Federal Highway Act, only $75 million of federal funds were devoted to highway construction (Leuchtenburg 1993:184 [1958]; Miller 2003:190).

This changed in the 1920s, with the Bureau of Public Roads planning a new national highway system. As the 1916 act, the 1921 Highway Act allocated funds to state legislatures, so that local authorities could undertake highway construction projects. Laissez-faire presidents persistently reduced public expenditures,[23] but not

---

23 Secretary of the Treasury, Mellon, cut federal spending from a war-time high of $18 billion in 1918 to $6 billion in 1920, and less than $3 billion in 1927. During Roosevelt's

with respect to road construction, which in terms of public expenditures in the 1920s was second, only behind education. No industry employed more men, or spent more money, than construction of highways and buildings. By 1929, total expenditures on roads and streets (local, state and federal) amounted to $2 billion a year,[24] or a full two per cent of US GNP. Between 1920 and 1929, the mileage of rural and municipal roads increased from 369,000 to 662,000 miles, with an additional 190,000 miles of federally supported highway (Atack and Passell 1994:578; Brinkley 2003:333p; Leuchtenburg 1993:184 [1958]; Moss 1995:138).

The result was a huge stimulus to the car industry. By the end of the 1920s "… paved roads and repair shops and filling stations had become so plentiful that the motorist might sally forth for the day without fear of being stuck in a mudhole or stranded without the benefit of gasoline or crippled by a dead spark plug" (Allen 2000:139 [1931]). In 1900, there was not a single filling station in the entire US.[25] By 1929, there were more than 120,000. Highway construction resulted in the first drive-in restaurants, roadside diners and hot-dog stands, the first motels, officially numbered highways, the first shopping center, the first public parking garage, the first automatic traffic lights, used-car lots, etc. By the late 1920s, cars were affordable, it was fairly easy to finance the purchase of a car, and the necessary road and service infrastructure making it a viable alternative to the railroad was largely in place. By 1928 it was possible to drive all the way from New York to Kansas on paved highways.[26] The prosperity of the 1920s would have been impossible without the automobile industry—car manufacturing created 1.5 million new jobs. But this expansion would not have been possible without infrastructure improvements (Allen 1961:108pp; Brinkley 2003:334; Leuchtenburg 1993:185 [1958]; Miller 2003:174, 191).

It was still true that federal involvement was modest. While increasing, with $75 million appropriated annually for highway construction, this still only made for a modest amount of total highway spending. As late as 1927, 53 per cent of all highway funds were provided locally, the federal government only accounting for 10 per cent of total spending. Large-scale federal involvement had to wait until the depression, when the federal government fed huge payments to the states in return for public works projects. Thus, the Works Progress Administration of Roosevelt's built a total of 650,000 miles of roads up until 1943 (Cowan 1997:234; Miller 2003:190; Moss 1995:229). While by 1940 only a fraction of today's highway network had yet been built, to quote Leuchtenburg (1993:184 [1958]): "Road building gave the

New Deal, federal spending gradually rose again, hitting $8.4 billion in 1936 (Mitchell 2003c:667).

24 Heilbroner and Singer (1994:128) state $1.4 billion per year.

25 Before the Model T, gasoline was bought at hardware stores, by the bucketful, and not at curbside filling stations as became commonplace during the 1920s (Brinkley 2003:334; Leuchtenburg 1993:185 [1958]).

26 Although it was still not advisable to travel southwest of St. Louis in the rainy season or to negotiate the mountain passes west of Salt Lake City in the winter (Leuchtenburg 1993: 185 [1958]).

auto industry a larger government subsidy than railroads received in their entire history".

Smithian growth was probably the main reason for the impressive performance of the US automobile industry. After all, by the 1920s, the US car industry was already by far the biggest in the world. However, subsequent Smithian growth rested on foundations provided by the government. Without infrastructure investments, the car would not have transformed the US as comprehensively as it did. It would not have developed from a rich man's plaything into a necessity for the common man. In the rapidity of this development, the US was without equal.

Vested Interests, Social Cohesion, and Political Consensus?

The first half of the twentieth century was marked by a weakening Republican political hegemony, a Progressivist intermezzo, the Great Depression and the coming together of new political alliances as a Democratic hegemony gradually emerged. As before, the main domestic issues were tariffs, the level of involvement of the federal government, and the overall level of federal spending.

On tariffs, the long-standing Republican alliance was slowly unraveling. Industry had been more or less unanimously pro-tariff for the simple reason that US wages were higher than in Europe. But with the dawn of the twentieth century, growth industries like car manufacturing were capital- rather than labor-intensive. For these, access to a world market without trade barriers was far more important than domestic tariffs. Thus, the battle for political influence between labor- and capital-intensive industries became ever more intense, with capital-intensive industries in the end winning out. However, it took until 1932, with the election of the Democratic president Franklin D. Roosevelt, before the US really changed its stance on tariffs. By the end of World War II, both Republicans and Democrats had become avid free traders.

Infrastructure developments had *fueled* growth in the automobile industry rather than sparking it in the first place. The same applies to vested interests. Car production was fueled by a comparative lack of vested interests constraining the automobile industry. A major conflict of interest did exist—that between labor-intensive (old, traditional politically dominant industries) and capital-intensive industry. The conflict was resolved in favor of capital-intensive industries, but not until the late 1920s, at a time when the US was already dominating world car production. US car production increased tremendously during the 1920s. Hence, the vested interest conflict was resolved at more or less the time in history when the Great Depression set in, hitting the car industry hard, which although gradually recovering, never hit 1929 production figures again until after World War II (see Table 5.5).

However, while the story is one of Smithian growth more than Schumpeterian, the business environment was conducive for the car industry, and this was much related to vested interests. First, federal and state spending on road infrastructure was vigorously fought by the railroads. The argument made on the part of the railroad companies, was that road expenditures amounted to an unfair public subsidy for a competing branch of transportation. However, this did not prevent in particular state and local government from accelerating their funding of road infrastructure (Atack and Passell 1994:578).

Second, this was an era of almost complete laissez-faire with respect to business regulations. Most industries, including the car industry, faced virtually no impediments. During the 1920s, the car industry was under highly favorable conditions, with strongly pro-business governments. During the Republican administrations of Harding (1920–1923) and Coolidge (1923–1928), Secretary of Commerce Hoover (president 1928–1932) stimulated big business by encouraging trade associations, information sharing, and by acting as a "clearing-house for information on business opportunities abroad" (Heilbroner and Singer 1994:133; Rae 1984:69). Investments soared, as did profits, increasing by 62 per cent between 1923 and 1929. President Coolidge declared that "the man who builds a factory builds a temple" (Heilbroner and Singer 1994:133). Attitudes toward the car were overwhelmingly positive, with industrialists like Henry Ford rising to folk hero status, and others like Chrysler, Durant, Willys and Nash not far behind (Moss 1995:142; Parrish 1994:52; Rae 1984:69). Kurth (1979:29) makes the point that in Europe, the countries that managed to create rapidly growing car industries after World War II were those that came closest to having institutions and policies emulating the US during the 1920s.[27]

However, while the car was seen by politicians, industrialists and the common man as a tremendous asset, the positive attitude had not been a given. During the first decade of the new century, the car received a very mixed reception. Britain has become infamous for its red-flag act, until 1896 preventing cars from driving faster than four miles per hour, and requiring someone to walk 60 paces in front of the car with a red flag (and a red lantern at night)—a result of pressure from railroad and horse carriage companies trying to restrict competition. Some US states were no better. In 1900, Vermont mandated that "a person of mature age" walk one-eighth of a mile in front of the car with a red flag. Cities like San Francisco, Cincinnati and Savannah set speed limits as low as eight miles per hour (Leuchtenburg 1993:185 [1958]; Ruiz 1984:21). Brinkley (2003:114) speaks of a zeitgeist that was remarkably hostile, particularly in rural areas. Rifles were fired at motorists, as the car symbolized not only progress, but also wealthy people flaunting their prosperity, showing off their fancy playthings. On roads that were narrow and in poor condition, inconsiderate and reckless driving by the rich endangered pedestrians to such an extent that articles started comparing the attitude of the rich and reckless to that of the French nobility before the French Revolution. Even future president Woodrow Wilson in 1906 warned against the car's potential for social unrest, stating that nothing had done more to spread socialist attitudes than the car (Brinkley 2003:115)!

Hence, the US was about as skeptical of the car as most European countries. This changed with the introduction and steadily declining price of the Model T, which

---

27 In other words, the countries that could start afresh after the war—Germany, Japan and Italy.

rapidly became affordable even for the average industrial worker or farmer. From now on, the US was on a different path than Europe. In the US, mass production spread, while in Europe, car production was treated more as a craft. To Ruttan (2001:460) European craftsmen would never agree to work under mass production conditions. Freeman and Louçã (2001:279) stress how mass production met with contempt. Thus, with a few partial exceptions, until after World War II, the European car industry consisted of crafts production for the upper classes. Tellingly, the first European car manufacturer to embrace a strategy of unadulterated mass production of cheap, reliable cars for the common man was the car manufacturer set up by the European head of state catering the most shamelessly to the masses—Adolf Hitler and Volkswagen![28] Although note the Smithian component: This was a factory set up by the German state. In a country far scarcer in capital than Britain or France, major investments in physical capital had to be made, not by private interests, but by the state. Hence, from 1937 the German people's car project was taken over and funded by the state (Wood 1985:202p).

Third, while labor-intensive industries dominated American politics, they were no longer equally strong. The political and economic coalition based around the Republican Party was breaking down. Because US industrial wages were high compared to Europe, labor-intensive industries were pro-tariff. But these industries were running out of steam. Capital-intensive industries flourished because of US comparative advantage in capital and in mass-production technology. Because of their capital intensity, these suffered less from high industrial wages, and survived from exports rather than a sheltered domestic market. Hence, they lobbied for free trade rather than protection (Ferguson 1984).

The tariff issue was tenuous throughout the period as tariff policy was always one of the most visible manifestations of federal involvement in economic policy-making. In one sense, tariff policies were of less relevance to car manufacturing, as US automobile imports were negligible. Yet, US tariffs triggered retaliatory tariffs from Europe, increasing the price of US cars in Europe. This had detrimental effects on US car producers, which can most easily be seen by how major corporations like Ford and GM found it preferable to purchase European firms, or set up European affiliates, in order to circumvent European tariffs, rather than market US cars in Europe (Rae 1984:69).[29]

Tariff legislation bears witness of the relative strength of the labor-intensive industries. Ferguson (1984:61) speaks of the "System of '96" [1896], as being the stable coalition of political and economic power prior to World War I. It rested

---

28 Hitler was also a great admirer of Henry Ford (who beyond being a revolutionary industrialist was a strong anti-Semite, and a source of continuing inspiration for Hitler), among other things reading Ford's autobiography while imprisoned in 1923–1924. This was when Hitler had the idea of how to solve the unemployment problem: By the government building a network of roads and then initiating mass production of a small car cheap enough for the man in the street (Brinkley 2003:413; Wood 1985:200)!

29 In its first year alone, the 1930 Smoot–Hawley tariff led to retaliatory tariffs from 26 nations (Hiscox 2002:60).

on a Republican hegemony and on the unity of industry and major finance, with a business community that was nationalistic, protectionist and labor-intensive, consisting of industries like steel, textiles, coal and shoes, enemies of labor and strongly for governmental laissez-faire. However, by World War I, these industries were challenged, economically and industrially by capital-intensive industries, and politically by labor and middle-class citizens and professionals giving rise to a Progressivist movement demanding greater federal responsibility in economics and politics, and regulations protecting the consumers.

While no Progressive candidate ever became president, the movement put its mark on politics. Republican president Theodore Roosevelt (1900–1908) pushed Progressivist ideas as he forced regulations on the railroads and federal inspections and standards. President (and fellow Republican) William Howard Taft had extended on Roosevelt's policies, by seeking tariff reform. However, vested interest groups and lobbyists for all practical purposes controlled the Senate. The result was the 1909 Payne–Aldrich Tariff Act, which contrary to Taft's intentions split the Republican Party into progressive and conservative factions by increasing tariffs rather than reducing them (Ferguson 1984; Hiscox 2002:57; Hofstadter 1955:172; Moss 1995:74pp).[30]

The Republican split led to Roosevelt leaving the party to run as a Progressive candidate in 1912. With Roosevelt and Taft fighting each other, Democrat Woodrow Wilson, who also ran on a platform strongly akin to Progressivism, seized the presidency. Unlike Taft, Wilson fought the lobbyists and succeeded, implementing the 1913 Underwood–Simmons Tariff Act, which on average reduced import tax from 40 to 29 per cent. But the "System of '96" fought back, and post-World War I presidencies saw a decline of Progressivism, with Harding, Coolidge and Hoover all devoted to laissez-faire and a minimalist state. These administrations raised tariffs back to pre-war levels, through the emergency tariff of 1921, the Fordney–McCumber tariff act of 1922 and the Smoot–Hawley tariff of 1930, after pressure from old industries like textiles and steel. In order to appease capital-intensive industry, the 1922 act included provisions for the president to negotiate trade agreements based on reciprocity, and the president given the authority to himself raise or lower tariffs by up to 50 per cent. The car industry managed to avoid the tariff increases. Hence, with the Smoot–Hawley tariff increase, tariffs on cars actually *fell to their lowest level ever*, namely 10 per cent (see Table 5.9) (Ferguson 1984:86; Hiscox 2002:59; Kurth 1979:27; Leuchtenburg 1993:109 [1958]; Moss 1995:76pp, 88, 142; Parrish 1994:52).[31]

---

30 For a small and nascent car industry, an *ad valorem* tariff of 45 per cent may actually have been beneficial during the early years as the industry was not very capital-intensive yet, not to a great extent exporting to Europe, and with European cars technologically more sophisticated. However, this was soon to change.

31 Of 37 tariff changes during Harding and Coolidge, tariffs were raised 22 times. Lower tariffs on a general level had to wait until Franklin D. Roosevelt (Hiscox 2002:59).

The tension between the "System of '96" and the new industries (Ferguson (1984:61): the "Multinational Bloc"), was strong throughout the 1920s. With the US changing from a debtor to a creditor nation during World War I, the onus was now with capital. Hence, leading labor-intensive industries sought to protect their vested interests ever more intensely. However, the Multinational Bloc was gaining power. Capital-intensive firms had been growing strongly ever since World War I (by 1948, oil companies and car companies were the largest US industrials). Hence, at the 1928 election, Republican presidential candidate Herbert Hoover, despite his reputation as champion of US domestic industry, rejected the protectionist political platform offered to him by the old and trusted Republican supportive cast, instead siding with the multinationalists and tariff reductions. The Democrats responded by having Al Smith run on the first high-tariff Democratic platform ever. The 1928 election was the first election where demands for lower tariffs won through on a permanent basis for the first time (Ferguson 1984:78, Hiscox 2002:59p).

Ambiguity was the case in 1932 as well, as Hoover ran against the Democratic challenger Franklin D. Roosevelt. Roosevelt won the election, and stayed in the White House until his death in 1945. But more important than tariffs, after five years of spectacular rise, 1929 saw the New York stock market crash, with the Great Depression following. Thus, what marked most of the pre-war years of Roosevelt's presidency were his attempts to combat the depression—the New Deal. Car production plummeted from 5.3 to 1.3 million (1932), 100,000 businesses failed (1929–1933). GNP dropped from $80 to $42 billion, 6,000 banks went bankrupt, and in 1934 unemployment peaked at 25 per cent. Part of the recovery plan was the National Recovery Administration (NRA), whereby industries would regulate competition and pay their employees minimum wages. This arrangement met with support from labor-intensive industry like textiles, where regulating competition might have tangible benefits. Capital-intensive industries were distinctly lukewarm, with Ford, General Motors and Chrysler all reluctant to sign on. Generally, industries with good long-term economic prospects opposed the NRA, which started to self-destruct almost immediately. With conflict between protectionists and free-traders, big corporations and small firms, buyers and suppliers, Roosevelt instead turned toward free trade and capital-intensive industries. In 1934, he gave Secretary of State Cordell Hull the authority to negotiate bilateral tariff reduction treaties.[32] Twenty-two such treaties were negotiated between 1934 and 1939. The combination of free trade and New Deal was heavily fought by the labor-intensive industry, which formed a massive protectionist bloc. Simultaneously, as Republican presidential candidate Alfred Landon criticized Hull's treaties, business leaders left the Republican Party in droves. Overall, the New Deal was at best only a partial success. By 1937 unemployment was still 14 per cent, and Roosevelt was largely responsible for triggering a new depression (even bigger than the 1929 Crash) as he slashed

---

32 Kindleberger (1986:233) states that although Roosevelt had opposed the Smoot–Hawley tariff, he actually had little faith in the reciprocal trade agreements, and did it primarily to appease Hull.

federal expenditures and raised taxes. Yet, the outcome was the forging of a new historic bloc of capital-intensive industries, investment banks and internationally oriented commercial banks, spun around a Democratic political platform of social welfare, oil price regulation and free trade. These elements were all in place by 1938 and constituted the core coalition in American politics for decades to come. The Depression had changed the presidency, vastly increasing it in size, power and scope (Ferguson 1984:43, 85pp; Heilbroner and Singer 1994:175; Kindleberger 1986:271p; Moss 1995:231, 240pp; Parrish 1994:312).

The above suggests that the vested interest argument has some explanatory power. Clearly, as time progressed, vested interests lost in power. However, it took until the late 1930s before US administrations came down solidly on the side of the new industries. By then, the US had dominated world car production for three decades. And then came the Great Depression. Car production fluctuated enormously and far more so than in Europe. Looking at production figures, it is evident that this industry was different from the carrier industries of previous chapters in one respect. It was not just the world's first mass production industry, but also the first mass *consumption* industry. This explains both why the car industry in the US grew to become so much bigger than in Europe, and why European production figures remained much more stable. In Europe, the car was still to a very great extent a luxury item. Thus, there was no mass consumption from which a dramatic slow-down could occur. In the US, Smithian factors triggered the industry's growth and its recessions.

Because of the relatively modest contribution of vested interests, it is also less likely that consensus and cohesion were of importance. The evidence seems to bear this out. To paraphrase Kindleberger (1986:234) on the US and Britain's repeal of the Corn Laws: In both cases, the change in commercial policy was rooted in structural economic change. In Britain, manufacturing interests fought agricultural interests, in the US labor-intensive stood against capital-intensive industries. In Britain, manufacturers benefited from lower tariffs, in the US capital-intensive industries did. But in Britain, manufacturing interests could rely on spokesmen (Cobden, Bright) to eloquently articulate their position, and explain why favoring agriculture greatly harmed Britain. Relatively early on this became the accepted consensus, even if vested interests were powerfully represented in Parliament and government. In the end, this consensus was so strong that a Conservative government, controlled by land-holding aristocrats, went against its immediate class-interests to vote for the repeal.

No similar situation existed in the US. The 1930s switch to free trade and consumer oriented policies did not arise from any conscious effort to promote growth industries. No consensus spread as in Britain. Instead, labor-intensive industries kept their stronghold on economic policy-making. It took the most serious economic depression in modern history and a very turbulent presidential campaign (1936) before the US came decisively down on the side of capital-intensive industry. This was one coalition of vested interests being substituted by a different one rather than a consensus spreading in favor of capital-intensive industry. The new coalition was a long-lived one, cemented by structural change and permanent increase in federal spending finally brought about by World War II.

It is true that Republicans became less adamant about protectionism as the century progressed, and the Democrats less staunchly free-trade. Roosevelt himself did not have much of an opinion, and seems to have embraced tariff reductions partly because his co-workers convinced him, and partly because it was politically opportune. In the 1932 presidential campaign, he insisted on being vague, admitting that his position was fairly close to that of the Republicans (Ferguson 1984:89pp).

Hiscox (2002:56pp) demonstrates that party cohesion (which is not how this notion is otherwise employed in this book) within both the parties fell between 1897 and 1930. He (ibid.:137pp) argues that this reflects the fact that the composition of the support base of the parties was changing. The Republicans were drawing greater support from the South and the West, where export industries were important, and the Democrats increased their influence in the Northeast, where textile and steel industries were dominant. By the 1930s, there was not much difference in the support base of the parties. Rather than consensus spreading, as late as 1936, Roosevelt had to endure very strong attacks against his political platform. The American Liberty League (formed in 1934 by the DuPont family, which owned the largest chemical company in the US [33]) accused the New Deal of destroying the American capitalist system, whereas on the left, he was fiercely criticized for not going far enough (Ferguson 1984:89pp; Moss 1995:223pp).

One may argue that tariffs were not the only relevant issue, and vested interests were countered successfully in other areas, as in the construction of highway infrastructure. However, while highway expenditures increased greatly, the federal government simultaneously scaled down its overall spending. In the 1920s, Secretary of the Treasury Mellon dramatically slashed federal spending. If anything, if the previous decade had emphasized a greater role for government, the political consensus of the 1920s was one of economic laissez-faire and "back to normalcy" (as put by president-to-be Harding during the 1920 campaign). Granted, the role of the government increased during the 1920s, and so even if Progressivism declined, progressivist policies found a permanent place in American politics. Still, while the federal government was spending more on roads and highways, the spending spree on the part of local and state governments was what really accelerated road construction. A federal commitment to building infrastructure existed, but was not clearly scaled up until the Great Depression, when federally financed road building was used to combat unemployment. Still, as mentioned earlier, 1920s local and state spending provided car manufacturers with a subsidy larger than that ever given to the railroads.

When push comes to shove, vested interests, social cohesion and political consensus only played a limited part in the rise of the US automobile industry. First, while tariffs were a problem for capital-intensive industries in general, the US car

---

33 This should not come as a surprise. It is widely held that the US chemical industry survived from British and German competition only because of US tariffs (Ferguson 1984).

industry was not hit extremely hard. It primarily supplied its domestic market, and imports from Europe were no grave threat. It was a problem in the sense that tariffs in European countries made it more convenient for US manufacturers to produce cars *in* Europe rather than to export. And it was a problem in the sense that during the 1930s, when the US domestic market crashed, European tariffs made it more or less impossible for US manufacturers to compensate for their losses by exporting. Second, vested interests, or their absence, do not explain the *initial* rise of the US car industry. The US produced five times as many cars as France as early as 1910 and *50 times as many* by the end of World War I. This was due to a combination of technological breakthroughs in mass production and Smithian factors. The infrastructure and vested interest stories came into play primarily at a time when the US was already supremely dominant.

Conclusions

Compared to the other industries the automobile industry deviates somewhat. We find the same mechanisms as in the other chapters. But these mechanisms were fairly minor players. In one sense, this is not a surprise. Mass-production technologies were revolutionary and the impact breathtaking. Yet, from a different perspective, they were hardly revolutionary at all. The US already had a comparative advantage in machine tools production and in interchangeable parts production. Mass-production technologies had very obvious precursors, and the US had an advantage within these precursors. Putting these precursor technologies together into what emanated as true mass-production technologies, was conceptually no extreme leap, but rather a fairly logical development of already existing technologies.

Because mass-production technologies are conceptually quite simple, human capital was of less importance. While endowed with what was rapidly becoming the best elementary education in the world, the US still lagged behind Europe in higher education. However, most of the entrepreneurs in the car industry were practical rather than scholarly men (Henry Ford was most uncomfortable reading in public even at an adult age, and his writing skills left a lot to be desired). To the extent that the US benefited from its education system, it did so from having a large pool of skilled workers to draw on. However, once car manufacturers followed Henry Ford's mass-production example, skills were the least useful qualification an autoworker might possess. Assembly line mass production meant that each worker would only do a certain number of very simple operations, and then repeat these again and again. Granted, Detroit attracted engineers and industrialists from all over the world. And within a couple of decades, any car manufacturer of size had a research department. However, it is doubtful that the US benefited more from this than any other country. Early car manufacturing drew on relatively well known techniques, and Europe was ahead of the US both in terms of higher education and in the technological sophistication of its cars. In some industries, this might spell disaster. In the car industry, the ability to produce cheaply and efficiently accounted for more than having the edge in terms of technology or product design. The American car revolution was not one of the US producing better cars, it was one of producing them radically more cheaply and efficiently.

Also, the US was richly endowed in a number of important Smithian advantages. In three areas, the US had vital advantages. The US had a higher GDP per capita and higher worker wages, giving rise to a level of mass consumption unequaled by Europe. The US was also more richly endowed in capital, which was of tremendous importance in an industry that was distinctly capital-intensive. In both areas, World War I played to the advantage of the US and to the detriment of Europe. While Europe went from capital-abundant to capital-scarce, the US went from scarce to abundant, being a debtor prior to the war and a major creditor afterwards. Europe became radically more capital-scarce at exactly the time when the car industry was becoming radically more capital-intensive! With World War I, an era of free trade ended. European countries put up gradually rising protective tariffs, preventing the creation of a large European market, and preventing European manufacturers from reaping the benefits of economies of scale. In contrast, the US benefited from a large domestic market.

In terms of mass production technologies, Europe was able to catch up. A number of European industrialists traveled to Detroit to learn how to set up mass-production facilities in their respective countries. Still, Europe never came close to catching up in terms of production. This strongly suggests that there was more to the US lead than technological sophistication, pointing strongly in the direction of Smithian explanations. In Europe, the car never became a mass consumption item until after World War II. When Europe caught up with the US in terms of production, it was not because of finally mastering mass production, but a mix of producing small, functional cars for the masses, and the purchasing power of the masses gradually increasing.

Yet, the role of the state was more than negligible. The state contributed by providing a highway infrastructure, without which the explosive expansion of the US car industry would have been implausible. For the car to be a conceivable mass consumption item there had to be roads on which cars could be driven, filling stations for gas, service stations for repairs, etc. In this area, the US state contributed crucially, even if by modern standards, the overall infrastructure investments strike us as rather modest. Still, at this stage, the industry was already by far the biggest in the world, which cannot be attributed to efforts of the state.

Much the same applies to vested interests, social cohesion and political consensus. The period saw a transition from a Republican to a Democratic political hegemony, a transition from political coalitions built on the support of labor-intensive industries to coalitions built on capital-intensive industries, a transition from economic and political laissez-faire to a greater degree of economic and political activism, and a transition from protectionism toward free trade. This was a period of political turmoil and a period where old and dominant industries had to relinquish their grip on political power. However, again the timing of events suggests that this was a contributory factor rather than the immediate cause. The transition was not really completed until the 1930s, at a time when the US was already dominant. Possibly, the vested interest story is more interesting if seen from a European perspective—Freeman and Louçã (2001:279) talk about European hostility toward mass-production techniques. It may be the case that a relative lack of US vested interests is revealed only when directly juxtaposed against Europe. However, anecdotal evidence seems to indicate that the constraints on European car manufacturers had less to do with politics, and more to do with attitudes against mass production. Also, persisting with crafts methods of production was far more rational for European manufacturers, since Europe was much scarcer in capital, finding it hard to make the heavy investments necessary for mass production tooling and equipment.

Finally, a word of caution must be added to the point about Smithian growth. By the end of World War I the US was the world's largest car producer by far. Percentage-wise, the most dramatic growth in US car production took place between 1910 and 1920, whereas Smithian arguments about capital primarily apply to the post-World War I period. Hence, again it is harder to provide an explanation for this early phase of growth than it is for the next decade of sustained growth. Thus, of the Smithian arguments, purchasing power for the average worker seems the most likely candidate. As the world's first mass consumption industry demand was crucial, which brings us back to where we started: The reason why the US car industry became a mass consumption industry has to do with the mass-production technological breakthrough. Henry Ford revolutionized car production. Between late 1913 and early 1914 he reduced the time needed to assemble a Model T by 88 per cent, to a little over an hour and a half. This fueled an enormous increase in production, and is a major part of the reason why US production figures rose so dramatically.

In the final analysis, when all causal variables have been weighed and found to some extent wanting, maybe we need to recognize that in this case, and more than for the other industries, the US car industry owes its success to one man—Henry Ford. It is just that it cannot come as any surprise that this man was an American. The US had a major comparative advantage in technologies thought of as precursors to mass production, and it had a larger potential demand for a contraption like the car, by virtue of having the highest worker wages of the world.

Chapter 6

Information and Communication Technologies

A World Economy in Transition: ICTs and Globalization?

This chapter has to be of a more speculative nature than the previous four, since the focus with respect to information and communication technologies (ICTs) and industries is on developments that are still in the present and to some extent in the future. During the 1970s and early 1980s, several scholars (e.g. Kennedy 1989) predicted the decline and fall of the US, based on decreasing shares of world manufacturing output, falling labor productivity and defense expenditures far superseding those of its nearest rivals. The 1990s instead saw the US re-establish itself as the number one economic (and military) power, with Japan since 1990 stuck in a more or less continuing recession. A crucial reason for this is the success that the US has experienced in ICTs. While both the US and Japan are highly successful ICT *producers*, only the US has been able to successfully *utilize* its ICTs. This has greatly boosted the economy and propelled the US on a most impressive growth spurt.

ICTs and ICT industries are the obvious choice for a present-day leading sector. First; while aware of the hype that has surrounded ICTs, especially up until the dot.com bubble burst in 2001, ICTs have spawned exceptionally rapidly growing industries. Over the past few years, we have seen ever more evidence pointing in the direction that ICTs are having a strong positive impact on productivity figures (TFP, labor productivity), especially in the US. There is a large, and growing, literature emphasizing the importance of ICTs for present and future growth and development (e.g. Castells 2000a; Freeman and Louçã 2001; Mowery and Rosenberg 1998; Nelson 1996; OECD 2001a; Perez 2002).

Second, ICTs have one characteristic central to most influential technologies; its generic nature. It is becoming ever more evident that the main boost to national economies around the world does not stem primarily from computer *manufacture* (or other ICT producing industries), but from the utilization of ICT *services*, especially in the knowledge-intensive part of the service industries (like banking and insurance). Thus, ICTs have improved the productivity both of manufacturing and in the services.

The fact that this chapter comments on phenomena still very much underway, increases the risk of short-term swings and fluctuations unduly biasing the chapter. Ten–fifteen years ago one faced the challenge of explaining how companies invested like never before in ICT, but without any visible productivity improvements emanating from these investments. In a famous statement, Robert Solow in 1987 claimed, "you can see the computer age everywhere but in the productivity statistics". Five years ago, the focus was on ICTs and the Asian crisis (1997–1998). In the final years before 2001, ICT enthusiasts were finally becoming confident about the effect of ICTs on productivity, as studies suggested rising productivity figures, especially so in the US. ICTs were giving rise to a "New Economy" with different rules and dynamics. Then the dot.com bubble burst, making previous claims about the end of business cycles sound ridiculous. Now, as the world economy has been carefully growing its way out of recession, optimism, combined with more solid evidence that ICTs are positively influencing productivity figures, is again starting to characterize the literature.

Hence, for a chapter on ICTs, I have sought to rely on data for which there is widespread consensus. The dot.com bubble represented a temporary setback. ICTs were well overdue for a crash. But hopefully, the crash will give way to steady and more realistic growth in the ICT industries. Optimism, crises and crashes notwithstanding, there are a number of things that we can agree pretty conclusively on, forming the foundations for a chapter on ICTs as the present driver of the economy.

For instance, there is no doubt that the world economy has undergone major changes over the past couple of years, often summarized under the heading globalization. To some scholars, these changes are less than revolutionary (e.g. Gray 1998:61pp; Hirst and Thompson 1999). To others, they are substantial, particularly because of developments closely linked with the rapid progress and utilization of ICTs—the level of financial and capital flows, electronic money, and the emergence of a global, electronic economy.

While this chapter is not about globalization, one focus seems to unite most globalization accounts: The technological revolution launched by ICTs, and the shift away from manufacturing industries. Also prominent is a belief in ICTs as the engine of today's world economy. The OECD (2001a:5) stresses that something new *is* taking place. Economic growth today depends on success within knowledge-based services rather than manufacturing industry (ibid.:12pp; 2000b:8pp, 43, 49pp, 52pp), and employment growth is considerably stronger amongst knowledge workers than other workers (OECD 2001a:14).[1]

Granted, there has been considerable disagreement as to the effect of ICTs on the economy, but disagreement has slowly given way to a growing consensus that ICTs are having an effect. There was never any disagreement on the fact that a structural transformation has been going on for a long time in all Western economies, in the

---

1   Employment growth figures show knowledge workers to be considerably more sought-after than other workers. For the US and EU, 1992–1999, the annual employment growth for knowledge workers was 3.3 per cent. For service workers the corresponding figure was 2.2 per cent, management workers 1.6 per cent, data workers 0.9 per cent, and finally goods-producing workers –0.2 per cent (OECD 2001a:14). Wage patterns are even more extreme. Data from the US shows that the wages of knowledge workers have risen much faster than the wages of other professions. Real earnings of knowledge-intensive workers (1985–1998) grew by 17 per cent as compared to 5.25 per cent for the average employee and a real earning *cut* of 2.5 per cent for workers in goods-producing companies (OECD 2001c:55).

sense of manufacturing giving way to service industries, in particular knowledge-intensive services. Table 6.1 pits the US and Japan against each other for the period of 1950–1991. While the table suggests the same development in both countries, it also suggests that Japan has been much slower in undergoing this transition.

Table 6.1 Distribution of Employment, US vs. Japan, 1950–1991(%)

	1950		1970		1991	
	US	Japan	US	Japan	US	Japan
Agriculture and mining	14.4	50.3	4.6	19.8	3.5	7.2
Manufacturing	33.9	21.0	33.0	34.1	24.7	33.7
Services	51.4	28.6	62.6	46.0	71.8	58.4
– of which knowledge-intensive services	4.8	1.5	8.2	4.8	14.0	9.6

Source: Castells (2000a:304pp).

The 1970s saw a conspicuous productivity slowdown hitting most Western economies. Labor productivity growth in the US fell to 0.8 per cent annually for 1973–1980, down from a consistent 2.5 per cent between 1913 and 1970 (Freeman and Louçã 2001:297). Total factor productivity (TFP) dropped to as low as 0.08 per cent annually—even less than during the early years of the Industrial Revolution (Sachs and Larrain 1993:558)![2] This was due both to low productivity in manufacturing and to two oil price shocks. More importantly, it was also because of sagging productivity in the service sectors not exposed to free trade.[3]

But since the mid-1990s, the US has again been forging ahead. Between 1990 and 2000, US GDP growth exceeded that of Japan for seven out of 10 years. Since the 1980s, US *trend* GDP per capita growth rates (1990–1999) have increased from 2.1 to 2.2 per cent., which sounds innocuous, but compares favorably to Japan, which saw a decline from 3.2 to 1.5 per cent (OECD 2001c:15).[4] Returns from ICT

2   Increasing very cautiously for 1979–1993 to 0.4 per cent annually (Castell 2000a:82). Different scholars calculate somewhat different figures, but the overall picture is the same. Castells (2000a:82) even reports negative TFP growth for 1973–1979 (–0.4 per cent). Maddison concludes that in the US, the residual's contribution to overall growth for the period 1973–1984 was 0 per cent (Boskin and Lau 1996:99).

3   Even in Japan, TFP growth declined. While greater than US figures, Japanese TFP growth (1973–1979) fell to an annual 1.3 per cent (down from 5.6 per cent (1960–1973)). Again, productivity in sectors not open to free trade was the main culprit.

4   Average growth for the 1990s in Japan was a very low 1.1 per cent (Rosecrance 1999:131).

investments take most of the credit for US growth, and is also the reason why Japan has been falling clearly behind.

US labor productivity and TFP have shifted dramatically upwards. Since 1995, labor productivity has averaged almost 3 per cent a year—twice the average rate of the previous two decades (*Economist* 2003a). OECD (2001c:21) figures show that TFP growth has increased by an annual average of 0.3 per cent,[5] whereas in Japan it fell substantially (by an annual average of almost 0.9 per cent). In the US, TFP growth rose from 0.5 per cent (1985–1995) to 1.5 per cent (1995–2000). In Japan, it fell from three per cent to 1.25 per cent, even turning negative (–0.2) between 1990 and 1995 (*Economist* 2000; OECD 2000a:24; 2001d:44).[6] Despite half a century of catch-up, Japanese productivity was still lower than in the US, using 11 per cent more effort and 20 per cent more capital per worker (Farrell 2003:146p).[7]

However, it may be more instructive to look at the specific contribution of ICTs to growth. While scholars disagree somewhat as to the actual figures, they all agree that the US is on top, Japan near the bottom. The OCED (2001c:20) concludes that between 1990 and 1995, the difference between the US and Japan was only slight, ICTs boosting GDP growth by 0.4 per cent in the US, 0.3 per cent in Japan. But for 1995–1999, the difference is considerable: 0.9 per cent for the US, and still only 0.3 for Japan. Yusuf and Evenett (2002:105) present more dramatic figures. During 1990–1995, ICTs contributed 0.31 per cent to annual Japanese GDP growth, rising to 0.38 per cent between 1995 and 2000. For the US, the figures were 0.97 per cent for 1990–1995, and a remarkable 1.71 per cent for 1995–2000. If this is true, the contribution of ICTs to US GDP growth was actually greater than total Japanese GDP growth for this period! There are figures indicating that for 1995–1999, investments in IT and TFP gains in the production of IT goods together may have accounted for 98 per cent of the total increase in US productivity growth (*Economist* 2003a).[8] van Ark, Inklaar and McGuckin (2003:17), and van Ark and Inklaar (2003:11) convincingly show that the reason why the US is so far ahead has less to do with ICT *producing industries*, and all to do with ICT *using services*. US ICT producing industry exhibits extremely impressive productivity growth (1995–

---

5   1980–1989 vs. 1990–1999.

6   There are figures suggesting that the computer industry contributed to around 50 per cent of overall TFP growth, in other words as much as every other industry put together (OECD 2000a:51).

7   This is particularly conspicuous in industries like retailing, where Japanese labor productivity is only around 50 per cent of US overall productivity (Japanese productivity is 88 per cent of the US in modern retailing, but only 19 per cent in the traditional sectors). In food processing it is as low as 39 per cent (Farrell 2003:154; William W. Lewis 2004:39; Sakakibara 2003:44p).

8   Others present more modest findings. However, even conservative estimates are impressive, as the 60 per cent for the 1990s, reported by a Jorgenson and Stiroh 2000 Brooking Paper (cited in van Ark 2002:5).

2000): 23.7 per cent annually.[9] But they only account for 2.6 per cent of GDP, and so their overall effect on the economy is modest. More importantly, in ICT using services, productivity growth has increased from an annual 1.9 per cent between 1990 and 1995 to an impressive 5.4 per cent for 1995–2000. As ICT using services account for as much as 26.3 per cent of total GDP (2000), these are figures that strongly influence the overall economy. The contrast with Japan is stark. For ICT producing industries, the Japanese figures are mirror-images of the US, with 22.7 per cent annual productivity increase (1995–2000), and a 3.3 per cent share of GDP. However, in ICT using services, productivity growth 1995–2000 was 0.0 per cent,[10] down even from the 1990–1995 figure of 1.5.

Hence, productivity growth figures make a very credible case for the utilization of ICTs as the main reason for US economic breakaway and Japanese stagnation. Also, qualitative evidence suggests a Japan where companies have only reluctantly introduced new technologies, and only after they have been shown to be effective in the US. And a Japan that has failed to demonstrate leadership in the information age, lagging substantially behind most of the industrialized countries in adoption and use of ICTs (OCED 2000a:51; World Economic Forum 2002:232). The World Economic Forum (2003:457) singles out the government's lack of success in ICT promotion as one of Japan's greatest competitive disadvantages.[11] Quantitative evidence bears witness of a dual economy with impressive productivity in export sectors, such as automobiles and computer production, but conspicuously low productivity in the non-export service industries. The dual nature of ICTs makes the sector hard to assess in some respects. While Japan has one of the most successful computer industries in the world, it has not managed to avoid a decade and a half of economic recession. In other words, if we focus on ICTs as hardware, Japan is a tremendous success. However, since services have outgrown manufacturing in terms of employment, and since service industries have often lagged in terms of productivity, success with respect to ICTs becomes a story not about having a large ICT-producing industry, but of being able to utilize ICTs in other sectors. This is where the US has forged ahead. Japan has been very good at treating its ICT industries as traditional mass production industries. Hence, as Rosecrance says:

> As long as industry and manufacturing were the standards of excellence in economics, Japan prospered. It still excels in these important sectors; but while "manufacturing matters," it matters much less than it once did. Achievement is now measured not by

---

9   Or as much as an annual 41.7 per cent if we are to believe Castells (2000a:93). According to Castells (2000a:148), the US IT sector accounts for eight per cent of US GDP, but contributed to an average 35 per cent of GDP growth between 1995 and 1998. William W. Lewis (2004:88) goes further: Manufacturing of microprocessor chips and computers accounted for 20 per cent of TFP growth acceleration since the mid-1990s.

10   *The Economist* (2004d:82) even reports *negative* productivity growth in IT using services, 1995–2000.

11   On this indicator, Japan came in 46 out of 80 countries. The US was 15th (World Economic Forum 2003:588).

manufacturing productivity increases, but by excellence in creative and information services: product design, fundamental research, and intelligent software. As Japan was mastering hardware, the world was beginning to shift to software. As Japan triumphed in tangibles, the world shifted to intangibles. It is Japan's failure to excel in both elements of economic strategy—manufacturing and services—that creates problems today. (1999:123)

In the following we shall see how weak Japanese governments have been unable to prevent an iron triangle of vested interests from controlling politics. While this system may have been beneficial during the mass-production era, it became a liability as the world economy changed. Vested interests have prevented structural change in finance, construction, retailing, wholesaling, food processing and a host of other sectors. This has harmed the Japanese economy by draining resources away from more productive investments. It has also been harmful in the sense that especially in finance and in retailing, Japan has been able to utilize ICTs for productivity improvements to a much lesser extent than the US. Japan could not adjust its institutions and policies so as to benefit from the opportunities provided to ICTs by these new industries. Instead, it was the US that profited. The federal government provided the country with the world's best university system, abundant funding for ICTs relevant for national security purposes, and a political environment that from the 1980s could more or less unanimously agree that liberalization and deregulation was essential with respect to future US growth. As a result, the US has profited from its ICTs in a way Japan has been unable to.

ICT Industries

Providing a brief history of ICTs is tricky. First, ICTs is not a very homogeneous group, and thus it is not obvious on what to focus. Second, many of the crucial ICT developments occurred between 1945 and 1970, that is preceding the time period highlighted in this chapter. Third, the secret to economic success has been less about ICT manufacturing, and much more about ICTs utilization, especially in the knowledge-intensive service industries. The following section is divided into two subsections, one dealing with ICT manufacturing, and one dealing with network technologies. For both, I have chosen to go far back in time, starting with World War II for computer production and, for network technologies, back to developments coming out of US reactions to the 1957 Sputnik launch.

Computers, Semiconductors and Software

The honors of producing the first successful computer probably go to Germany, which between 1936 and 1942 developed the Z3 and the Z4 for aircraft design calculations. While more advanced than contemporary American attempts, the factory was closed down as a consequence of allied bombing in 1944. Computing machines were also developed by the British, who were trying to come up with a machine to crack the codes from the German Enigma machine. Compared to other war efforts, the British COLOSSUS was groundbreaking. After the war, the machine was dismantled, among other reasons because of Churchill's view that it had to be kept a secret (Freeman and Soete 1999:171; Nairn 2002:313).

Instead, computer production came to be dominated by the US. Scholars routinely name the ENIAC (Electronic Numeral Integrator and Computer) as the world's first fully electronic digital computer, built between 1942 and 1946. It was more than 30 meters long, weighed 30 tons, and employed the simultaneous use of 70,000 resistors and 18,000 vacuum tubes. It filled a room the size of a squash court, and its electricity consumption was so enormous that it caused the lighting of Philadelphia to twinkle when it was turned on. Following the ENIAC came the EDVAC (Electronic Discrete Variable Automatic Computer), which spurred the British to renew work based on their wartime activities, creating the EDSAC (Electronic Delay Storage Automatic Computer) (Castells 2000a:42; Cowan 1997:294; Freeman and Soete 1999:172; Mowery and Rosenberg 1998:2, 136; Nairn 2002:318).

The first commercial computer was the 1950 UNIVAC-1 (Universal Automatic Computer). Early funding had been provided by a betting consortium, which wanted computing power for racecourse betting[!], but when it withdrew, the research team was forced to look for a buyer. Hence, Remington Rand bought the rights to the technology and became the early leader in computer manufacture (Castells 2000a:42; Mowery and Rosenberg 1998:138; Nairn 2002:320p).

IBM was absent during the early phase, surviving by virtue of demand vastly outstripping supply. Hence it could compete, even with products distinctly inferior to those of Remington Rand. IBM rapidly caught up, and was propelled into the lead in 1964 with the System 360.[12] The 360 was more of a commercial breakthrough than a technological marvel. It created a family of IBM computers in different price ranges, all compatible with each other, running on the same operative system and other software. As a consequence, IBM managed to preserve its position throughout the 1970s, and was not truly challenged until the dawn of the microcomputer (Bresnahan and Malerba 1999:94pp; Castells 2000a:42; Mowery and Rosenberg 1998:145; Nairn 2002:322).

With the 1971 invention of the microprocessor, the computer industry faced a new revolution, enabling computers that were smaller, faster and cheaper. In 1975 Ed Roberts produced the *Altair*.[13] While crude, it attracted the interest of Paul Allen and Bill Gates, who saw it as a perfect base from which to run their new BASIC programming language software. Employing BASIC, the Altair in 1976 also became the basis for the Apple computer, by Steve Jobs and Stephen Wozniak. By the time IBM realized the potential of the microcomputer, there were already a number of

---

12 The System 360 was a family of six mutually compatible computers and 40 peripherals, all with the ability to work together (Chandler and Cortada 2000:221).

13 This was an extremely crude and simple computer. It had no keyboard, no screen, no printer, and not even a permanent storage. However, it only cost $397 (or just above $1,000 in today's currency) (Nairn 2002:354).

new firms entering the business—Atari, Apple, Commodore, Radio Shack, Tandy, etc. Hence, in 1980, IBM started a microcomputer program of its own, trying to claw back its dwindling market share. In the process of developing what came to be known as the Personal Computer, IBM ensured its own survival as a computer manufacturer by outsourcing components and software, essentially putting its brand name on a product completely developed by others. This meant that IBM clones sprang up on a large scale, including in Japan. This hampered IBM sales. At the same time, it made the computer industry standardize around two designs, the Apple and the IBM. Because of the sheer number of IBM clones, IBM effectively diffused a new standard for microcomputers, enabling it to compete against the Apple Macintosh, even though the Apple was probably the superior design (Castells 2000a:43; Nairn 2002:364pp).

Europe's computer industry lost out, but Japan succeeded. Four years of negotiations (1956–1960) between IBM and MITI (Ministry of International Trade and Industry) led to a compromise. IBM insisted on working independently in Japan, MITI wanted a joint venture. In the end, IBM was allowed to work independently, but only if it gave up its patents in Japan. Still, Japanese manufacturers were dependent on alliances with US companies for manufacturing licenses and technical assistance. These alliances, combined with the 1962 MITI program to encourage cooperation between Japanese computer manufacturers—and tariffs of around 25 per cent—meant that Japanese computer manufacturers controlled 52 per cent of the domestic market by 1966, rising to almost 60 per cent by 1970 (up from 18 per cent in 1961). Still, the IBM System 360, and the later 370 (1970), made it evident that Japan had fallen behind. MITI tried to reorganize Japanese computer manufacturing, but the single most important factor behind Japanese catch-up was fortuitous. Gene Amdahl—one of IBM's leading designers on System 360 and 370—left IBM in 1970, but could not find funding to set up his own business. Hence, in 1971 he turned to Fujitsu, which within three years went on to produce Amdahl computers in Japan. This was the difference between the industry's success and its immediate failure (Bresnahan and Malerba 1999:104; Chandler 2001).

While IBM is still the world's largest producer of large-scale mainframe and supercomputer systems, Fujitsu, NEC and Hitachi follow next. In desktops, IBM is also the largest,(with Compaq second), and Fujitsu, Toshiba and NEC in 3rd, 4th and 5th position. In the Japanese market, Fujitsu passed IBM in terms of market share in 1979. While the US must still be considered number one in computer manufacturing, Japan has come a very close second for more than a decade (Bresnahan and Malerba 1999:104; Chandler 2001:223p).

In semiconductors, a world market originally dominated by the US is today controlled by Japan. The first major breakthrough substituted vacuum tubes for relays. Hence, vacuum tubes were a crucial component of any electronic circuit between 1915 and 1950, first employed in the lighting industry, and then in radios (Cowan 1997:292; Nairn 2002:314, 325).

However, most stories about the origin of the semiconductor start with the 1947 invention of the transistor, by a team of physicists at Bell Laboratories (that is, the research arm of AT&T). The transistor was considerably smaller than the vacuum tube, it required far less power to operate, it was much more reliable, and it did not need to be heated up. The transistor made possible the processing of fast-paced electric impulses in a binary manner, enabling coding of logic and communication with the machine, as well as between machines. Transistors are put together in processing devices called semiconductors (or chips). While revolutionary, it was unreliable and difficult to produce. Yet, with time, scaling-up of production was extremely successful, with the US leaping ahead. The transistor became extremely useful, employed in radios, television sets, hearing aids, calculators, etc., as well as in computers. AT&T licensed the transistor to anyone who wanted to produce it, and this ensured rapid diffusion (Castells 2000a:40; Cortada 2000:177; Freeman and Louçã 2001:306; Langlois and Steinmueller 1999:22; Nairn 2002:325).

The 1957 Integrated Circuit was the next breakthrough (invented by Jack Kilby and Bob Noyce). This led to semiconductor prices falling by 85 per cent between 1959 and 1962, with production increasing by a factor of 20 during the 1960s. From $50 in 1962, prices fell to $1 by 1971. Originally, 3–12 transistor equivalents could be packed into one IC. This increased to 4,000 in the 1960s, to over 500,000 in the 1970s, and to 100 million in the 1980s. During the first decade, the US reigned supreme. As of 1958, US semiconductor production netted a nominal $236 million as opposed to only $19 million in Japanese semiconductor manufacture. By 1961, the figures had increased to $607 million for the US, and $78 million for Japan (Castells 2000a:40; Cowan 1997:293; Langlois and Steinmueller 1999:23pp, 32; Mowery and Rosenberg 1998:128).[14]

In 1971, Intel invented the microprocessor, for all practical purposes a computer on a chip. But this was also the decade in which Japanese IC manufacturers were actually catching up with the US, not in microprocessors, but in DRAM memory chips. This was an area in which US companies during the early 1970s controlled 95 per cent of the world market. However, profit margins were low, and when an industry recession delayed the US 16K DRAM chip in 1976, Japanese firms rapidly achieved a market share of 41 per cent. Different production decisions in Japan and the US with respect to the 64K chip allowed Japanese firms to increase their share. By 1990, Japanese firms controlled 98 per cent of the market, four of the five largest semiconductor producers of the world being Japanese (Castells 2000a:40pp; Chandler 2001:155, 240; Freeman and Louçã 2001:307; Langlois and Steinmueller 1999:41p)!

1985 saw unprecedented losses in the US IC industry, with Intel hit especially hard. Intel withdrew from the DRAM market in 1985, restructured and survived by specializing in higher-margin, more design-intensive chips, like microprocessors. Hence, with its main emphasis on microprocessors, Intel by 1994 had regained a

14 While the gap between Japan and the US was overwhelming, compared to Europe, Japan was not doing badly. Hence West German production rose from a net $10 million in 1958 to $30 million in 1961. Corresponding British figures were $8 million and $32 million (Langlois and Steinmueller 1999:29).

31 per cent world market share in microcomponents. Out of the world's top six semiconductor producers, three were once again from the US, with Intel the biggest. The US and Japan have essentially divided the IC market between them. Japanese (and Korean) companies dominate the memory chip market, with US firms controlling microprocessors (Chandler 2001:155, 240; Freeman and Louçã 2001:308; Langlois and Steinmueller 1999:47pp).

No branch of the computer industry is more symbolic of the information age than software. It is a special case in the sense that it requires little physical capital, relying almost solely on human capital. In this field, the US has been very dominant, with no serious Japanese challenge. Two of the central decisions affecting the development of the software industry were made by IBM. In 1969, IBM accidentally created a market for independent software producers by announcing that it would now price software and services separate from computers, "unbundling" hardware and software sales. Second, in 1981, when IBM entered the microcomputer market, it did so by outsourcing among other things the software component of microcomputer development, encouraging the industry to write software for the IBM PC (Castells 2000a:42p; Chandler and Cortada 2000:295; Cortada 2000:203; Mowery 1999:144; Nairn 2002:353pp).

Having a strong domestic hardware industry does not necessarily lead to a strong software industry. Yet, the US definitely benefited from its hardware sector. Because of strong government and Department of Defense demand for hardware, US software benefited as early software production to a large extent was custom software for federal demand. But also, the Japanese market (figures from 1991) was to an unusual extent dominated by mainframe computers (70 per cent), compared to the US (45 per cent). Since mainframes normally come with their own tailor-made software, there was a much greater incentive for the unbundling of hardware and software in the US than in Japan. Also, a relative lack of network-based computing in Japan was a considerable handicap for any domestic software industry; part of the dominant US position is routinely attributed to the strong user-producer interactions in the US software industry (Mowery 1999:150; Mowery and Rosenberg 1998:162p).[15] As a consequence, the packaged software market in Japan is less than one-quarter the size of the US market, and US firms control 75 per cent of world packaged software production.

Network Technologies

The origins of the Internet go back to 1957 and the Soviet launch of the Sputnik—the world's first artificial satellite. The Sputnik caught the US by surprise and gave rise to fears that Soviet ballistic missile technologies might take out major parts of the US command structure in one massive first strike. Hence, the Department of Defense in 1958 formed ARPA (Advanced Research Projects Agency), with the explicit

---

15 In terms of software products fitting local needs, the US was number one out of 75 countries, Japan only 30th (World Economic Forum 2002:347).

purpose of ensuring US scientific superiority. ARPA had two major objectives. First, computers should be able to talk to each other in order to share information. Second, and more importantly, the links between each computer should be made so robust that cutting one link would not crash the system. Thus, the network would be made independent of any command and control center and have an entirely decentralized structure (Castells 2000a:45; Nairn 2002:332pp).

In 1969, ARPA gave rise to the world's first computer network, the ARPANET. Over the next few years, a pilot project including four American universities was initiated, connecting mainframe computers to telephone lines. By 1970, it was extended to 11 universities, by 1973 there were 45 hosts and by 1977 111, most of these still in the military sphere, but also including 16 university campuses. In 1983 ARPANET was split into ARPANET for scientific purposes, and MILNET for military use. Also, by this time, other networks were forming, the National Science Foundation (NSF) creating the NSFNet, consisting of the scientific network CSNET (Computer Science Research Network) and the BITNET for non-science scholars. In 1989, ARPANET was incorporated into the NSFNet, which was a loose superstructure of networks called the ARPA–INTERNET, still supported by the Department of Defense and the NSF. When ARPANET was closed down the next year, the NSFNet became what eventually developed into today's Internet, growing from 200 hosts in 1980, reaching 1,000 four years later and accelerating rapidly, with 159,000 hosts in 1989, the first million passed in 1993, 10 million hosts in 1995 and 100 million in 2000. However, as of the early 1990s, the network was still under government control, and restricted to non-commercial use. It was not privatized until 1995 (Castells 2000a:46; Chandler 2001:171pp).

Before the noncommercial Internet could merge with commercial networks, it had to be made usable. Major breakthroughs were the World Wide Web and the browser. The world wide web (WWW) was created at CERN in Geneva, and provided a new system for organizing information (hypertext), and a standard format for Internet addresses (URL, or uniform resource locator). The WWW software was distributed for free over the Internet, and made it feel less like a "library that has no card catalogue" (Chandler 2001:173). Further, the first browser, Mosaic, written at the NSF National Center for Supercomputing Applications, was released in 1993. It gave the Web a graphically richer face, as well as making it easier to exploit hypertext. Internet development had also been feeding off the computer counterculture of hacking. Hence, in 1978 the modem was invented by two Chicago students.

The overwhelming majority of these developments occurred in the US. In terms of international comparisons, the US ranks ahead of most countries on most network related criteria. In particular, it ranks ahead of Japan, which has been downright slow at utilizing its impressive ICT *manufacturing* skills. Out of 29 OECD countries (2001 figures), the US ranked number one in the number of Internet hosts per 1,000, with Japan 16. The US was also number one in the amount of web sites created per 1,000 inhabitants, Japan 26th. In terms of broad band penetration rates, Japan did somewhat better, at 11th from 30, with the US 3rd. But in terms of Internet subscribers per 100 inhabitants, Japan was a lowly 19 out of 26, with the US 5th.

The same applies to Internet and electronic commerce transactions, with Japan 18 out of 29, with the US 2nd (OECD 2001e:71pp). In the World Economic Forum's (2002:233, 303) Networked Readiness Index, Japan is only 21st out of 75 countries, with the US first.[16] Erecting an information infrastructure is not synonymous with actual utilization of ICTs in particular knowledge-intensive service industries. These figures are not proof that the US is more eagerly utilizing its ICTs, but they plausibly point in the direction of Japan being a distinct laggard in erecting an Internet and information infrastructure, with the US at the same time being the leader in the field.

For computers, semiconductors, software and network technologies, many of the crucial developments took place significantly earlier than the time period highlighted in this chapter. However, to paraphrase Castells (2000a:53, 85), these developments did not start to come together until the 1970s. The microprocessor was invented in 1971, and the microcomputer in 1975. The Xerox Alto, which was the matrix of many software technologies, was developed in 1973. ARPANET was set up in 1969, diffusing throughout the 1970s, helped by the network protocol TCP/IP invented in the 1973. It took another two decades before this new technological paradigm diffused and consolidated to the extent that ICTs positively affected productivity rates, growth rates, TFP rates, etc. Hence, despite 1950s and 1960s computer production, for the start of this paradigm, we still have to look to the 1970s.

The Role of the State

Human Capital

For ICTs a focus on basic indicators like literacy and enrollment rates hardly makes much sense. While literacy and enrollment are obviously still important, they are not distinguishing indicators of educational performance in contemporary developed, industrialized countries. Still, modern growth literature to an ever greater extent focuses on human capital (e.g. Gilpin 2000; OECD 2001b), including primary education.

Both the US and Japan have done well in terms of basic education. This was an area in which Japan was never far behind in any case. Japan was catching up early on, and the state's conscious efforts to improve elementary and higher education is credited with making a very significant contribution to Japan's rapid economic growth ever since the nineteenth century (e.g. Dore 1982:105pp [1965]; Young 1998:59). Morris-Suzuki (1994:80) points out that compulsory primary education was introduced in 1871, a full 20 years ahead of Britain.

---

16 Sections written by Chowdhury (2002:232) and Ratnathicam and Kirkman (2002:303).

Both countries attained full literacy decades ago,[17] and for every age group, both the US and Japan are far above the OECD average in terms of the amount of population with at least upper secondary education.[18] Both countries are also well above the average with respect to expenditure on educational institutions per student. However, with a number of different indicators, the quality of basic education differs significantly, as seen for instance from PISA surveys.[19] In reading literacy, mathematical literacy and scientific literacy (for 15-year-olds) Japan performs conspicuously better than the US.[20] Japan ranks between 3rd and 10th (out of 32) for overall reading literacy, as opposed to 10th and 20th for the US, although a greater proportion of American students rank at the very highest proficiency level. In mathematical and scientific literacy the difference is greater. In both, Japan ranks among the first three, with the US down at the OECD average (OECD 2002a:69pp; 2002b:39).[21] Other surveys confirm this. Yusuf (2003:186) lists Japan 4th and 5th (out of 38) in secondary education science and mathematics skills, with the US 18th and 19th.[22]

Despite the above, major criticism has been raised against the Japanese education system. Interestingly, this criticism seems to reflect the dualism of this chapter— that of ICTs as mass production vs. generic technology with particular benefits for knowledge-intensive services. The Japanese education system has been good at producing people with basic skills, especially in the natural sciences, but far less so at producing graduates with strong abilities for innovative thinking and creativity. Schools have been transformed into what Cheng and Hsuing (1998:122p) label a "recruiting agency for the factory", created to meet industry's demand for "a stable supply of malleable labor". This is backed up by PISA surveys (OECD 2002a:329) for "quality and use of school resources" (15-year-olds, 2000), which ranks Japan bottom out of 27 OECD countries. The survey included use of school libraries, use of science laboratories, and the use of computers in school. Japan did poorly in all

---

17 See for instance CIA's *World Factbook 2006*, which reports 99 per cent literacy for both Japan and the US.

18 For the age group 25–64, 88 per cent of Americans, 83 per cent of the Japanese had at least upper secondary education (OCED average 64 per cent). For the 55–64 group; US 83 per cent, Japan 63 per cent, OECD average 49 per cent. For the 25–34 group; US 88 per cent, Japan 94 per cent, OECD average 74 per cent (OECD 2002a:37).

19 Programme of International Student Assessment. Survey includes 32 mostly OECD countries.

20 The data are based on samples that make an exact rank of a country impossible. However, it is possible to report the range of rank order positions within which the country mean lies with a 95 per cent likelihood.

21 In mathematical literacy, Japan ranks 1–3, the US 16–23, and in scientific literacy 1–2 compared to the US 11–21 (OECD 2002a:69pp; 2002b:39).

22 However, in the World Economic Forum (2003:581) Global Competitiveness Report, Japan is only 27th out of 80 countries in the quality of math and science education. Granted, the US is worse, in 38th. Still, it suggests that Japan may not be as far ahead of the US in certain areas of basic education as other statistics indicate.

three subsections, but especially so in the availability and use of computers. Also in the ratio of students to computers, Japan was only marginally above the OECD average. The US was nowhere near the top of the list, but nevertheless ranked in the top third (OECD 2002a:329). In a World Economic Forum (2002:361) study, the US was 7th out of 75 countries with respect to Internet access in schools, Japan only 32nd.

The OECD (1999a:50) makes it clear that education and training in Japan must be made more conducive to creativity and entrepreneurship (Barker and Goto 1998:258; Castells 2000b:265; Rosecrance 1999:110). What worked in an era of mass production may not work equally well with ICTs. Thus, there is a clear recognition that a focus on the creation of new, fundamental knowledge is required for Japan to be successful in the future.

In most respects both countries have devoted sizable funding to basic education. That US mathematical and science literacy scores are highly mediocre, cannot be a good sign. The advantage that Japan holds in this area may explain why it has been good at ICT-related *production*. However, the primary contribution to growth stems from the *utilization* of ICTs, which is an area where Japan has fallen behind. This goes well with question marks hanging over Japanese basic education with respect to its alleged lack of creativity, and the utilization of school resources. It also goes well with the differently structured linkages in the US and the Japanese industry–state–academic networks, leading to widespread diffusion in the US and the virtual opposite in Japan.

The relevance of human capital becomes more obvious once we shift the focus toward higher education. The transformation undergone by the US higher education system following World War II cannot be underestimated. The pre-war system had been more about interaction between academia and industry than about advanced technology, with the individual states bearing the brunt of the financing, not the federal government. However, from 1940 to 1945, federal R & D expenditures soared from \$83.2 to \$1,313.6 million.[23] The present large-scale, well-funded US higher education system is the legacy of wartime expenditures, and has resulted in a federal commitment to university research that has lasted for more than half a century. It has also resulted in a system where nongovernmental institutions have retained most of the responsibility for R & D, even if the funding has been provided by the federal government (Mowery and Rosenberg 1993:39; Mowery and Rosenberg 1998:23; Nelson and Romer 1996:49).

Following the war, the Vannevar Bush report (*Science: The Endless Frontier*) recommended a large-scale US effort on science and technology. The government should coordinate and fund US research activities, but with private and academic involvement. He also suggested the foundation of what eventually became the National Science Foundation (NSF). Bush's recommendations were not followed in terms of the institutional structure that he suggested. Still, the massive post-war

---

23 Of this, the Department of Defense accounted for an increase from \$29.6 to \$423.6 million (in 1930 dollars).

expansion of the US science system is a legacy of the wartime program overseen by Bush and by the report (Mowery and Rosenberg 1998:31p; Nairn 2002:390; Nelson and Romer 1996:49).

As a consequence, science-based industries were complemented by a system of research universities at the world research frontier within both science and engineering. A number of new institutions contributed with public funding: NSF, National Institutes of Health, the Department of Defense, the Atomic Energy Agency, the National Aeronautics and Space Agency, and the Department of Agriculture (Ruttan 2001:438).

The expansion of publicly funded research in US universities is one of the characteristic features of the US system. Federal R & D support grew from $500 million in 1935–1936 to $2.4 billion in 1960 and $16.8 billion in 1995.[24] In addition to this, the federal government supported investments in physical equipment and facilities for advanced research. The amount of financial aid for students in higher education has been increased, and the amount of scientific personnel increased strongly. As a consequence, US universities have developed from prewar mediocrities into the world's finest science institutions, with a combined R & D rivaling that of Germany, France, Britain and Japan put together. At the same time, industry research spending has also increased dramatically. As a consequence, the number of scientists in industrial research rose from 50,000 in 1946 to almost 600,000 by the mid-1980s.[25] Since the 1980s, many US firms have cut back on expenditures for basic research. Hence, corporate laboratories have been closed down. Also, as other economies have caught up with the US in GDP per capita, the US advantage in basic research has been eroding (Mowery and Rosenberg 1993:48pp; 1998:30pp, 46).

Modern Japanese universities had a genuinely practical purpose from the outset, established in the Meiji era with the explicit intent of importing Western knowledge and ideas to assist in developing the nation, with engineering and applied sciences, technology and agriculture elevated to university status.[26] A high level of education was perceived as necessary for Japan to catch up with the West. By 1930, Japan had 30 universities, with a total enrollment of 40,000 students (Beauchamp and Rubinger 1989:41; Jansen 2000:541; Kennedy 1989:266; Nakayama 1989:33pp).

The education system expanded during the interwar years through the creation of basic research institutions, national industrial laboratories and improvements to science and technology education. Supplying critical firms and industries with the necessary technology and knowledge for catch-up was an expressed goal, and the military's emphasis on science and technology for military progress strongly contributed to the process. The Science Council was founded in 1933 in order to

---

24 In 1987 dollars, hence these figures are not directly comparable with the above figures illustrating the overall wartime R&D expansion. University research as share of GNP doubled between 1960 and 1985 (Mowery and Rosenberg 1993:47; 1998:35).

25 Odagiri and Goto (1993:104) state a total of 949,000 "R & D personnel" (1988). Hence, there is considerable disagreement as to these figures.

26 Tokyo University was founded in 1870.

promote basic research, with most of the funding going to engineering projects, and with an emphasis on militarily relevant technology (Odagiri and Goto 1993:83pp).

Still, Japanese ICT industries with a few exceptions sprang up independently of pre-war companies. And because of World War II, Japan had to start from behind, importing technology from abroad. Hence, as in the US, government institutions had a very explicit impact on education efforts, in particular through MITI. MITI early on searched for new and promising industrial sectors to promote, and singled out microelectronics, calling for a transformation of Japanese society to accommodate these technologies (Castells 200b:228, 250pp; Odagiri and Goto 1993:85pp).

However, it is also the case that Japanese R & D to a large extent has depended on industry rather than government or academia. While total R & D expenditures have been above that of most Western nations, the government's share has traditionally amounted to less than 20 per cent, as compared to almost 50 per cent in the US. Whereas in the US, roughly one third of total business R & D has been funded by the government, Japanese companies have relied almost exclusively upon their own funds. The share of services in business R & D was particularly low, Japan 19th out of 19 OECD countries (in contrast to the US, which was 3rd). Over the past decade, Japanese higher education has come under increasingly strong criticism. Obviously, one should be careful criticizing this system, since the alleged detrimental features of the system were very much prevalent prior to the 1990s as well, and at that time hailed as positives rather than negatives. However, voices have been raised over the fact that the university sector has played a very minor role in knowledge generation (Barker and Goto 1998:258; Odagiri and Goto 1993:104; OECD 2001e:23; Porter 1990:397).

Castells (2000b:251p) claims that fundamental weaknesses in Japanese science have limited Japan's ability to generate new technology. The science system is good at adapting technology, but not at generating it. This has to do with the university system: Graduate schools are weak and doctoral programs geared toward in-house promotion. Universities are "degree-granting bureaucracies, primarily aimed at cultural reproduction and social selection, not centers of innovation and training for autonomous thinking." The system is unable to generate a critical mass of researchers and programs to come up with radical innovations, despite a wealth of engineering graduates. More funding has yielded more of the same: More bureaucratically minded graduates in bureaucratically organized centers. Japan is still toward centralized mass-production and manufacturing rather than knowledge-intensive services.[27]

However, on a number of higher education indicators, Japan stacks up well against the US. OECD (2001e) figures suggest that Japan has not only caught up with, but even passed the US in terms of per capita number of research scientists.[28]

---

27 The OECD (2002a:134) adds to this by providing figures that suggest that social rates of return to education are markedly lower in Japan than in the US.

28 Japan: 97 per 10,000 (1999); US 81 (1997). In 1981, it was the other way around, with the US 62 to Japan 54. Both countries are considerably above the OECD average (OECD 2001e).

On patenting, Japan was behind, but only modestly so. Out of 14 industrialized countries, the US and Japan were one and two in terms of patents per capita (1968–1997), the only major difference being that the increase in patenting was considerably more rapid in the US (Yusuf and Evenett 2002:61).[29] While the Japanese government effort has been modest in terms of R & D expenditures, in overall terms, Japanese figures compare very favorably with the US (3.0 per cent of GDP vs. 2.6 per cent for the US) (Yusuf 2003:179). In basic research as percentage of GDP, the two were fairly similar, the main difference being the US university sector, which overwhelms the Japanese (OECD 2001e:39). In terms of investments in knowledge overall, US expenditures amounted to 6.0 per cent of GDP, as opposed to Japan's 4.7 per cent (1998), a difference accounted for by spending on higher education, where the Japanese figure fell well below the OECD average (OECD 2001e:146).[30] Of the OECD countries, no country had a larger share of population with at least upper secondary level education, and no country spent more per student on tertiary education than the US. Japan was 7th (of 29) on the first measure, 9th (of 25) on the second. While this indicates a stronger role for the US than the Japanese government in human capital investment, what it also shows is that Japan allocates about the same amount of funding as the OECD average (OECD 2001e:15, 146).[31]

On other indicators, the Japanese performance looks shadier. Science–innovation links have developed rapidly over the past decade or two,[32] nowhere more so than in the US, and of the major OECD countries nowhere less so than in Japan. In the US, the number of scientific citations in patents has multiplied by 6–7, as opposed to merely doubling in Japan (OECD 2001c:49). The US also tops an OECD survey on spin-offs from publicly funded research, most of these being in ICTs and in biotechnology. The figures indicate that the number of spin-offs in North America was 3–4 times higher than in any other OECD country (OECD 2001c:51). While Japan was not a part of the survey, other surveys support the basic finding that the Japanese science–innovation link is weak. In a survey of the relative impact[33] of scientific papers (1996–2000), Japan was rock-bottom (Yusuf 2003:209). Also, Japan lags far behind in terms of indicators like articles in international academic journals.[34] In terms of world university rankings (based on research productivity

---

29 2.8 per cent for Japan, 5.3 per cent for the US. Patents per 100,000 1992–1997: US 25.2, Japan 19.0 (Yusuf and Evenett 2002:61).

30 US 1.9 per cent of GDP, Japan 0.6 per cent (OECD 2001e:39).

31 While behind in R&D expenditures, the US made up for this in particular through spending on higher education (1.9 per cent vs. 0.6 per cent). Here, the Japanese figure fell well below the OECD average (OECD 2001e:146).

32 Measured as the average number of scientific papers cited in patents taken in the US by country of origin (OECD 2001c:49).

33 Relative impact = sum of fields in which countries received more than the world average number of citations out of 22 broad categories. In Japan, no field received an above average number of citations (Yusuf 2003:209).

34 Roughly 50,000 as compared to 250,000 for the US (Hobday 1995:64). However, since most journals are published in English, there is a fairly heavy bias against Japan on this

within economics), the highest ranked Japanese universities was Osaka in 105th, followed by the University of Tsukuba in 116th and Tokyo University in 136th. This, in contrast to US universities, which held the first 17 spots (Kalaitzidakis, Mamuneas and Stengos 2001:18pp). The overall image is one of Japan comparing favorably to the US on "stocks" type knowledge indicators, but less well on "flow" type indicators. In other words, while both countries have been successful in producing knowledge and human capital, the US has been superior with respect to utilizing it.

Human Capital and ICTs   The importance of interaction between the science system and the business sector, and the fact that technological innovation today makes more intensive use of scientific knowledge than ever before, is becoming ever more recognized (OECD 2000b:28). Moreover, evidence is substantial that the contribution of the US federal government in terms of providing R & D, human capital and knowledge, has had a very direct impact on the growth of early ICT industries and on the US dominance in ICTs.

Some of the most important breakthroughs in ICTs came about through US government funding, through universities or private R & D laboratories benefiting from basic research and government funding of privately conducted R & D. US universities were instrumental in the development of the first computers following World War II. The project leading up to the 1943 ASCC (Automatic Sequence Controlled Calculator), or the Harvard Mark I, was begun in 1936 at Harvard, under the leadership of Howard Aiken, with the funding and cooperation of IBM. The team of scientists behind the 1946 ENIAC was sponsored by the Army. It faced resistance from both the NDRC (National Defense Research Committee) and the MIT, but the enthusiastic endorsement of Princeton mathematician John von Neumann, working on the Manhattan Project, did much to enhance the reputation of computer research in both the federal government and the science community. Hence, the Army also funded the successor machine, EDVAC (Bresnahan and Malerba 1999:127; Freeman and Soete 1999:171pp; Mowery 1999:145; Nairn 2002:313pp).

While this may not bear witness of strong initial government resolve, it does highlight the indisputable contribution of human capital to ICTs. Up until the mid-1950s, development of computer technology relied almost solely on university researchers, either through university research projects or in direct cooperation with industry or the Army. From the mid-1950s, computer hardware was developed by the computer industry itself, but the universities were responsible for numerous advances in software. For this, they continued to benefit from continuously rising federal R & D support. By the late 1950s, contributions from the NSF and the Department of Defense far outstripped private-sector R & D efforts, with DARPA (Defense Advanced Research Projects Agency) accounting for the majority of federal

---

indicator. In terms of scientific and technical articles per capita, the US was 11th out of 28 OECD countries, with Japan 17th, and with a share of physics and chemistry articles twice that of the US (OECD 2001e:62p).

financing. Federal support for the purchase of mainframe computers was crucial for the institutionalization of these departments. Likewise, DARPA and NSF funding contributed to legitimizing the field of computer science. The training of scientists and engineers at these newfound computer science departments was of utmost importance, and the US found itself with a very sizable advantage over Europe and Japan, which suffered from shortages in skilled personnel (Mowery 1999:145, 159; Mowery and Rosenberg 1998:35p, 140pp).

The state was also instrumental in giving the US a first-mover advantage in semiconductors. It is true that the transistor did not arise from university research, and neither did the technologies of semiconductor production. In semiconductors, the main contribution made by US universities was instead one of developing courses and graduate programs to supply the industry with skilled scientists and engineers. In this area, the US was far ahead of other countries. The transistor drew heavily on basic research, particularly in physics, and thus could hardly have been invented without the contribution of the university system. However, the actual invention stemmed from research at Bell Laboratories. Still, until the 1960s, government sponsored R & D accounted for 25 per cent of all R & D going into semiconductors. However, it should be kept in mind both that many of the federal projects were failures, and that inventions happened at the hands of companies that had not received support. Military R & D had only a modest impact on actual innovation. Hence, despite the considerable research contribution on the part of the federal government, the federal contribution may actually have been greater in terms of providing a huge demand for semiconductors, rather than through the actual research (Castells 2000a:68; Langlois and Steinmueller 1999:21pp, 35p; Mowery and Rosenberg 1998:134p).

US software development has also benefited from defense-related R & D. First and foremost, the US software industry is founded on a research and personnel infrastructure that has given the US a major advantage in terms of access to skilled scientists and software engineers, as well as entrepreneurs. The software industry has benefited greatly from federal funding in universities and industry, with defense-related projects the primary source until the 1980s. There are few examples of actual software products derived directly from military funding. Instead, the software industry has benefited from funding and investments originally targeted at the hardware industries and from the large R & D infrastructure emanating from postwar federal R & D efforts (Mowery 1999:156; Mowery and Rosenberg 1998:161p).

In software, the role of the state has been less direct. However, when comparing the US to other countries, what has been conspicuous outside of the US is a shortage of skilled software developers and engineers. The growth of the academic discipline of computer engineering in the US, combined with generous funding, created a skill-base unrivaled elsewhere. This has created a US advantage not limited to software, but particularly strong in this industry, as the software industry is extremely knowledge-intensive compared to its physical capital requirements, and because software has been characterized by a steady stream of new entrants into the market, rather than dominance by the established computer firms (Mowery and Rosenberg 1998:165).

The state has also played a part in the diffusion of technologies through licensing and intellectual property rights. Intellectual property rights are a cornerstone of long-term growth. However, as seen in the chemical industry chapter, there is a trade-off between innovation and diffusion. If intellectual property rights are too tight, it stifles diffusion by providing the inventor with too much protection. The US government has seen to it that intellectual property rights have been leniently interpreted, stepping in and making decisions that, deliberate or not, have led to diffusion.

A prime example is the process that led to the diffusion of the transistor. Through Bell, AT&T had a monopoly on transistor production. In 1949, the Department of Justice filed an antitrust suit against AT&T, with the understanding that AT&T either had to release the technology, or develop a new line of business around the commercial sale of transistor products. Thus, AT&T decided to license the transistor to anyone interested in producing it, in order to get the federal government off its back, and hoping that by allowing widespread access, the technological progress of other firms would spill over back into telephony, and thus benefit AT&T. The suit was settled in 1956, AT&T agreeing to restrict itself to telecommunications, while licensing its semiconductor patents at nominal rates to any interested party. That same year a case was also settled with IBM. The Department of Justice succeeded in opening up the computer industry to competition and new entries by making the patents of IBM (as well as RCA and AT&T) available to all entrants (Chandler 2001:90p; Langlois and Steinmueller 1999:22; Mowery and Rosenberg 1998:125).

The other main example comes from software, again in the shape of an antitrust suit against IBM. In 1969, the Department of Justice filed against IBM for impairing the development of independent electronic data-processing companies. One of the charges was that IBM had sold hardware, software and services only as a single package. Hoping for a quick settlement, IBM responded to the charge by unbundling its software. The result was a virtually new market opening up for independent software applications, starting with applications for the IBM Series 360 and 370 (Chandler 2001:121; Mowery and Rosenberg 1998:162).

Thus, through antitrust legislation, the US has shied away from very strong intellectual property rights. In other respects this has also been the case, especially with respect to software. Nelson and Romer (1996:64) ask the following question: "What if someone had been able to patent the blinking cursor?" If such had been the case, innovation would have significantly slowed. Instead, basic software concepts are not granted strong property rights, whereas software *applications* (packaged software) are protected. Thus, there is a distinction between concepts and final applications, not unlike product vs. process patents in the chemical industry.

The opposite point applies to Japanese software—intellectual property protection is too weak, seriously hampering the growth in the packaged software industry (Mowery 1999:154). The licensing of MS-DOS to Japanese desktop manufacturers was delayed by Microsoft's concern with weak property rights. While protection for software has improved, Japan is still behind the US in this area. At the same time, the developments triggered by antitrust suits against IBM would never have happened in Japan for the simple reason that mainframe computers controlled such a large part of the market that there was never much of an incentive for individual software producers in any case.

The role of the Japanese state has been unfortunate in other ways, too. The shortage of software engineers is a reflection of the reluctance with which the university system has adapted to the requirements of the software industry. Computer science departments are a rarity in Japanese universities, and the quality of existing computer curricula far below that of the US. This is an industry where the technical and market uncertainties are far greater than in other computer based industries, which is something that the Japanese R & D model has not been well suited to dealing with. Overall, the smaller role played by Japanese universities in ICT industries has reduced the overall pool of scientists as well as the flow of knowledge, affecting software in particular. The Japanese model has instead been one where research has been carried out by specialized research institutes not directly connected with the higher education system (Mowery 1999:153p; Mowery and Rosenberg 1998:36, 141; Porter 1990:706).

In other sectors, like semiconductors, Japanese efforts have been more successful. The 1975–1980 VLSI (very large scale-integrated circuits) program was a government effort at deepening the level of technological competence. Five computer manufacturers were supervised by MITI in a three-year project aimed at increasing the transistor count of Japanese ICs so as to compete with the US in the DRAM market. The manufacturers were forced to agree on pooling their efforts in a single laboratory.[35] The result was a Japanese semiconductor industry that by the end of the 1980s had overtaken the US (Chandler 2001:130, 240; Langlois and Steinmueller 1999:44p).

However, generally Japanese firms and the Japanese government would not by themselves carry out basic research, instead depending on a strategy of "digestion of foreign technology", with US firms allowed only through the direct export or licensing and technology sales. Purchasing by the NTT (Nippon Telegraph and Telephone) may have played a role in stimulating demand, but both NTT demand and MITI coordination efforts were less important for the Japanese computer industry than domestic competition between Japanese firms (Langlois and Steinmueller 1999:30). Japanese attempts to boost the mainframe industry were not particularly successful (similar subsidies in Europe were also distinct failures). Instead, the most conspicuous moment of technological catch-up was a fluke, Gene Amdahl in 1971 bringing the design and competency from the IBM System 370 with him to Fujitsu (Chandler 2001:193).

While there are areas where the Japanese state has been instrumental in fostering a domestic computer industry, the case for human capital having an impact on ICTs is more easily made for the US. However, there is one more area that more

---

35 And did so reluctantly. For all practical purposes, the manufacturers agreed on the MITI joint laboratory idea in order to get private research subsidies. Hence, only 15–20 per cent of the overall budget went to the joint laboratories, with the rest going to the private research laboratories of the computer manufacturers (Langlois and Steinmueller 1999:45).

obviously reflects the differences between the US and Japan: Despite the deliberate and conscious attempts of the MITI at fostering linkages, the link between science and industry, universities and the commercial sectors has been far stronger in the US. Overall, the universities have been the missing link of the Japanese R & D system, with R & D depending on large corporations (Porter 1990:706). The link between universities and ICT industries has been far stronger in the US. This reflects what we have seen above; Japan has been better at "stock" type than "flow" type knowledge.

Since before World War II, the main strength of US universities has been a focus on university–industry interaction. US higher education was geared toward commercial opportunities rather than first-class science. While US higher education improved, the university–industry link persisted, with interactions between inventors, basic research and applied research uniquely strong, among other things because government agencies like the Department of Defense provided generous support for mission-oriented basic research. In the late 1980s and early 1990s, cooperative R & D and government support happened through for instance the SEMATECH project, funded by the Department of Defense, with the federal government seeking to help major firms cooperate in microelectronics so as to re-establish themselves in among other things semiconductors. The mobility of researchers, scientists and engineers on average changing jobs every four years is unrivaled, compared for instance to Japan where only 20 per cent of engineers change jobs even once in a lifetime (Castells 2000a:68; Freeman and Louçã 2001:308; Mowery and Rosenberg 1998:23; Nelson and Romer 1996:50p; OECD 2001c:50). As seen above, the science-link is stronger in the US and basic research yields more spinoffs than anywhere else (Mansfield 1996:132; Nelson and Romer 1996:55; OECD 2001c). With Mowery and Rosenberg (1998:140): "U.S. universities provided important channels for cross-fertilization and information exchange between industry and academia, but also between defense and civilian research efforts in software and in computer science generally." In other words, this is not only about university–industry interaction, but also about civilian spinoffs from military projects.

In comparison, despite conscious efforts, similar links do not exist in Japan. This is because the university sector has never been heavily involved, because Japan has never managed to produce a sufficient number of computer engineers, and because defense-related R & D has played no part. MITI has been the main coordinating organ of industrial policies with research associations (RAs) the most convenient way by which to distribute MITI subsidies for technology development programs. MITI early on searched for new industrial sectors and singled out microelectronics. However, most of the 26 "Technopoles" constructed through MITI's Technopolis Program in the 1980s and 1990s were failures. The purpose was to create a number of mini Silicon Valleys. For all practical purposes, it turned into an agglomeration of branch plants with scant network effects if any (Castells 2000b:228, 250pp; Odagiri and Goto 1993:87p). An OECD and WBI (2000:144pp) report concluded that the links between central societal actors were much closer in the US than in Japan. According to the report's "Knowledge Assessment Scorecard Indicators", using 20 indicators to evaluate the utilization of human capital, the US scored badly only on foreign direct investment (although Japan actually did worse). On every other indicator, the US was at, or very close to the top. In contrast, the Japanese scorecard showed strongly fluctuating values. Research collaboration between university and industry was one indicator where Japan finished far behind, ranking in the second third from a group of 60 countries, including 30 developing economies.

For decades scholars praised MITI targeting industries and coordinating policy actions in order to build technological competencies and improve competitiveness. Today the tendency is toward seeing MITI as having been too eager to limit domestic competition, with success as much despite as because of government intervention. The unwillingness of Japanese companies to go along with government plans of industry consolidation and mergers may have been a blessing. Attempts by European countries to create "national champions" in the computer industry all went terribly wrong. Instead, MITI belatedly realized the benefits of strong domestic competition, scaling back its role, and not targeting industries as aggressively as it once did (Chandler 2001; Porter 1990:414).

The differences between the US and the Japanese education systems fall very much in line with how the countries have performed with respect to ICTs. US success has been founded on its superior utilization of ICTs, whereas Japan has been excellent at mass-manufacturing, but not at all at making good use of these technologies. The same duality is found in the Japanese education system, which has been far more successful in knowledge production than in its utilization. On a number of indicators, Japan stacks up very well against the US. But the Japanese system is too formal and rigid to foster the innovative skills required in a world where success depends more on knowledge-intensive services than on manufacturing. Also, Japan has suffered from a fairly chronic skill shortage in its computer industries (despite churning out more engineers a year than the US). However, the main reason why the US science system has worked better has to do with the utilization of knowledge. There is ample evidence that US research efforts have been more successful in setting up an ICT industry than Japanese efforts. True, in terms of building human capital and technological competency, the Japanese state has channeled efforts through the MITI, but for the most part, Japan has caught up in ICTs by utilizing technologies already invented elsewhere. In the US, ICT breakthroughs have come about from the federal government generously funding a university system through the formation of computer science departments and the education of a wealth of computer science graduates able to fill jobs in the computer industry and start their own firms. But also, the links between the university system and industry have been much closer than virtually anywhere else, ensuring the rapid diffusion and utilization of knowledge. This has made the US ICT sector very dynamic, which combined with the network technologies described earlier explains why the US education system has been better at promoting successful ICT companies and utilizing ICTs in other industrial sectors than Japan.

(Cold) War and Government Demand

US ICT industries also benefited from direct government support in the shape of government demand and procurement for ICT goods. During the early years, federal support gave the US ICT industries a major competitive advantage over similar industries in Europe and Japan. Government support was also heavily instrumental in the growth of network technologies. Earlier chapters have emphasized the importance of wars. In ICTs, early US dominance to a great extent stemmed from a science system emanating from two world wars. But also, from victory in World War II sprang a superpower rivalry and a Cold War. Cold War meant that even though initial demand for ICT products was low, the miltary almost single-handedly provided ICT manufacturers with funding and demand. This gave US producers an enormous early advantage. The fear of the Soviet Union ensured a continuous interest in these technologies, as the US military very clearly perceived the advantages of technological superiority in warfare.

There are two components to the contribution of the military. First, the military funded R & D and performed research of its own. In 1950, more than 90 per cent of federal R & D spending was controlled by the Department of Defense and the Atomic Energy Agency. By 1960, defense research accounted for 80 per cent of federal R & D funds, staying at around 50 per cent until the early 1980s, and then rising again, dropping below 50 per cent for only three years since World War II. Second, the military accounts for a very large proportion of early ICT demand. Defense-related funding from the federal government, both for universities and private interests was very substantial indeed. However, it is still true that military R & D itself had only a modest impact on innovation, and that especially in semiconductors, recipients of military R & D were not successful. The future semiconductor giants were firms that survived without military contracts. Hence, it is probably true that the role of the military (and by extension, the government) was primarily one of providing a demand for ICT products, rather than actual R & D (Langlois and Steinmueller 1999:69; Mowery and Rosenberg 1998:32, 134).

Military funding was most important in the early days of the industry. When the MIT and the National Defense Research Committee opposed John Mauchly and John P. Eckert's plans for "High-Speed Vacuum Tube Devices for Calculating", the Army Ordnance—occupied with the computation of firing tables for artillery—funded the project that eventually became the ENIAC. A 1944 Army grant ensured that work would start on the EDVAC. The navy and air force supported Project Whirlwind at MIT (in order to create a flight simulator), and the Census Bureau supported the UNIVAC. The 1951 IAS computer, was funded by among others the Army and the Navy, and gave rise to IBM's 1953 Model 701.[36] Military procurement

---

36 However, military demand was *not* the reason for IBM's success. If anything, government funding was intended to boost Remington Rand, in order to preserve a level of competition in the computer industry. IBM viewed this as "government-funded competition" (Bresnahan and Malerba 1999:89p).

and demand presented a major incentive for new entrants into the computer industry, which duly happened in the late 1950s and 1960s (Bresnahan and Malerba 1999:89, 128; Mowery and Rosenberg 1998:136, 144; Nairn 2002:315pp).

In semiconductors, military procurements were even more obvious. First, government sponsored R & D represented 25 per cent of overall semiconductor R & D. While the major breakthroughs in transistors were developed privately, they were developed very much with military demand in mind. Hence second, military demand was what gave US semiconductors an early edge. By 1960, the US produced 90 per cent of the world's Integrated Circuits. Out of total US semiconductor production, 40 per cent was produced for defense-related purposes, peaking at 48 in 1960. Jack Kilby's IC was invented with very little of the research having been supported by the military. However, until 1962, an estimated 100 per cent of IC production went to military procurements.[37] The Apollo project was another large-scale customer. Government demand was indeed successful in creating a successful IC industry. Civilian demand increased as prices dropped, in other words toward the end of the 1960s (Langlois and Steinmueller 1999:25pp; Mowery and Rosenberg 1998:124pp).[38]

Software also benefited from defense-related R & D and procurement. Military demand for software accounted for a substantial amount of the software industry's profits, but unlike computers and semiconductors, there are few examples of civilian spinoffs. Military funding for the R & D infrastructure probably played a greater role than actual demand for software products. Overall, defense-related spending dropped off over the past few decades, and does not have the same impact today as it did in the 1950s and 1960s (Mowery 1999:156; Mowery and Rosenberg 1998:162).

Finally, network technology initiatives were also prompted by the military. Network technologies would ensure that even in the case of a massive nuclear first strike, the system would still survive. When ARPANET was founded, it included four universities, but the main emphasis was on the military, as the original purpose was to open the net to research institutions cooperating with the Department of Defense. The military involvement did not cease until 1990 (Castells 2000a:46; Chandler 2001:171).

Japan could to some extent free-ride on US military efforts, but fundamentally, US military R & D and procurements benefited US ICT industries, not foreign ones. The argument has been made that in Japan, where defense-related R & D for very obvious reasons did not play much of a role, the consumer electronics market was used to build up a domestic market in much the same way as the US defense market.

---

37 Among other things because of the 1960–1962 Minuteman missile program, and then because of the Vietnam War. By 1965, defense production share of total production was down to 72 per cent, by 1969 36 per cent. However, because of the rapid production of ICs, 36 per cent in 1969 accounted for more than 20 times the total production of 1962, when defense procurements accounted for 100 per cent (Langlois and Steinmueller 1999:37; Mowery and Rosenberg 1998:133).

38 In 1963, defense production share of total IC production was as high as 94 per cent. By 1968 this had fallen to 37 per cent (Mowery and Rosenberg 1998:129, 133).

This, combined with the VLSI program, allowed Japan to catch up in memory chips (Freeman and Soete 1999:182; Langlois and Steinmueller 1999:44p). In a most indirect way the military still played a role. The Japanese industrial structure was largely put in place in particular during the interwar years, at a time when military concerns were strong. Military R & D was very highly prioritized, which is the reason why now that this structure is geared toward civilian production instead, Japan can still show for a very high R & D intensity. Shifting its priorities toward civilian production, Japan could militarily free-ride on the US, thus devoting its creative resources to civilian purposes (Fukushima 1996:57; Nelson 1996:282).

Military support has not provided US firms with a permanent lock on the market. Rather, the point is that the US protected these industries while they were still young and vulnerable, and that, planned or not, it turned out to be highly efficient, at least for a while. Up until the 1970s, technological initiatives on the part of the Department of Defense were crucial, with DARPA (Defense Department Research Agency) playing a role not dissimilar to that played by MITI. And while military procurements do not play as great a role as they once did, according to a World Economic Forum (2003:580) survey of 80 countries, the US was 5th, with Japan no better than 17th in terms of government procurements for ICT equipment (Castells 2000a:68p; Nelson 1996:294; Schultze 1996:107). US ICT industries emerged out of a Cold War context, where technological superiority over the Soviet Union was considered crucial. This had the side-effect of boosting ICT industries on a scale impossible to any other country.

> … during the decisive 1950s and 1960s, military contracts and the space program were essential markets for the electronics industry, both for the giant defense contractors of southern California and for the start-up innovators of Silicon Valley and New England. They could not have survived without the generous funding and protected markets of a US government anxious to recover technological superiority over the Soviet Union…the state, not the innovative entrepreneur in his garage, both in America and throughout the world, was the initiator of the information technology revolution. (Castells 2000a:68p)

Deregulation, Liberalization and Financial Reform

The distinction between Schumpeterian and Smithian growth is often fluent. Smithian growth components have economic impacts that are distinctly Schumpeterian, and the other way around. Government procurements was one of the causes of US advantage in ICTs. Increased demand is generally considered Smithian. In this case, government demand and procurements greatly increased the size of the domestic market for ICTs *but also* contributed to the US *technological* lead in ICTs vs. Europe and Japan.

This section also deals with issues that might be interpreted as Smithian. It can easily be argued that deregulation and liberalization affected ICTs first and foremost through the expansion of markets. However, since ICTs mark a shift away from traditional manufacturing, they are economically important also because as generic technologies they have substantially improved the productivity of other industries, primarily in the services. In the Iron chapter, infrastructure developments—as in railroads—were treated as Schumpeterian. Railroads, in addition to the obvious

Smithian effect of enlarging and connecting markets, had immediate impacts on technology and industry by providing iron producers with a huge source of demand for iron products and by ensuring an easy supply of coal for iron smelting. With ICTs, there are effects that resemble these. There is Smithian growth, as ICTs are infrastructure technologies (as railroads were), expanding markets, increasing trade and improving the flow of capital, goods and information. But this expansion would have been impossible if not for the technological breakthrough represented by ICTs (the iron industry would have been hamstrung if not for the supply of coal provided by railroads). Hence, Smithian growth rests upon Schumpeterian foundations.

The precise impact of these changes is disputed. However, what is not in doubt is that by the 1970s, a growing body of experts was making the case that government meddling, taxes, regulations and reduced incentives were stifling US growth and productivity. There was credible evidence that the 1970s had seen a sharp increase in the regulatory burden on industry, and that tax rates on investments had risen to unprecedented levels. Inflation had turned tolerable nominal tax rates into very high effective rates (Johnson 1997:915; Krugman 1994:55, 65pp).[39]

Deregulations started with President Jimmy Carter, introducing tax breaks, removing business regulations on corporations, and deregulating industries like airlines, trucking and oil. This was to a large extent a success. Carter's lead was followed by President Ronald Reagan, and then by President George Bush. Finally, President Bill Clinton extended Reagan's policies of deregulation and liberalization to the international arena (Castells 2000a:140pp; Gilpin 2000:250; Johnson 1997:919; Krugman 1994:69pp).

Assessing Reagan's achievements is difficult (Krugman 1994:78). Taylor (1995:781pp) stresses that on deregulation, often thought of as his main economic achievement, he was less than consistent. Deregulation started in 1975 and was almost complete by the time Reagan was elected. Instead, his 1986 Tax Reform Act is hailed by *The Economist* (2004b:15) as one of his most important domestic achievements, flattening rates, simplifying rules and removing loopholes. On deregulation, Reagan's main achievement was one of preventing a backlash of re-regulation. To Krugman (1994), Reagan essentially lucked out on the business cycle. No permanent upswing in growth and productivity occurred until the final months of Bush's presidency, stemming from productivity growth associated with new technologies. However, it still seems likely that there were some effects. Krugman (1994:162) acknowledges that the banking system had become quite inefficient by the late 1970s, and that financial reform was crucial.

Hence, financial institutions were deregulated. Savings and loan association (S&L) banks had prospered when financial markets were still highly regulated, with depositors protected by the national insurance system. This arrangement stimulated "moral hazard"—as in letting banks gamble with the money of their depositors— since the money was guaranteed by the insurance system. Banking was deregulated

---

39 Nominally, the tax on profits from investing in equipment was 42 per cent. The effective rate was closer to 75 per cent (Krugman 1994:71)!

at a time when many of the S&L were nearly bankrupt (Krugman 1994:162). The inevitable result was the federal government spending in excess of $100 billion to pay off depositors of bankrupt S&Ls (Krugman 1994:161pp; Zinn 1995:570).

Reagan and Clinton had quite different views on the role of the state. Hence, it is ironic that Clinton's policies in many ways were a continuation of Reagan's rather than a reversal. Clinton's beliefs in the role of government in building national industry meant an emphasis on "managed trade". The perception that Japan engaged in unfair trade practices, free-riding on the US, meant that it would be the policy of the US to force Japan to open its economy in particular to US high-technology products. Simultaneously, he extended Reagan's deregulation and liberalization to international trade and finance. This happened partially through direct US pressure on governments (in cooperation with G7 countries like Britain), and by using the precursor to NAFTA, the FTA, to put extra pressure on the Uruguay Round GATT negotiations, through a veiled threat of going it alone through regional free trade agreements. Further, the strategy was pursued through the IMF, which was instructed to prescribe these policies "in the strictest possible terms" (Castells 2000a:140). The World Bank and the WTO also supported international deregulation and liberalization of goods, services and capital. (Castells 2000a:136pp; Friedman 2000:382, 444; Gilpin 2000:250pp. Krugman 1994).

Castells (2000a:140) describes how these policies were part of a concerted all-out effort of Clinton's to unify all economies around one set of homogeneous rules, with the flow of capital, goods and services determined exclusively by the markets. The consequence was a world economy increasingly deregulated and liberalized, and one in which the US shaped the basic architecture and infrastructure. The Clinton administration aided the dynamism of the new economy—by removing restrictions on private business, and by using US influence to open markets all around the world (Castells 2000a:140p).

While there is doubt as to the impact of 1980s US reform, there is no disagreement that the regulatory burden of Japan was, and still is, substantially higher, that attempts at regulatory reform in Japan have been far less successful, and that government over-regulation stifling innovation and entrepreneurship has been a contributory cause of Japanese stagnation. Vested interests (see next subchapter) have resisted deregulation, and as a consequence, the Japanese economy is one of the most heavily regulated in the world. Markets are controlled through permits and regulations, with producers given priority over consumers (Gilpin 2000:281; Grimond 2002). OECD (2001c:82) figures support this: In a survey of barriers to entrepreneurship, Japan was 18th out of 21 OECD economies.[40] Mirroring this, figures on entrepreneurial activity put Japan last out of 16 countries, with the US at number one (OECD 2001c:74). Part of the reason for this can be found in the lack of a well-functioning venture

---

40 Japan scored particularly poorly on "regulatory and administrative opacity". The country was also below the mean on "administrative burdens on start ups". The OECD (2001c:83) shows the relationship between administrative barriers to start-ups and TFP growth to be statistically significant at the 0.05 level (T=−2.32).

capital market, where regulations have stifled Japanese growth. Pension funds have been the main source of venture capital in the US, which has the world's largest venture capital market. In Japan, venture funds have been raised mainly through corporations. In the US, venture capital investment has to a great extent targeted new technology, and was especially important in the establishment of microelectronics firms in the 1950s–1960s. Also, the sheer size of the US venture capital market dwarfs that of Japan. Equity markets, from where high-risk projects like venture capital investments derive much of their funding, are vastly more developed in the US. The NASDAQ was founded in 1971, with almost 5,000 firms listed. The Japanese equivalent, Mothers, was established as late as 1999, with only 29 firms (Mowery and Rosenberg 1993:49; OECD 2001c:79).

While there have been attempts at reform, more striking is how little has actually changed. Regulations, favorable tax treatment and subsidies have preserved a system where productivity is lower than in the US. Belated and reluctant Japanese deregulation of *some* sectors has put Japan at a disadvantage, as other countries, like the US, started the process earlier, and are better adapted to a world of global flows and global competition (Castells 2000b:251; Gordon 2003:325; Sakakibara 2003:44p).

The financial system is normally singled out as one of the main culprits behind Japan's problems, and justifiably so. It was sheltered to a high degree. Banking was politically regulated with a lack of accounting transparency. From the 1960s through to the 1980s, Japan was protected from global financial markets. Sheltered by the state, banks were gradually involved in ever more risky loans. With high levels of personal savings and very low interest rates, banks were left with huge cash balances lent back to local companies. Banks fiercely competed for customers, with loans going to ever less qualified customers for even less qualified projects, often to preferred customers based on informal obligations rather than profit evaluations. By the time Japan embraced global financial markets, Japanese banks and securities companies had built a financial pyramid based on continued high growth rates and the repayments of risky loans. Hence, Japan saw a large number of bad loans for a very extended period of time (Castells 2000b:234pp; Chiu and Lui 1998:150; Friedman 2000:185; Moe 2004).[41]

Reagan was saved in 1984 by a sudden and fortunately timed economic upsurge. Overall US economic performance during Reagan and Bush was neither spectacular nor horrible. The growth during Clinton's presidency had started during Bush, six months before the election (Krugman 1994:128p). The US economy was beginning to grow rapidly because the technological revolution in ICTs was finally paying dividends in the sense of jobs and productivity improvements. While it is true that

---

41 Japan's total of non-performing loans was adjusted from 3.5 per cent in 1996 to 12 per cent in 1997. In comparison, at the height of the aforementioned US S&L crisis, the comparable figure was 5.6 per cent. Net liabilities of Japanese bankrupt companies in 1997 occupied a larger share of Japanese GDP than was the case in the US even at the height of the Great Depression (Asher and Smithers 1999:38p; Hsieh 2000:14)!

US growth to some extent was triggered by ICTs, over the past decade, the US also experienced a productivity revolution in sectors like retailing, with Wal-Mart in particular contributing strongly (William W. Lewis 2004). While this productivity growth is not close to that experienced by ICTs, the large number of people employed in retailing and in similar sectors means that the effect on the overall economy has nevertheless been huge. This growth is only to a limited extent linked with the utilization of ICTs.

Still, the US had positioned itself perfectly for taking advantage of the new international economy. Reagan only represented the first wave of deregulation and liberalization, extending mainly to the domestic sphere. It had some positive impact on the overall economy, but only indirectly on ICTs. ICTs were of much greater importance in the second wave. This wave, often referred to as globalization, would have been impossible without the breakthrough in ICTs. Without these breakthroughs, global, interdependent financial markets with virtually instant and limitless capital flows could not have arisen. However, this global economy could not have developed without deliberate policies of deregulation, privatization and liberalization of trade and investment (Castells 2000a:147).

The US lead in ICTs was part of the reason why the US was able to create this new economic infrastructure. Being the lead country, the US was uniquely positioned to take advantage of the benefits accruing from utilizing ICTs in manufacturing and in the services (Castells 2000a:139). Because of its exposure to the international economy, the incentive to utilize ICTs has been considerably greater than in Japan. Japan strongly resisted abandoning its sheltered financial system. Doing so, it deprived some of its most knowledge-intensive services of the incentive to modernize, as in utilizing ICTs. Japanese businesses have been very reluctant to make good use of ICTs. The strong tendency of the state to protect them from exposure to international competition is among the most important explanations for this reluctance. Deregulation and the breakthrough of ICTs changed the game. No longer could the Japanese state shelter the economy, provide cheap capital to privileged businesses and still determine monetary and industrial policies. As it belatedly abandoned this model, the financial system essentially crashed.

Thus, we can distinguish between two phases of government-led globalization. In the 1980s, conservative free-marketers, most prominently Thatcher and Reagan, pushed for deregulation and liberalization of finance and investment. But not until the 1990s was this extended to the rest of the world, Clinton being the main force for a networked, global economy. Since the end of World War II, the US has been the main proponent of a world order based on free trade. An open international economy was seen as the best way to prevent another depression and to economically forestall the Soviet Union. But also, policies for an open and integrated international economy were in the US interest for other reasons: Technological advantage, superior managerial flexibility, the presence of US multinationals, and US hegemony in international trade and finance (Castells 2000a:142). It was developments particularly in ICTs that made it increasingly hard for other countries to ignore global market forces. Deregulation of financial markets and liberalization of cross-border transactions led to a ten-fold increase between 1980 and the late 1990s in investment by pension funds, mutual funds and institutional investors in the US. Deregulation and liberalization also led to an acceleration of speculative capital flows, greatly increasing the vulnerability of countries to international market forces. These processes occurred earlier and faster in the US than elsewhere. Hence, the US shift toward an open international economy occurred earlier than elsewhere, benefiting in particular two industries that gained from applying new ICT technologies—IT and finance (Castells 2000a:104p, 148; Friedman 2000:381p Rosecrance 1999:146).

Vested Interests, Political Consensus, and Social Cohesion

The dualism between production and utilization of ICTs puts its stamp on this section, too. With respect to ICT industries, Japan rapidly caught up with the US. No vested interests prevented this. On the contrary, in both countries, ICT industries enjoyed special treatment by the state. But in the utilization of ICTs, Japan has fallen far behind. In the US, no vested interests were strong enough to block the deregulation and liberalization of the US economy. The US (along with Britain), took the lead in creating a globalized world economy, and consequently came much better prepared for this than Japan. Productivity improvements in the knowledge-intensive service industries have been among the most prominent contributors to impressive US economic and productivity growth. US service industries have eagerly taken advantage of the benefits from an integrated and deregulated world economy, whereas Japan has only hesitantly and belatedly joined in. Vested interests, often referred to as an "iron triangle" of politicians, bureaucrats and special interests, have consciously blocked Japanese structural change. To this day a modern and competitive export sector coexists with sheltered and backward industries (first and foremost service industries—retailing, wholesale and food processing), with very low productivity compared to the US.[42]

Because of vested interests, first, non-modern sectors have been sheltered, without incentives to change. Second, because of the very low productivity in these sectors, and because services account for a huge part of a nation's total employment, this has been a major drag on the economy, reducing overall demand, including that for ICT equipment. Finally, because vested interests have blocked structural change, the sectors that have had the potential to utilize ICTs the most intensely—banking, insurance, and financial services—have been deprived of the opportunity and incentive to do so. Because of vested interests, Japan still treats its ICT industries as traditional mass manufacturing rather than as knowledge-intensive services, and has suffered from this.

---

42 Japan's big export industries only contribute 10 per cent of Japan's GDP. At 7.5 million employees, retailing dwarfs the most important export industry—cars (220,000 employees). Housing construction accounts for 2.3 million employees, food processing for 1.3 million. These three industries are all at less than 50 per cent of US productivity (William W. Lewis 2004:24, 28).

In previous chapters, we have had the benefit of hindsight. For each of the previous time periods, there is a massive literature, and so with respect to issues like vested interests, consensus and cohesion, scholars have reached a rough consensus. With ICTs, we do not yet have this advantage. Since we cannot know whether or not present data reveal general trends or just temporary swings, the conclusions must be tentative. Hence, caution should be advised. I have sought to steer clear of controversial data, trying to form a conclusion based on a narrative that there should be broad consensus about. Political consensus and social cohesion in the US does to a considerable extent explain why the US managed to transform its economy from the 1980s onwards. The lack of such is an obvious reason why Japan during the same time period has had problems implementing policy decisions that go against vested interests.

Both in the US and Japan, ICT-industries were favored industries. Hence, old and dominant industries did not block their growth and progress. Granted, the US did not offer infant industry protection. First-mover advantage in ICTs meant that the US was pretty much dominant in every facet of ICT production in any case and thus coped well without protection. Moreover, government and army procurement provided the industry with a massive initial boost.

However, in the 1980s, as Japan challenged US ICT supremacy, attitudes changed. ICT interests had the ear of several presidents, and in 1985 Reagan announced a major shift in US policy following "unfair trading practices of other countries". Concerns over industrial decline were eroding support for free trade, especially when confronted with Japan, which was perceived as playing by different rules, destroying US high-technology industries. Thus, Reagan combined multilateral, unilateral and regional trade policies, encompassing a commitment to a multilateral trading regime with low trade barriers, with US initiatives leading to the Uruguay Round of GATT, eventually (1995) resulting in the World Trade Organization (WTO). Simultaneously, a policy of "managed trade" sought to force other countries (read: Japan) to open their markets to US goods and investments. A third component of the new trade policies sought to forge closer ties with other North American economies, resulting in the US–Canada Free Trade Agreement (FTA, 1988), under Clinton (1994) extended to Mexico to form the NAFTA (Gilpin 2000:232).[43]

Hence, to the extent that vested interests affected the development of ICT-industries, they sided with them rather than against them. As early as 1977, US semiconductor firms founded the SIA (Semiconductor Industry Association), seeking to force Japan to eliminate semiconductor duties. As Japan challenged the US in semiconductors, the SIA lobbied successfully for the Semiconductor Chip Protection Act (SCPA), which sought to protect intellectual property in US chip design. Of greater importance was the 1986 Semiconductor Agreement, which led to a semiconductor agreement that essentially cartelized the world semiconductor market, with the

---

43   In addition to the expected benefits of free trade, there was also the notion that NAFTA would serve the US as a lever when facing trade negotiations against in particular the EU (Gilpin 2000:239).

US allotted a 20 per cent share.[44] While clear indication that it was fashionable to support high-technology industries, documentation that the agreement significantly affected the profitability of Silicon Valley is lacking (Gilpin 2000:232pp; Langlois and Steinmueller 1999:58). Clinton extended on this, perceiving a government role in supporting strategic industries, for practical purposes implying high-technology industries like ICTs (Silicon Valley strongly supported Clinton's election) (Gilpin 2000:253; Krugman 1994:266).

As mentioned before, MITI singled out ICTs as particularly promising as early as the 1960s. Specific sectors were provided with different types of state support, mostly channeled through MITI. Hence, while the strategic trade theory of the US was introduced in the late 1980s, MITI had been practicing industrial policies along these lines for decades already. Far earlier than in the US, a vested interest backing ICTs had formed, and US pressure for policy change against Japan among other things stemmed from the VLSI circuit project supported by MITI (and the NTT), whereby Japan conquered the semiconductor market. From the outset of the Japanese computer industry, MITI had refused to give in to IBM demands until in 1960 a compromise was reached, whereby IBM exchanged its patents in return for access to the Japanese market. Following this, in 1961, MITI and the nascent Japanese computer industry formed the JECC (Japanese Electronic Computer Company), jointly owned by Fujitsu, Toshiba, Hitachi, NEC, Mitsubishi Electric, Oki Electric and Matsushita. The JECC provided below-market rate funding and purchased finished computers. Combined with high tariffs, this ensured a rapid rise of Japanese computer manufacturers.[45] Other MITI initiatives, like the 1980s Technopolis Program may not have been overly successful, but do illustrate how vested interests favored ICTs rather than working against them (Castells 2000b:229, 248pp; Chandler 2001:190pp; Nye 1991:167).

No US Vested Interests Blocking Deregulation and Liberalization   However, the US and Japan differed in a vital respect. In Japan, vested interests were successful in blocking deregulation and liberalization. In the US, no such thing was allowed to happen. On the contrary (with Britain), the US led the process. In 1999 Alan Greenspan made the point that while 300,000 US jobs were destroyed every week because of new technologies, 300,001 were created.[46] In the US, a president like

---

44 The agreement followed upon US threats with increased trade barriers, lest Japan open its telecommunications and microelectronics sectors (and others) to international competition. Disagreement as to the interpretation of "20 per cent" led to considerable tension. Japan perceived 20 per cent as a "reasonable target". The US insisted on interpreting it as mandatory. Ironically, the Semiconductor Agreement violated the new GATT framework for international trade that the US had just been instrumental in putting in place (Gilpin 2000:235).

45 Although it is not altogether obvious to what extent MITI's policies were successful. MITI has belatedly starting realizing the benefits of strong domestic competition, scaling back and not targeting industries as aggressively as it once did (Chandler 2001).

46 *The Economist* (2004c:91) reports that the US economy on average destroys around 30 million jobs a year, and creates slightly more, which should yield somewhere around 600,000

Reagan when faced with the air traffic controllers' union could destroy organized labor by firing 12,000 striking air traffic controllers. It is a country where hiring and firing is relatively easy. It is a country where Schumpeterian creative destruction has been allowed to work (*Economist* 2004a:25; Friedman 2000:373). Hence, the US has more easily been able to take advantage of new technologies than other countries. This is what happened toward the end of the 1980s and the early 1990s, as computers, fax machines, printers, voice recognition software and other technologies greatly improved the quality of US services and manufacturing (Rosecrance 1999:145).

As mentioned earlier, US S&L banks fared badly when finance was deregulated in the 1980s. However, compared to the crisis in the Japanese financial system, there are striking differences. In the US, insolvent banks were not kept on artificial life-support, and were closed down once depositors had been paid off. In Japan, vested interests have for practical purposes made it impossible to do the same. Insolvent banks have remained in business, with the state persistently bailing them out. In other words, the government has not had the strength to resist the power of the financial sector, and has allowed inefficient structures to live on, blocking change and incurring ever increasing costs to the economy (Gordon 2003:325; Krugman 1994:162).

It is a recurring theme of the US that despite interest group lobbying, there are certain ideas that interest groups have not been able to block, namely policies of deregulation and liberalization. In this area, political consensus has been strong. By the late 1970s, the notion that Western economies were bogged down by inefficiencies and rigidities, and the West receding into stagnation and decline was widespread. Pressure was gradually building in favor of deregulation, tax cuts and liberalization and against government-directed economic policies. Carter started the process, but what gave it its major impetus was the rise of the conservative movement, spearheaded by Margaret Thatcher, who became British PM in 1979. Reagan latched onto her ideas during the 1980 presidential campaign, attacking the size and role of the state, curbing expenditures, reducing taxes and removing regulations.[47] Controversial at first, by 1985, Western Europe was adopting similar policies. By the end of the Cold War, even former socialist countries subscribed to what had become a new neoliberal economic orthodoxy. Hence, Reagan's task (later Bush and Clinton) was greatly aided by the fact that he was at the forefront of what was quickly becoming a global (not including Japan) ideological movement. Eight years of Ronald Reagan took large amounts of economic decision-making out of the hands of politicians, leaving it to the market (Castells 2000a:138; Friedman 2000:104p; Johnson 1997:919pp; Knutsen 1999:288; Krugman 1994:69pp, 78; Micklethwait and Woolridge 2004:88; Zinn 1995:563).

The pervasiveness of this orthodoxy can be seen in the policies of Reagan's successors. Democrats and Republicans essentially agreed on removing business regulations, cutting welfare programs, deregulating S&L banks, and more. Bill

---

jobs a week.

47 By 1981, the marginal tax rate had fallen from 70 per cent to 28 per cent.

Clinton, who explicitly declared to reverse 12 years of Republican policies, continued and extended on important parts of Reagan's legacy. Clinton made it abundantly clear that the Reagan years had permanently changed politics, and that there was no going back, by declaring "the end of welfare as we know it" and "the end of big government". He cut back on federal spending and implemented tax reform that could just as well have come from the Republicans. True, he differed from Reagan and Bush in his emphasis on communitarian ideas of consensus, solidaric trust and a social safety net (Knutsen 1999:288; Micklethwait and Woolridge 2004:11, 117pp). But these ideas did not seek a return to the past. Friedman (2000:106) portrays the economic differences between Clinton and Bob Dole during the 1996 presidential election as very slight. They both recognized that they were subject to international flows of capital and that deviating far from the preferred policies of international investors would unduly harm the economy. There was broad agreement on low tariffs, removing foreign investment restrictions, getting rid of quotas and domestic monopolies, increasing exports, deregulating capital markets, opening banking and telecommunication systems to private ownership and competition. Clinton extended deregulations to the international economy and became one of the world's foremost promoters of an open international, liberal economic world order. Here, he could rely on considerable bipartisan consensus (Castells 2000a:140pp; Rosecrance 1999:146).

Clinton believed in activist policies in order to stimulate growth, with industrial prosperity in particular depending on high-value added industries such as ICTs. In this area as well, he could rely on bipartisan support (Krugman 1994:248pp). Hence, activist Clinton and laissez-faire Reagan both advocated managed trade policies. During Reagan, this had developed pragmatically as a means to appease protectionists in Congress, but it fit well with a worldview whereby other countries (read: Japan) were free-riding on the US, playing by different rules and destroying US high-tech industries. Clinton's strategic trade theories implied the embracing of managed trade on a conceptual level as well. Hence, as Clinton was working to deregulate the world economy, he combined this with managed trade specifically designed to benefit US exporters, in particular high-tech industries. And as Reagan, Clinton met with approval from both Congress, vested interest groups and the public (Castells 2000a:140; Gilpin 2000:232, 254).

The above suggests that the necessary political consensus between Republicans and Democrats for structural change did exist. It is less clear to what extent this mandate also stemmed from the people. There is a rich literature on declining US social cohesion. Fukuyama (1999:27) makes the point that around 1965 a large number of indicators serving as negative measures of social capital all started moving sharply upwards—crime rates, divorce rates, suicides, etc. Others have made the same observations.[48] Surveys indicate that the trust that Americans have in

---

48 Between 1960 and 1990 US population increased by 41 per cent. However, violent crime increased by 560 per cent, teenage suicides by 200 per cent and divorce rates by 200 per cent (Johnson 1997:965).

other humans and in public institutions has decreased. In 1993, 37 per cent believed that "most people" can be trusted, down from 58 per cent in 1960. In 1958, 73 per cent trusted the federal government to do what is right "most of the time" or "just about always". By 1994, this had fallen to 15 per cent. Putnam (1995b) asserts that while trust is high and stable for those born in 1930 and earlier (roughly 50 per cent), it declines rapidly for those born in 1940 and onwards, down to only 23 per cent for those born in 1965. Trust in other words declined sharply during Watergate and the end of the Vietnam War.[49] Wuthnow's (2002:72) figures suggest that trust in government decreased from 65 per cent in 1964 to 41 in 1972, and to 26 per cent during Watergate (1974). While there has been some decline in trust in Japan as well, the US has been hit far worse. Still, in the 1999 World Values Survey, the US actually ranked ahead of Japan (Dayton-Johnson 2001:4; Fukuyama 1999:59p, 129; OECD 2001b:44).[50]

However, while this seems to point in the direction of a decline in social cohesion, divorce rates have dropped since the 1980s. Levels of trust in major institutions have improved throughout the 1990s. Crime rates have dropped substantially since 1991–1992 (falling by 15 per cent since the early 1990s), and dramatically so in the biggest cities. Murder rates in the thirteenth century were three times what they were in the seventeenth century, seventeenth-century murder rates three times as large as in the nineteenth century, and early nineteenth-century murder rates twice as high as 1970s murder rates. Hence, when scholars talk about the destruction of the social fabric, the decline of trust and cohesion, compared to previous time periods,

---

49 Knutsen (1999:250) suggests that there were crucial events preceding Vietnam and Watergate too. The end of World War II helped sustain US cohesion by welding a US "us" as the protector of the free world, in opposition to an alien, communist "them". This began to change in the 1960s. The assassination of John F. Kennedy and the murders of Robert Kennedy and Martin Luther King shook the US. 1968 saw the Tet offensive in Vietnam—widely perceived as the first major instance when the US public realized that the war in Vietnam was faring genuinely badly. It was becoming harder to preserve a national identity around the US as untainted, as the force of good in the world, fighting communism. This coincided with Nixon's announcement that the US would no longer exchange dollars for gold (1971), rapidly followed by oil crisis (1973). Surveys show that from 1975 onwards, Americans considered economic issues more important than security issues, supporting the view that the cohesion spun around a Cold War mythology was breaking down.

50 The US was 8th, with Japan 13th out of 42 countries. 48.5 per cent of Americans agreed that "in general, people can be trusted", as opposed to 37.5 per cent in Japan. Both countries were in the upper third, but far off the Scandinavian countries, with Norway the only country beating 60 per cent (Dayton-Johnson 2001:4). This meant that the US and Japan had actually switched positions compared to a 1995 OECD survey of 25 countries, where Japan was 8th and the US 13th. Interestingly, the figures had almost exactly reversed as well, with 35.6 per cent of US respondents declaring that "most people can be trusted", as opposed to 46 per cent in Japan (OECD 2001b:44).

present-day murder rates are among the lowest in human history (Fukuyama 1999:8, 31, 271; Johnson 1997:967)![51]

Fukuyama (1999) argues that technological progress and structural change always brings disruption. But once the period of disruption is over, social order will begin to remake itself. This is what has happened since the early 1990s, with trust increasing and crime rates dropping. The reason why trust declined more in the US than elsewhere, in particular Japan, is: One, Americans have always been more profoundly skeptical against government power and authority than others. Two, compared to Japan, the degree of structural change has been far greater in the US. In Japan, the transition from manufacturing to services has been slow.

Did an increase in cohesion in the American people made it easier for the state to pursue structural reform? This is the argument: A sense of unity arose after World War II, lasting until the 1960s (Putnam 1995b; Zinn 1995:620). Following Vietnam and Watergate, the 1970s saw decline, stagnation, pessimism and doubts as to the US role in the world. Knutsen (1999:288) asserts that Reagan's 1980 presidential campaign was "driven by deep, patriotic concerns about America's impotence". He replaced the doubts and indecisions of the 1970s with "conviction politics". He resurrected patriotism and confidence by upping the Cold War rhetoric, referring to the Soviet Union as the evil empire, and restoring the feeling of US moral legitimacy (Johnson 1997:919). And he did it by pitching the US against Japan in a second cold war, one of international trade. As US core industries were performing poorly, Japan was repeatedly accused of unfair trade, stealing US businesses, buying US property and US companies, and trade restrictions put in place. Thus, social cohesion has been rising compared to the 1970s, and this has more easily enabled US presidents to pursue policies that might otherwise have alienated large shares of voters. However, it is hard to produce conclusive evidence. The story makes sense, but drawing strong conclusions seems risky if not foolhardy.

Moreover, since the 1990s, US politics has seemed extraordinarily tumultuous. George Bush's presidency imploded. Bill Clinton won the 1992 and 1996 elections, but failed to get close to 50 per cent of the vote. His presidency was marred by scandals, alienating large parts of socially conservative voters. The presidency of George W. Bush has not exactly been ushering in bipartisanship. The political climate has hardened. Republicans and Democrats show more hostility toward each other than for decades and the nation seems split down the middle. But despite animosity and hostility, there has been widespread consensus in important areas. US presidents have drawn on considerable political consensus with respect to issues like international trade, deregulation and liberalization. Within a few years of Reagan,

---

51 However, the US is far ahead of other countries in terms of voluntary associations. Although the overall membership numbers have declined, the overall number of voluntary associations in the US has doubled, from 10,000 in 1970 to 23,000 by 1990 (Skocpol 2002:130). According to the World Values Survey (1999), more than 70 per cent of Americans were a member of one or more groups and more than 45 per cent a volunteer for one or more. The corresponding figures for Japan were 30 and 13 per cent (Dayton-Johnson 2001:6).

deregulation, liberalization, less state and more market, had become economic orthodoxy. Clinton extended this legacy to the international scene. US policy-making has exhibited considerable consensus in areas that have directly affected economic performance. US political elites have been at the forefront of developments that have promoted structural economic change by opening up the world economy, thereby greatly driving growth in the service industries. In a comparatively Schumpeterian US economy of creative destruction, this has been far easier than in Japan. These are developments that have been beneficial with respect to the utilization of new technologies, such as ICTs. Political consensus has prevented vested interests from blocking such change, very much in contrast to what has been the case in Japan.

Japan: An Iron Triangle of Vested Interests   If the US arrested its decline, Japan is the success story that turned sour, from industrial miracle to being stuck in a recession that has lasted for a decade and a half. Following World War II, political stability has been virtually continuously guaranteed by the Liberal Democratic Party (LDP). With the exception of a ten-month intermezzo in 1993, the LDP has been in power since 1958. Vested interests have played a very prominent role. Two notions deserve particular attention. The first is the one of an "iron triangle" constituted by the LDP, the bureaucracy and vested interest groups preventing structural reform. Because linkages between these actors are so close and cemented, deregulation and liberalization has met with extremely stiff resistance. The second notion is the one of a "dual economy", which is what the iron triangle is protecting. A highly efficient and internationally competitive export-oriented manufacturing sector has coexisted with a distinctly low-productivity domestic manufacturing and service sector (food processing, textiles, retail, construction, medical services etc.) protected by regulations and subsidies. The domestic service industry, which accounts for three quarters of Japanese employment, has an overall productivity of only 63 per cent of the US (Grimond 2002; OECD 2001d:44; Sakakibara 2003:ix, 42pp).

This dual structure, including an emphasis on government financed construction projects to a degree that defies any economic rationale, and a reluctance to deregulate and liberalize banking and finance, means that sectors that in the US have undergone dramatic productivity improvements have remained largely unchanged in Japan. Qualitative data speak of the reluctance with which ICT equipment has been employed in Japanese firms, and quantitative data suggest ever more strongly that compared to the US, ICTs have not had nearly as great an impact on growth and productivity in Japan.[52] van Ark and Inklaar's (2003) attempt at measuring productivity differences in US and Japanese service industries strongly supports this.

The relationship between the LDP and the bureaucracy has led to a very opaque decision-making structure, with strong ties to preferred special interest groups. The government is relatively impotent compared to the party. Prime ministers come and

---

52 For instance, Japanese TFP growth in banking has been weak. The one example of a service sector that has been successfully deregulated in Japan, with accompanying TFP increases, is telecommunications (OECD 2001c:46).

go, controlled by faction leaders behind the scenes, people devoted to protecting the status quo rather than promoting reform. Bills may be drafted by the government, but not without the instruction of party committees or research groups. When the bill is drafted, another LDP organ—the Council for Policy Coordination—approves it before it goes to the LDP General Council for final approval. Similar processes take place with respect to the budget. Interactions between vested interests and politicians take place through LDP committees and research groups. While government ministers and state secretaries are not allowed to interact with such interests, there are no general restrictions on politicians (Grimond 2002; Sakakibara 2003:47pp).[53]

The bureaucracy has a very close relationship with the party, whereas the relationship between the party and the government is rather one of mistrust. Bureaucrats in the different ministries develop only loose ties to their own ministers (the average tenure of a government minister is less than a year), whereas personal ties between bureaucrats and LDP parliamentarians are strong and long-lasting. Hence, decision-making largely takes place behind closed doors, by actors that have no formal role in the process (Sakakibara 2003:55p), and is often limited to a tug-of-war between factional interests within the LDP. Beyond communist countries, it is hard to find states with a more powerful party than the LDP (ibid.:49). Hence, the party spans a very broad coalition of interests and patronages. Castells (2000b:232) portrays the LDP as a coalition of political factions at the hub of power, exchanging "votes for money, money for favors, favors for positions, positions for patronage, then patronage for votes, and so on". It has also created a party that is strongly averse to change. To quote Grimond (2002): "Its two main purposes—rent-seeking and self-perpetuation through electoral success—have both flourished under the status quo. Almost every interest-group imaginable is represented within its ranks, and it takes care to look after them."

The close connections between politics and bureaucracy can be seen in the prominent roles played by specific Japanese ministries. The Ministry of Finance, controlling MITI and the Bank of Japan, is the most important, as its main function has been to coordinate and help Japanese business through credit, export and import allocations and support for technological development. Other ministries, like the Ministry of Construction, the Ministry of Agriculture and the Ministry of Transport have had more political functions, channeling private funds into the political campaigns of the LDP in return for political favors. This has been an integral part of politics. Banks were shielded in return for financing political parties. Big business, wary of the threat of socialism, never saw any alternative to the LDP, and has made generous financial contributions to the LDP and to individual party members (Castells 2000b:227pp; Fukushima 1996:57).

True, the bureaucracy has enjoyed great prestige. For decades, the successes of the MITI were scrutinized and envied by Western countries that toyed with the idea of emulating Japan. Japanese bureaucrats were successful in increasing the

---

53 They are even allowed to take financial contributions from vested interests, and cannot be prosecuted for bribery. The same goes for government bureaucrats (Sakakibara 2003:50).

productivity of its market economy through selective state intervention (Castells 2000b:229). However, the system also encouraged corruption and moral hazard. When it is commonly understood that firms can buy politicians in order to ensure favorable regulations, the system does not operate in a way that ensures economically sound solutions. Hence, from the late 1980s onwards, Japan was rocked by political scandals. The 1992 Sagawa Express scandal revealed not only that politicians had been bribed in return for political favors, but that underworld (Yakuza) connections had been used to support political allies and to deter the opposition (Castells 2000b:233; Gordon 2003:313).[54]

The iron triangle thus is a coalition very much opposed to change. An extremely politicized administration subsidizes an inefficient agricultural sector and contributes to upholding the dual economy. In the US, expenses related to agriculture accounts for one per cent of the federal budget. The corresponding Japanese figure is 6.3. In retailing, government loan guarantees and subsidies to traditional retailers along with regulations that restrict large-scale retailing provides an incentive for small-scale, traditional retailers not to exit, and means that the share of employment derived from traditional stores is 55 per cent in Japan, as opposed to 19 in the US.[55] Retailing is an area where productivity differences with the US are particularly striking. Japan is a nation of "small-timers": Small shopkeepers—mom-and-pop stores—are the backbone of Japanese retailing. They are also the backbone of the LDP (Farrell 2003:148pp; William W. Lewis 2004:46p; Sakakibara 2003:138p). Regulations are responsible for the low productivity levels in the non-export sectors, but reform would have put thousands of firms out of business and hundreds of thousands out of work (Gilpin 2000:281). Cuts in the labor force have been marginal, with no major restructuring of business taking place, despite elaborate plans (Gordon 2003:327; Grimond 2002). It is also from the service sector—construction, retailing, wholesaling—that the bulk of the enormous amount of bad loans has arisen. It is here that we find what *The Economist* (2004d:81) has labeled "'zombies'—companies that are competitively dead, but sustained by their banks, continue to walk the Earth and give healthier firms nightmares."

---

54 A concrete example of government protection having negative effects in ICTs can be found in software. Protection of hardware meant higher hardware costs than in the US and slower rates of domestic adoption. This hampered the growth of a domestic software market. The protection of the domestic market meant that Japan was dominated by mainframe producers with tailor-made software, as opposed to the US, where rapid diffusion of desktop computers led to an unbundling of hardware and software and a dynamic and independent software industry (Mowery 1999:150p; Mowery and Rosenberg 1998:162).

55 The Large-scale Retail Store Law prohibited the building of stores larger than 1,000 square meters. In 2000, it was replaced by the Large-scale Retail Location Law. Large stores are no longer prohibited, but entry subject to social screening criteria by local authorities (where the local shopkeeper normally carries a lot of clout), for all practical purposes even increased entry-barriers, further cementing the dual economy (William W. Lewis 2004:31p; Sakakibara 2003:46).

Instead of restructuring, one of the main ways in which Japan has tried to boost its economy is a way more symbolic of the dual economy and the iron triangle than either agriculture or retailing, namely construction. Lavish construction projects have been a prime breeding ground for vested interests. "The country is littered with airports that no one uses, bridges that carry no traffic and roads that go nowhere" (Grimond 2002). Japan is using more concrete per year on public works projects than the entire US (Nathan 2004:219)! Japanese infrastructure investments have grown gradually in terms of share of GDP, and by 1996 amounted to a full six per cent. During the 1950s and 1960s, these investments were of great social benefit (marginal productivity of social overhead capital of 25–35 per cent), but the productivity of these projects has fallen ever since, and today marginal productivity figures are very close to zero (Sakakibara 2003:36).[56]

Local government makes the iron triangle even harder to reform. For practical purposes, the central government finances most local construction projects, leading to incentives for gross local overspending. In most government-subsidized projects, the central government funds 50 per cent of the project directly, but indirect funding and subsidies means that the real share is closer to 90. Because of indirect subsidies, even locally funded projects have more than 50 per cent state funding (Sakakibara 2003:119). Thus, beyond doubt is the fact that major rigidities in the Japanese state are still upheld through a conglomerate of vested interests with major influence on political decision-making. As long as this structure is upheld, Japan will struggle with low productivity in sectors encompassing a majority of the employment. This lowers overall demand and investments, and the maintenance and protection of the dual economy significantly reduces the incentive to invest in new technologies.[57] Vested interests have effectively prevented Japan from deregulating, liberalizing and otherwise creating the incentives necessary for the country to embrace the potential of knowledge-intensive service industries (Gordon 2003:317; Grimond 2002; Nathan 2004:218p).

Still, where vested interests in the gravest and most direct manner have affected both the economy in general and the utilization of ICTs is with respect to business and financial networks. Businesses have traditionally been organized in business networks, *keiretsu*, guided by the state bureaucracy and aided through trade policy, technology policies and credit (Whitley 1998:220pp), connected to tight social

---

56 The system goes back to PM Kakuei Tanaka (elected in 1972), who secured his local power base through pork-barrel projects resulting in tunnels, bridges, highways and high-speed trains to the backcountry. He resigned in 1974 because of corruption and bribery scandals. Similar scandals have been commonplace ever since. Construction companies have been happy to fund the campaigns of their local members of the Diet, as well as contributing generously to infrastructure committees in the LDP.

57 However, the underutilization of ICTs is just one of the reasons why Japanese retailing (and construction, food processing, etc.) have such low productivity levels. Zoning laws, tax regulations and subsidies have distorted competition and allowed small and inefficient mom-and-pop stores to survive. Hence, the productivity of these sectors could be greatly increased, even without ICT equipment (William W. Lewis 2004:30).

networks of professional, well-trained technocrats and enmeshed in extensive quasi-contractual networks of reciprocal obligation and trust. This has implied a network of dense mutual obligations and market agreements that made informal partnerships prominent: Firms trade with a small but specific number of preferred partners on a long-term basis, based on keiretsu obligations and not on profit evaluations. This provides for a business structure not well adapted to structural change (Castells 2000a:190, 200; 2000b:220pp, 235; Henderson 1998:366; Moe 2004).

Also, it has made it extremely hard for start-ups to raise cash as big banks have preferred to pump capital into companies affiliated with them, regardless of profit perspectives. Thus, unlike in the US, there is no dynamic, second tier of small, aggressive start-ups challenging the big companies (not even in the computer industry[58]). Furthermore, capital for hostile takeovers is not easily available. The Japanese economy has been far more genteel than the US economy, but also less efficient at Schumpeterian creative destruction, and less well adapted to major structural change. Emphasis has been on safeguarding the weak, and public and vested interests would have been strongly opposed to any policy action making it easier to close down firms. Hence, politicians have steadily been pumping money into companies so inefficient that they should rather have been allowed to go bust (Asher and Smithers 1999:53; Castells 2000a:191; Friedman 2000:60; Fukuyama 1995:165; Gilpin 2000:282; Henderson 1998:373p; Whitley 1998:222).

The business–government system served Japan well for three decades, but the blurring of lines between business and government made business take for granted that the state would bail it out. By the mid-1990s, the ICT revolution, combined with the gradual shift away from manufacturing had changed the global environment. Practices that had worked during economically and politically stable times became a liability during times of rapid change, sheltering the central actors of the existing system rather than embracing new actors, technologies and businesses (Moe 2004; OECD 1999a; Perkins 2000:240). The guidance of MITI in financial and monetary affairs turned out to be a weakness. The link between business and finance was hugely dysfunctional, and there for everyone to see.

Vested interests were also prevalent with respect to finance. The keiretsu enjoyed privileged financial access, often guaranteed by the government. Lack of transparency and legal norms in bank lending allowed for huge loans without any basis in realistic profit expectations.[59] Each keiretsu was led by a major banking company. The bank would be obliged to lend to a certain number of preferred customers, with the

---

58 In the computer industry—a sector in which in the US, IBM's domination has steadily been challenged and undermined by smaller startups—the Japanese continue to rely on four large producers: NEC, Hitachi, Fujitsu and Toshiba (Fukuyama 1995:165).

59 Asher and Smithers (1999:39): "Japanese companies in the financial services world are legendary for their practices of hiding insolvent assets ... and for misleading creditors and government credit investigators regarding their real state of operational health." Dattel (1999:62p) makes the point that the problems were never in manufacturing, where Japan is still world class. But whereas manufacturers deal in physical products, financial institutions deal in abstractions. It is much easier to hide "flaws" in an abstraction than in a physical

keiretsu first among these. Banks thus had a vested interest in lending over profit. Banks would also have to lend money on the basis of advice from the Ministry of Finance, the Yakuza, and the LDP (Castells 2000b:235). In the words of Grimond (2002), "banks were treated as quasi-public-sector organisations to be used to get Japan's post-war business back on its feet". However, with the deregulation of the international economy, Japanese banks could no longer depend on the state to bail them out (Castells 2000b:234pp; Chiu and Lui 1998:150; Friedman 2000:185; Pye 2000:253).

Lending money to preferred customers has led to a staggering series of bad loans. This would have been a problem with or without the deregulation and liberalization of international finance. However, Japan's problems have been strongly exacerbated by the inability to adjust smoothly from sheltered to global financial markets. Protection undoubtedly led to Japanese banks becoming inefficient, lacking strong incentives to modernize and adapt. This problem was recognized by politicians in the early 1990s following the 1989–1990 stock market crash and property bubble. However, the Ministry of Finance has been very reluctant to implement any decisive reform. This was very much contrary to US advice and practice, where insolvent banks were simply allowed to fail instead of taxing the economy by remaining on government life-support. Instead, in the more genteel Japanese economy, the extent of bad debt has been downplayed in order to make it politically feasible for the government to help out leading banks and customers. 1998 saw an initiative to use public funds to take over the banks and liquidate their debts, thereby rebuilding banks overwhelmed by bad debts. However, at the same time the government also expanded loan guarantee limits, guaranteeing loans to inefficient businesses. While this made political sense, it increased the number of bad loans and has been persistently prolonging the banking crisis. Any structural reform is costly to banks, depositors and taxpayers, not to say politicians, and the presence of such interests have so far prevented any significant structural reform from taking place. While liquidating some bad debts, banks have been continuously picking up new debt until the very last few years (Gilpin 2000:280; Gordon 2003:325; Rosecrance 1999:124; Sakakibara 2003:51).[60]

In general, vested interests have played a far more prominent role than in the US. From the late 1970s onwards, deregulation, liberalization and financial reform, on a domestic and an international scale, became recurring themes in US politics. In Japan, an iron triangle of vested interests have sheltered and protected a dual economy, preventing structural change. Ironically, the two most successful sectors of the Japanese economy—car manufacturing and electronics—are the only two not

---

product. Thus, whereas Japanese cars are as reliable as ever, Japanese financial institutions got away with secrecy and misinformation.

60   The problem of bad loans has been accentuated by the fact that often, former regulators from the Ministry of Finance (and other ministries) have retired from government into post-retirement positions as directors of suspect and bankrupt lenders (Gordon 2003:317).

to have strong connections with the political system or to have been systematically milked by the LDP (Grimond 2002).

The reason why vested interests have been so powerful has to do with the weakness and lack of relative autonomy of the Japanese state. While policy decisions have been made to support key industries, the LDP has for most of its existence itself been a coalition of vested interests. The fact that the LDP reigned unchallenged for four decades meant that policies would be carried out without much opposition from the Diet. However, the government, including the PM, has traditionally not been strong, but controlled completely by the party. Hence, the government has very little relative autonomy. Industrial policy has been in the hands of a vested interest complex favoring industries like computers and semiconductors, but which has also protected a hopelessly inefficient dual economy. Relative government autonomy exists only in relation to other political parties. This might be construed as political consensus, but only in the sense that it leaves the power with one unrivaled party. But while unrivaled in the Diet, the government is anything but unrivaled behind the scenes, where politics is conceived by the party, in conjunction with the bureaucracy and with vested interests. Prime ministers have come and gone, "frequently controlled by faction leaders behind the scenes and unable to do much before some scandal or failure unseated them. The factions they serve … are [mostly] vehicles for distributing party and ministerial posts; they seldom promote reform" (Grimond 2002). The LDP leadership has rarely been pro-reform (Castells 2000b:225pp; Sakakibara 2003:47pp).

To a great extent, politics has been in the hands of vested interests. This does not have to be unequivocally bad. If they are the "right" vested interests it may in fact be very effective. However, during times of change, this is rarely the case. What characterizes vested interests is exactly the fact that they advocate policies that go in favor of their own narrow interests, no matter whether this is for the good or the bad of the economy as a whole. But in times of change, the status quo is inevitably upset by new technologies and new growth industries. Hence, as vested interests keep promoting policies in their own favor, these are policies that often go distinctly against the interests of new industries. In Japan, one of the very pervasive beliefs has been the one that comparative advantage is inextricably linked with manufacture and that continued economic success depends on Japan's ability to produce competitive high-quality industrial goods. Hence, Japan has only been weakly influenced by the movement toward deregulation and liberalization (Gilpin 2000:263).

In addition to being a weak state, social cohesion has been dropping. While the decline was less than in the US, it is abundantly clear that trust has decreased, with the percentage declaring that "in general, people can be trusted" now lower than in the US (Dayton-Johnson 2001:4). Politics has become markedly more volatile. Between 1955 and 1989, the average time in power for a Prime Minister, was 3.7 years. Since 1989, this has dropped to 1.4. Thus, Japan has had 11 PMs since 1989. Moreover, the hegemony of the LDP has been challenged, and in 1989, for the first time since 1958, the party lost its majority in one of the houses of the Diet.[61] Since the 1993 vote of no confidence and resignation of the LDP government, the party found it hard to recover its former strength, even though it was soon back in power. It was replaced by a coalition government consisting of the Japan Renewal Party (Shinseito) and the New Japan Party (Nihon Shinto), although the coalition lasted for only 10 months.[62]

Bribery scandals and Yakuza ties are among the reasons why the LDP lost its political preeminence. Moreover, with the end of the Cold War external pressure on the LDP to maintain unity and discipline despite factional rivalries diminished. While politics consensus may not have dramatically dropped, conflicts are definitely more out in the open. The result in any case is that both the government and the party are weakened, which does not make the task of implementing structural reform any easier (Castells 2000b:232p, 245; Fukuyama 1999:59p; Gordon 2003:312pp, 321; Grimond 2002; William W. Lewis 2004:46p).

There is a fair bit of irony to this. As the 1990s progressed, politicians came under ever greater pressure to implement structural reforms. An increasing number of Japanese politicians, businessmen and scholars readily admit that the iron triangle stifles growth and prevents the restructuring necessary for Japan to develop along the same lines as other industrialized economies. The irony is that exactly at the time when the executive has started to assert itself more heavily against the party and vested interests, it has been weakened by scandals and rejected by its traditional voters. As government tried to carve out an independent role for itself, it lost what was its main strength, namely the lack of an effective opposition (Gordon 2003:320pp). Maybe these developments were inevitable. In order to trigger reform within the LDP, first the party needed to come under such pressure that it perceived of there being a clear incentive. And maybe in a system where politics has been at best opaque, sooner or later corruption and bribery would come out in the open, triggering scandals and weakening the dominant party to such an extent that reform is perceived as necessary. However, the short term effect may well be one of weakening the executive further on the expense of vested interests.

We should not underestimate the willingness to reform. Yaushiro Nakasone (PM 1982–1987) clearly saw that economic and political reforms would be crucial for future growth. Thus, as early as 1985, he set up a policy deliberation council to investigate economic reform. The council's report concluded that liberalizing trade and financial services was vital, so that Japan could rely less on exports and more on

---

61 The Diet is split into two chambers, the House of Representatives, which is the stronger of the two, and the House of Councillors. The LDP lost its majority in the House of Councillors but retained a narrow majority in the House of Representatives (Gordon 2003:313).

62 Primarily because the LDP used any means possible to reclaim power. It forced the PM, Hosokawa Morohiro, out of office by accusing him of dubious financial dealings (falsely so). His replacement, Tsutomo Hata, lasted only two months, as by mid-1994, the LDP formed an alliance with its arch-rival, the Japan Socialist Party (JSP), promising the JSP the PM if they agreed to the alliance. The alliance damaged the JSP, which was perceived as selling out by large amounts of its voters.

domestic demand. The report was also met with widespread acclaim by the public (Aoki 1995:xii; Fukushima 1996:58pp). So, while only weakly influenced by the global ideological shift toward deregulation and liberalization, such forces were not absent. However, reform has still been slow, with powerful forces resisting calls for change.[63] Maybe the biggest triumph of the reform movement has been a destructive one. Because of resistance within the LDP, the 1980s saw factions split from the party to form separate parties. Two of these, the Japan Renewal Party and the New Japan Party, were instrumental in forming the coalition that in 1993 broke the LDP monopoly on power. The fact that the LDP now actually has to compete for votes means a far more serious check on corruption and a more genuine willingness to restrain the power of vested interests.

In 2001 PM Junichiro Koizumi came to power with the clear understanding that Japanese politics has to be reformed. While facing heavy resistance, he set up a wide-ranging structural reform program, with the writing off of bank debts high on the agenda, and including a new commercial code, weakening the role of insiders (OECD 2001d:13, 103). This has been partially successful. Japanese banks are still extremely unprofitable, but a gradual turnaround has taken place, with bank debts halved since 2001. The exception is the regional banks, which are still suffering huge numbers of bad loans especially from small, local companies (*Economist* 2004d:83; Emmott 2005). Koizumi has been more intent than most of his predecessors to reduce the influence of vested interests. There are now tentative signs that an accumulation of small changes are beginning to have a positive effect. While the LDP has been weakened throughout the 1990s, Koizumi called a snap election in 2005 over the question of postal reform. This was seen as an election for or against economic reform. Part of the LDP split, but Koizumi was rewarded for his platform of economic reform with a landslide win, which brought the LDP 296 out of 480 seats in the Diet. The LDP is back, and it seems more willing now, than before, to recognize the need to break the power of the iron triangle. However, while he has changed the face of Japanese politics, Koizumi has now stepped down so it is hard to predict what will happen next (Emmott 2005; Gordon 2003:321pp; Grimond 2002; OECD 2001d:13, 53).

Hence, comparing the US and Japan, it is very obvious that in banking, probably more so than in any other sector, the differences have been huge. The US embraced an open international economy with full mobility of factors of production. Japan shunned it. Japanese banks, sheltered and protected, did not have the opportunity or incentive to modernize in the same way as US banks. Hence, TFP growth in Japanese banking has been weak (for 1996–1999 even weaker than in retailing) (OECD 2001d:46), whereas banking and finance in general, primarily through the

---

63 Fukushima (1996:64) lists one such example, which he characterizes as typical: Upon calls to deregulate petrol stations (1995) (only station attendants are allowed to pump fuel, as it is considered flammable, and thus must be left to the experts …), the National Fire Prevention Agency demanded a three-year study to determine whether self-service stations could ever be safe.

efficient utilization of ICTs, have been among the primary contributors to US TFP and labor productivity growth.[64]

Japanese society puts a great value on harmony and frowns upon conflict. On the face of it, this sounds like a society rich in political consensus and social cohesion. This is wrong. It could of course be argued that the reason why vested interests have been allowed to play such a major part is not because politicians are weak and vested interests strong, but because in a harmonious and consensual society, different interests are included because their views are considered important. However, what may seem like consensus and cohesion for practical purposes means that politics has been governed by vested interest coalitions, with the government at best playing second fiddle. As a result, Japan has not been able or willing to attempt any restructuring of its economy until very recently. The so-called iron triangle has successfully preserved the dual structure of the economy, and this has resulted in the Japanese service industries taking up a relatively small share of employment, and falling far behind in terms of productivity. The absence of reform has meant that the Japanese service sector has lacked both the opportunity and the incentive to invest heavily in technological equipment like ICTs. Data show quite clearly that productivity improvements in Japanese services, in particular banking, have been very slow compared to the US. And data also quite clearly show that when it comes to the utilization of ICTs and the impact of ICT using service industries, Japan is very much a laggard, very much in contrast with the US.

Tellingly, in the US no vested interests controlled policy-making. Instead, presidents enjoyed considerable autonomy. Not because other branches, like the legislature, were impotent, but because of considerable consensus as to the direction in which the country was heading with respect to issues like international trade, deregulation and liberalization. In the comparatively Schumpeterian US economy, promoting policies of structural change, was far easier than in Japan. US presidents did not find themselves checked and controlled by all and sundry vested interests. Ironically, it is not Japan with its emphasis on harmony and consensus, but the far more conflictual US, which has been able to exhibit political consensus around such policy issues. Maybe this is in the nature of the beast. Structural change almost by necessity implies conflict. This may be easier to accomplish in a country where the consensus is about the importance of conflict and change, than in a country that suppresses change in order to avoid conflict and preserve consensus and harmony.

Conclusions

Writing a definitive story of something that is still on-going is always hard. History is an endless stream of events. Breaking off that stream and dividing chunks of

---

64 Measures of the performance of US financial services, taking into account quality adjustments made possible by new technology, estimate a 1977–1994 growth of over seven per cent a year. The average TFP growth of Japanese banking (1986–1999) was 2.2 per cent (OECD 2000b:52pp; 2001c:46).

history into epochs does violence to the concept of history itself. The four previous chapters dealt with time periods that comprised the invention of a new technology, the rise of that industry to economic predominance, and its peak. For this fifth time period, no peak has yet arrived. Further, this fifth period is different in the sense that it sees a shift away from traditional mass-manufacturing and toward the services, in particular knowledge-intensive services. The chapter is about a time period that has yet to peak. And its focus is on something far less tangible than the rise of a manufacturing industry, namely the rather *in*tangible process of how structural change has affected not just ICT industries, but on macro processes affecting the utilization of ICTs in production processes in general. For all these reasons, the conclusions must be tentative.

But let us throw caution aside for a few pages: The dual nature of ICTs presents us with another problem. In the utilization of ICTs, Japan has clearly been a laggard. However, with respect to ICT *industries*, Japan has been a good number two, in certain sectors even number one. Hence, Japan is treated as a laggard based on its performance in *utilizing* ICTs. This makes sense. It is evident that countries have been able to benefit greatly from ICTs without themselves having strong ICT industries. While ICT manufacturing has undoubtedly brought benefits to both the US and Japan, these are small industries in terms of employment share and turnover. The contribution to GDP and TFP growth has come not primarily as a result of the rise of specific new industries, but from the utilization of ICTs in the services (as well as in manufacturing). Hence, explosive productivity increases in ICT manufacturing have had less of an impact on the overall economy than merely strong increases in the ICT using service industries. This applies most notably to the US. This is also the main area in which Japanese productivity has stagnated.

It is very obvious that human capital has been crucial. The link between science and industrial development has been closer for ICTs than for any of the other industries and technologies in this book. With both the US and Japan, we see an absolutely massive expansion of the science system following World War II. For the US, the early lead that it enjoyed in all branches of ICTs had much to do with the human capital advantage that it had over other countries. While Japan has by no means been a laggard in terms of education, in certain ICT sectors like software, it has been sorely lacking in human capital. The Japanese education system has come under heavy criticism over the past few years for stifling creativity and for not being able to cope with the requirements of a business environment characterized by more uncertainty and putting more stress on the need for flexibility.

For several of the previous time periods, wars have been important. In this chapter, the impact arose from *cold* war. The start of the Cold War fueled strong beliefs that the best way to prevent a Soviet attack was to stay technologically ahead. The impact was enormous, especially during the early phase of US ICT manufacturing, and ensured an early lead for the US. While the semiconductor industry is a good example that military demand and procurements do not necessarily provide any permanent advantage, there is no doubt that US ICT industries benefited greatly from their links with the military.

While close links and interaction between science and industry were an important component to US success, it is less obvious that we can explain differences between the US and Japan with recourse to the so-called science link (the relationship between science and industry). Data do indeed show that the link has been far stronger in the US, and that spinoffs from scientific research have occurred more readily in the US than elsewhere. At the same time, for several decades the links between different actors in the Japanese economy were strong, knowledge diffusing rapidly, and the MITI taking on special responsibility for financing projects and promoting links between different economic actors. What is beyond doubt is that this is an area in which the US has excelled. What is less beyond doubt is that Japan was much worse, with the exception for the most recent decade.

It may well be that the most important contributions made by the state in fostering ICT *industries* has been the massive increase in human capital investments. With respect to the utilization of ICTs in the services, human capital has undoubtedly been important, but probably not crucial. The growth has been most pronounced in the knowledge-intensive services. Success in ICTs seems intertwined with something akin to globalization. Countries that have embraced globalization have at the same time provided their ICT industries and ICT using services with greater opportunities and incentives to grow. The technological breakthroughs provided by ICTs were a necessary condition for globalization to occur in the first place. Beyond this, among the most prominent policies conducive to globalization initiated by the world's governments, have been policies of international deregulation, liberalization and financial reform, creating an open international economy with full mobility of factors of production, among other things including virtually limitless capital flows.

In this area, the US was at the forefront, with Japan being extremely reluctant. With Margaret Thatcher, whose ideas and policies he latched on to, Ronald Reagan spearheaded what in less than a decade became a new neoliberal economic orthodoxy, with a focus on deregulation, liberalization, financial reform, and the opening of industries to international competition. With Clinton, these policies were extended to the international scene. The US, having started this process earlier than any other country (except for Britain), was uniquely suited to taking advantage of the benefits of globalization, its service industries achieving high productivity levels and being internationally competitive. It provided US service industries, especially in banking and finance, with both the opportunity and incentive to modernize and increase its productivity further, by the efficient utilization of ICTs. These were opportunities and incentives withheld from Japanese service industries, as deregulation and liberalization were blocked by Japanese vested interests. The so-called iron triangle insists on preserving a dual economy consisting of a very backward, traditional and low-productivity service sector. It also diligently sheltered the financial system from international competition. When Japan finally and most reluctantly opened its financial markets, its banks were unable to compete.

The reason for the lack of vested interests blocking structural change in the US has to do with the speed with which these ideas rose to ideological preeminence. Both Democratic and Republican presidents marketed similar ideas in these areas, not facing much resistance from the legislature, enjoying considerable political consensus. Virtually the opposite was true of Japan, where politics for all practical purposes was run by vested interests. During the first post-war decades this was not a big problem, as the vested interests running the country essentially were the "right" vested interests. However, as times changed, and new technologies and industries rose, vested interests kept promoting policies going in their own favor. In times of stability, this may not be a problem. During times of change, it almost always is. And the past few decades *have* been a time of change. In Japan, impotent governments were almost completely controlled by LDP factions that in turn were heavily influenced by the bureaucracy and by vested interests. A case could also be made that this was not only about consensus but also about cohesion. When Reagan came to power, the US was demoralized, struggling politically and economically. While hard to measure, it has been argued that among Reagan's prime achievements was his ability to turn this mood around. Newfound optimism and a greater level of social cohesion in the populace made it easier for him to carry out policies with considerable redistributional effects, as well as carrying him through the serious economic crisis that set in during his first term in office. The point can hardly be verified, but it deserves mentioning.

The point about Reagan reveals one of the main dangers with respect to making assessments about present-day phenomena or people. These are politicized issues. These are political characters that people are strongly opinionated about. Still, there is little doubt that the biggest impact that ICTs have had on growth and productivity has occurred through the utilization of ICTs in the knowledge-intensive services. In this area, the US has been vastly more successful than Japan. What does this imply for the future? It could mean that Japan has a huge potential for growth, since it has much catching up to do. Or it could mean that Japan has lost its chance, and will keep lagging. In any case, with the US being the forerunner in ICTs and Japan a laggard, what is certain is that the US has a solid head start, and that Japan is again playing catch-up.

Chapter 7

Conclusions

Technological progress and industrial leadership are crucial for a state's economic growth and development, and ultimately for the state's prestige in the international system. Is there a role for the state in encouraging and promoting technological progress and industrial leadership, and if so, what is it? Is it true that with every rise of a great power—politically, economically, technologically, industrially—there is also an inevitable fall? If not, is there anything that the state can do in order to prevent it? Or at worst, how have certain states been able to prolong their periods of dominance and leadership?

This book suggests that there are systematic variations that can be scientifically traced with respect to these questions. However, these are macro questions in the extreme, and there is no neat and easy way in which to provide them with neat and easy answers. A project like this requires a theory that is so parsimonious that the project is actually doable, and at the same time not so simplistic that it neglects the historical context and the subtler details of each and every case. Hence, macro projects seek to make sense out of what may initially look like complexity and chaos. Yet, it is my hope that this book contributes to making its way around some of this complexity, ultimately providing some system to the chaos.

This requires finding a useful angle. The angle for this book is the state, and its role in promoting one out of several types of growth, Schumpeterian growth. More precisely, what is the role of the state in promoting technological progress and industrial leadership? For this, Joseph Schumpeter—flowing naturally from the emphasis on Schumpeterian growth—combines with Mancur Olson to form the theoretical underpinnings of the book. In his emphasis on key industries in different historical eras, Schumpeter provides a mechanism that can account for the rise and fall of nations. Certain industries have been more important than others, and hence, a nation's economic growth, prosperity and ultimately its position and stature in the international system, hinges on its performance within these industries. However, no industry lasts forever. Sooner or later, a country will run out of new investment opportunities in what were once profitable industries, and maturation, saturation, and ultimately, stagnation and depression, will set in. The economy will stumble into a recession until and unless it can find investment opportunities in new industries, typically derived from technological breakthroughs.

Olson provides a different mechanism. He provides the mechanism for why leadership often changes from one country to another as a consequence of the Schumpeterian economic fluctuations. One might expect the lead nation to have an inherent advantage with respect to persisting as the lead nation when the next revolutionary technology (and industries) comes along. But this may not be true. The lead nation may have a hard time adapting to a new economic reality, tied up as it is in institutional structures, tariff policies, education policies, patent systems etc. of yesteryear, benefiting the old industries and proving highly resistant to change. Olson (1982) emphasizes the gradual silting up of rigidities that happens over time as vested interests grow powerful enough to influence and exert control over policy-making. Fitting Olson into a Schumpeterian context yields the conclusion that the reason why the lead nation may have a hard time adapting is because of resistance against altering the status quo being exerted by powerful pressure groups, i.e. industrial lobbies, seeking to protect the interests of their own industries. Structural economic change is blocked by old and mature industries in an effort to preserve profits and employment in sectors that are no longer the engine of the economy. In doing so, they make life harder for the new and promising industries of the future. In contrast to this, countries where no strong vested interests existed in the first place, new and promising industries would not find their growth hampered because of outdated regulations, arrangements and institutions protecting old and unprofitable industries.

To this, a mechanism is needed in order to explain why some states manage to retain their relative autonomy when faced with vested interest groups, whereas others do not. Here, a number of scholars (e.g. Dayton-Johnson 2001; Fukuyama 1995; Knutsen 1999; Putnam 1995a, 1995b) emphasize the importance of ties holding a nation together. Hence, only in countries characterized by a high degree of political consensus and social cohesion does the state stand a realistic chance of curbing the power of vested interests. Only in such countries does the state have the necessary political autonomy and popular support to pursue policies of structural economic change without having to fear being overthrown, either through elections or in a coup.

In addition to the above, very much in line with the Schumpeterian approach, belongs a focus on human capital. If technological progress is among the main mechanisms by which industrial leadership is achieved, one would expect human capital to be of importance. Hence, the main variables circumscribing this book are human capital, vested interests, and consensus and cohesion. These are the variables through which the state promotes technological and industrial leadership.

Human Capital, Vested Interests and Consensus and Cohesion

In one sense, every chapter in this book is a finished project in itself. Still, the chapters are of value primarily as the component parts of a greater whole, in providing the necessary empirical foundation for the overall project. Nonetheless, each chapter largely supports the general story of human capital, vested interests, and consensus and cohesion.

This does not mean that they all support the general story to exactly the same extent. There is no reason why industrial growth would play itself out in exactly the same manner on each and every occasion. For instance: In general, as time has passed, most industries have become more knowledge-intensive. The sciences have progressed and become more advanced, leading to new industries being more knowledge-intensive. Clearly, the technology required for the cotton textiles revolution of the late eighteenth century was nowhere near path breaking if judged by present-day standards. But in the late eighteenth century, it was.

However, the individual chapters support the story to a large extent. This is very obvious in the case of chemicals and ICT industries, both highly knowledge-intensive, drawing heavily on scientific research. Germany benefited greatly from its superb education system. The US increased its R & D efforts tremendously as a consequence of World War II and never looked back. In the same manner, the British chemical industry suffered from a lack of human capital, caused among other things by German chemists leaving Britain to take up positions in the German industry instead. To what extent Japan has been deficient in human capital with respect to ICTs is a more contentious question. The effort of the Japanese state was considerable and Japanese catch-up rapid. But Japan fell short in one important respect. The impact of ICTs has primarily been transmitted through their utilization, not the manufacturing of ICT equipment. In this respect, the Japanese human capital record is checkered at best, with numerous reports criticizing the rigor and the lack of flexibility and creativity in Japanese education (Castells 2000b:251; OECD 1999a).

Neither in Germany nor in the US did vested interests unduly block economic policy-making. No powerful German cotton textile industry existed. In Britain, cotton textiles as well as a number of other interests put constraints on the state, very much stifling any initiative for policies of structural change. In Germany, no such interests had the power to block change. Much the same applies to the present-day US. Despite considerable initial opposition against policies of deregulation, liberalization and financial reform, no groups had the power to prevent politicians from pushing fairly wide-ranging changes through. In contrast to this stands Japan, where an array of vested interests have accumulated power over more than half a century to the extent that for decades it has almost been political suicide not to adhere to these interests.

In terms of consensus and cohesion, the German case fits less convincingly. Bismarck did not seek to cultivate any political consensus, and with respect to cohesion, one of the reasons why Emperor Wilhelm II ultimately forced him to resign was the fact that he was struggling to hold the country together. Blatant nationalist policies (Weltpolitik) from the end of the nineteenth century were in part a result of the Emperor's personal megalomania, and an attempt to use nationalism to counter the growth of socialism. But for Britain the argument works better. Britain struggled with dwindling social cohesion from the late nineteenth century onwards, even if socially calm and stable. Also, the political consensus of the mid-nineteenth century had given way to considerable disagreement. Here as well, nationalism worked, as the Conservatives used the politics of Empire and patriotism, of Queen and country to wrest the working-class vote away from the Whigs.

For the US and Japan, the argument works well. In the US during the 1980s, political consensus rapidly spread, hailing the virtues of deregulation and liberalization, including policies of globalization. Within less than a decade these ideas had become the new economic orthodoxy in the Western world. However, in Japan, no such consensus existed. If anything, in Japan consensus instead centered on the need for stability and the preservation of a political ideal where harmony of interests took center stage over structural change. This ideal more or less explicitly implies that politics be molded in cooperation with a number of favored interest groups.

The Cotton Textile chapter also fits well. Since cotton textiles represents the first phase of industrialization, technological change was slow, and its impact on the overall economy only moderate. Also, education systems were not yet very well developed. Still, Britain was far better endowed in human capital than France. The cotton textile industry quite clearly shows how human capital was important even at this early stage of industrialization. With respect to vested interests, and consensus and cohesion, Britain also had powerful advantages. In Britain, the ruling elites were united, crushing attempts at physical resistance against industrialization fiercely and without hesitation. French political elites were far more hesitant. They were not unambiguously pro-industrialization, structural reform was persistently blocked by the nobility, and the regime did not enjoy any groundswell of public support, something which became abundantly clear in 1789.

The Iron and Automobile chapters both deal with industries in which innovation was more piecemeal. Both were immensely important industries, but to a lesser extent derived from technological breakthroughs. Hence, as expected, human capital was less important, even if the Iron chapter suggests that Britain continued to benefit from its overall human capital advantage. British iron production was technologically far more sophisticated than the French. But as importantly, with respect to vested interests, consensus and cohesion, the overturning of vested interests symbolized by the Corn Laws, and forging a new political consensus from the 1840s onwards, were huge advantages compared to France, where vested interests blocked reform, among other things with respect to railroad construction, and where governments enjoyed scant autonomy. The only time when French ruling elites exhibited any degree of political consensus, was when government positions were controlled by the far right, which was staunchly against reform in any case!

This leaves the automobile industry as the only deviant case. It is not deviant in the sense that human capital, vested interests, and consensus and cohesion were immaterial. The US had considerable competency in areas that were crucial for mass manufacturing, it eventually combated vested interests that were stifling capital-intensive industries, and a consensus did develop on the importance of these new industries. However, all these developments took place at a stage where the US car industry was already by far the world's largest. Hence, Smithian factors seem to have been more instrumental in triggering growth than Schumpeterian factors. In many ways, this should not come as a major surprise, since of all the five technological breakthroughs, mass production technologies come closest to being a microinvention rather than a macroinvention. As elaborated upon earlier, we should expect less Schumpeterian and more Smithian growth for microinventions than we should for macroinventions.

With the partial exception of the car industry, all five time periods and industries support the story. Overwhelmingly, those countries that achieved technological and industrial success had a human capital advantage. Not surprisingly, the human capital variable was more important the more knowledge-intensive the industry. Also, human capital in general has become more important as time has passed. The Industrial Revolution was not a revolution as in being a clear and decisive break with the past. Sciences and technologies were not yet very sophisticated, and the mechanically gifted layman was able to intuitively grasp most of the sciences, without much formal education. Hence, human capital requirements were far less than was the case a century later. But in general, those countries that were behind in terms of human capital, failed to achieve industrial leadership. This applies to France for cotton textiles and iron, for Britain and chemicals, and for Japan with respect to the utilization of ICTs. Contrary to this, Britain had a human capital advantage both in cotton textiles and iron, Germany had a clear advantage in chemicals, and the US was strong with respect both to the production and the utilization of ICTs.

However, there is more to the story. Does it matter if human capital was acquired formally, through a state-sponsored education system, or informally, through for instance on-the-job training? Early British human capital advantage was *not* a consequence of a well-funded, government-sponsored education system. The French state was far more activist with respect to higher education, and France was ahead of Britain in nearly all the sciences. And still, there is no doubt that Britain had a far larger pool of mechanically skilled people than France, which is something that was of crucial importance with respect both to cotton textiles and iron. The early Industrial Revolution was the work of mechanically gifted experimenters and tinkerers, largely without much formal training, not of highly educated experts. This is exactly the kind of human capital that Britain possessed, and which France was very short of. Hence, more important than formal training was informal training, as long as it was the right kind of training. However, it is also obvious that this was not an approach to human capital that Britain could reap benefits from for all eternity. By the late nineteenth century, the sciences had advanced to such a degree that gifted amateurs no longer could have any hope of contributing. As Britain refrained from reforming its education system until the very end of the nineteenth century, it fell woefully behind in chemicals. Hence, by the late nineteenth century formal education was very much a requirement for all but the technologically most unsophisticated technologies.

This brings me to the next point. Once knowledge is produced, it needs to be utilized. A country may have the world's finest scientists and experts, but if their knowledge does not move beyond academic circles, it is unlikely to benefit the economy. Hence, the diffusion of knowledge is as crucial as producing it in the first place. Here as well, the cotton textile industry brings the point across clearly. British inventions were rapidly diffused throughout the country, from business networks,

Dissenter networks, through close ties between finance and industry, through scientific journals and through an infrastructure system that allowed rapid travel. In France, access to the crucial inventions both within cotton textiles and iron came as a result of the slow diffusion of these inventions across the Channel. Once the French Revolution, the Revolutionary and the Napoleonic Wars started, this process of diffusion came to an almost complete halt. Mechanisms for transmitting such knowledge within France without foreign impetus seemed close to non-existent. One of the most conspicuous differences was how France was good at invention, with Britain good at application (of French inventions). The Swiss calico printer Ryhiner in 1766 (cited in Mokyr 1990:115) asserted that "... for a thing to be perfect it must be invented in France and worked out in England". A similar story applies to present-day ICTs too. A crucial difference between the US and Japan is their ability to utilize these technologies. The US has led the world, Japan is a laggard. Japan has been excellent at mass manufacturing ICT equipment, but has failed to utilize it, thus losing out on major productivity improvements in its service industries.

However, the chemical industry serves as an example that formal training is crucial as well. The reason for the German human capital advantage was first and foremost its superior higher education system, churning out highly skilled scientists at a rate much higher than in Britain. There are few signs that Britain had become any worse at diffusion. But diffusion without a proper knowledge base could only go so far. Chemical knowledge in Germany was widespread, going back as far as the early nineteenth century, when German states, competing with each other, all invested in chemical laboratories. Later on, German chemical firms invested heavily in industrial laboratories, performing their own research in addition to drawing on the university sector. While knowledge was rapidly diffused, the German success had more to do with an excellent system of the *production* of knowledge.

Does this suggest much of a role for the state? Again, the story needs fine-tuning. The role of the state has increased over time. When the sciences grow more complex, more is required of the education systems in order to produce sufficiently skilled experts. Hence, no state could anymore get away with the amount of education effort and involvement common during the late eighteenth century. The British state neglected the education system during the early Industrial Revolution, and despite this, Britain grew to become an industrial superpower. However, this no longer constitutes a viable recipe for success, and became evident toward the latter part of the nineteenth century as Germany caught up with and then surpassed Britain.

But this means that the role of the state may be less important. Often, the diffusion of knowledge has taken place through processes that have essentially side-stepped the state. In Britain, what was of importance was links between inventors, industrialists, and finance. In France, where the state actually actively sought to promote such links, it failed dismally. On the other hand, present-day experience tells us that in the US, the state has been successful in promoting such links, for instance through specialized applied research-institutes, and by taking a role in the spread of military knowledge for civilian purposes. The Japanese case points to a state that was successful in promoting the diffusion of ICT manufacturing knowledge, but where Japan later fell short because of its inability to utilize ICTs in the new service industries.

Hence, there are bound to be processes of diffusion that sidestep the state. The empirical record suggests that this may even be an area in which the state should only carefully meddle. With respect to the activist French state, which deliberately sought to promote diffusion in order to catch up, it should not be forgotten that in a very different manner, the British state actually played a role too. In order to have a future as a scientist in France, one was dependent on being on good terms with the political establishment. As a scientist, you worked either *for* the state or *against* it. Personal economic gain was rarely the incentive. Not so in Britain, where the government recognized the importance of technology transfer and sought not to interfere. British engineers and scientists rarely had to subject themselves to hidden political or military agendas. While acknowledging the only indirect role of the state in these processes, this does not take away from the fact that overall, the role of the state has been considerable with respect to the production of human capital.

Even during the early phase of the Industrial Revolution, human capital was more important than we have earlier assumed. However, the link between human capital and industrial leadership has naturally been stronger in the more knowledge-intensive industries. The link is obvious with respect to Germany and chemicals, although this argument cannot be made completely without qualification. With respect to ICTs, the contribution of the US higher education system is undisputed. However, even in cotton textiles and in iron it is possible to trace a distinct contribution to industrial development from human capital.

How about the automobile industry? On the one hand, mass-production technologies, while having a revolutionary impact on industrial production, were not technologies that required a sophisticated understanding of scientific principles. Rather, they could be grasped fairly easily, and perfected through trial-and-error. Which is essentially what Henry Ford, whose formal schooling had not even endowed him with the ability to read without stuttering, did. As much as a technological breakthrough, mass production was an organizational breakthrough. Hence, one should not expect human capital, neither in the shape of primary education nor higher education to have had a tremendous impact. On the other hand, the US already had an advantage in precision tooling and in interchangeable parts. Hence, from a human capital point of view, it should not come as a surprise that the combining of the two to yield true mass-production technologies occurred in the US, and not in any other countries. While this cannot explain why Henry Ford was the one to make the breakthrough, it tells us that the US for decades already had been producing people with the right kinds of skills and mind-set to come up with a concept like mass production.

In the final analysis, has human capital been important with respect to technological progress and industrial leadership? The answer is a fairly resounding yes. With the partial exception of the automobile industry, human capital has been important in every time period. Naturally, the degree to which it has been crucial has varied, and there have been differences between different time periods with respect to the importance of formal training compared to informal, the importance of schooling compared to diffusion, and the importance of primary schooling compared to higher education. But this does not take away from the fact that the link between human capital and industrial growth has been amply demonstrated for each and every time period.

The second main variable in the book is vested interests. To what extent can vested interests explain why some countries have been able to take advantage of opportunities for industrial growth presented by new technology, whereas others have remained mired in a slowly stagnating status quo? The empirical evidence provides solid support for the theory. In every case of industrial leadership (with the partial exception of the US automobile industry), the country that achieved leadership managed to overcome what were often considerable vested interests. The countries that failed were all characterized by inability or unwillingness to pursue economic policies that went against the interests of powerful interest groups.

The vested interests of one time period are not the same as for another period. This follows more or less by necessity from the Schumpeterian part of the theoretical framework. For each time period, new industries have grown to establish themselves as the new engine of the economy. In the same way, the forces fighting against change and seeking to preserve the status quo are not likely to be the same forces that fought against change 50 years earlier.

In Britain, agricultural interests sought to block manufacturing interests, but failed, most conspicuously so with the repeal of the Corn Laws. In the latter part of the nineteenth century, religious interests were successful at blocking education reform. During the same period, cotton textile interests were lukewarm with respect to government involvement in education and also effectively prevented patent and tariff reform. The French king had to fight the nobility over financial reform as well as over the guild system, not very successfully so. Industry lobby groups were successful in pushing tariffs, for the purpose of protecting the existing industrial structure rather than modernizing. The state bureaucracy blocked railroad reform, and the Catholic Church managed to prevent education reform. In Germany, no strong cotton textile sector already existed. Hence, what in Britain were powerful vested interests had no bearing on German economic policies. Thus, the German chemical industry fairly easily got the attention of the German state, which was willing to include special provisions for dyestuffs with respect both to tariff policies and the patent system. In the US free trade vs. protectionism was a major issue during the first half of the twentieth century, the battle raging between protectionist labor-intensive industries and free traders in the capital-intensive industries. And in the present era, the US has successfully steered clear of vested interests in pushing for policies of deregulation and liberalization, whereas Japanese politics is caught in a web of interest groups, regulating and stifling the business sector and the services, and channeling vast sums of money into sheltered and highly inefficient sectors.

In general, the vested interest argument fits well for all the cases (with the partial exception of the US automobile industry). French economic development and industrial growth was clearly hampered by an array of vested interests, whereas one of the reasons why Britain was so hugely successful in iron was because of the links forged between iron and coal through the construction of a railroad network that could cheaply and efficiently transport coal to the iron ore. In France, vested interests in railroad construction were deeply entrenched in the state bureaucracy, preventing economic reasoning from driving the construction of railroads. France ended up with the finest railroads in the world. But since they were also prohibitively expensive and time-consuming to build, railroad construction occurred at a much slower pace than in Britain. And because the state bureaucracy considered railroads far too important for business interests to have a say, railroads were of negligible relevance to industry. Where Britain built a *network*, France built a *hub and spokes* system, every road leading straight to Paris. Regarding chemicals, the contrast between German and British vested interests is illustrative. Britain had the world's most successful cotton textile industry. It also had the world's largest chemical industry, but its influence on politics was negligible, completely drowned out by cotton textiles. In Germany, no major industries were in a position to do the same, and thus, German politicians and the German bureaucracy were extremely receptive to a promising industry starting more or less from scratch. However, the Britain of the late eighteenth and early to mid-nineteenth century also shows us that the British state had earlier been quite successful at preventing vested interests from blocking change. The government was very unambiguously and fiercely clamping down on attempts at physical resistance against new machinery. Processes of industrialization were not to be disturbed, unlike what was the case, for instance, in France. Finally, a present-day example: In Japan, over the past few decades, it is quite evident that vested interests have stifled growth and development, and that the government rarely has been in a position to pursue policies independently of such interests.

Hence, in most cases, the vested interest argument fits really well. As with human capital, the only somewhat deviant case was the US automobile industry. True, the US overcame vested interests favoring labor-intensive over capital-intensive industries. However, victory did not arrive until the 1930s, at a time when the US car industry had for decades already been producing more than 80 per cent of the world's total amount of cars. Hence, it is not likely that this was the reason for the initial success of the car industry. Furthermore, as most US cars were produced with the domestic market in mind, it is hard to say to what extent tariff reductions benefited the industry, although tariffs were reason enough for both Ford and General Motors to establish European subsidiaries instead of selling American cars in Europe. Most likely, Smithian factors, like demand, drove most of the developments in what was not only a mass-production industry, but also a mass consumption one.

Overall, the evidence strongly supports the theory, even more unambiguously so than for human capital. It strongly indicates that there was, and still is, a causal connection between the absence of vested interests (or the overcoming of vested interests) and industrial growth and leadership. This implies an important role for the state in preventing vested interests from becoming too powerful.

The third and final of the main variables, is political consensus and social cohesion. The evidence provides solid support for the theory here as well. However, this is at the same time the one variable that exhibits the largest range of variation in terms of the different ways that it materialized (or failed to). Hence, this is the variable that requires the most interpretation. In the Introduction, I stressed the fact that I do not deal with how consensus and cohesion form in the first place. The only thing that I care about is that it actually exists. Also, consensus and cohesion do not by necessity guarantee the desired outcome. Rather, the importance of consensus and cohesion is along the lines of no state being able to go against powerful vested interests unless it can fall back on considerable levels of political consensus and social cohesion. Hence, it is easy to imagine situations where consensus and cohesion exist, but around the wrong policies. If so, the outcome will be stagnation and stasis, not structural change and industrial leadership. In several cases, most particularly in nineteenth-century France and to some extent in present-day Japan, this seems to have been exactly what happened. The ruling elites were pretty much in agreement as to where the country would be headed. However, the only reason why these ruling elites were in unison was because they could agree on the preservation of the status quo, and on preventing major structural change.

Observing the absence of consensus and cohesion may actually be easier than observing its presence. This is probably most obvious in the case of France, for cotton textiles and iron. With a few exceptions, French regimes were very weak. First, based on the amount of social revolutions and riots alone, we can conclude that social cohesion was low. French regimes could not rely on any groundswell of popular support to save them if times were tough. With respect to political consensus, the growing sense of unity in interests and outlooks that marked British ruling elites toward the end of the eighteenth century never found a parallel in France. Instead, the relationship between the monarch and the nobility was tenuous, at times openly hostile. While most educated men would agree that the state's finances were in dire need of reform, no consensus could ever be carved out. Post-1815 governments were distinctly weak. If day-to-day survival is a government's most pressing priority, then policies will invariably become policies of not offending powerful interests. Hence, post-1815, during those periods when France was characterized by political consensus, the reason was that power rested with the extreme right, that is, with people that perceived structural change as unequivocally bad. Hence, political consensus rested with people determined to preserve the status quo. In short, very few French regimes had the kind of relative autonomy necessary to pursue policies independently of vested interests. Often they lacked the willingness as well.

Conspicuously, the main exceptions to this pattern occurred during periods of autocracy, as only Napoleon, and his less illustrious nephew, Napoleon III, had the necessary autonomy—and the willingness—to go against vested interests. It is debatable whether these were periods of political consensus. Speaking of consensus during periods of dictatorship inevitably has a hollow ring to it. However, what is important here is that only during those periods when French politics was *not* marred by strife and a complete lack of political consensus and social cohesion, did French rulers actually manage to go against vested interests. It took until Napoleon III for France to have a leader who was powerful enough to go against vested interests among other things to reform railroad construction and the financial system. And it became very evident later on that even an Emperor's position rests on an alliance of interests that need to be satisfied. Hence, when providing support for Italian unification, Napoleon III lost the support of one his most important allies, the Catholic Church and had to backtrack plans of reforming education. Later on, he also alienated business interests.

Present-day Japan is another good example, although with a slightly different twist. In Japan, for most of the post-war era, governments have been reluctant to go against vested interests. To the extent that political consensus has existed, it has centered around the preservation of the existing status quo rather than on structural change. Japanese governments have routinely been rendered impotent when faced with resistance—not in the Japanese Diet, where the LDP has normally had a clear majority—but from within the LDP. Since Japanese governments have been chronically weak, the most important political consensus that Japanese PMs have to seek is with the upper echelons of the LDP itself. This is a consensus that has very frequently been absent, as the party has relied heavily on votes from exactly those groups that would be jeopardized by large-scale structural change.

What is more important, consensus or cohesion? This seems an empirical rather than a theoretical question, but the evidence tends in favor of consensus. This might be because the mechanisms through which cohesion works are harder to trace. A lack of political consensus has very observable effects on policy-making, lack of social cohesion less so. In particular, it is hard to empirically observe how the existence of social cohesion has made it less risky for political elites to pursue policies of structural change. However, there is no doubt that social cohesion has also been important. Mid-nineteenth-century France endured two revolutions (1830, 1848) and one *coup d'état* (1851). It is conspicuous how little support the outgoing regimes had in the people. The Bourbon Monarchy (1815–1830) and the July Monarchy (1830–1848) engendered little enthusiasm, but persisted for as long as they could produce economic growth and reasonable protection for business. When they could no longer do this, and business interests withdrew their lukewarm support, both quickly floundered. The same applied to the short-lived Second Republic (1848–1851). When these regimes encountered problems, they fell at the first hurdle, as there was no groundswell of support to fall back on for political legitimacy. Social cohesion applies to Britain as well. The reason why Britain found it impossible to go against the cotton textile industry to raise tariffs in the late nineteenth century, was not only because of the cotton textile industry lobbying against it, but because a tariff increase would have been political suicide. The Corn Laws raised the cost of living for the average worker by 15–20 per cent (Lindert 2003:329; O'Rourke 1994:133). Hence, tariffs symbolized the exploitation of the workers and the channeling of hard-earned wages into the coffers of idle landowners. Even the Conservatives, otherwise favorably predisposed toward protectionism, refused to address the issue, knowing full well that it would lose them the next election. Instead, they turned their focus outward, toward nationalist policies of Empire, colonialism and national glory.

The best examples of consensus and cohesion playing a positive role can probably be found with respect to Britain and to the present-day US. For both cotton textiles and iron, political consensus was one of the reasons why the British process of industrialization was so successful. This was a consensus that had developed in the 1760s, manifesting itself in a shared understanding among the political elites over the importance of suppressing physical resistance against industrialization, and otherwise not meddling in the affairs of business. The consensus lasted until the end of the Napoleonic Wars. Hence, the main early to mid-nineteenth-century domestic political struggle was over the Corn Laws. Whig appeals for repeal met with little success, and it took the Conservative Government of Robert Peel, and the willingness of large parts of the Conservative Party to vote against their normally favored agricultural interests, before the repeal was finally passed in 1846. Hence, manufacturing could not defeat the vested interests of agriculture and nobility until the rise of major political consensus in favor of structural change.[1] In the present-day US, political clashes between Democrats and Republicans have become fierce lately. However, in certain areas, there are only minor differences between the two. Reforms most commonly associated with President Reagan were actually introduced by Carter, and a decade or so later extended to the international arena by Clinton. The new political consensus was one of liberalization and deregulation, supported internationally through the increased political support for conservative parties all over the West. Thus, Reagan, Bush and Clinton all enjoyed broad bipartisan support for economic and political measures that promoted structural change in general, and ICTs and knowledge-intensive services in particular.

In addition to the by now familiar deviant case of the US automobile industry, one other case deserves discussion and interpretation, namely Germany and chemicals. Bismarck's period as German Chancellor hardly ushered in political consensus. Bismarck in fact went out of his way *not* to forge ties with any of the political parties, and instead preferred to make temporary alliances as best he saw fit. Granted, following his successful wars against Denmark, Austria and France, the considerable opposition that he had been met with in the Prussian Landtag evaporated, and for the following couple of years he had considerable leverage. However, he took little interest in economic affairs, switching overnight from free trade to protectionism, seemingly without giving it much thought or concern (Klug 2001:225). Hence, he did not use his leverage for the benefit of industry. But at a lower level, political consensus was important as the bureaucracy was characterized by a widespread belief in the importance of creating favorable conditions for business. The German chemical industry met with little skepticism whenever it requested the state for favors. Still, the main reason why this was so easy for the German chemical industry was the absence of strong established vested interests in the first place.

---

1   As mentioned in the Iron chapter, the repeal was not without consequences for the Conservatives. The party split, and was forced out of government, not to return for several decades. Hence, for the Conservatives, going against vested interests actually turned out to be a highly risky political decision.

Finally, the US automobile industry is again the only deviant case, and again for the same reasons. A political consensus gradually did spread, but no sooner than the 1930s. Ferguson (1984:85pp) writes that Roosevelt's new historic bloc of capital-intensive industries and internationalists, investment banks and internationally oriented commercial banks, around a political platform of social welfare, oil price regulation and free trade were not all in place until 1938. And at this time, the US car industry had long dominated world production. As with the vested interest argument, the consensus argument has some explanatory leverage, but it cannot explain what triggered the growth of the industry in the first place.

While the empirical evidence provides considerable support for consensus and cohesion, it is also clear that more interpretation is required here than for human capital and vested interests. Consensus and cohesion have taken a wide array of different forms in different countries and come about in very different ways. Without the end of the Cold War and the rise of a neoliberal economic and political consensus, deregulation and liberalization would have been far harder to push through any Western parliament. In Germany, consensus came about, not through the deliberate actions of the Chancellor, who was fairly aloof in matters of economics, but through the state bureaucracy, and through other government officials and individual members of the Reichstag. In laissez-faire Britain, no deliberate strategy existed for supporting new industries, but the state was unambiguously against meddling with free enterprise, and as it was pro-industry, attempts to physically prevent industrialization were fiercely countered. The repeal of the Corn Laws followed after a serious economic crisis (1837–1842), which converted a great number of British politicians to the belief that manufacturing industry and exports were the only way out of the crisis, and that hence, agricultural interests had to be curbed, although the immediate cause may have been the 1846 Irish famine. This means that an external shock contributed greatly to the formation of a new political consensus, whether this shock was the famine or the recession.

The fact that consensus and cohesion have manifested themselves in different manners is not a problem. What matters is not how consensus and cohesion arose in the first place, but whether they exist or not. And what matters is whether or not states actually benefit from consensus and cohesion in curbing vested interests, and not if it results from fortuitous accidents or from deliberate policies. Obviously, if states have managed to curb vested interests primarily by accident, it becomes considerably harder to make predictions about government policy. On the other hand, the mechanism by which vested interests are curbed is the same whether it happens by accident or not. However, it does suggest that this is an area where more work is needed.

Smithian Growth, Tariffs and War

As mentioned in the Introduction, beyond Schumpeterian, there are several other types of growth. It is no surprise that a number of cases also exhibit Smithian features. First, since technology has become ever more important as a source for economic growth and industrial prowess, it is reasonable to assume that Smithian growth becomes relatively more important the farther back in time we go. The early Industrial Revolution took place with technologies that by present standards were distinctly primitive, and the figures show that productivity growth figures were very moderate indeed. Second, industries are not all equally knowledge-intensive. One would expect Smithian growth to be of greater importance the less knowledge-intensive the industry is.

Thus, Smithian growth seems the better explanation for the US automobile industry, which was the least knowledge-intensive of the five industries. Here, demand factors were of great relevance. And because the car industry was not only a mass-production industry, but also one of the first genuine mass *consumption* industries, car sales were extremely sensitive to demand factors.

Smithian factors also played a role for cotton textiles and iron, and even for chemicals and ICTs, demand factors were of importance. In the German chemical industry, Germany initially failed to capitalize on its human capital advantage, as the supply of German chemists far outstripped domestic demand for such experts. Hence, they went to Britain instead, where they were instrumental in the growth of the early modern British chemical industry. However, once demand for chemists had risen in Germany, most of them left Britain to take up employment at home, leading to a massive influx of skilled chemists to Germany, but also to a brain-drain from Britain that permanently damaged British chemicals. With respect to ICTs, government and military procurements were one of the reasons why the US took an early lead—in other words another demand-type explanation.

While discarding most of the Smithian arguments for the rise of the Industrial Revolution, arguments about property rights and transaction costs both seem valid with respect to explaining why Britain industrialized, instead of, for instance, France. With respect to iron, resource endowments were of considerable importance, and far more so than for cotton, since the transportation of iron and coal for quite obvious reasons is more laborious and expensive than the transportation of cotton. Britain had a definite advantage over France in that iron and coal were often located in immediate geographic proximity of each other, and that the easy access to waterways made transportation comparatively easy even before the construction of railroads. However, this argument should only be taken so far. If resource endowments are a problem, this provides a very obvious role for the state in countering these problems. The typical fashion in which this was achieved was through the construction of railroads. In this, the French state did not perform, held back as it was by powerful vested interests.

However, each industrial period also contains a number of more time-specific explanations. Tariffs are one of the most obvious of these. Tariffs have been part of a relatively small array of economic policies that can be traced essentially as far back in time as trade. However, there is no such thing as one correct tariff policy. Different economic situations call for different tariff policies. A small and vulnerable industry might well benefit from infant industry protection. Old and stagnant industries will also often lobby for protection. But in their case, tariffs would just delay necessary structural change in the economy, and be detrimental to the development of new industries, even if it helps the old industry. Furthermore, even in small and vulnerable industries, tariffs do not always have the desired effects. Here as well, there is always the chance that granting an industry protection gives it the opportunity to persist with inefficient practices rather than modernizing. Other industries are already competitive. For these, tariff protection raises the overall costs of the economy, as well as potentially triggering retaliatory tariffs from other countries. If so, tariff reductions would be the recommended recipe, not tariff increases. Finally, there are often differences between labor-intensive and capital-intensive industries. In labor-intensive industries, the wage bill accounts for a proportionately large part of the industry's overall costs. Hence, in high-wage countries, labor-intensive industries are likely to lobby for protection. Capital-intensive industries on the other hand, can be less concerned with their wage-bills. They instead typically gain from exploiting economies of scale, which means that the primary concern is not on wages, but on acquiring access to as large a market as possible. This drives capital-intensive firms toward international free trade instead of protection. Different tariff policies were required of Britain in the early nineteenth century compared to in the late nineteenth century and between the nineteenth century and present-day US. Hence, very pragmatically the conclusion is that tariff policies must adapt to the historical and economic circumstances of each specific country and industry.

Also striking is the effect of war. In several of the chapters, tariffs and war have been merged, for the reason that they both represent (very) different cases of shutting off the domestic market from foreign competition. As with tariffs, wars can work in different ways. They may provide the industry with protection from competition, but without being a stimulus to modernize, as can be seen with cotton textile and iron production in France during the Napoleonic Wars. Cotton textiles in particular expanded rapidly, but expansion was short-lived as once peace arrived, France was technologically and cost-wise far behind Britain, which was by then swamping the French market with cheap products.

However, wars may have effects beyond the sheltering of markets. External shocks to the system may have the potential to trigger change. Defeat in the Napoleonic Wars triggered education reform in Prussia. The US seems to have benefited from World War II, in the sense that it massively raised the research involvement of the federal government, creating a high-technology superpower out of what had previously been a low-technology country. The Cold War presented US political elites with a strong rationale for permanently increasing the federal government's involvement. These conflicts all broke the power of vested interest groups, enabling the state to make important institutional reforms that would not have been politically doable if not for the crisis.

Other wars have had more fortuitous effects. Britain gained greatly from the Napoleonic Wars compared to France. The technology diffusion across the Channel, on which France had been more or less dependent, stopped and, by the end of the wars, British cotton textiles and iron stood head and shoulders above France in terms of technological sophistication, price and total production. World War I had fortuitous effects for the US. Prior to the war, Europe had been capital-abundant and the US capital-scarce. After the war, the roles switched. While it is true that exports across the Atlantic never accounted for a high percentage of either American or European sales, it is conspicuous that as the car industry grew more capital-intensive, Europe became less able to compete in capital-intensive industries, whereas the US became more competitive.

Obviously, war is not always good! Wars may generate new vested interests instead of breaking them up. Hence, the Napoleonic Wars were the main reason why the British Parliament passed a set of Corn Laws. These raised the costs of the entire country, wage-workers as well as industry, and were not repealed until 1846. Of course, France did not benefit from them either. France fell further behind, and once the wars were over, the same old interest groups became even more powerful. The wars led to the fragmenting of authority and the delegitimization of the new rulers, rather than a fresh start. While it is hard to say anything conclusive, what is interesting is how wars at times seem to have had the effect of forging a new political consensus, working through the same Schumpeterian and Olsonian mechanisms as specified in the Introduction.

Infrastructure has also been important, particularly so with respect to iron, but also for the automobile industry and to a lesser extent cotton textiles. If we define infrastructure broadly, we can probably even make a case for the construction of an information infrastructure as crucial for the success of ICT industries and services. In the Schumpeterian world, where industries and economies are in a constant state of flux, there is no guarantee that the infrastructure adequate for one industrial era will also be so for the next. Without the proper infrastructure, industrial leadership will be hard to achieve. In one way, it resembles other basic conditions for growth, like property rights. This is also an area in which it becomes evident that there is a significant overlap between the Schumepterian and Smithian forms of growth.

The Way Ahead

Do any of the cases exemplify technological process and industrial leadership to such an extent that we can talk of this as an archetypal case? Are ICT industries more representative than cotton textiles? Does the present-day US embody the process of technological and industrial leadership better than nineteenth-century Britain? Every time period and industry is different, and every country contains complex social and political processes that must be understood in the historical context within which these countries were inscribed. There are major differences between each and every case, and it is impossible to single out one of them as more archetypal than the rest. Instead, this book takes five fairly different key industries from five time periods in five countries, stretching over a period of a quarter of a millennium, and still manages to find systematic similarities between them.

Still, particular cases may be more instructive with respect to future technological progress and industrial leadership than others. ICT industries are definitely more representative of present-day growth processes than for instance cotton textiles. The recipe for the future is not one of adopting late eighteenth-century British laissez-faire policies, but must fall much closer to US policies.

If we look back in time instead, the cotton textile industry should be more representative than ICTs. Growth processes prior to the Industrial Revolution hinged even less on technological progress than was the case with cotton textiles. But the conclusion is not obvious. If since the Industrial Revolution, the world economy has been driven by the rise and fall of *industries*, how would this apply to the pre-industrial era? One possible solution can be found with Modelski and Thompson (1996), who suggest that even before the Industrial Revolution, certain economic activities, primarily involving different brands of long-distance trade, brought special benefits to a country. To frame it in Schumpeterian terms, monopoly-like profits could be had for instance from being the undisputed number one in the pepper trade. To what extent was a country's advantage in long-distance trade dependent on human capital? For instance, good seamanship consistently favored Britain over France. The quest for an invention that made it possible to measure longitudes obviously also hints at the importance of human capital, even if the effect of human capital on economic growth was less than what later became the case. Also, since pre-industrial societies did not suffer from industrial ups and downs, the importance of curbing vested interests may have been less pressing. However, vested interests come in many forms, and there is no reason why they might not block Smithian growth in the same manner as they have in this book blocked Schumpeterian growth. One example is financial reform, which was in all likelihood among the most important reasons why England (later Great Britain) had a more prosperous economy than France, and why England was better able to finance its wars (e.g. Kennedy 1989).

Still, the pace of change has accelerated greatly since the Industrial Revolution, and therefore the consequences of vested interests blocking structural change have become far graver. Much the same can be said for consensus and cohesion. In countries where the pace of structural change is slow, the importance of consensus and cohesion would be less. In line with both Epstein (2000) and North and Weingast (1989), it is overwhelmingly probable that pre-industrial growth was primarily Smithian rather than Schumpeterian. For that reason as well, even if the Schumpeterian and Olsonian mechanisms still hold, the relevance is considerably less than for the industrial era.

One of the goals of this book has been to say something about the complexities of economic growth and development. Why has such a universally desirable goal been so hard to achieve? The book started by taking as its vantage point the rise and fall of the great powers. No power has managed to stay on top forever. Rise has been followed by stagnation and decline. This is exactly the story told in this book, but with the emphasis on economic rise and fall, more specifically on the rise and fall of breakthrough technologies and key industries. In the extreme long term, economic growth is a cyclical process that depends on more than just the optimization of fiscal policies, interest rates, budget deficits, exchange rates, and the balance of trade. It depends on the successful utilization of new technologies for the achievement of industrial growth and leadership.

Hence, different industries have been the driving force of the world economy during different historical epochs. Leadership has shifted, powers have waxed and waned. The fact that the US has been the world's dominant power for a century or so does not make it any less naïve to assume that the cycle has finally come to a full stop. At its prime, Great Britain produced 50 per cent of the world's iron and cloth—the world's two dominant industries at the time. It produced two-thirds of all the coal, which was the most important fuel in the world. And it accounted for 25 per cent of overall world trade. Only half a century later, the Empire on which the sun never set, was being surpassed by both the US and Germany. Wohlforth (2002:104) points out that in terms of military capabilities, no leading power has ever held a greater advantage over the other great powers than the US today. Counterbalancing should not be expected when it is beyond the capabilities of other powers to do so. However, while militarily unchallenged, in terms of gross world product, the US is far less ahead. The US accounts for 23 per cent of world gross product, the EU 20 per cent, and China 12 per cent.

While there is no reason why the decline and fall of the US would be imminent, a main point of this book is that success is never final. The foundations, on which economic success rests, constantly change, because of new technologies being invented and new key industries arising. Only by constantly being at the forefront of technological developments, by utilizing new technologies to create growth industries, and by preventing old leading industries from protecting the old order and blocking structural change, can powers stay ahead of the competition. Success does not necessarily breed success. On the contrary, it may sow the seeds of its own destruction. Success is never permanent, but has to be reproduced, over and over again. This is a tall order! It should come as no surprise that rise more or less inevitably has led to fall. It is an order that is so tall that even the world's presently undisputed superpower will find it hard to stay on top if it takes it status for granted.

The mechanisms suggested in this book should not apply only to great powers. Small powers and Third World countries are less likely to achieve industrial *leadership*, or be at the scientific frontier. (Making a distinction between great powers and less great powers is somewhat arbitrary in any case.) Smaller powers cannot expect to achieve the same kind of leadership, but if so, the major difference is one of degree and not one of kind. If we focus less on industrial leadership *per se*, and more on technological progress, the ability to utilize new technology for industrial purposes, and the ability to pursue policies of structural change, should be important nevertheless. It is not only great powers that have been able to grow rich and prosperous. Some of the wealthiest countries today are small powers, and human capital, vested interests, and consensus and cohesion should be relevant to these powers too. The crucial question is probably rather; to what extent do small powers grow wealthy through innovation, and to what extent through emulation and utilization? It could well be that in terms of human capital, smaller powers would focus more on the diffusion of knowledge than its actual production. The emphasis on preventing the economy from being frozen in an old and stagnant status quo, the importance of preventing rigidities from silting up the economy, the importance of structural economic change, all remain undiminished, whether this be a great power or not. Both the destruction and the creation phase of Schumpeter's waves of creative destruction must be allowed to play themselves out. This is a tall order for politicians, as policies of structural economic change always have significant redistributive effects. In other words, politicians will have to make decisions that almost by default create losers. Often, the losers are tangible, as in the very concrete loss of jobs, whereas the benefits are far less tangible, and harder for people to see.

This means that the book touches upon issues of major relevance to present-day politics as well. We live in a day and age where most countries are democracies. The pressure on politicians to come up with fast and easy solutions to most societal problems, preferably without a single human being losing out, makes it increasingly hard to pursue policies of structural change, unless one wants to lose the next election. Most Western countries are facing large-scale demographic problems in the future as birth rates drop and people stay alive for longer. Especially in Continental Europe, it has turned out to be exceedingly difficult for politicians to go against the power of the labor unions, despite the widespread consensus that reforms with respect to pensions, unemployment benefits and social security in general are essential (e.g. *Economist* 2003b). While not being an industrial issue *per se*, not having the political consensus or the necessary cohesion in the people to go against vested interests, resisting the reform of established social security arrangements could result in European welfare states locked in a downward spiral, unable to break out.

Finally, the literature is ripe with arguments about what is the better form of government with respect to economic growth and development—centralization, decentralization, democracy, authoritarian rule, strong state, weak state, etc. The argument made here suggests that using too blunt an instrument will not yield credible results. Technological change and industrial leadership, economic growth and development have been achieved under very different kinds of regimes. Laissez-faire Britain was extremely decentralized, as was the US for most of its history. Germany rose to industrial leadership while being highly authoritarian. While not included here, present-day Chinese growth also takes place under very authoritarian conditions. And it is widely recognized that the growth experienced by Japan from the 1868 Meiji Restoration onwards was both highly impressive as well as achieved under often distinctly repressive regimes (e.g. Maddison 1991:207pp; Morris-Suzuki 1989:72). But Japan has also grown rapidly under democracy, and so has Germany. This has triggered speculation that in addition to the more laissez-faire Anglo-American model, there might also be a well-functioning growth model more along corporatist, welfarist lines.

When industrial growth can be achieved in such a variety of different regimes, the recommendation must be that we search for what actually unites these. This is what this book has done. It has looked at processes *within* centralized, decentralized, democratic, authoritarian, strong and weak states. It suggests that the main role for the state should be one of promoting structural change when such is required. This is something that a wide array of different states might be capable of. And this in fact happened. What matters is less whether the state is centralized or decentralized, weak or strong, authoritarian or democratic, but what takes place within these states. What matters is what the state actually does—its ability and willingness to pursue policies of structural change. And hence, what matters is whether or not the state is in possession of sufficient political consensus and social cohesion for political elites to be able to go against powerful vested interests resisting change.

One important implication stems from both the theory and the empirical cases: The future is never won once and for all. This book establishes a mechanism whereby past success can very easily lead to future failure, but where failure does not follow as a necessity. The future needs to be won, over and over again.

Bibliography

Abramovitz, Moses, "Resource and Output Trends in the United States Since 1870", *The American Economic Review*, 46(2) (1956): 5–23.

Acemoglu, Daron, Simon Johnson and James A. Robinson, "The Colonial Origins of Comparative Development", *The American Economic Review*, 91(5) (2001): 1369–1401.

Aghion, Philippe and Peter Howitt, "A Model of Growth Through Creative Destruction", *Econometrica*, 60(2) (1992): 323–51.

Ahlström, Göran, *Engineers and Industrial Growth: Higher Technical Education and the Engineering Profession During the Nineteenth and Early Twentieth Centuries* (London: Croom Helm, 1982).

Allen, Frederick Lewis, *The Big Change: America Transforms Itself, 1900–1950* (New York: Bantam Books, 1961).

Allen, Frederick Lewis, *Only Yesterday: An Informal History of the 1920's* (New York: Perennial Classics, 2000 [1931]).

Amsden, Alice H., *The Rise of "The Rest"* (New York: Oxford University Press, 2001).

Anderson, C. Arnold, "Patterns and Variability in the Distribution and Diffusion of Schooling", in C. Arnold Anderson and Mary Jean Bowman (eds), *Education and Economic Development* (Chicago: Aldine Publishing Company, 1965a), pp. 314–44.

Anderson, C. Arnold, "Literacy and Schooling on the Development Threshold", in C. Arnold Anderson and Mary Jean Bowman (eds), *Education and Economic Development* (Chicago: Aldine Publishing Company, 1965b), pp. 347–62.

Antràs, Pol and Hans-Joachim Voth, "Factor Prices and Productivity Growth during the British Industrial Revolution", *Explorations in Economic History*, 40 (2003): 52–77.

Aoki, Masahiko, *Information, Corporate Governance, and Institutional Diversity* (Oxford: Oxford University Press, 1995).

Ark, Bart van, "Measuring the New Economy", *Review of Income and Wealth*, 48(1) (2002): 1–14.

Ark, Bart van and Robert Inklaar, *ICT Production and Use in Germany, Japan and the United States* (2003): http://www.eco.rug.nl/medewerk/inklaar/papers/ictgermanyjapan.pdf. [11-01-2004]

Ark, Bart van, Robert Inklaar and Robert H. McGuckin, *ICT and Productivity in Europe and the United States*, Paper for the SOM PhD Conference, De Nieuwe Academie, Groningen (2003): http://www.eco.rug.nl/medewerk/inklaar/papers/ictdecompositionrev2.pdf. [06-12-2004]

Armytage, W.H.G., "Education and Innovative Ferment in England, 1588–1805", in C. Arnold Anderson and Mary Jean Bowman (eds), *Education and Economic Development* (Chicago: Aldine Publishing Company, 1965), pp. 376–93.

Arora, Ashish and Alfonson Gambardella, "Evolution of Industry Structure in the Chemical Industry", in Ashish Arora, Ralph Landau and Nathan Rosenberg (eds), *Chemicals and Long-Term Economic Growth* (New York: John Wiley & Sons, 1998), pp. 379–413.

Arora, Ashish, Ralph Landau and Nathan Rosenberg, "Introduction", in Ashish Arora, Ralph Landau and Nathan Rosenberg (eds), *Chemicals and Long-Term Economic Growth* (New York: John Wiley & Sons, 1998a), pp. 3–23.

Arora, Ashish, Ralph Landau and Nathan Rosenberg, "Conclusions", in Ashish Arora, Ralph Landau and Nathan Rosenberg (eds), *Chemicals and Long-Term Economic Growth* (New York: John Wiley & Sons, 1998b), pp. 515–22.

Arora, Ashish and Nathan Rosenberg, "Chemicals: A U.S. Success Story", in Ashish Arora, Ralph Landau and Nathan Rosenberg (eds), *Chemicals and Long-Term Economic Growth* (New York: John Wiley & Sons, 1998), pp. 71–102.

Asher, David and Andrew Smithers, "Japan's Key Challenges for the 21st Century", in Karl D. Jackson (ed.), *Asian Contagion* (Boulder: Westview, 1999), pp. 29–57.

Ashton, Thomas Southcliffe, *The Industrial Revolution 1760–1830* (London: Oxford University Press, 1997 [1948]).

Atack, Jeremy and Peter Passell, *A New Economic View of American History from Colonial Times to 1940* (2nd edition) (New York: W.W. Norton, 1995).

Azariadis, Costas and Allan Drazen, "Threshold Externalities in Economic Development", *Quarterly Journal of Economics*, 105(2) (1990): 501–26.

Bairoch, Paul, "International Industrialization Levels from 1750 to 1980", *The Journal of European Economic History*, 11(2) (1982): 269–333.

Bairoch, Paul, *Economics & World History* (Chicago: University of Chicago Press, 1993).

Barker, Brendan and Akira Goto, "Technological Systems, Innovation and Transfers", in Grahame Thompson (ed.), *Economic Dynamism in the Asia-Pacific* (London: Routledge, 1998), pp. 250–74.

Barro, Robert and Xavier Sala-i-Martin, *Economic Growth* (Cambridge: MIT Press, 1995).

Barzun, Jacques, *From Dawn to Decadence* (New York: HarperCollins, 2000).

Beauchamp, Edward R. and Richard Rubinger, *Education in Japan* (London: Garland Publishing, 1989).

Beaudoin, Steven M., "Chronology", in Steven M. Beaudoin (ed.), *The Industrial Revolution*, (Boston: Houghton Mifflin, Boston, 2003), pp. xviii–xx.

Berg, Maxine, "Revisions and Revolutions: Technology and Productivity Change in Manufacture in Eighteenth-century England", in Peter Mathias and John A. Davis (eds), *Innovation and Technology in Europe* (Oxford: Blackwell, 1991), pp. 43–64.

Berger, Helge and Mark Spoerer, "Economic Crises and the European Revolutions of 1848", *The Journal of Economic History*, 61(2) (2001): 293–326.

Berghoff H. and R. Möller, "Tired Pioneers and Dynamic Newcomers? A Comparative Essay of English and German Entrepreneurial History, 1870–1914", *Economic History Review*, XLVII (2) (1994): 262–87.

Best, Geoffrey, *War and Society in Revolutionary Europe, 1770–1870* (Bungay: Fontana Paperbacks, 1982).

Best, Geoffrey, "The French Revolution and Human Rights", in Geoffrey Best (ed.), *The Permanent Revolution* (Chicago: University of Chicago Press, 1989), pp. 101–27.

Bethell, Tom, *The Noblest Triumph* (London: Macmillan Press, 1998).

Birnbaum, Pierre, *The Idea of France* (New York: Hill and Wang, 1998).

Boot, H.M., "How Skilled were Lancashire Cotton Factory Workers in 1833", *The Economic History Review*, New Series, 48(2) (1995): 283–303.

Born, Karl Erich, "Structural Changes in German Social and Economic Development at the End of the Nineteenth Century", in James J. Sheehan (ed.), *Imperial Germany* (New York: Franklin Watts, 1976), pp. 16–38.

Boskin, Michael J. and Lawrence J. Lau, "Contributions of R & D to Economic Growth", in Bruce L.R. Smith, and Claude E. Barfield (eds), *Technology, R & D, and the Economy*, (Washington DC: The Brookings Institutions and American Enterprise Institute, 1996), pp. 75–107.

Bossenga, Gail, "Protecting Merchants: Guilds and Commercial Capitalism in Eighteenth-Century France", *French Historical Studies*, 15(4) (1988): 693–703.

Braudel, Fernand, *Civilization & Capitalism 15th-18th Century* (Los Angeles: University of California Press, 1979).

Braudel, Fernand, *The Identity of France: Volume One, History and Environment* (London: Fontana Press, 1989).

Braudel, Fernand, *The Identity of France: Volume Two, People and Production* (London: Fontana Press, 1991).

Bresnahan, Timothy F. and Franco Malerba, "Industrial Dynamics and the Evolution of Firms' and Nations' Competitive Capabilities in the World Computer Industry", in David C. Mowery and Richard R. Nelson (eds), *Sources of Industrial Leadership*, (Cambridge: Cambridge University Press, 1999), pp. 79–132.

Brezis, Elise S., Paul R. Krugman and Daniel Tsiddon, "Leapfrogging in International Competition", *The American Economic Review*, 83(5) (1993): 1211–19.

Brinkley, Douglas, *Wheels for the World* (New York: Viking, 2003).

Brose, Eric Dorn, *Technology and Science in the Industrializing Nations* (New Jersey: Humanities Press, 1998).

Burns, Michael, "Families and Fatherlands", in Robert Tombs (ed.), *Nationhood and Nationalism in France* (London: HarperCollins Academic, 1991), pp. 50–62.

Cameron, Rondo, "A New View of European Industrialization", in R.A. Church (ed.), *The Coal and Iron Industries* (R.A. Church and E.A. Wigley (eds), *The Industrial Revolutions* (vol. 10)) (Oxford: Blackwell Publishers, 1994), pp. 3–25.

Cameron, Rondo and Larry Neal, *A Concise Economic History of the World* (Oxford: Oxford University Press, 2003).

Caron, François, "The Evolution of the Technical System of Railways in France from 1832 to 1937", in Renate Mayntz and Thomas P. Hughes (eds), *The Development of Large Technical Systems* (Frankfurt-am-Main: Campus Verlag, 1988), pp. 69–103.

Caron, François (1998), "The Birth of a Network Technology", in Maxine Berg and Kristine Bruland (eds), *Technological Revolutions in Europe* (Cheltenham: Edward Elgar, 1998), pp. 275–91.

Cars: Cars Store Billeksikon (vol. 4), "Austin", in Björn-Eric Lindh, (ed.) (Göteborg: Brepols, Nordbok, 1988a), pp. 249–83.

Cars: Cars Store Billeksikon (vol. 25), "Morris" in Björn-Eric Lindh (ed.) (Göteborg: Brepols, Nordbok, 1988b), pp. 1950–65.

Cars: Cars Store Billeksikon (vol. 26), "Opel", in Björn-Eric Lindh (ed.) (Göteborg: Brepols, Nordbok, 1988c), pp. 2050–77.

Cars: Cars Collection (vol. 14), "Henry Ford", in Gunnar Almgren (ed.) (Smeets: Publicity A/S, 1987), pp. 28–45.

Castells, Manuel, "The Rise of the Network Society", in *The Information Age* (vol. I) (Malden: Blackwell, 2000a).

Castells, Manuel, "End of Millenium", in *The Information Age* (vol. III) (Malden: Blackwell, 2000b).

Central Intelligence Agency, "The World Factbook 2006" (2006): http://www.cia.gov/cia/publications/factbook. [09-24-2006]

Chambliss, J.J., "Development of National Systems of Education", in *The New Encyclopædia Britannica*, (2003): http://www.britannica.com/eb. [09-10-2003]

Chandler, Alfred P., Jr., *Inventing the Electronic Century* (New York: The Free Press, 2001).

Chandler, Alfred P., Jr., and James W. Cortada, "The Information Age", in Alfred P. Chandler, Jr., and James W. Cortada (eds), *A Nation Transformed by Information*, (Oxford: Oxford University Press, 2000), pp. 281–99.

Chandler, Alfred P., Jr., Takashi Hikino and David Mowery (1998), "The Evolution of Corporate Capability and Corporate Strategy and Structure Within the World's Largest Chemical Firms", in Ashish Arora, Ralph Landau and Nathan Rosenberg (eds), *Chemicals and Long-Term Economic Growth* (New York: John Wiley & Sons, 1998), pp. 415–57.

Chang, Ha-Joon, *Kicking Away the Ladder* (London: Anthem Press, 2002).

Cheng, Lucie and Ping-Chun Hsiung, "Engendering the 'economic miracle'", in Grahame Thompson (ed.), *Economic Dynamism in the Asia-Pacific* (London: Routledge, 1998), pp. 112–36.

Chesnais, François, "The French National System of Innovation", in Richard R. Nelson (ed.), *National Innovation Systems* (Oxford: Oxford University Press, 1993), pp. 192–229.

Chiu, Stephen W.K. and Tai-Lok Lui, "The Role of the State in Economic Development", in Grahame Thompson (ed.), *Economic Dynamism in the Asia-Pacific* (London: Routledge, 1998), pp. 137–61.

Chowdhury, Mridul (2002), ".jp", in World Economic Forum, *The Global Information Technology Report 2001–2002* (Oxford: Oxford University Press, 2002), pp. 232–3.

Cipolla, Carlo M., *Literacy and Development in the West* (Harmondsworth: Penguin Books, 1969).

Clark, Gregory, "Too Much Revolution", in Joel Mokyr (ed.), *The British Industrial Revolution* (Boulder: Westview Press, 1999), pp. 206–40.

Coleman, D.C. and Christine MacLeod, "Attitudes to New Techniques: British Businessmen, 1800–1950", *Economic History Review*, XXXIX(4) (1986): 588–611.

Colley, Linda, *Britons: Forging the Nation 1707–1837* (New Haven: Yale University Press, 1992).

Collins, James B., *The State in Early Modern France* (Cambridge: Cambridge University Press, 1995).

Cookson, Gillian, "Innovation, Diffusion, and Mechanical Engineers in Britain, 1780–1850", *The Economic History Review*, New Series, 47(4) (1994): 749–53.

Cortada, James W., "Progenitors of the Information Age", in Alfred P. Chandler, Jr. and James W. Cortada (eds), *A Nation Transformed by Information* (Oxford: Oxford University Press, 2000), pp. 177–216.

Cowan, Ruth Schwartz, *A Social History of American Technology* (New York: Oxford University Press, 1997).

Crafts, N.F.R., "Economic Growth in France and Britain, 1830–1910", *The Journal of Economic History*, XLIV(1) (1984): 49–67.

Crafts, N.F.R., "Real Wages, Inequality and Economic Growth in Britain, 1750–1850", in Peter Scholliers (ed.), *Real Wages in 19th and 20th century Europe* (New York: Berg Publishers Limited, 1989), pp. 75–95.

Crafts, N.F.R., "Microinventions, Economic Growth, and 'Industrial Revolution' in Britain and France", *The Economic History Review*, New Series, 48(3) (1995a): 591–8.

Crafts, N.F.R., "Exogenous or Endogenous Growth? The Industrial Revolution Reconsidered", *The Journal of Economic History*, 55(4) (1995b): 745–72.

Crafts, N.F.R., "The First Industrial Revolution", *The American Economic Review*, 86(2) (1996): 197–201.

Crafts, N.F.R., "Forging Ahead and Falling Behind", *The Journal of Economic Perspectives*, 12(2) (1998): 193–210.

Crafts, N.F.R. and C. Knick Harley, "Output Growth and the British Industrial Revolution", *The Economic History Review*, New Series, 45(4) (1992): 703–30.

Crafts, N.F.R., S.J. Leybourne et al., "The Climacteric in Late Victorian Britain and France", *Journal of Applied Econometrics*, 4(2) (1989): 103–17.

Crafts, N.F.R. and T.C. Mills, "The Industrial Revolution as a Macroeconomic Epoch", *The Economic History Review*, New Series, 47(4) (1994): 769–75.

Crosby, Alfred W., *Ecological Imperialism* (New York: Cambridge University Press, 1986).

Crouzet, François, "An Annual Index of French Industrial Production in the nineteenth century", in Rondo Cameron (ed.), *Essays in French Economic History* (Homewood, Illinois: Richard Irwin, 1970), pp. 245–78.

Crouzet, François, *Britain Ascendant* (New York: Cambridge University Press, 1990).

Crouzet, François, "Introduction" in François Crouzet (ed.), *The Economic Development of France since 1870: Volume I* (Aldershot: Edward Elgar, 1993), pp. ix–xix.

Crouzet, François, *A History of the European Economy, 1000–2000* (Charlottesville: University Press of Virginia, 2001).

Crouzet, François, "The Historiography of French Economic Growth in the Nineteenth Century", *The Economic History Review*, 56(2) (2003): 215–42.

Cuenca Esteban, Javier, "British Textile Prices, 1770–1831: Are British Growth Rates Worth Revising Once Again?", *Economic History Review*, XLVII(1) (1994): 66–105.

Cullen, L.M., "History, Economic Crises, and Revolution", in *Economic History Review*, XLVI(4) (1993): 635–57.

Darnton, Robert, *The Literary Underground of the Old Regime* (Cambridge: Harvard University Press, 1982).

Dattel, Eugene R., "Reflections of a Market Participant", in Karl D. Jackson (ed.), *Asian Contagion* (Boulder: Westview, 1999), pp. 59–81.

Dayton-Johnson, Jeff, *Social Cohesion and Economic Prosperity*, (Toronto: James Lorimer & Company Ltd., Publishers, 2001).

Deane, Phyllis and W.A. Cole, *British Economic Growth 1688–1959* (London: Cambridge University Press, 1962).

De Long, J. Bradford, "Overstrong Against Thyself", in Mancur Olson and Satu Kähkönen (eds), *A Not-So-Dismal Science* (Oxford: Oxford University Press, 2000), pp. 138–67.

Diamond, Jared, *Guns, Germs and Steel* (London: Vintage, 1997).

Donnelly, J.F., "Representations of Applied Science", *Social Studies of Science*, 16(2) (1986): 195–234.

Dore, Ronald P., "The Legacy of Tokugawa Education", in Marius B. Jansen (ed.), *Changing Japanese Attitudes Toward Modernization* (Rutland, Vermont: Charles E. Tuttle Company, 1982 [1965]), pp. 99–131.

Dosi, Giovanni, "Technological Paradigms and Technological Trajectories", *Research Policy*, 11 (1982): 147–62.

Dow, Christopher, *Major Recessions* (Oxford: Oxford University Press, 1998).

Downs, Anthony, *An Economic Theory of Democracy* (New York: Harper, 1957).

DuPlessis, Robert S., "Transitions to Capitalism in Early Modern Europe", in Steven M. Beaudoin (ed.), *The Industrial Revolution*, (Boston: Houghton Mifflin, 2003), pp. 71–80.

Easterlin, Richard A., "A Note on the Evidence of History", in C. Arnold Anderson and Mary Jean Bowman (eds), *Education and Economic Development* (Chicago: Aldine Publishing, 1965), pp. 422–9.

Easterlin, Richard A., "Why Isn't the Whole World Developed?", *The Journal of Economic History*, XLI(1) (1981): 1–19.

Easterlin, Richard A., *Growth Triumphant* (AnnArbor: University of Michigan Press, 1998).

Eckstein, Harry, "Case Study and Theory in Political Science", in Fred I. Greenstein and Nelson W. Polsby (eds), *Handbook of Political Science* (London: Addison–Wesley, 1975), pp. 79–137.

Economist, The, "Explaining the Mystery", January 4th 1992, 17.

Economist, The, "Solving the paradox", September 21st 2000, http://www.economist.com. [06-15-2004]

Economist, The, "The new 'new economy'", Sept 11th 2003a, http://www.economist.com. [06-15-2004]

Economist, The, "Computing the gains", October 23rd 2003b, http://www.economist.com. [06-15-2004]

Economist, The, "Special Report: The Reagan Legacy", June 12th–18th 2004a, 8379(371), 24–6.

Economist, The, "Fiscal outrages in America: Veto one for the Gipper", June 19th–25th 2004b, 8380(371), 15.

Economist, The, "Trade Disputes", September 18th–24th 2004c, 8393(372), 91.

Economist, The, "Dead firms walking", September 25th–October 1st 2004d, 8394(372), 81–3.

Eichengreen, Barry, "Monetary, Fiscal, and Trade Policies in the Development of the Chemical Industry", in Ashish Arora, Ralph Landau and Nathan Rosenberg (eds), *Chemicals and Long-Term Economic Growth* (New York: John Wiley & Sons, 1998), pp. 265–306.

Ejrnæs, Mette and Karl Gunnar Persson, "Market Integration and Transport Costs in France 1825–1903", *Explorations in Economic History*, 37 (2000): 149–73.

Elbaum, Bernard and William Lazonick, "The Decline of the British Economy", *Journal of Economic History*, XLIV(2) (1984): 567–83.

Emmott, Bill, "The sun also rises", *The Economist*, October 6th 2005, http://www.economist.com/surveys. [02-28-2005]

The New Encyclopædia Britannica (15th edition), "Royal Society" (Chicago: Encyclopædia Britannica Inc., 1994), vol. 10, p. 220.

The New Encyclopædia Britannica (15th edition), "United Kingdom" (Chicago: Encyclopædia Britannica Inc., 1994), vol. 12, p. 143.

Epstein, S.R., *Freedom and Growth* (London: Routledge, 2000).

Evans, Chris and Göran Rydén, "Kinship and the Transmission of Skills", in Maxine Berg and Kristine Bruland (eds), *Technological Revolutions in Europe* (Cheltenham: Edward Elgar, 1998), pp. 188–206.

Evans, Eric J., *The Forging of the Modern State* (Harlow: Longman, 1983).

Fagan, Brian, *The Little Ice Age* (New York: Basic Books, 2000).

Fagerberg, Jan, "Technology and International Differences in Growth Rates", *Journal of Economic Literature*, 32(3) (1994): 1147–75.

Fairchilds, Cissie, "Three Views on the Guilds", *French Historical Studies*, 15(4) (1988): 688–92.

Farber, David, *Sloan Rules* (Chicago: University of Chicago Press, 2002).

Farrell, Diane, "Asia: The Productivity Imperative", in World Economic Forum, *The Global Competitiveness Report 2002–2003* (Oxford: Oxford University Press, 2003), pp. 145–62.

Fearon, James D, "Counterfactuals and Hypothesis Testing in Political Science", *World Politics*, 43(2) (1991): 169–95.

Feinstein, Charles, "Changes in Nominal Wages, the Cost of Living and Real Wages in the United Kingdom over two Centuries, 1780–1990", in Peter Scholliers and Vera Zamagni (eds), *Labor's Reward* (Aldershot: Edward Elgar, 1995), pp. 3–36.

Ferguson, Thomas, "From Normalcy to New Deal", *International Organization*, 38(1) (1984): 41–94.

Fox, Robert, "Science, Practice and Innovation in the Age of Natural Dyes, 1750–1860", in Maxine Berg and Kristine Bruland (eds), *Technological Revolutions in Europe* (Cheltenham: Edward Elgar, 1998), pp. 86–95.

Freeman, Christopher, "The 'National System of Innovation' in Historical Perspective", *Cambridge Journal of Economics*, 19 (1995): 5–24.

Freeman, Christopher and Francisco Louçã, *As Time Goes By* (Oxford: Oxford University Press, 2001).

Freeman, Christopher and Carlota Perez, "Structural Crisis of Adjustment, Business Cycles and Investment Behaviour", in Giovanni Dosi, Christopher Freeman et al. (eds), *Technical Change and Economic Theory* (London: Pinter Publishers, 1988), pp. 38–67.

Freeman, Christopher and Luc Soete, *The Economics of Industrial Innovation* (Cambridge: The MIT Press, 1999).

Fremdling, Rainer, "Transfer Patterns of British Technology to the Continent", *European Review of Economic History*, 4 (2000): 195–222.

Friedman, Thomas, *The Lexus and the Olive Tree* (New York: Anchor Books, 2000).

Fukushima, Kiyohiko, "The Revival of 'Big Politics' in Japan", *International Affairs (Royal Institute of International Affairs 1944–)*, 72(1) (1996): 53–72.

Fukuyama, Francis, *Trust* (New York: The Free Press, 1995).

Fukuyama, Francis, *The Great Disruption* (New York: The Free Press, 1999).

Fulbrook, Mary, *A Concise History of Germany* (Cambridge: Cambridge University Press, 1992).

Furet, François, *Revolutionary France 1770–1880* (Oxford: Blackwell, 1995).

Galor, Oded, "Convergence? Inferences from Theoretical Models", *The Economic Journal*, 106(437) (1996): 1056–69.

Giddens, Andrew, *Runaway World* (London: Routledge, 2000).

Gilbert, Felix and David Clay Large, *The End of the European Era* (New York: W.W. Norton, 2002).

Gilpin, Robert, *War and Change in World Politics* (Cambridge: Cambridge University Press, 1981).

Gilpin, Robert, *The Political Economy of International Relations* (Princeton: Princeton University Press, 1987).

Gilpin, Robert, "Economic Evolution of National Systems", *International Studies Quarterly*, 40(3) (1996): 411–31.

Gilpin, Robert, *The Challenge of Global Capitalism* (Princeton: Princeton University Press, 2000).

Gilpin, Robert, *Global Political Economy* (Princeton: Princeton University Press, 2001).

Goldin, Claudia, "The Human-Capital Century and American Leadership", *The Journal of Economic History*, 61(2) (2001): 263–92.

Gordon, Andrew, *A Modern History of Japan* (Oxford: Oxford University Press, 2003).

Gordon, Robert B., "Realizing the Ideal of Interchangeability", in Gary J. Kornblith (ed.), *The Industrial Revolution in America* (Boston: Houghton Mifflin, 1998), pp. 88–98.

Gordon, Robert B. and Patrick M. Malone, *The Texture of Industry* (Oxford: Oxford University Press, 1994).

Graff, Harvey J., *The Legacies of Literacy* (Bloomington: Indiana University Press, 1987).

Gray, John, *False Dawn* (New York: The New Press, 1998).

Greasley, David and Les Oxley, "Endogenous Growth or 'Big Bang'", *The Journal of Economic History*, 57(4) (1997): 935–49.

Greasley, David and Les Oxley, "British Industrialization, 1815–1860", *Explorations in Economic History*, 37 (2000): 98–119.

Greenfeld, Liah, *The Spirit of Capitalism* (Cambridge: Harvard University Press, 2001).

Greif, Avner, "The Fundamental Problem of Exchange", *European Review of Economic History*, 4 (2000): 251–84.

Griffiths, Trevor, Philip Hunt and Patrick K. O'Brien, "Inventive Activity in the British Textile Industry, 1700–1800", *The Journal of Economic History*, 52(4) (1992): 881–906.

Griffiths, Trevor, Philip Hunt and Patrick K. O'Brien, "The Curious History and Imminent Demise of the Challenge and Response Model", in Maxine Berg and Kristine Bruland (eds), *Technological Revolutions in Europe* (Cheltenham: Edward Elgar, 1998), pp. 119–37.

Grimond, John, "A Survey of Japan", *The Economist*, April 18th 2002, http://www.economist.com/surveys. [06-15-2004]

Hage, Jerald, Maurice A. Garnier and Bruce Fuller, "The Active State, Investment in Human Capital, and Economic Growth", *American Sociological Review*, 53(6) (1988): 824–37.

Hamilton, Gary, "Asian Business Networks in Transition", in T.J. Pempel (ed.), *The Politics of the Asian Economic Crisis* (Ithaca: Cornell University Press, 1999), pp. 45–61.

Harley, C. Knick, "Reassessing the Industrial Revolution", in Joel Mokyr (ed.), *The British Industrial Revolution* (Boulder: Westview Press, 1999), pp. 206–40.

Harris, Ron, "Political Economy, Interests Groups, Legal Institutions, and the Repeal of the Bubble Act in 1825", *The Economic History Review*, New Series, 50(4) (1997), 675–96.

Heilbroner, Robert and Aaron Singer, *The Economic Transformation of America Since 1865* (Fort Worth: Harcourt Brace, 1994).

Held, David, Anthony McGrew et al., *Global Transformations* (Cambridge: Polity Press, 1999).

Henderson, Jeffrey, "Danger and opportunity in the Asia-Pacific", in Grahame Thompson (ed.), *Economic Dynamism in the Asia-Pacific* (London: Routledge, 1998), pp. 356–84.

Hirst, Paul and Grahame Thompson, *Globalization in Question* (Cambridge: Polity Press, 1999).

Hiscox, Michael J., *International Trade & Political Conflict* (Princeton: Princeton University Press, 2002).

Hobday, Michael, *Innovation in East Asia* (Cheltenham: Edward Elgar, 1995).

Hobsbawm, Eric J., *The Age of Revolution* (London: Weidenfeld & Nicolson, 1962).

Hobsbawm, Eric J., *Industry and Empire* (London: Penguin Books, 1969).

Hobsbawm, Eric J., *The Age of Capital* (London: Abacus, 1975).

Hobsbawm, Eric J., *The Age of Empire* (London: Abacus, 1987).

Hodgson, Geoffrey, "An Evolutionary Theory of Long-Term Economic Growth", *International Studies Quarterly*, 40(3) (1996): 391–410.

Hoffman, Philip T., *Growth in a Traditional Society* (Princeton: Princeton University Press, 1996).

Hoffman, Philip T. and Jean-Laurent Rosenthal, "New Work in French Economic History", *French Historical Studies*, 23(3) (2000), 439–53.

Hofstadter, Richard, *The Age of Reform* (New York: Vintage Books, 1955).

Holsti, Kalevi J., *The State, War, and the State of War* (Cambridge: Cambridge University Press, 1996).

Hoppen, K. Theodore, *The Mid-Victorian Generation* (Oxford: Oxford University Press, 1998).

Horstmeyer, Micheline, "Industry within Political, Social and Public Policy Context", in Ashish Arora, Ralph Landau and Nathan Rosenberg (eds), *Chemicals and Long-Term Economic Growth* (New York: John Wiley & Sons, 1998), pp. 233–64.

Hounshell, David A., *From the American System to Mass Production, 1800–1932* (Baltimore: Johns Hopkins University Press, 1984).

Howitt, Peter, "Endogenous Growth and Cross-Country Income Differences", *The American Economic Review*, 90(4) (2000): 829–46.

Hsieh, Wen-jen, "The East Asian Financial Crisis", in Chyungly Lee (ed.), *Asia-Europe Cooperation after the 1997–1998 Asian Turbulence* (Aldershot: Ashgate, 2000), pp. 1–32.

Hudson, Pat, *The Industrial Revolution* (London: Edward Arnold, 1992).

Huntington, Samuel P., *The Clash of Civilizations and the Remaking of World Order* (New York: Simon & Schuster, 1996).

Jackson, Karl D., "Introduction", in Karl D. Jackson (ed.), *Asian Contagion* (Boulder: Westview, 1999), pp. 1–27.

Jacob, Margaret C., *Scientific Culture and the Making of the Industrial West* (Oxford: Oxford University Press, 1997).

Jacob, Margaret C., "The Cultural Foundations of Early Industrialization", in Maxine Berg and Kristine Bruland (eds), *Technological Revolutions in Europe* (Cheltenham: Edward Elgar, 1998), pp. 67–85.

James, Harvey S., Jr., *British Industrialization And The Profit Constraint Hypothesis* (1996): http://wueconb.wustl.edu/eprints/eh/papers/9612/9612003.abs. [03-02-1999]

Jansen, Marius B., *The Making of Modern Japan* (Cambridge: The Belknap Press, 2000).

Johnson, Paul, *A History of the American People* (New York: Harper Perennial, 1997).

Jones, Eric L., *Growth Recurring* (Oxford: Oxford University Press, 1988).

Judd, Denis, *Empire* (New York: Basic Books, 1996).

Justman, Moshe and Mark Gradstein, "The Industrial Revolution, Political Transition, and the Subsequent Decline in Inequality in nineteenth century Britain", *Explorations in Economic History*, 36 (1999): 109–27.

Kalaitzidakis, Pantelis, Theofanis P. Mamuneas and Thanasis Stengos, *Rankings of Academic Journals and Institutions in Economics*, Discussion Paper 2001–10, Department of Economics, University of Cyprus (2001): http://www.econ.ucy.ac.cy/papers/0110.pdf. [07-01-2004]

Kale, Steven D., "French Legitimists and the Politics of Abstention, 1830–1870", *French Historical Studies*, 20(4) (1997): 665–701.

Keck, Otto, "The National System for Technical Innovation in Germany", in Richard R. Nelson (ed.), *National Innovation Systems* (Oxford: Oxford University Press, 1993), pp. 115–57.

Kennedy, Paul, *The Rise and Fall of the Great Powers* (London: Fontana Press, 1989).

Khan, B. Zorina and Kenneth L. Sokoloff, "Patent Institutions, Industrial Organization and Early Technological Change", in Maxine Berg and Kristine Bruland (eds), *Technological Revolutions in Europe* (Cheltenham: Edward Elgar, 1998), pp. 292–313.

Kim, Jong-Il and Lawrence J. Lau, "The Sources of Economic Growth of the East Asian Newly Industrialized Countries", *Journal of the Japanese and International Economies*, 8(3) (1994): 235–71.

Kindleberger, Charles P., *Manias, Panics, and Crashes* (New York: John Wiley & Sons, 1978).

Kindleberger, Charles P., "Financial Institutions and Economic Development", *Explorations in Economic History*, 21(2) (1984), 103–24.

Kindleberger, Charles P., *The World in Depression* (Berkeley: University of California Press, 1986).

Kindleberger, Charles P., *World Economic Primacy* (New York: Oxford University Press, 1996).

Kindleberger, Charles P., *Comparative Political Economy* (Cambridge: MIT Press, 2000).

Klug, Adam, "Why Chamberlain Failed and Bismarck Succeeded", *European Review of Economic History*, 5 (2001), 219–50.

Knutsen, Torbjørn L., *A History of International Relations Theory* (Manchester: Manchester University Press, 1992).

Knutsen, Torbjørn L., *The Rise and Fall of World Orders* (Manchester: Manchester University Press, 1999).

Knutsen, Torbjørn L. and Helge Høibraaten, "Demokrati og dialog", in Gunnar Fermann and Torbjørn L. Knutsen (eds), *Virkelighet og vitenskap* (Oslo: Ad Notam Gyldendal, 1998), pp. 223–300.

Krasner, Stephen D., "Approaches to the State", *Comparative Politics*, 16(2) (1984): 223–46.

Krause, Wolfgang and Douglas J. Puffert, "Chemicals, strategy, and tariffs", *European Review of Economic History*, 4 (2000): 285–309.

Krugman, Paul, *Peddling Prosperity* (New York: Norton, 1994).

Kurth, James R., "The Political Consequences of the Product Cycle", *International Organization*, 33(1) (1979), 1–34.

Landes, David S., *The Unbound Prometheus* (New York: Cambridge University Press, 1969).

Landes, Davis S., "What Room for Accidents in History?", *Economic History Review*, XLVII(4) (1994), 637–56.

Landes, David S., *The Wealth and Poverty of Nations* (New York: W.W. Norton, 1998).

Landes, David S., "The Fable of the Dead Horse; or, The Industrial Revolution Revisited", in Joel Mokyr (ed.), *The British Industrial Revolution* (Boulder: Westview Press, 1999), pp. 128–59.

Langlois, Richard N. and W. Edward Steinmueller, "The Evolution of Competitive Advantage in the Worldwide Semiconductor Industry, 1947–1996", in David C. Mowery and Richard R. Nelson (eds), *Sources of Industrial Leadership* (Cambridge: Cambridge University Press, 1999), pp. 19–78.

Lenoir, Timothy, "Revolution from above", *The American Economic Review*, 88(2) (1998): 22–7.

Leuchtenburg, William E., *The Perils of Prosperity, 1914–1932* (Chicago: University of Chicago Press, 1993 [1958]).

Lewis, W. David, *Iron and Steel in America* (Greenville, Delaware: The Hagley Museum, 1976).

Lewis, Gwynne, *France 1715–1804* (Harlow: Pearson Education Limited, 2004).

Lewis, William W., *The Power of Productivity* (Chicago: University of Chicago Press, 2004).

Lindert, Peter H., *Democracy, Decentralization, and Mass Schooling before 1914* (2001): http://aghistory.ucdavis.edu/wp104.htm. [10-26-2002]

Lindert, Peter H., "Voice and Growth", in *The Journal of Economic History*, 63(2) (2003): 315–50.

Lipset, Seymour Martin and Gabriel S. Lenz, "Corruption, Culture and Markets", in Lawrence E. Harrison and Samuel P. Huntington (eds), *Culture Matters* (New York: Basic Books, 2000), pp. 112–24.

Lloyd-Jones, Roger, "The First Kondratieff", *Journal of Interdisciplinary History*, 20(4) (1990): 581–605.

Lloyd-Jones, Roger and M.J. Lewis, *British Industrial Capitalism since the Industrial Revolution* (London: UCL Press, 1998).

Lucas, Robert E., "On the Mechanics of Economic Development", *Journal of Monetary Economics*, 22(1) (1988): 3–42.

Lundvall, Bengt-Åke, *Aalborg High Level Workshop on Innovation Systems and Innovation Policy* (Aalborg: Department of Business Studies, Aalborg University, 1998).

Lundvall, Bengt-Åke, *Innovation, Growth and Social Cohesion* (Cheltenham: Edward Elgar, 2002).

Lyons, Martyn, *Napoleon Bonaparte and the Legacy of the French Revolution* (London: Macmillan Press, 1994).

McClellan, James E., III and Harold Dorn, *Science and Technology in World History* (Baltimore: Johns Hopkins University Press, 1999).

McCloy, Shelby T., *Government Assistance in Eighteenth-Century France* (Philadelphia: Porcupine Press, 1977 [1946]).

McKeown, T.J., "The Politics of Corn Law Repeal and Theories of Commercial Policy", *British Journal of Political Science*, 19(3) (1989): 353–80.

McLean, Iain, "'The Politics of Corn Law Repeal': A Comment", *British Journal of Political Science*, 20(2) (1990): 279–81.

MacLeod, Christine, *Inventing the Industrial Revolution* (Cambridge: Cambridge University Press, 1988).

MacLeod, Christine, "Strategies for Innovation", *Economic History Review*, XLV(2) (1992): 285–307.

MacLeod, Christine, "James Watt, Heroic Invention and the Idea of the Industrial Revolution", in Maxine Berg and Kristine Bruland (eds), *Technological Revolutions in Europe* (Cheltenham: Edward Elgar, 1998), pp. 96–116.

McNeill, J.R. and William H. McNeill, *The Human Web* (New York: W.W. Norton, 2003).

McNeill, William H., *The Rise of the West* (Chicago: University of Chicago Press, 1963).

McNeill, William H., *Plagues and Peoples* (New York: Anchor Books, 1977).

Maddison, Angus, *Dynamic Forces in Capitalist Development* (New York: Oxford University Press, 1991).

Maddison, Angus, *The World Economy: A Millennial Perspective* (Paris: OECD, Development Centre Studies, 2001).

Maddison, Angus, *The World Economy: Historical Statistics* (Paris: OECD, Development Centre Studies, 2003).

Magnac, Thierry and Gilles Postel-Vinay, "Wage Competition between Agriculture and Industry in Mid-Nineteenth Century France", *Explorations in Economic History*, 34 (1997), 1–26.

Magraw, Roger, "'Not Backward but Different'? The Debate on French 'Economic Retardation'", in Martin S. Alexander (ed.), *French History since Napoleon* (New York: Oxford University Press, 1999), pp. 336–63.

Mankiw, N. Gregory, David Romer and David N. Weil, "A Contribution to the Empirics of Economic Growth", *The Quarterly Journal of Economics*, 107(2) (1992): 407–37.

Mansfield, Edwin, "Contributions of New Technology to the Economy", in Bruce L.R. Smith and Claude E. Barfield (eds), *Technology, R & D, and the Economy* (Washington DC: The Brookings Institutions and American Enterprise Institute, 1996), pp. 114–39.

Marczewski, Jan, "Some Aspects of the Economic Growth of France, 1660–1958", *Economic Development and Cultural Change*, IX(1) (1960): 369–86.

Marks, Robert B., *The Origins of the Modern World* (Lanham, Maryland: Rowman & Littlefield Publishers, 2002).

Mathias, Peter, "Who Unbound Prometheus? Science and Technical Change, 1600–1800", *Yorkshire Bulletin of Economic and Social Research*, 21(1) (1969): 3–16.

Mathias, Peter, "Resources and Technology", Peter Mathias and John A. Davis (eds), *Innovation and Technology in Europe* (Oxford: Blackwell, 1991), pp. 18–42.

Metcalfe, J. Stan, *Institutions and Progress*, CRIC Discussion Paper No 45 (Manchester: University of Manchester and UMIST, 2001).

Meyer-Thurow, Georg, "The Industrialization of Invention", *Isis*, 73(3) (1982): 363–81.

Micklethwait, John and Adrian Woolridge, *The Right Nation* (New York: The Penguin Press, 2004).

Miller, Nathan, *New World Coming* (New York: Scribner, 2003).

Mills, Terence C. and N.F.R. Crafts, "Trend Growth in British Industrial Output, 1700–1913", *Explorations in Economic History*, 33 (1996): 277–95.

Mitch, David, "Underinvestment in Literacy?", *Journal of Economic History*, XLIV(2) (1984): 557–66.

Mitch, David, "The Role of Education and Skill in the British Industrial Revolution", in Joel Mokyr (ed.), *The British Industrial Revolution* (Boulder: Westview Press, 1999), pp. 241–79.

Mitchell, Allan, "Private Enterprise or Public Service?", *The Journal of Modern History*, 69(1) (1997): 18–41.

Mitchell, B.R., *International Historical Statistics: Africa, Asia and Oceania* (Basingstoke: Macmillan Reference, 1998a).

Mitchell, B.R., *International Historical Statistics Europe: 1750–1993* (Basingstoke: Macmillan Reference, 1998b).

Mitchell, B.R., *International Historical Statistics: Africa, Asia & Oceania 1750– 2000* (Basingstoke: Palgrave Macmillan, 2003a).

Mitchell, B.R. *International Historical Statistics: Europe 1750–2000* (Basingstoke: Palgrave Macmillan, 2003b).

Mitchell, B.R., *International Historical Statistics: The Americas 1750–2000* (Basingstoke, Palgrave Macmillan, 2003c).

Modelski, George, "Evolutionary World Politics", in William R. Thompson (ed.), *Evolutionary Interpretations of World Politics* (London: Routledge, 2001), pp. 16–29.

Modelski, George and William R. Thompson, *Leading Sectors and World Powers* (Columbia: University of South Carolina Press, 1996).

Moe, Espen, "An Interpretation of the Asian Financial Crisis", *Asian Affairs: An American Review*, 30(4) (2004): 227–48.

Mokyr, Joel, *The Lever of Riches* (Oxford: Oxford University Press, 1990).

Mokyr, Joel, "Technological Inertia in Economic History", *The Journal of Economic History*, 52(2) (1992): 325–38.

Mokyr, Joel, "The Political Economy of Technological Change", in Maxine Berg and Kristine Bruland (eds), *Technological Revolutions in Europe* (Cheltenham: Edward Elgar, 1998a), pp. 39–64.

Mokyr, Joel, *The Second Industrial Revolution, 1870–1914* (1998b): http://www. faculty.econ.northwestern.edu/faculty/mokyr/castronovo.pdf. [10-05-2003]

Mokyr, Joel, "Editor's Introduction: The New Economic History and the Industrial Revolution", in Joel Mokyr (ed.), *The British Industrial Revolution* (Boulder: Westview Press, 1999), pp. 1–127.

Mokyr, Joel, "Innovation and its Enemies", in Mancur Olson and Satu Kähkönen (eds), *A Not-So-Dismal Science* (Oxford: Oxford University Press, 2000), pp. 61–91.

Mokyr, Joel, *The Gifts of Athena* (Princeton: Princeton University Press, 2002a).

Mokyr, Joel, *Thinking about Technology and Institutions*, paper for the Macalester International College Roundtable (2002b): http://www.faculty.econ.northwestern. edu/faculty/mokyr/macalester3.PDF. [10-05-2003]

Mokyr, Joel, *The Enduring Riddle of the European Miracle*, Conference on Convergence and Divergence in Historical Perspective: The Origins of Wealth and Persistence of Poverty in the Modern World, Riverside, CA (2002c): http:// www.faculty.econ.northwestern.edu/faculty/mokyr/Riverside.PDF. [10-05-2003]

Morgan, Kenneth, *The Birth of Industrial Britain* (London: Longman, 1999).

Morris-Suzuki, Tessa, *A History of Japanese Economic Thought* (London: Routledge, 1989).

Morris-Suzuki, Tessa, *The Technological Transformation of Japan* (New York: Cambridge University Press, 1994).

Moss, George Donelson, *The Rise of Northern America* (Upper Saddle River, NJ: Prentice Hall, 1995).

Mowery, David C., "The Computer Software Industry", in David C. Mowery and Richard R. Nelson (eds), *Sources of Industrial Leadership* (Cambridge: Cambridge University Press, 1999), pp. 133–68.

Mowery, David C. and Nathan Rosenberg, "The U.S. National Innovation System", in Richard R. Nelson (ed.), *National Innovation Systems* (Oxford: Oxford University Press, 1993), pp. 29–75.

Mowery, David C. and Nathan Rosenberg, *Paths of Innovation* (Cambridge: Cambridge University Press, 1998).

Murmann, Johann Peter, *Knowledge and Competitive Advantage* (Cambridge: Cambridge University Press, 2003).

Murmann, Johann Peter and Ernst Homburg, "Comparing Evolutionary Dynamics across Different National Settings", *Journal of Evolutionary Economics* 11 (2001): 177–205.

Murmann, Johann Peter and Ralph Landau, "On the Making of Competitive Advantage", in Ashish Arora, Ralph Landau and Nathan Rosenberg (eds), *Chemicals and Long-Term Economic Growth* (New York: John Wiley & Sons, 1998), pp. 27–70.

Nairn, Alasdair, *Engines that Move Markets* (New York: John Wiley & Sons, 2002).

Nakayama, Shigeru, "Independence and Choice", *Higher Education*, 18 (1989): 31–48.

Nathan, John, *Japan Unbound* (Boston: Houghton Mifflin, 2004).

Nelson, Richard R., "Recent Evolutionary Theorizing About Economic Change", *Journal of Economic Literature*, 33(1) (1995): 48–90.

Nelson, Richard R., *The Sources of Economic Growth* (Cambridge: Harvard University Press, 1996).

Nelson, Richard R., "Bringing Institutions into Evolutionary Growth Theory", *Journal of Evolutionary Economics*, 12 (2002): 17–28.

Nelson, Richard R. and Paul M. Romer, "Science, Economic Growth and Public Policy", in Bruce L.R. Smith and Claude E. Barfield (eds), *Technology, R &D, and the Economy* (Washington DC: The Brookings Institutions and American Enterprise Institute, 1996), pp. 49–74.

Nelson, Richard R. and Sidney G. Winter, *An Evolutionary Theory of Economic Change* (Cambridge: Harvard University Press, 1982).

Nord, Philip, "Social Defence and Conservative Regeneration", in Robert Tombs (ed.), *Nationhood and Nationalism in France* (London: HarperCollins Academic, 1991), pp. 210–28.

Nord, Philip, *The Republican Moment* (Cambridge: Harvard University Press, 1995).

North, Douglass C., *Structure and Change in Economic History* (London: W.W. Norton, 1981).

North, Douglass C., *Institutions, Institutional Change and Economic Performance* (New York: Cambridge University Press, 1990).

North, Douglass C., *Institution and Productivity in History* (1994): http://ideas. repec.org/p/wpa/wuwpeh/9411003.html. [09-26-06]

North, Douglass C. and Barry R. Weingast, "Constitutions and Commitment", *The Journal of Economic History*, 49(4) (1989): 803–32.

Nye, John V.C., "The Importance of Being Late", *French Historical Studies*, 23(3) (2000): 423–37.

Nye, Joseph S., Jr., *Bound to Lead* (New York: Basic Books, 1991).

O'Brien, Anthony Patrick, "The Importance of Adjusting Production to Sales in the Early Automobile Industry", *Explorations in Economic History*, 34 (1997): 195–219.

O'Brien, Conor Cruise, "Nationalism and the French Revolution", in Geoffrey Best (ed.), *The Permanent Revolution* (Chicago: University of Chicago Press, 1989), pp. 17–48.

O'Brien, Patrick Karl, "Path Dependency, or Why Britain Became an Industrialized and Urbanized Economy Long before France", *The Economic History Review*, New Series, 49(2) (1996): 213–49.

O'Brien, Patrick Karl, Trevor Griffiths and Philip Hunt, "Political Components of the Industrial Revolution", *The Economic History Review*, New Series, 44(3) (1991): 395–423.

Odagiri, Hiroyuki and Akira Goto, "The Japanese System of Innovation", in Richard R. Nelson (ed.), *National Innovation Systems* (Oxford: Oxford University Press, 1993), pp. 76–114.

OECD, *An Empirical Comparison of National Innovation Systems* (Paris: OECD, Working Group on Innovation and Technology Policy, 1997).

OECD, *Asia and the Global Crisis* (Paris: OECD, 1999a).

OECD, *Managing National Innovation Systems* (Paris: OECD, 1999b).

OECD, *Knowledge-Based Industries in Asia* (Paris: STI Report, 2000a).

OECD, *A New Economy? The Changing Role of Innovation and Information Technology in Growth* (Paris: OECD Publications, 2000b).

OECD, *The New Economy: Beyond the Hype: Final Report on the OECD Growth Project*, Paris: OECD Publications, 2001a).

OECD, *The Well-being of Nations*, Centre for Educational Research and Innovation (Paris: OECD Publications, 2001b).

OECD, *The New Economy: Beyond the Hype: The OECD Growth Project* (Paris: OECD Publications, 2001c).

OECD, *OECD Economic Surveys: Japan* (Paris: OECD Publications, 2001d).

OECD, *OECD Science, Technology and Industry Scoreboard* (Paris: OECD Publications, 2001e).

OECD, *Education at a Glance* (Paris: OECD Publications, 2002a).

OCED, *Education Policy Analysis* (Paris: OECD Publications, 2002b).

OECD, *Patents and Innovation*, OECD Publications (2004): http://www.oecd.org/ dataoecd/48/12/24508541.pdf [09-22-2004].

OECD and WBI, *Korea and the Knowledge-based Economy* (Paris: 2000)

Olson, Mancur, *The Rise and Decline of Nations* (New Haven Yale University Press, 1982).

Olson, Mancur, *Power and Prosperity* (New York Basic Books, 2000).

O'Rourke, Kevin, "The Repeal of the Corn Laws and Irish Emigration", *Explorations in Economic History*, 31 (1994): 120–38.

Pacey, Arnold, *Technology in World Civilization* (Cambridge: MIT Press, 1990).

Pakenham, Thomas, *The Scramble for Africa* (London: Abacus, 1991).

Parente, Stephen L. and Edward C. Prescott, *Barriers to Riches* (Cambridge: MIT Press, 2002).

Parrish, Michael E., *Anxious Decades* (New York: W.W. Norton, 1994).

Perez, Carlota, *Technological Revolutions and Financial Capital* (London: Edward Elgar, 2002).

Perkin, Harold, *The Origins of Modern English Society 1780–1880* (London: Routledge & Kegan Paul, 1969).

Perkins, Dwight H., "Law, Family Ties, and the East Asian Way of Business", in Lawrence E. Harrison and Samuel P. Huntington (eds), *Culture Matters* (New York: Basic Books, 2000), pp. 232–43.

Phillips, William H., "The Economic Performance of Late Victorian Britain", *The Journal of European Economic History*, 18(2) (1989): 393–414.

Phillips, William H., "Patent Growth in the Old Dominion", *The Journal of Economic History*, 52(2) (1992): 389–400.

Pierson, Paul, "The New Politics of the Welfare State", *World Politics*, 48(2) (1996): 143–79.

Pilbeam, Pamela, "Revolution, Restoration(s) and beyond", in Martin S. Alexander (ed.), *French History since Napoleon* (New York: Oxford University Press, 1999): 31–58.

Pipes, Richard, *Property and Freedom* (New York Vintage Books, 1999).

Pomeranz, Kenneth, *The Great Divergence* (Princeton: Princeton University Press, 2000).

Porter, Michael E., *The Competitive Advantage of Nations* (New York: The Free Press, 1990).

Price, Roger, *A Concise History of France* (Cambridge: Cambridge University Press, 1993).

Pugh, Martin, *Britain Since 1789* (New York: St. Martin's Press, 1999).

Putnam, Robert D., "Bowling Alone", *Journal of Democracy*, 6(1) (1995a): 65–78.

Putnam, Robert D., "Tuning In, Tuning Out", *PS Online*, Apsanet (1995b): http://www.apsanet.org/PS/dec95/putnam.cfm. [07-10-2004]

Pye, Lucian W., "'Asian Values': From Dynamos to Dominoes?", in Lawrence E. Harrison and Samuel P. Huntington (eds), *Culture Matters* (New York: Basic Books, 2000), pp. 244–55.

Pyenson, Lewis and Susan Sheets-Pyenson, *Servants of Nature* (London: W.W. Norton, 1999).

Quinault, Roland, "The Industrial Revolution and Parliamentary Reform", in Patrick K. O'Brien and Roland Quinault (eds), *The Industrial Revolution and British Society* (Cambridge: Cambridge University Press, 1993), pp. 183–202.

Rae, John B., *The American Automobile Industry* (Boston: Twayne Publishers, 1984).

Ratnathicam, Indran and Geoffrey Kirkman, ".us", in World Economic Forum, *The Global Information Technology Report 2001–2002* (Oxford: Oxford University Press, 2002), pp. 302–3.

Rebelo, S., "Long-Run Policy Analysis and Long-Run Growth", *The Journal of Political Economy*, 99(3) (1991): 500–21.

Reinert, Erik S., *Catching Up from Way Behind—a Third World Perspective on First World History*, Fremtek Working Paper 8/93 (Oslo, 1993).

Reinert, Erik S., *Competitiveness and its Predecessors—a 500-Year Cross-National Perspective*, STEP-report 3/94 (Oslo, 1994a).

Reinert, Erik S., *A Schumpeterian Theory of Underdevelopment—a Contradiction in Terms?*, STEP-report 15/94 (Oslo, 1994b).

Reinert, Erik S., *Det tekno-økonomiske paradigmeskiftet—konsekvenser for næringspolitikken*, Norsk Investorforum 3/96 (Oslo, 1996).

Da Rin, Marco, "Finance and the Chemical Industry", in Ashish Arora, Ralph Landau and Nathan Rosenberg (eds), *Chemicals and Long-Term Economic Growth* (New York: John Wiley & Sons, 1998), pp. 307–39.

Robertson, Paul L. and Richard N. Langlois, *Institutions, Inertia, and Changing Industrial Leadership* (1994): http://econwpa.wustl.edu/eprints/io/papers/9406/9406005.abs [05-15-2003].

Roche, Daniel, *France in the Enlightenment* (Cambridge: Harvard University Press, 1998).

Rocke, Alan J., "Group Research in German Chemistry", *Osiris*, 8 (1993): 52–79.

Rogowski, Ronald, *Commerce and Coalitions* (Princeton: Princeton University Press, 1989).

Roll, Richard and John Talbott, *Why Many Developing Countries Just Aren't* (Los Angeles: Finance Working Paper, 2001).

Romer, Paul, "Increasing Returns and Long-Run Growth", *The Journal of Political Economy*, 94(5) (1986): 1002–37.

Romer, Paul, "Endogenous Technological Change", *The Journal of Political Economy*, 98 (1990) 71–102.

Romer, Paul, "The Origins of Endogenous Growth", *The Journal of Economic Perspectives*, 8(1) (1994): 3–22.

Root, Hilton L., "The Redistributive Role of Government", *Comparative Studies in Society and History*, 33(2) (1991): 338–69.

Rosecrance, Richard, *The Rise of the Virtual State* (New York: Basic Books, 1999).

Rosenberg, Nathan, "Technological Change in Chemicals", in Ashish Arora, Ralph Landau and Nathan Rosenberg (eds), *Chemicals and Long-Term Economic Growth* (New York: John Wiley & Sons, 1998), pp. 193–230.

Rosenberg, Nathan and L.E. Birdzell, *How the West Grew Rich* (London: I.B. Tauris & Co. Ltd., 1986).

Rostow, Walt Whitman, *The Stages of Economic Growth* (Cambridge: Cambridge University Press, 1960).

Rostow, Walt Whitman, *How it all Began* (London: Methuen & Co Ltd, 1975).

Rostow, Walt Whitman, *The World-Economy* (London: Macmillan Press, 1978).

Ruiz, Marco (ed.), *100 År med Bilen* (Halden, Norway: J.W. Cappelens Forlag, 1984).

Ruttan, Vernon W., *Technology, Growth, and Development* (Oxford: Oxford University Press, 2001).

Sachs, Jeffrey D. and Felipe Larrain B. , *Macroeconomics in the Global Economy* (Hempstead, Hertfordshire: Harvester Wheatsheaf, 1993).

Sakakibara, Eisuke, *Structural Reform in Japan* (Washington DC: Brookings Institution Press, 2003).

Schama, Simon, *Citizens* (New York: Vintage Books, 1989).

Scherer, Frederik M., *Innovation and Growth* (Cambridge: The MIT Press, 1984).

Schofield, Roger S., "The Measurement of Literacy in Pre-Industrial England", in Jack Goody (ed.), *Literacy in Traditional Societies* (London: Cambridge University Press, 1968), pp. 311–25.

Schonhardt-Bailey, Cheryl, "Specific Factors, Capital Markets, Portfolio Diversification, and Free Trade", *World Politics*, 43(4) (1991): 545–69.

Schulze, Hagen, *Germany: A New History* (Cambridge: Harvard University Press, 1998).

Schultze, Charles L., "Comment", in Bruce L.R. Smith and Claude E. Barfield (eds), *Technology, R & D, and the Economy* (Washington DC The Brookings Instutions and American Enterprise Institute, 1996), pp. 107-113.

Schumpeter, Joseph Alois, *Business Cycles: A Theoretical, Historical and Statistical Analysis of the Capitalist Process* (NewsYork: McGraw-Hill, 1939).

Schumpeter, Joseph Alois, *Capitalism, Socialism and Democracy* (New York: Harper Torchbooks, 1942).

Schumpeter, Joseph Alois, *The Theory of Economic Development* (New Brunswick: Transaction Publishers, 1983 [1934]).

Schumpeter, Joseph Alois, "Capitalism", in Richard V. Clemence (ed.), *Essays on Entrepreneurs, Innovations, Business Cycles, and the Evolution of Capitalism: Schumpeter*, New Brunswick: Transaction Publishers, 1997a [1946]), pp. 189–210.

Schumpeter, Joseph Alois, "Economic Theory and Entrepreneurial History", in Richard V. Clemence (ed.), *Essays on Entrepreneurs, Innovations, Business Cycles, and the Evolution of Capitalism: Schumpeter* (New Brunswick: Transaction Publishers, 1997b [1949]), pp. 253–71.

Sewell, William H., Jr., *Work and Revolution in France* (Cambridge: Cambridge University Press, 1980).

Shorter, Edward and Charles Tilly, *Strikes in France, 1830–1968* (London: Cambridge University Press, 1974).

Sibalis, Michael David, "Corporatism after the Corporations", *French Historical Studies*, 15(4) (1988): 718–30.

Skocpol, Theda, "From Membership to Advocacy", in Robert D. Putnam (ed.), *Democracies in Flux* (Oxford: Oxford University Press, 2002), pp. 103–36.

Smith, Cecil O., Jr., "The Longest Run", *The American Historical Review*, 95(3) (1990): 657–92.

Solow, Robert M., "A Contribution to the Theory of Economic Growth", *Quarterly Journal of Economics*, 70 (1956): 65–94.

Standen, Anthony, "Chemical Industry", in *The New Encyclopædia Britannica* (2003): http://www.britannica.com/eb. [09-11-2003]

Stürmer, Michael, *The German Empire* (New York: Modern Library, 2002).

Sullivan, Richard J., "England's 'Age of Invention'", *Explorations in Economic History*, 26(4) (1989): 424–52.

Sullivan, Richard J., "The Revolution of Ideas", *The Journal of Economic History*, 50(2) (1990): 349–62.

Taylor, John B., "Changes in American Economic Policy in the 1980s", *Journal of Economic Literature*, 33(2) (1995): 777–84.

Taylor, Peter J., *The Way the Modern World Works* (Chichester: John Wiley & Sons, 1996).

Temin, Peter, "Two Views of the British Industrial Revolution", *Journal of Economic History*, 57(1) (1997): 63–82.

Thompson, William R., *The Emergence of the Global Political Economy* (London: Routledge, 2000).

Thompson, Willie, *Global Expansion* (London: Pluto Press, 1999).

Tilly, Charles, *The Contentious French* (London: Belknap Press, 1986).

Tilly, Charles, *Popular Contention in Great Britain 1758–1834* (Cambridge: Harvard University Press, 1995).

Tilly, Charles, *Contention & Democracy in Europe, 1650–2000* (Cambridge: Cambridge University Press, 2004).

Tilly, Richard H., "German Banking, 1850–1914", *The Journal of European Economic History*, 15 (1986): 113–52.

Tilly, Richard H., "Public Policy, Capital Markets and the Supply of Industrial Finance in Nineteenth-Century Germany", in Richard Sylla, Richard Tilly and Gabriel Tortella (eds), *The State, the Financial System and Economic Modernization*, Cambridge: Cambridge University Press, 1999), pp. 134–57.

Tipton, Frank B., *A History of Modern Germany Since 1815* (Berkeley: University of California Press, 2003).

Tombs, Robert, "Inventing Politics", in Martin S. Alexander (ed.), *French History since Napoleon* (New York: Oxford University Press, 1999), pp. 59–79.

Tortella, Gabriel, "Patterns of Economic Retardation and Recovery in South-Western Europe in the Nineteenth and Twentieth Centuries", *Economic History Review*, XLVII(1) (1994): 1–21.

Trebilcock, Clive, *The Industrialization of the Continental Powers 1780–1914* (London: Longman, 1981).

Unwin, George, Philip Soundy Unwin et al., "Publishing", in Robert McHenry and Yutorio C. Hori (eds), *The New Encyclopædia Britannica* (15th edition) (Chicago: Encyclopædia Britannica Inc., 1994), vol. 26, pp. 415–49.

Vaiciulenas, Albert, "Introduction", in Robert Tombs (ed.), *Nationhood and Nationalism in France* (London: HarperCollins Academic, 1991), pp. 103–7.

Van Horn Melton, James, *The Rise of the Public in Enlightenment Europe* (Cambridge: Cambridge University Press, 2001).

Verspagen, Bart, "Economic Growth and Technical change", *STI Working Papers 2001/1*, DSTI/DOC(2001)1.

Verspagen, Bart, "Evolutionary Macroeconomics", *The Electronic Journal of Evolutionary Modeling and Economic Dynamics*, 1007 (2002): http://www.e-jemed.org/1007/index.php. [02-10-2002]

Vincent, David, *The Rise of Mass Literacy* (Cambridge: Polity Press, 2000).

Walker, William, "National Innovation Systems: Britain", in Richard R. Nelson (ed.), *National Innovation Systems* (Oxford: Oxford University Press, 1993), pp. 158–91.

Wallis, John J. and Douglass C. North, "Measuring the Transaction Sector in the American Economy, 1870–1970", in Stanley L. Engermann and Robert E. Gallmann (eds), *Long-Term Factors in American Economic Growth* (Chicago: University of Chicago Press, 1986), pp. 95–161.

Waltz, Kenneth N., *Theory of International Politics*, New York: McGraw-Hill, 1979).

Webb, Augustus D., *The New Dictionary of Statistics* (London: George Routledge and Sons, 1911).

Webb, Steven B., "Tariffs, Cartels, Technology, and Growth in the German Steel Industry, 1879 to 1914", *The Journal of Economic History*, XL(2) (1980), 309–30.

Weber, Eugen, "The Nineteenth-century Fallout", in Geoffrey Best (ed.), *The Permanent Revolution* (Chicago: University of Chicago Press, 1989), pp. 155–81.

Wehler, Hans-Ulrich, *The German Empire 1871–1918* (Oxford: Berg, 1985).

Wetzel, David, *A Duel of Giants* (Madison: University of Wisconsin Press, 2001).

White, Eugene N., "Making the French Pay", *European Review of Economic History*, 5 (2001): 337–65.

Whitley, Richard, "East-Asian and Anglo-American Business Systems", in Grahame Thompson (ed.), *Economic Dynamism in the Asia-Pacific* (London: Routledge, 1998), pp. 213–49.

Winters, Jeffrey A., "The Determinant of Financial Crisis in Asia", in T.J. Pempel (ed.), *The Politics of the Asian Economic Crisis* (Ithaca: Cornell, 1999), pp. 79–97.

Wohlforth, William C., "U.S. Strategy in a Unipolar World", in G. John Ikenberry (ed.), *America Unrivaled* (Ithaca: Cornell University Press, 2002), pp. 98–118.

Womack, James P., Daniel T. Jones and Daniel Roos, *The Machine that Changed the World* (New York: Harper Perennial, 1990).

Woo-Cumings, Meredith, "The State, Democracy, and the Reform of the Corporate Sector in Korea", in T.J. Pempel (ed.), *The Politics of the Asian Economic Crisis* (Ithaca: Cornell, 1999), pp. 116–42.

Wood, Jonathan, "Volkswagen", in Jonathan Wood (ed.), *Great Marques of Germany* (London: Octopus Books Limited, 1985), pp. 196–221.

World Economic Forum, *The Global Information Technology Report 2001–2002* (Oxford: Oxford University Press, 2002).

World Economic Forum, *The Global Competitiveness Report 2002–2003* (Oxford: Oxford University Press, 2003).

Wright, Gordon, *France in Modern Times* (New York: W.W. Norton, 1995).

Wuthnow, Robert, "Bridging the Privileged and the Marginalized?", in Robert D. Putnam (ed.), *Democracies in Flux* (Oxford: Oxford University Press, 2002), pp. 59–102.

Young, Louise, *Japan's Total Empire* (Berkeley: University of California Press, 1998).

Yusuf, Shahid, *Innovative East Asia* (Washington DC: World Bank and Oxford University Press Copublication, 2003).

Yusuf, Shahid and Simon J. Evenett, *Can East Asia Compete? Innovation for Global Markets* (Washington DC: World Bank and Oxford University Press Copublication, 2002).

Zamagni, Vera, "An International Comparison of Real Industrial Wages, 1890–1913", in Peter Scholliers (ed.), *Real Wages in 19th and 20th century Europe* (New York: Berg Publishers Limited, 1989), pp. 107–39.

Zinn, Howard, *A People's History of the United States, 1492–Present* (New York: Harper Perennial, 1995).

Index

Abramovitz, Moses, 7
academic networks with government
    and/or industry, 132, 140–41, 162,
    212, 220–21, 246, 254–6, *see also*
    Britain; France; Germany; Japan;
    US
Académie Royale des Sciences, 47, 128
acids, 126
agriculture,
    Britain, 81, 103–6, 108, 256, 260–61
    share of GNP, 103
    transition away from, 103–5
    vested interests, 163
    distribution of employment, 201
    France, 33, 33n
    Germany, 161
    Japan, 238–9
Aiken, Howard, 216
alkalis, 126, 128, 131, 146, 148, 157
Allen, Paul, 205
Alsace-Lorraine, 85n, 101, 159n
Amdahl, Gene, 206, 219
American System of manufactures, 181–2
Anglicans, *see* church—Church of England
aniline purple, 129, 138, 143, *see also*
    mauve
aniline red, 129, 159, *see also* magenta
anti-Socialist Laws, 160, 161n
antitrust suits and legislation, 218
Apple Macintosh, 205–6
aristocracy, 64, 74, 104, 156, *see also* landed
    interests; nobility
Arkwright, Richard, 34n, 34–5, 54, 62–3
    Arkwright cotton mill, 35
armories, 57, 94, 182–3
ARPA, ARPANET, 208–10, 223
artisans, 46–8, 56–7, 73, 77, 166
assassination attempts, 114, 157, 234n
assembly line, 167, 171, 173, 181n
AT&T, 207, 218
Austin, 174, 175
Austria, 88, 147, 156, 159n, 164

Austro–Prussian commercial treaty, 156n
Austro–Prussian war, 159, 260
automobile industry, 166–98, 252–7, *see
    also specific companies*; *see also*
    mass production; US
    history and development, 171–6
    human capital, 176–81
    infrastructure developments, 187–9, 197
    as *mass consumption* industry, 194,
        197–8, 257, 262
    mass production, 166–70, 172–6
    Smithian growth, 183–7, 189–191, 194,
        196–8

Baeyer, Adolf von, 129
Balfour, Arthur, 151
bankruptcies, 84, 106n, 115, 193, 226, 227n
banks; banking, 54, 118, 199, 229, 247
    Bank Act (1844), 104
    Bank of France, 112–13
    Japan, 227, 236–8, 240–41, 244–5
    US, the, 185–6, 193–4, 225–6, 232–3
BASF, 129–31, 145n, 158, 183
Bayer, 130, 140, 159
Bell Laboratories, 206, 217–18
Benz, Karl, 171
benzene ring theory, 129
Berlin, 135, 137
Berthollet, Claude, 127–8
bicycle industry, 182
Birmingham Lunar Society, 46
Bismarck, Otto von, 157–61
    autonomy and consensus, 161, 251, 260
    economy and industry, 157n, 157–8, 165
    wars, 120, 120n, 159, 159n
Blanc, Honoré, 94, 182
bleaches, 126, 128, 147
Boulton, Matthew, 92n, 92–3
Bourbon, House of, 59, 72–3, 113–14, 259
    demise of, 110, 116, 120n
    vested interests, 109–10
Bourbon Restoration, 91, 100, 102